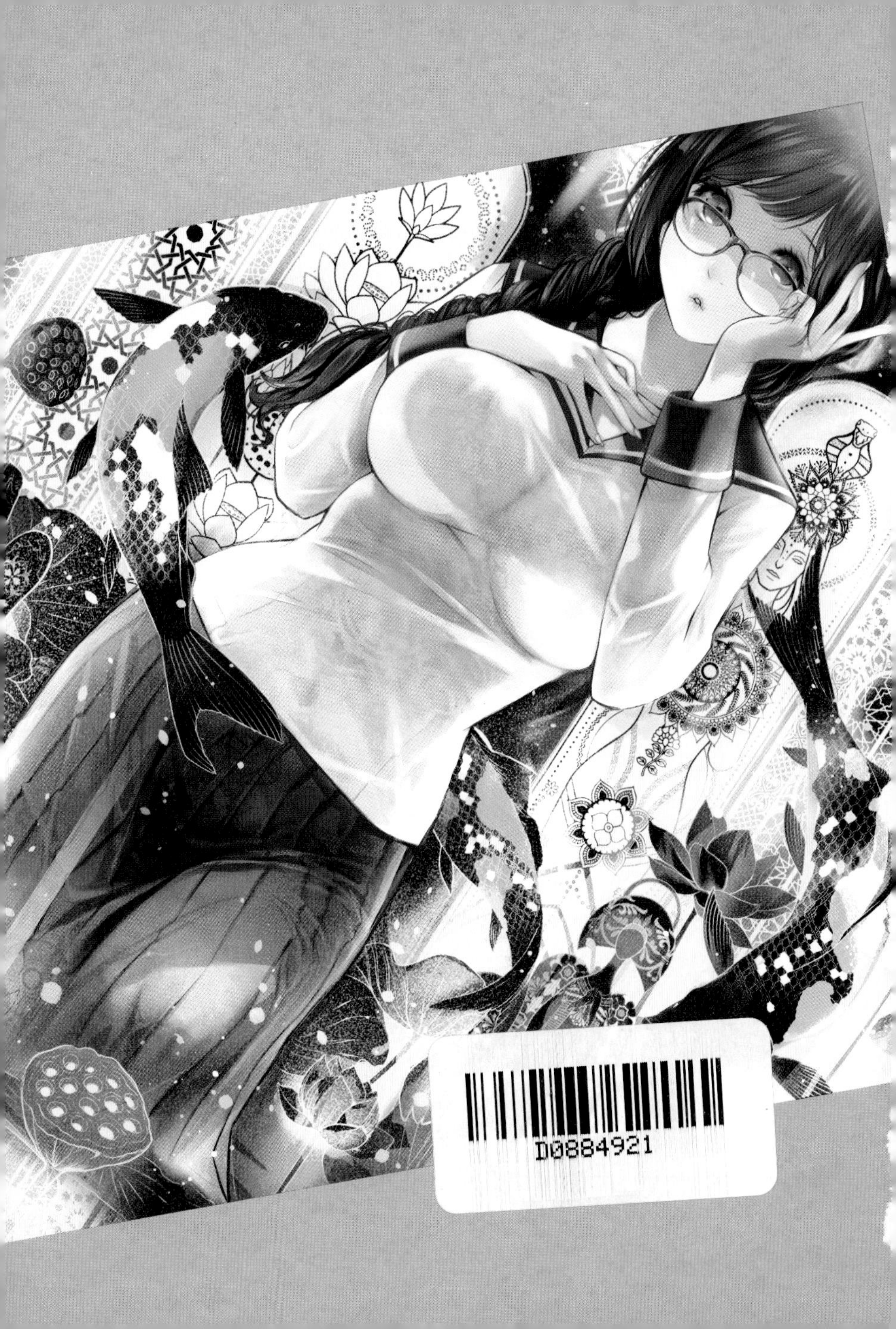

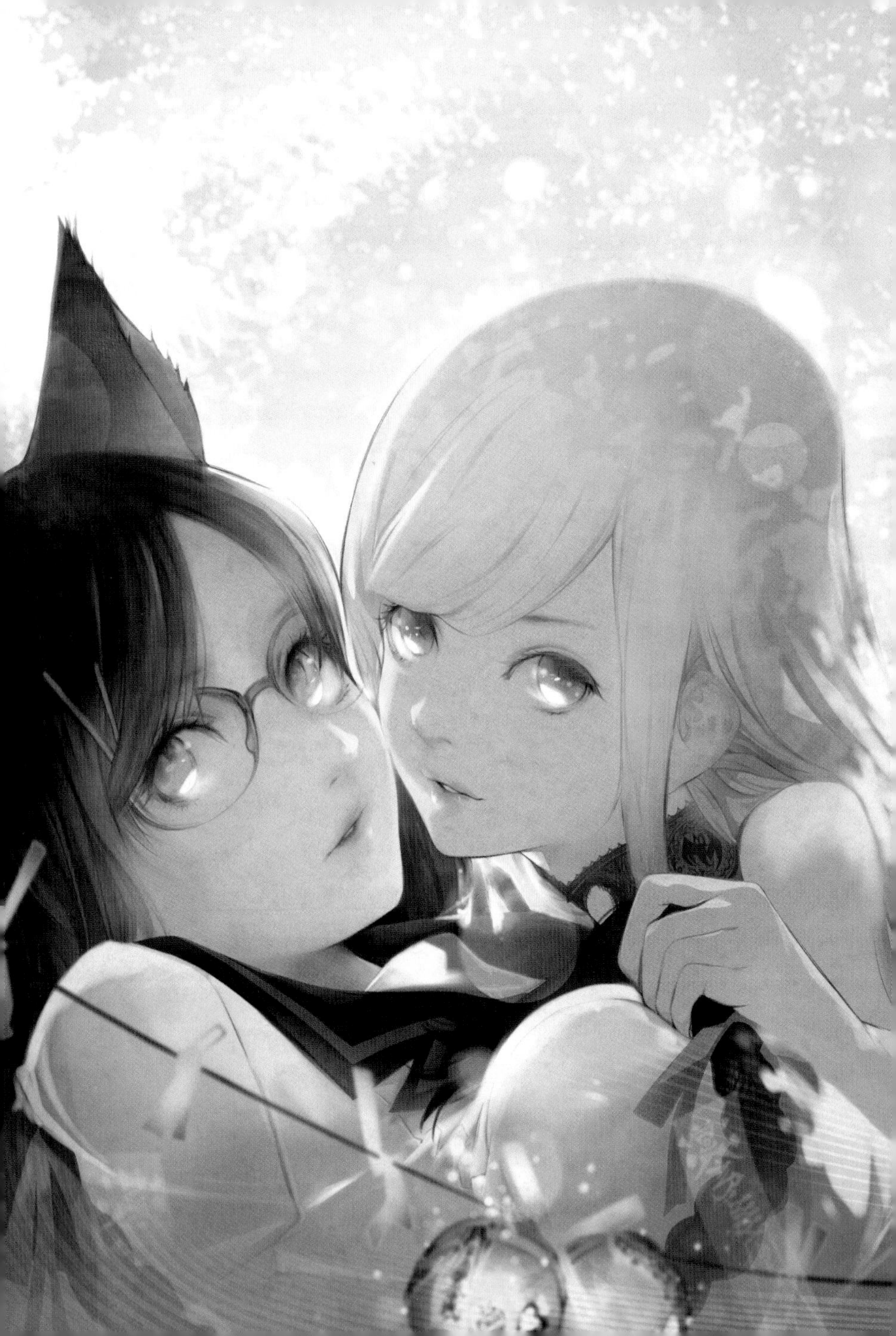

BAKEMONOGATARI

OH!GREAT

ORIGINAL STORY:
NISIOISIN

ORIGINAL CHARACTER
DESIGN: VOFAN

11

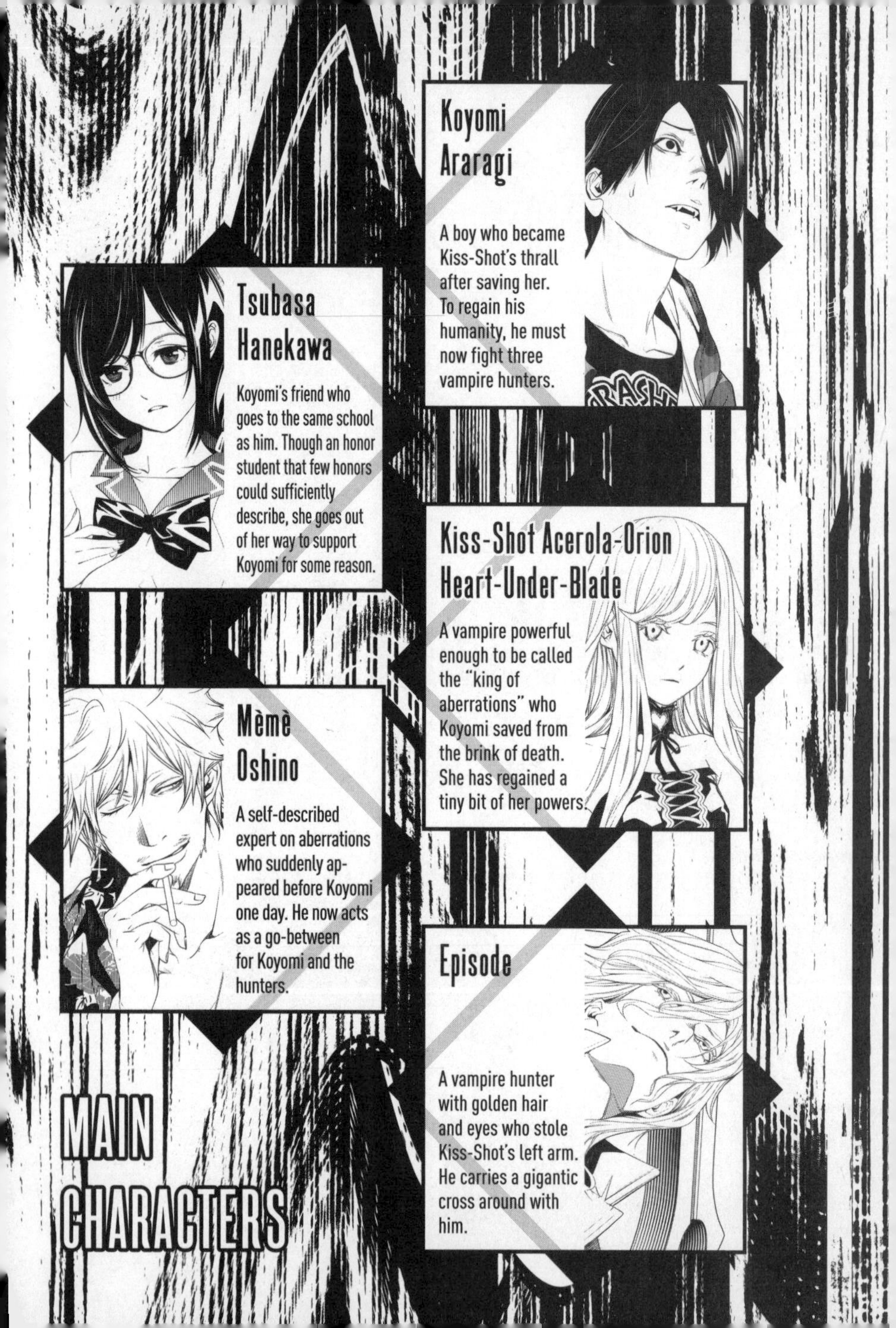
Koyomi Araragi
A boy who became Kiss-Shot's thrall after saving her. To regain his humanity, he must now fight three vampire hunters.
Tsubasa Hanekawa
Koyomi's friend who goes to the same school as him. Though an honor student that few honors could sufficiently describe, she goes out of her way to support Koyomi for some reason.
Kiss-Shot Acerola-Orion Heart-Under-Blade
A vampire powerful enough to be called the "king of aberrations" who Koyomi saved from the brink of death. She has regained a tiny bit of her powers.
Mèmè Oshino
A self-described expert on aberrations who suddenly ap-peared before Koyomi one day. He now acts as a go-between for Koyomi and the hunters.
Episode
A vampire hunter with golden hair and eyes who stole Kiss-Shot's left arm. He carries a gigantic cross around with him.
MAIN CHARACTERS

THE STORY SO FAR

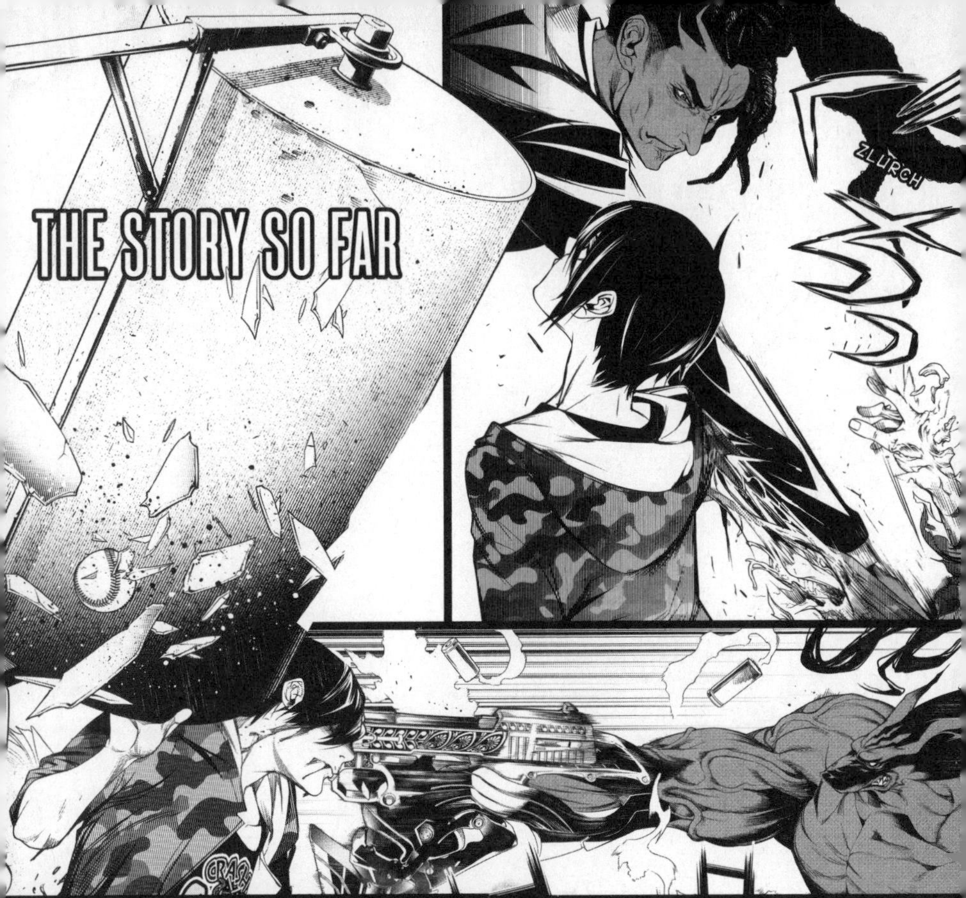
ZLURCH

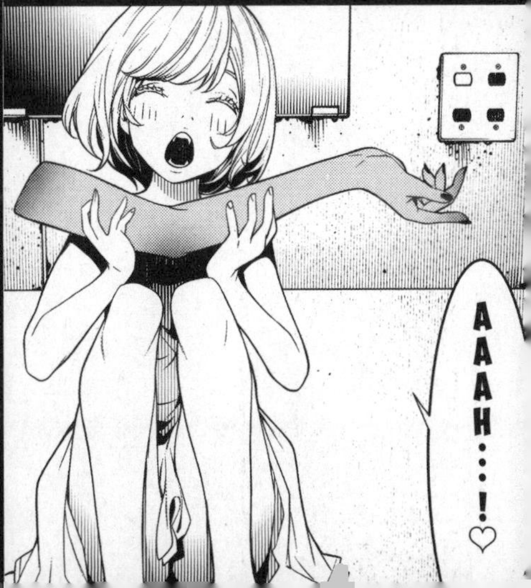
AAAH...!♡

During spring break, Koyomi Araragi saved the vampire Kiss-Shot Acerola-Orion Heart-Under-Blade. He was fully prepared to die for her but instead finds that he has become her vampiric thrall. To become human again, he must now fight three hunters who are after Kiss-Shot. For his first opponent, he took on the vampire Dramaturgy and, by some miracle, came out victorious.

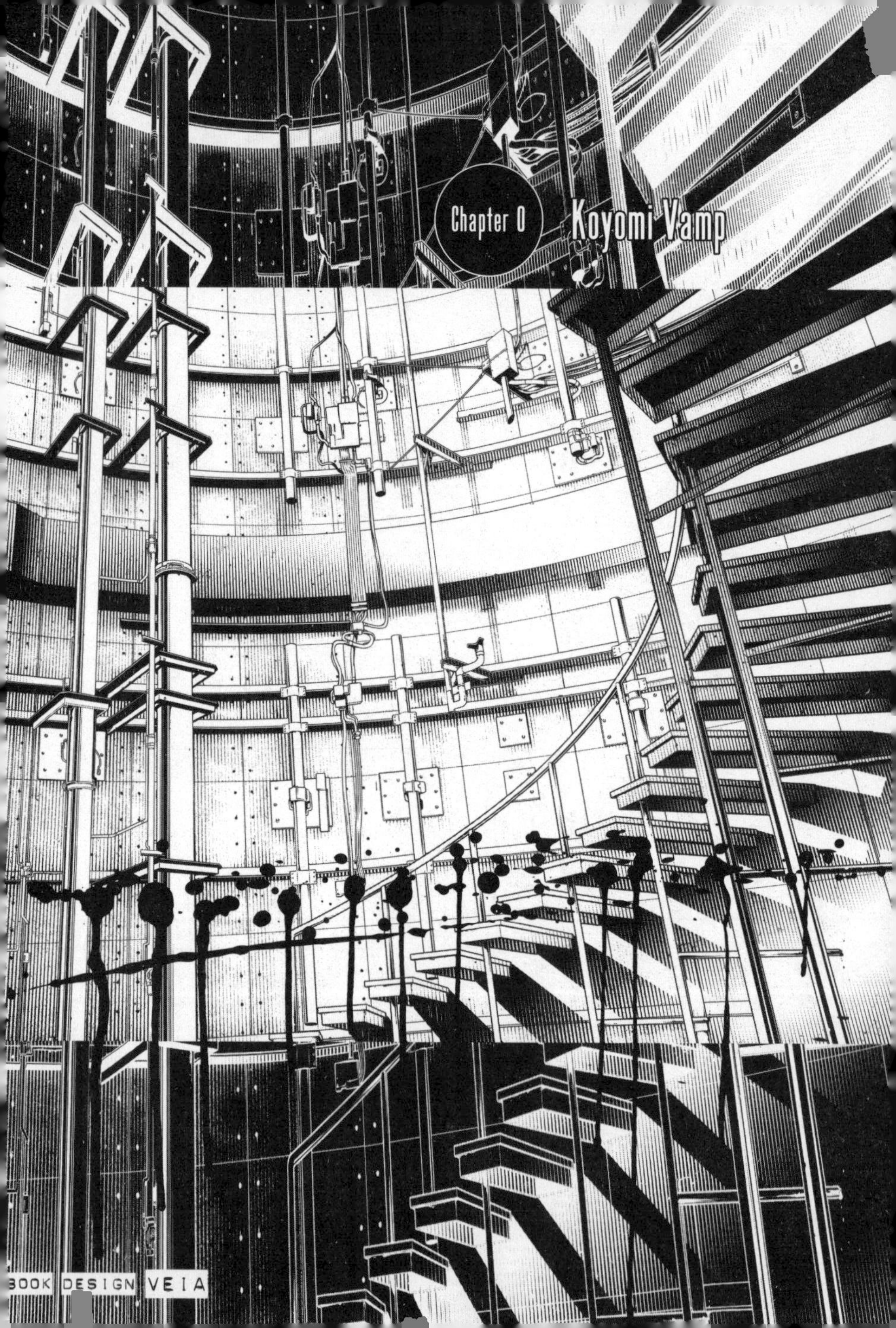
Chapter 0
Koyomi Vamp
BOOK DESIGN VEIA

BAKEMONOGATARI

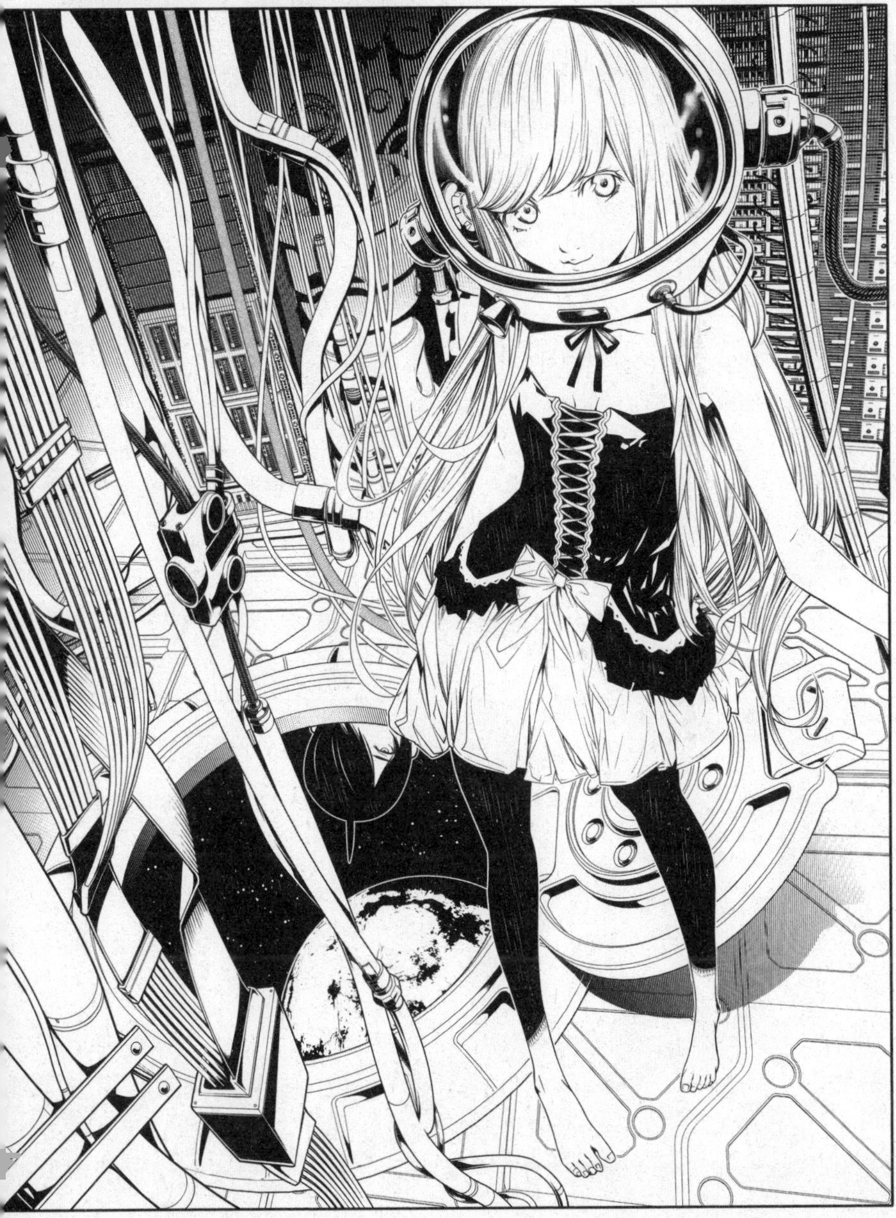

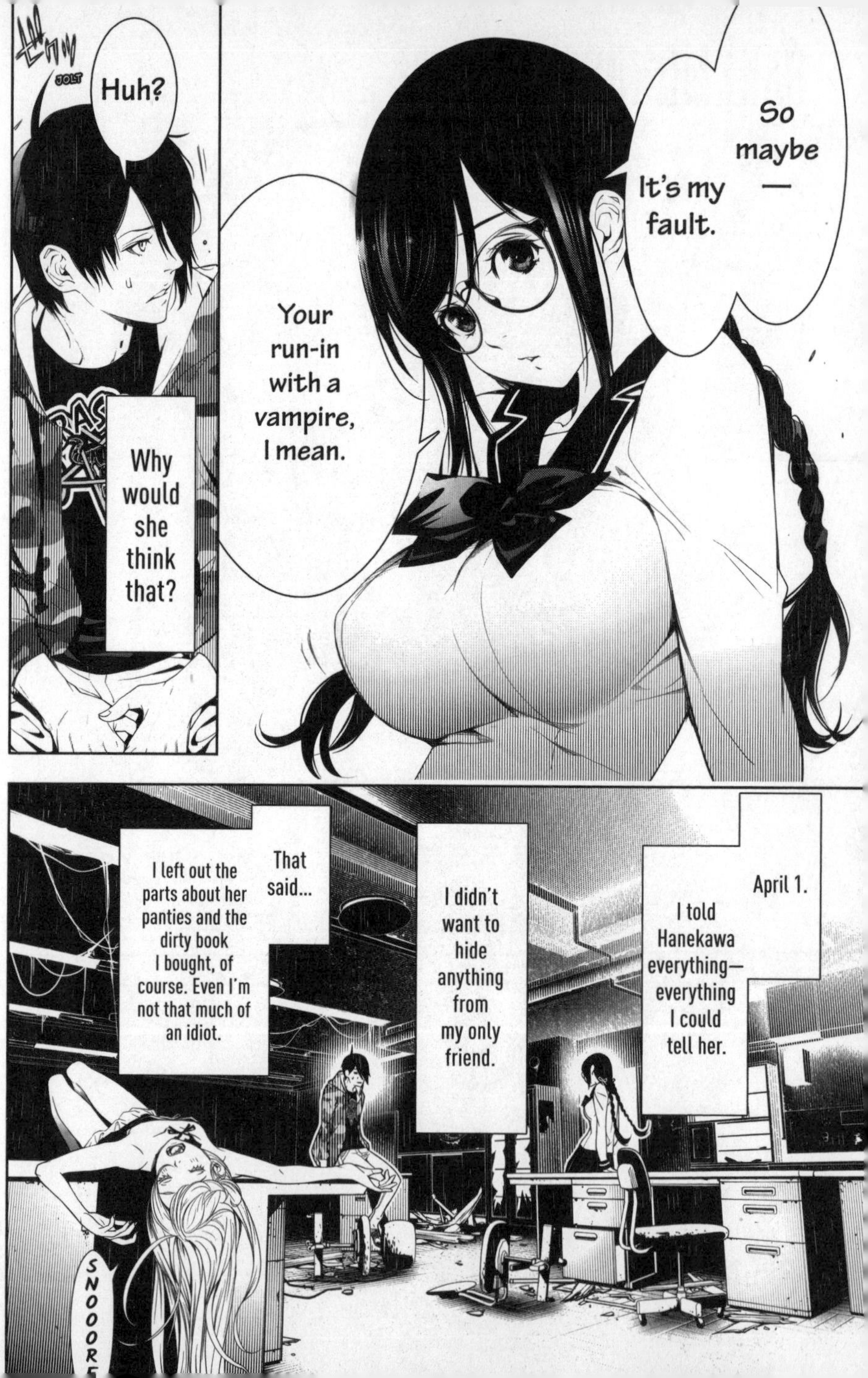
So maybe —
It's my fault.
Your run-in with a vampire, I mean.
JOLT
Huh?
Why would she think that?
April 1.
I told Hanekawa everything— everything I could tell her.
I didn't want to hide anything from my only friend.
That said...
I left out the parts about her panties and the dirty book I bought, of course. Even I'm not that much of an idiot.
SNOOORE

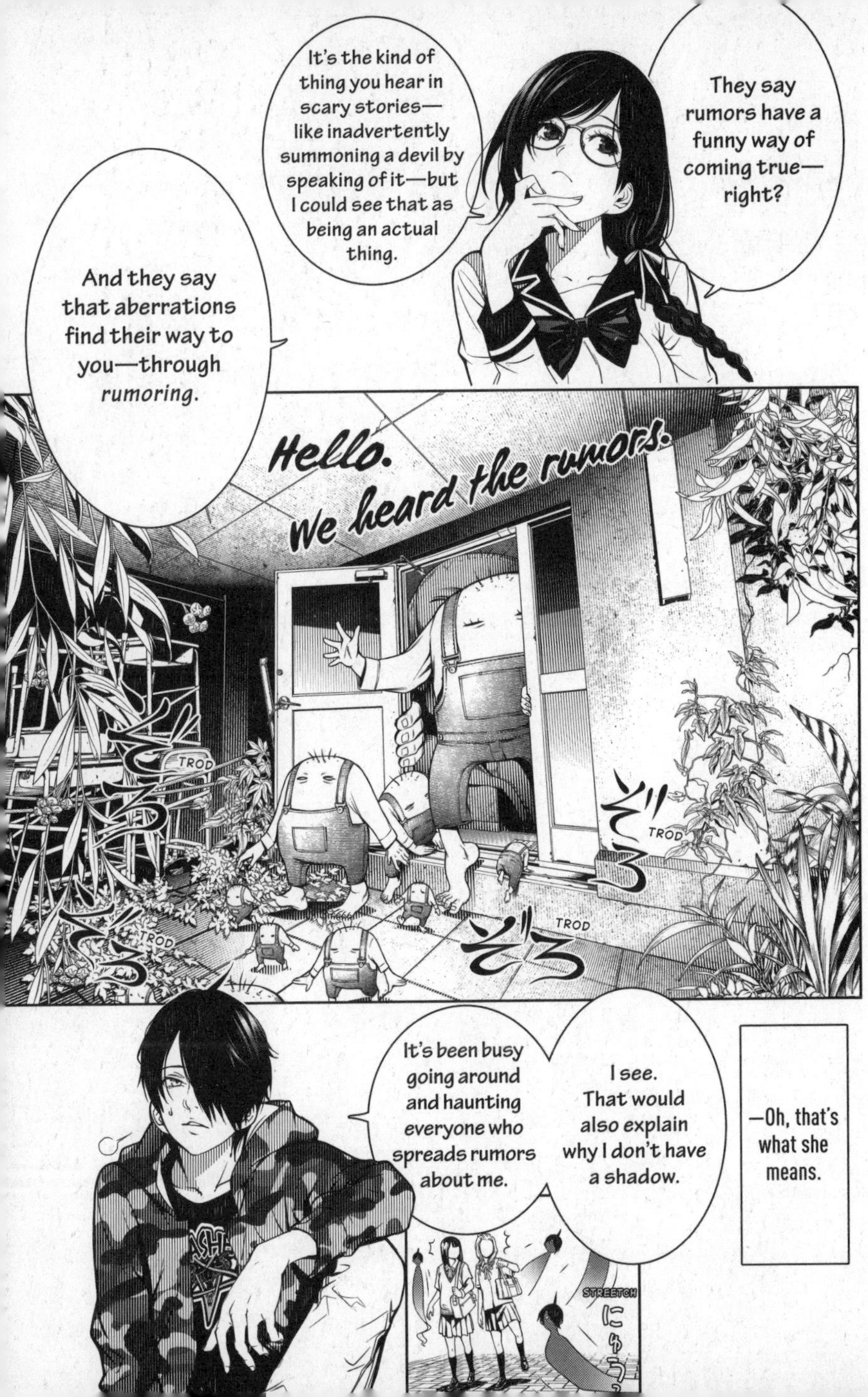
They say rumors have a funny way of coming true—right?
It's the kind of thing you hear in scary stories—like inadvertently summoning a devil by speaking of it—but I could see that as being an actual thing.
And they say that aberrations find their way to you—through *rumoring.*
Hello. We heard the rumors.
ぞろ
TROD
ぞろ
TROD
ぞろ
TROD
ぞろ
TROD
—Oh, that's what she means.
I see. That would also explain why I don't have a shadow.
It's been busy going around and haunting everyone who spreads rumors about me.
STREETCH

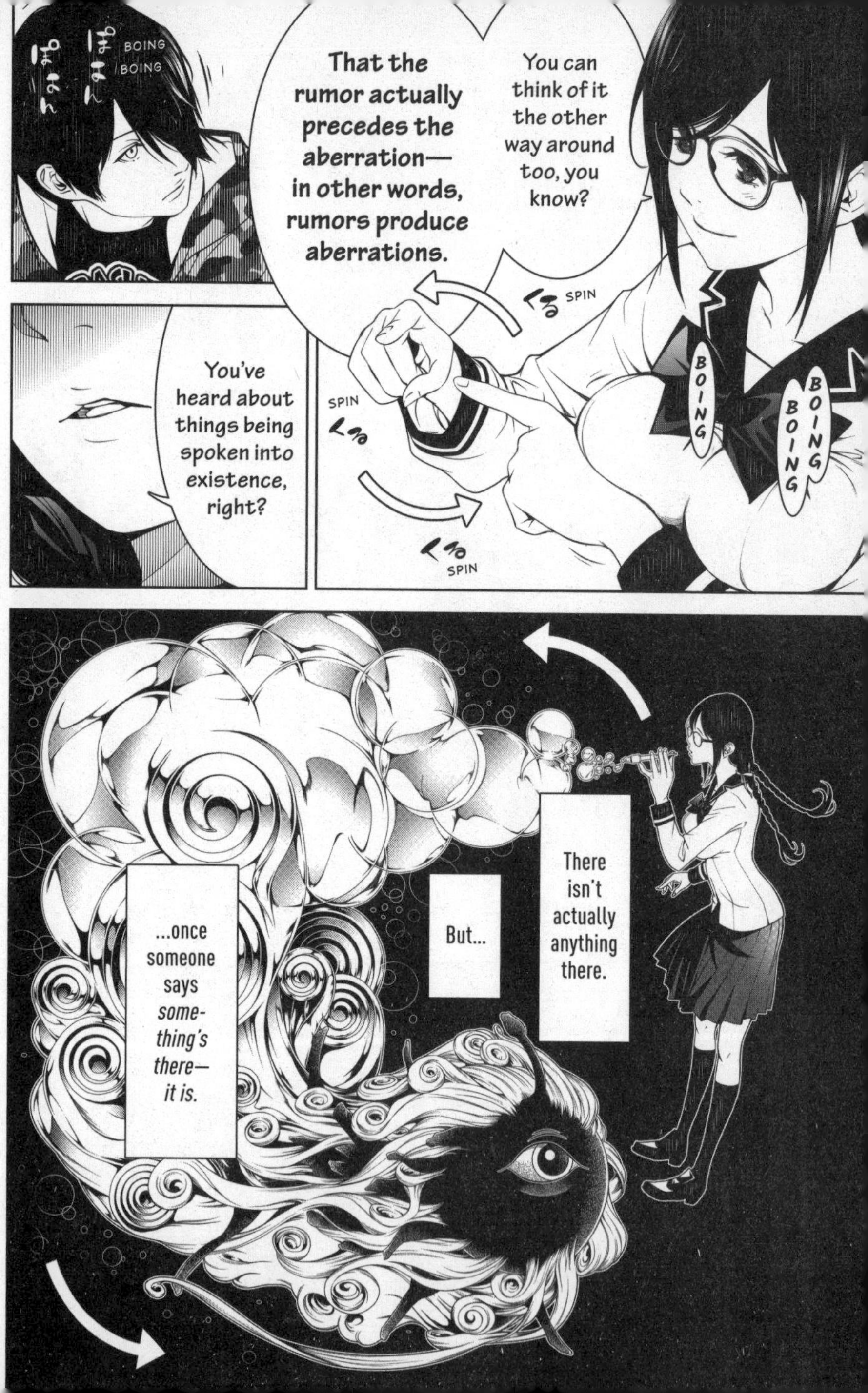

You can think of it the other way around too, you know?
That the rumor actually precedes the aberration—in other words, rumors produce aberrations.
SPIN
SPIN
SPIN
BOING BOING BOING
BOING
BOING
You've heard about things being spoken into existence, right?
There isn't actually anything there.
But...
...once someone says *something's there*—*it is.*

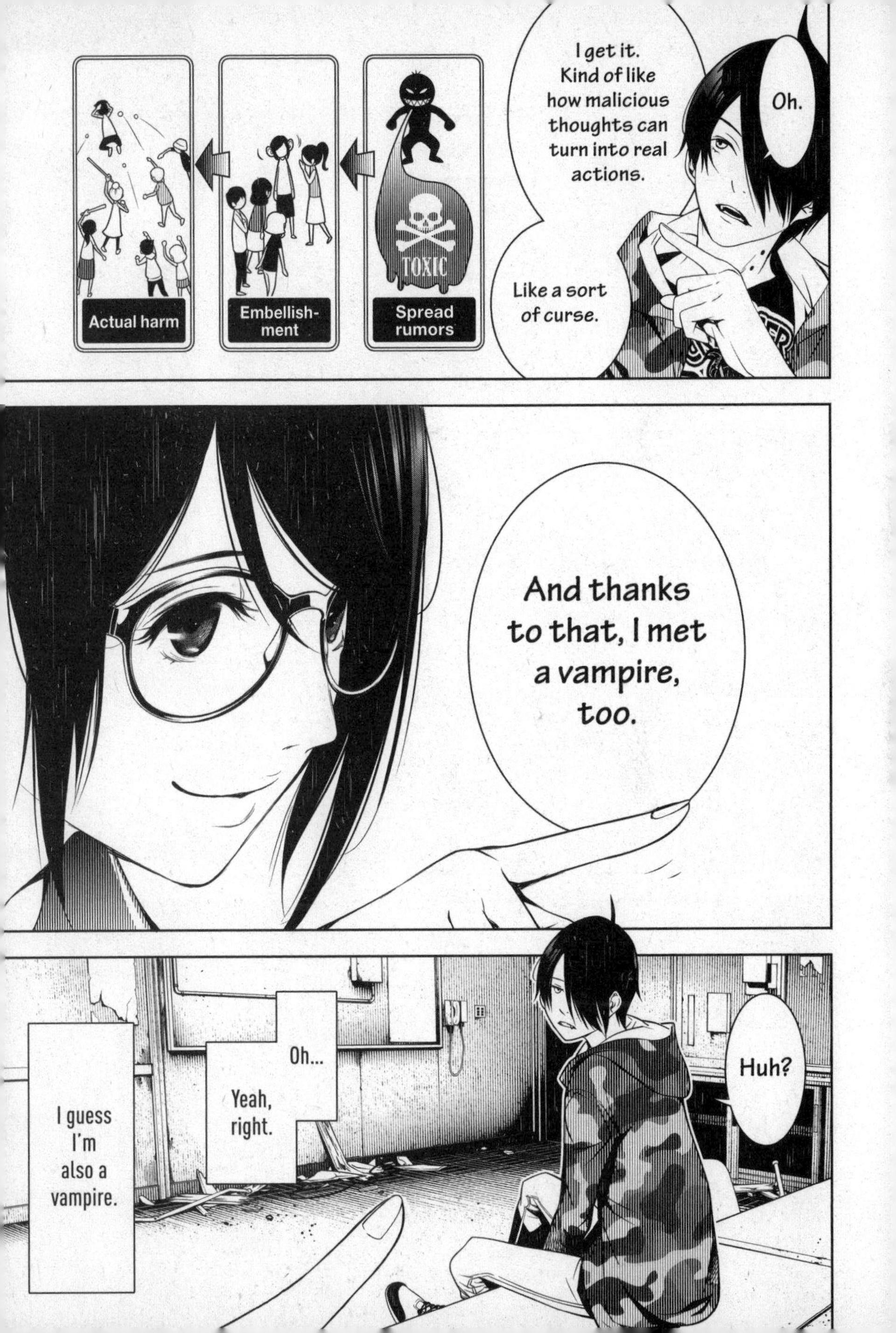
Oh.
I get it. Kind of like how malicious thoughts can turn into real actions.
Like a sort of curse.
Spread rumors
Embellish-ment
Actual harm
TOXIC
And thanks to that, I met a vampire, too.
Huh?
Oh...
Yeah, right.
I guess I'm also a vampire.

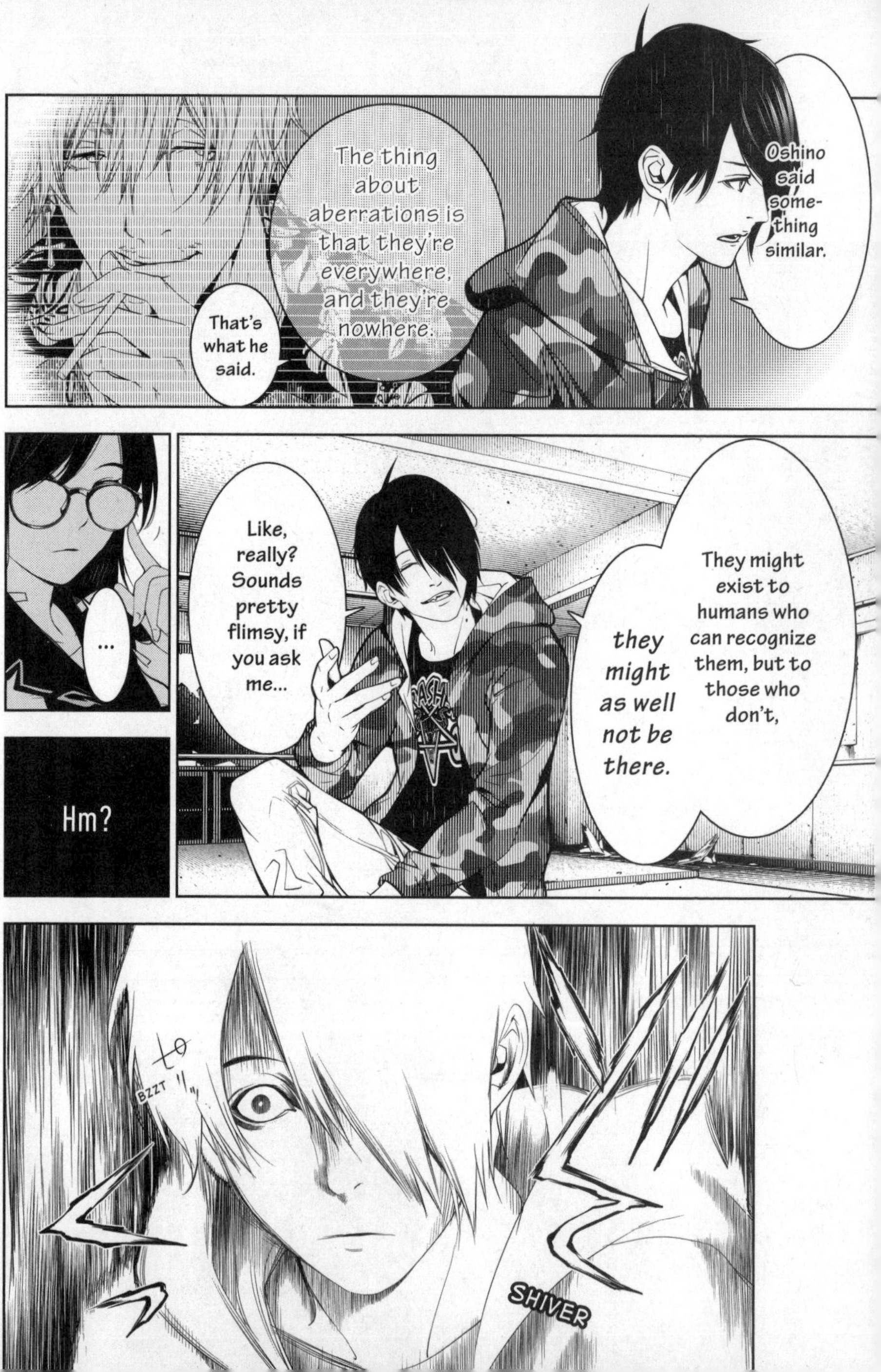
Oshino said some-thing similar.
The thing about aberrations is that they're everywhere, and they're nowhere.
That's what he said.
They might exist to humans who can recognize them, but to those who don't,
they might as well not be there.
Like, really? Sounds pretty flimsy, if you ask me...
...
Hm?
BZZT
SHIVER

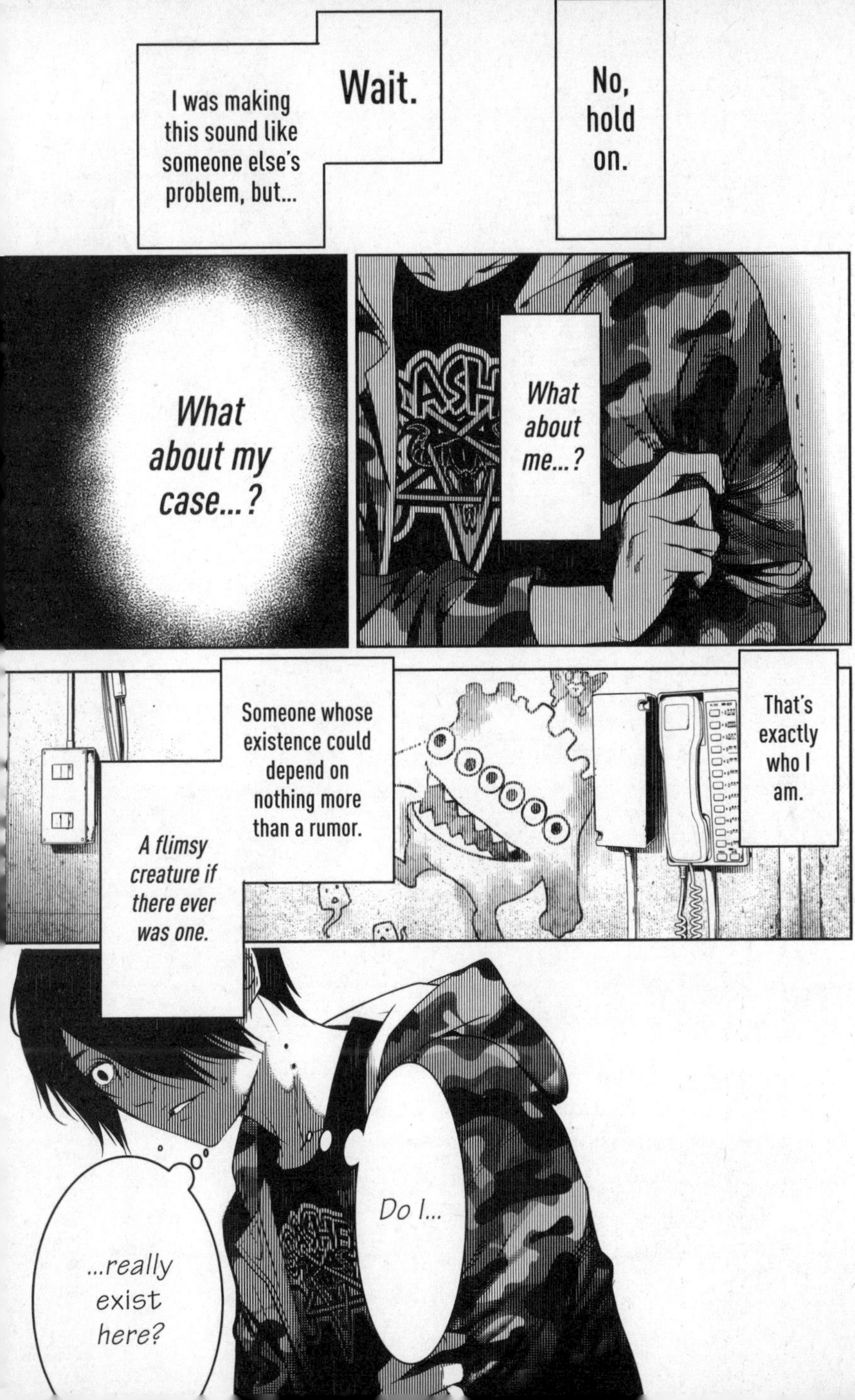

No, hold on.
Wait.
I was making this sound like someone else's problem, but...
What about me...?
What about my case...?
That's exactly who I am.
Someone whose existence could depend on nothing more than a rumor.
A flimsy creature if there ever was one.
Do I...
...really exist here?

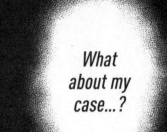

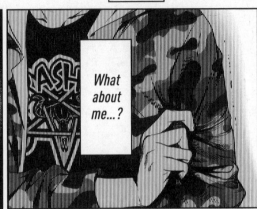

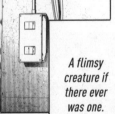

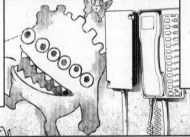

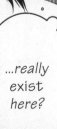

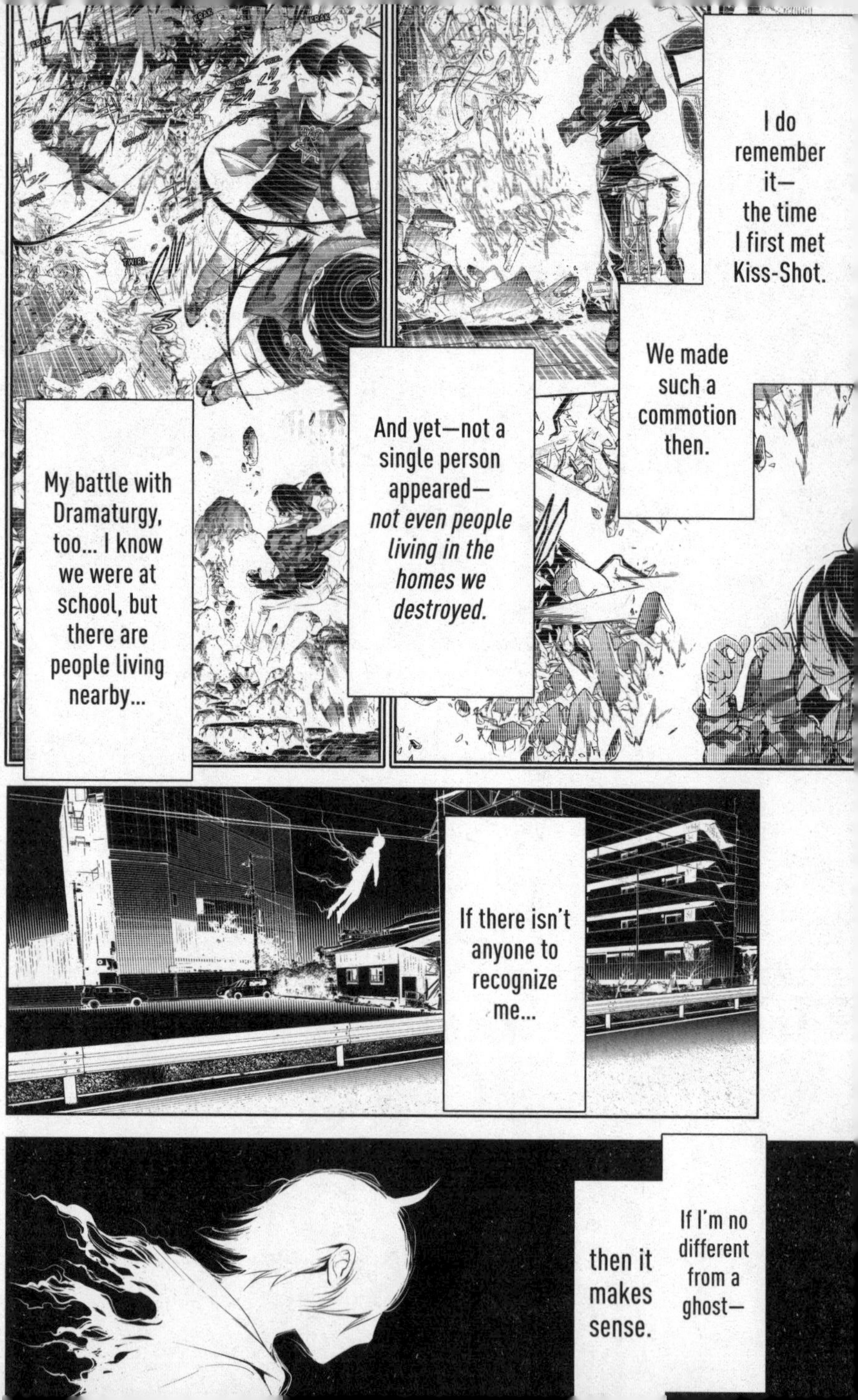
I do remember it—the time I first met Kiss-Shot.
We made such a commotion then.
And yet—not a single person appeared—*not even people living in the homes we destroyed.*
KRAK
TWIRL
My battle with Dramaturgy, too... I know we were at school, but there are people living nearby...
If there isn't anyone to recognize me...
If I'm no different from a ghost—
then it makes sense.

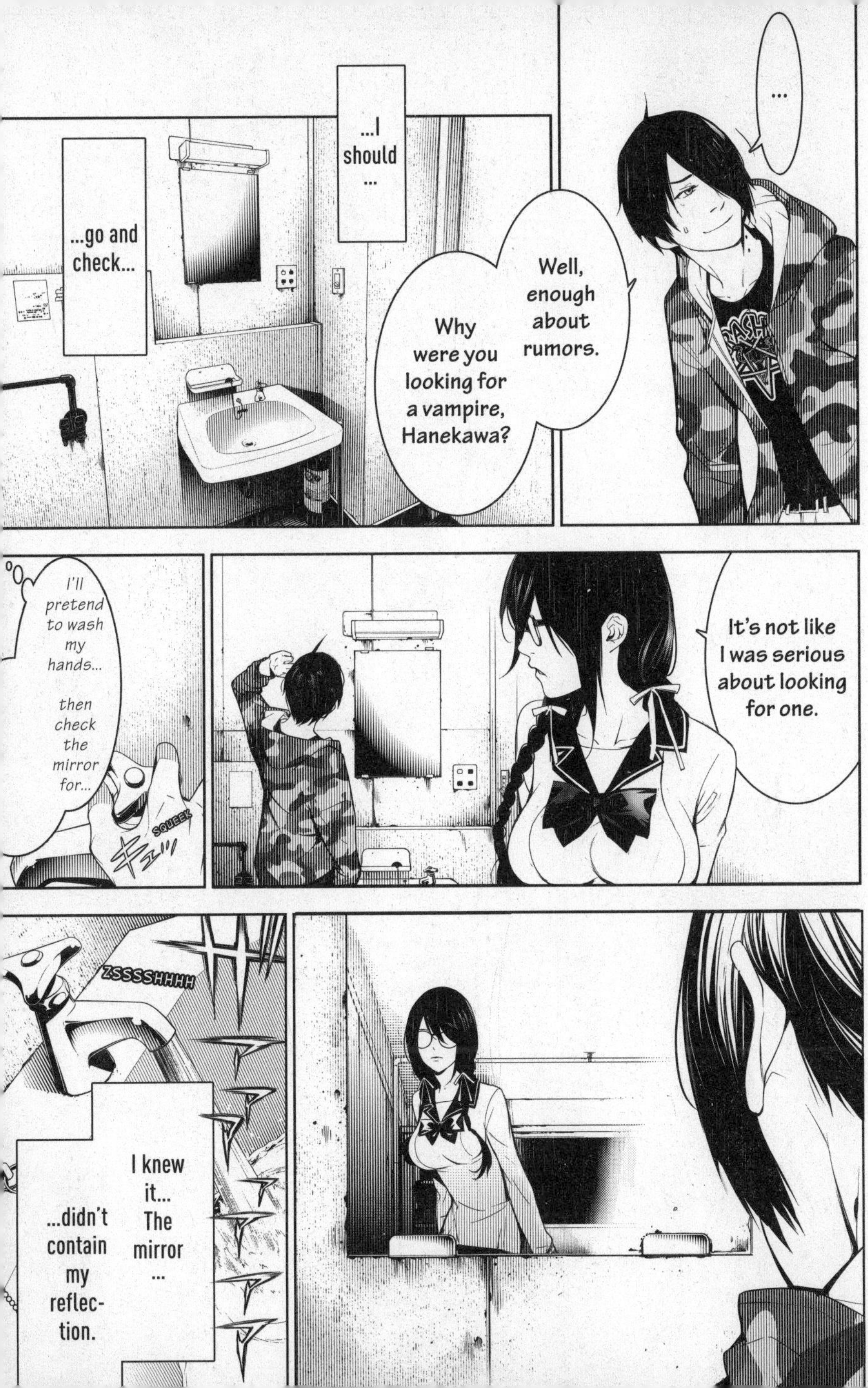
...
Well, enough about rumors.
Why were you looking for a vampire, Hanekawa?
...I should ...
...go and check...
It's not like I was serious about looking for one.
I'll pretend to wash my hands... then check the mirror for...
SQUEEK
ZSSSSHHHH
I knew it... The mirror ...
...didn't contain my reflec-tion.

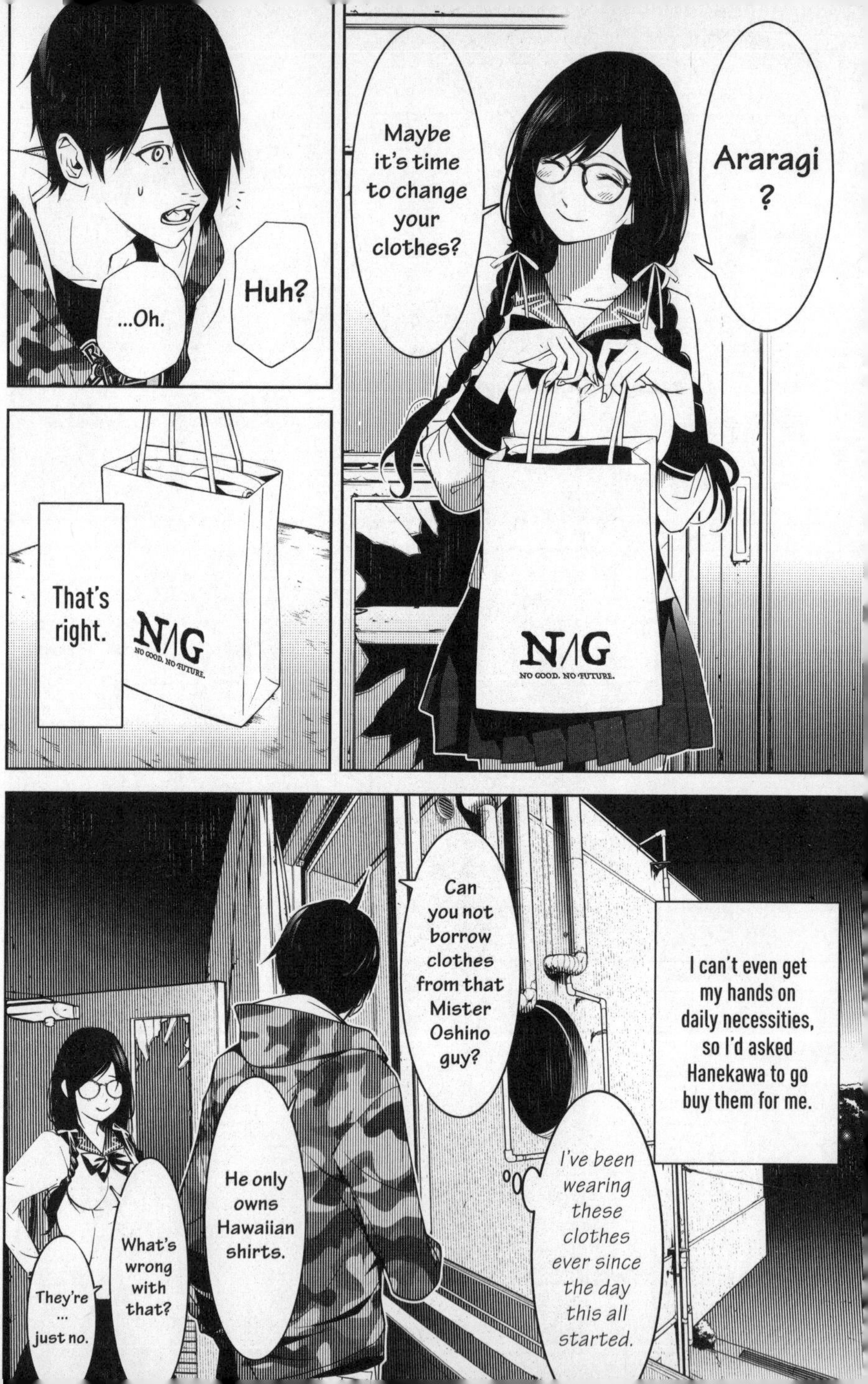
Araragi ?
Maybe it's time to change your clothes?
Huh?
...Oh.
NO GOOD. NO FUTURE.
That's right.
N/G
NO GOOD. NO FUTURE.
I can't even get my hands on daily necessities, so I'd asked Hanekawa to go buy them for me.
I've been wearing these clothes ever since the day this all started.
Can you not borrow clothes from that Mister Oshino guy?
He only owns Hawaiian shirts.
What's wrong with that?
They're ... just no.

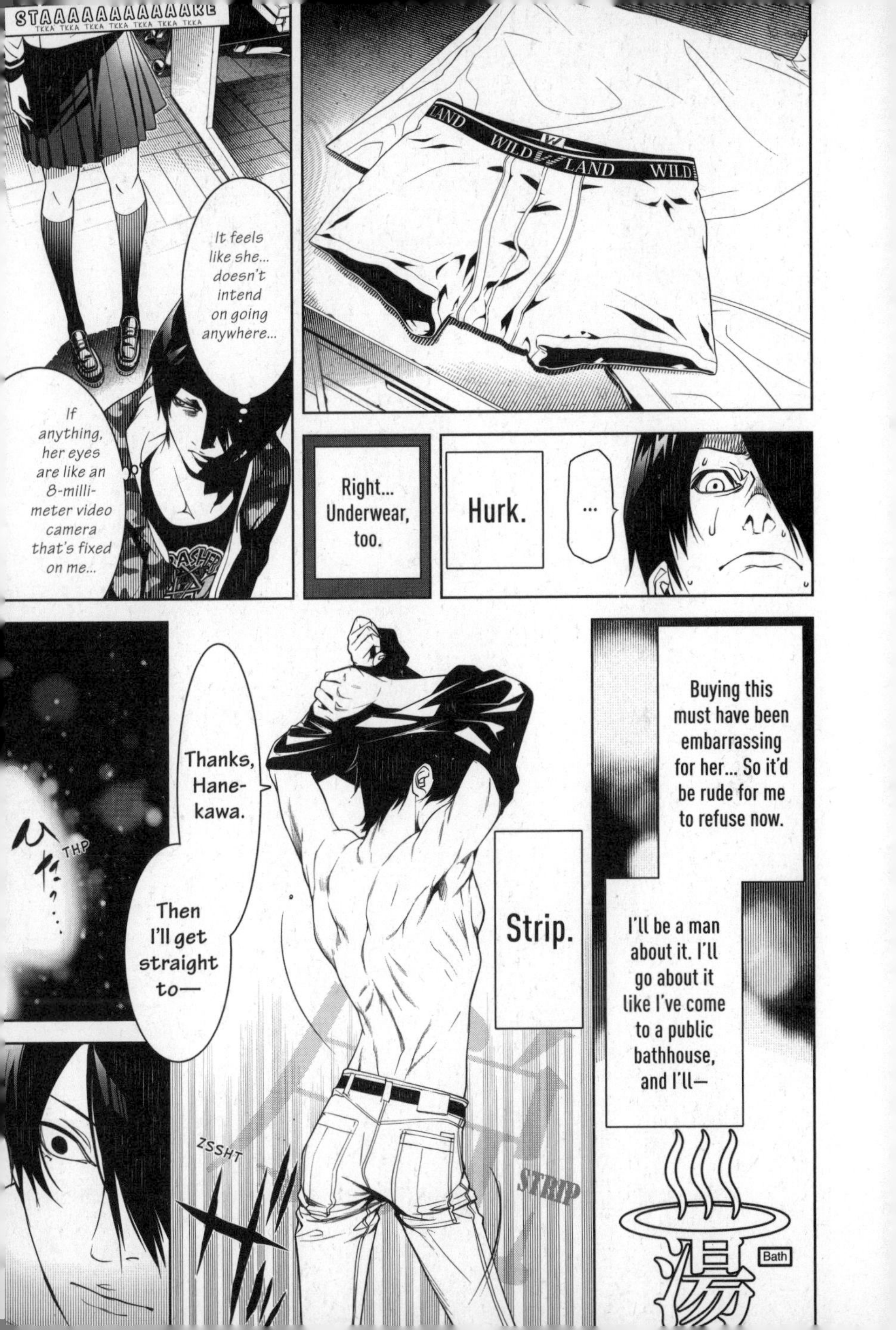
WILD LAND
WILD LAND WILD
...
Hurk.
Right... Underwear, too.
STAAAAAAAAAAARE
TKKA TKKA TKKA TKKA TKKA TKKA TKKA
It feels like she... doesn't intend on going anywhere...
If anything, her eyes are like an 8-milli-meter video camera that's fixed on me...
Buying this must have been embarrassing for her... So it'd be rude for me to refuse now.
I'll be a man about it. I'll go about it like I've come to a public bathhouse, and I'll—
湯
Bath
Strip.
STRIP
Thanks, Hane-kawa.
Then I'll get straight to—
THP
ZSSHT

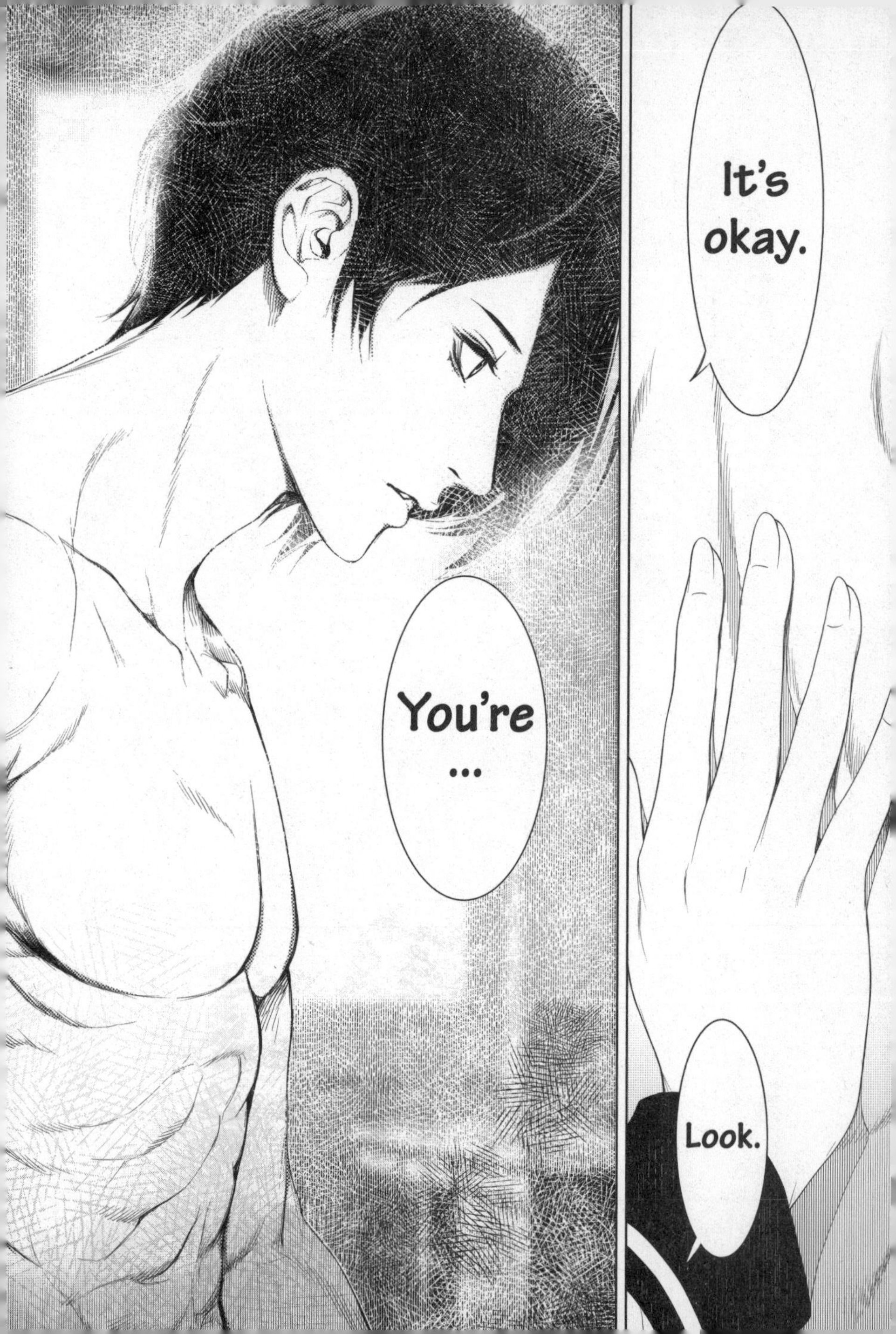
It's okay.
Look.
You're ...

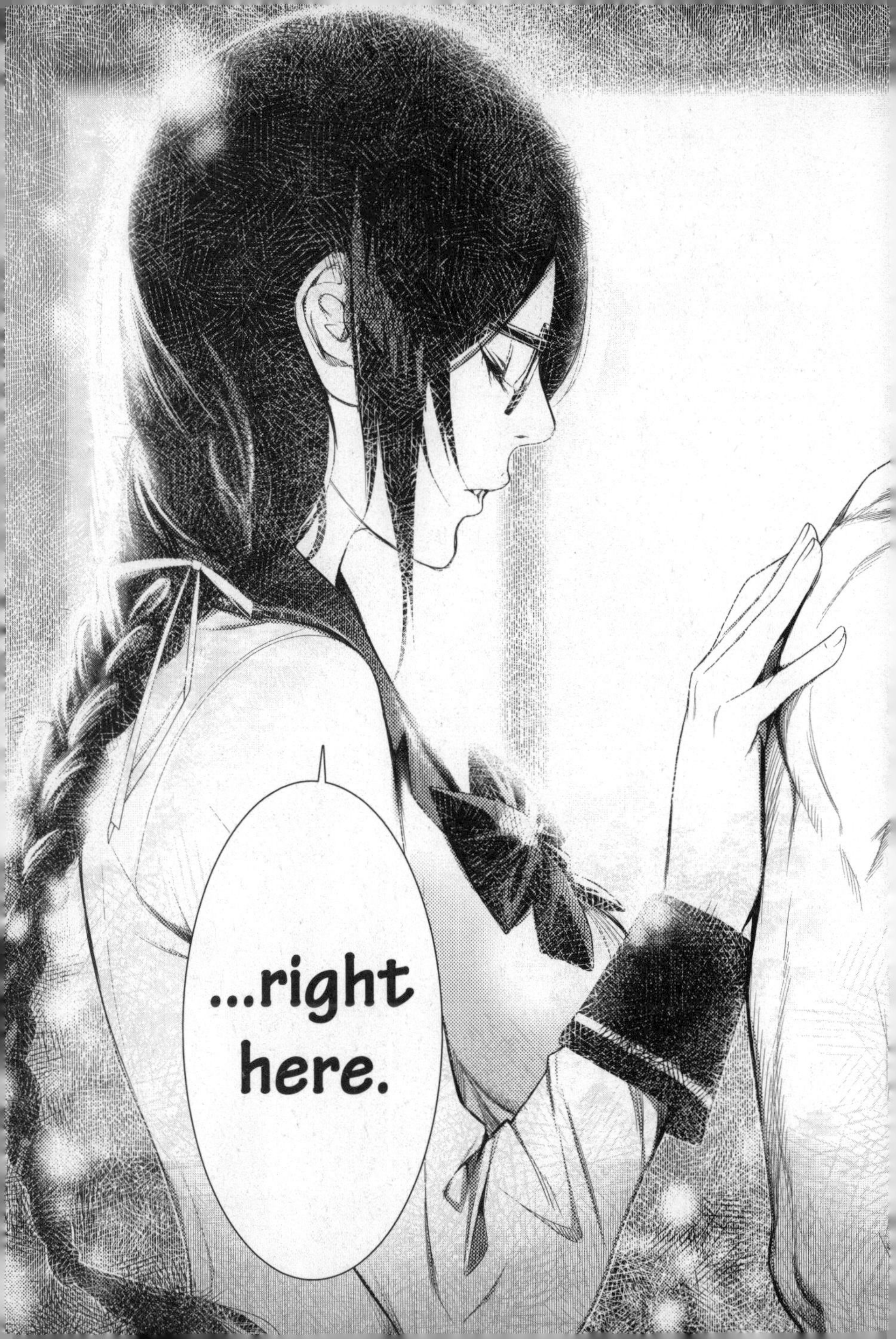
...right here.

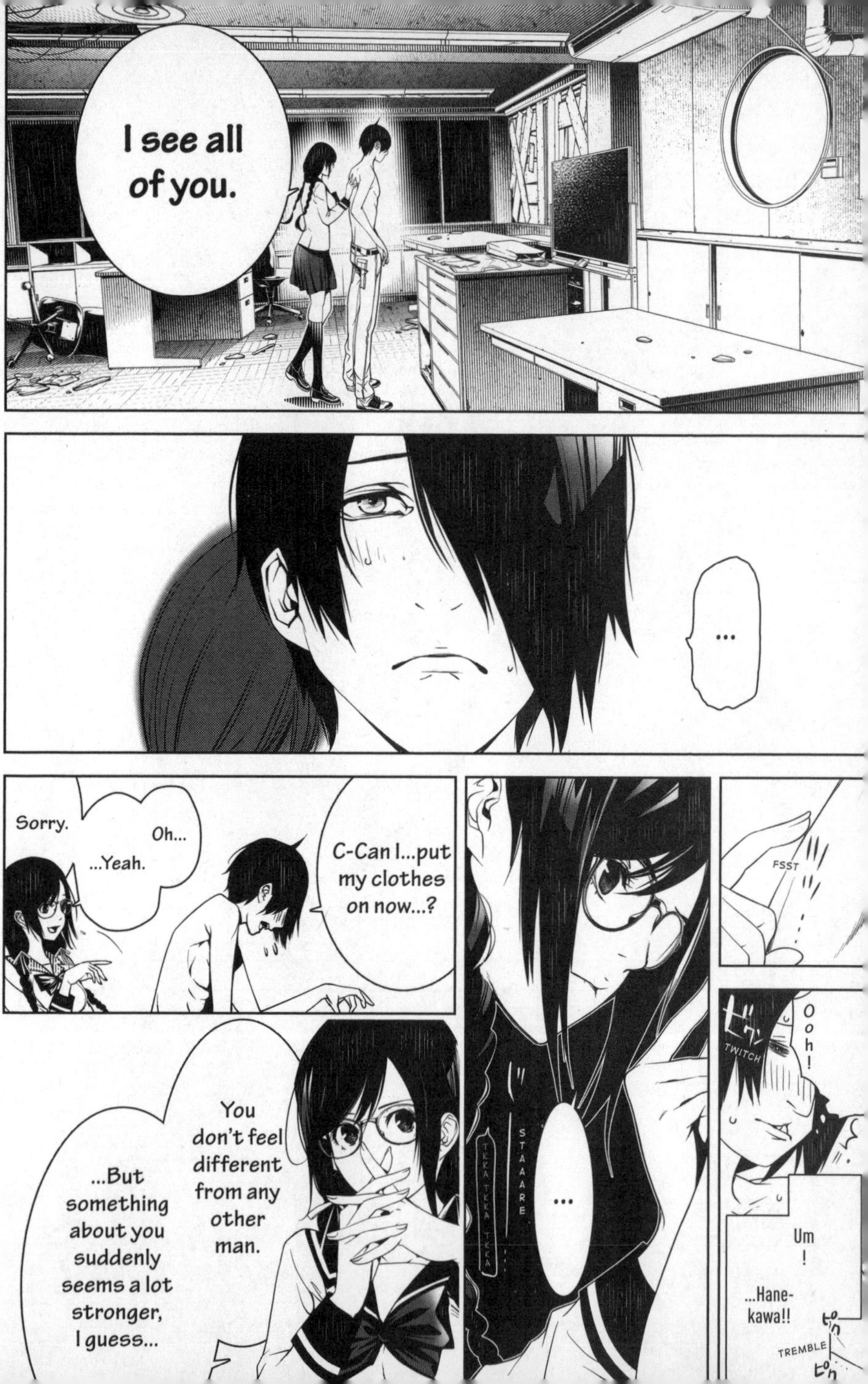
I see all of you.
...
FSST
TWITCH
Ooh!
Um!
...Hane-kawa!!
TREMBLE
STAAARE
TKKA TKKA TKKA
...
C-Can I...put my clothes on now...?
Oh... ...Yeah.
Sorry.
You don't feel different from any other man.
...But something about you suddenly seems a lot stronger, I guess...

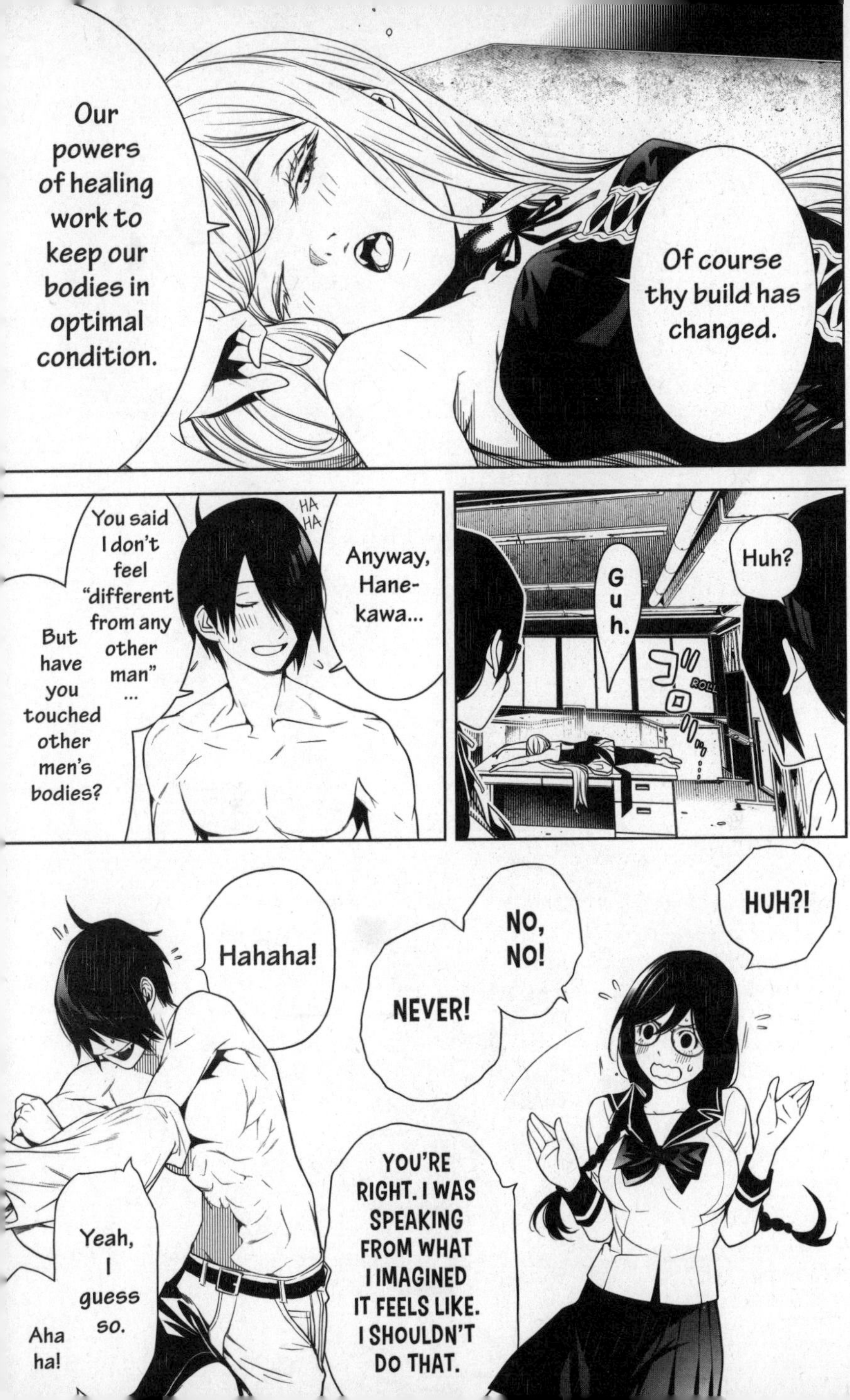
Of course thy build has changed.
Our powers of healing work to keep our bodies in optimal condition.
Huh?
Guh.
ROLL
Anyway, Hane-kawa...
HA HA
You said I don't feel "different from any other man"...
But have you touched other men's bodies?
HUH?!
NO, NO!
NEVER!
Hahaha!
YOU'RE RIGHT. I WAS SPEAKING FROM WHAT I IMAGINED IT FEELS LIKE. I SHOULDN'T DO THAT.
Yeah, I guess so.
Aha ha!

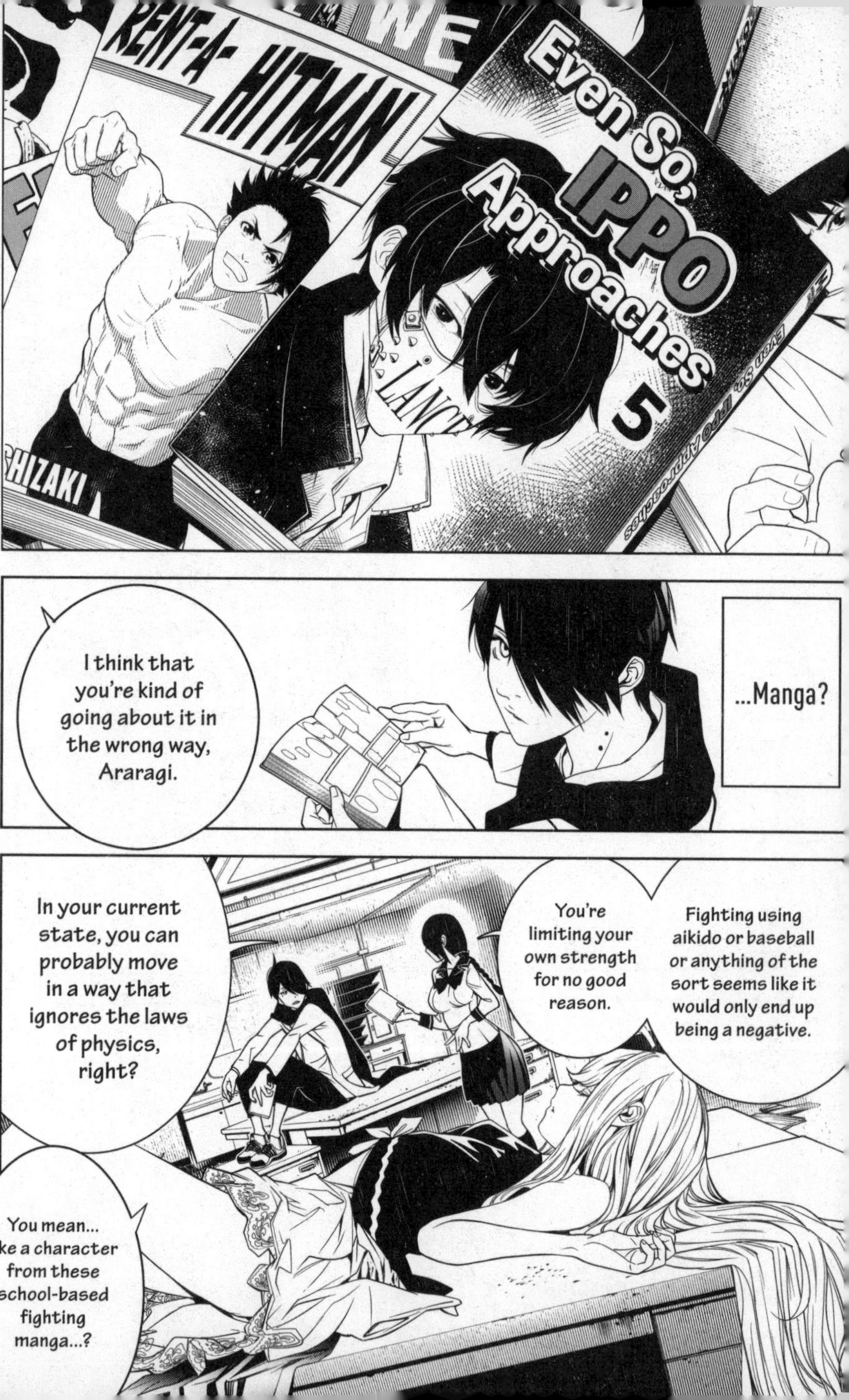
Even So, IPPO Approaches 5
Even So, IPPO Approaches
WE
RENT-A-HITMAN
HIZAKI
...Manga?
I think that you're kind of going about it in the wrong way, Araragi.
Fighting using aikido or baseball or anything of the sort seems like it would only end up being a negative.
You're limiting your own strength for no good reason.
In your current state, you can probably move in a way that ignores the laws of physics, right?
You mean... like a character from these school-based fighting manga...?

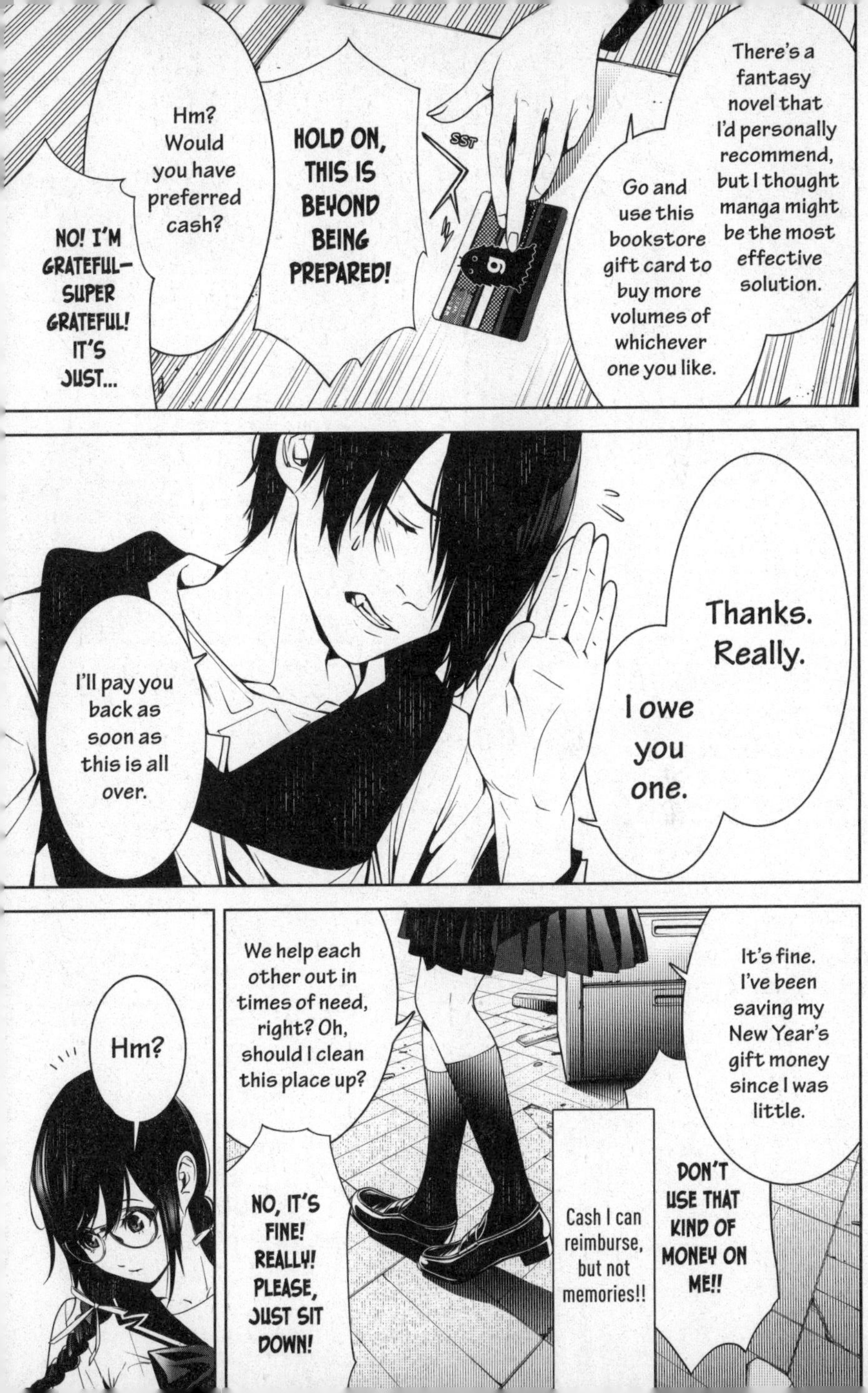
There's a fantasy novel that I'd personally recommend, but I thought manga might be the most effective solution.
Go and use this bookstore gift card to buy more volumes of whichever one you like.
SST
HOLD ON, THIS IS BEYOND BEING PREPARED!
Hm? Would you have preferred cash?
NO! I'M GRATEFUL— SUPER GRATEFUL! IT'S JUST...
Thanks. Really.
I owe you one.
I'll pay you back as soon as this is all over.
It's fine. I've been saving my New Year's gift money since I was little.
DON'T USE THAT KIND OF MONEY ON ME!!
Cash I can reimburse, but not memories!!
We help each other out in times of need, right? Oh, should I clean this place up?
NO, IT'S FINE! REALLY! PLEASE, JUST SIT DOWN!
Hm?

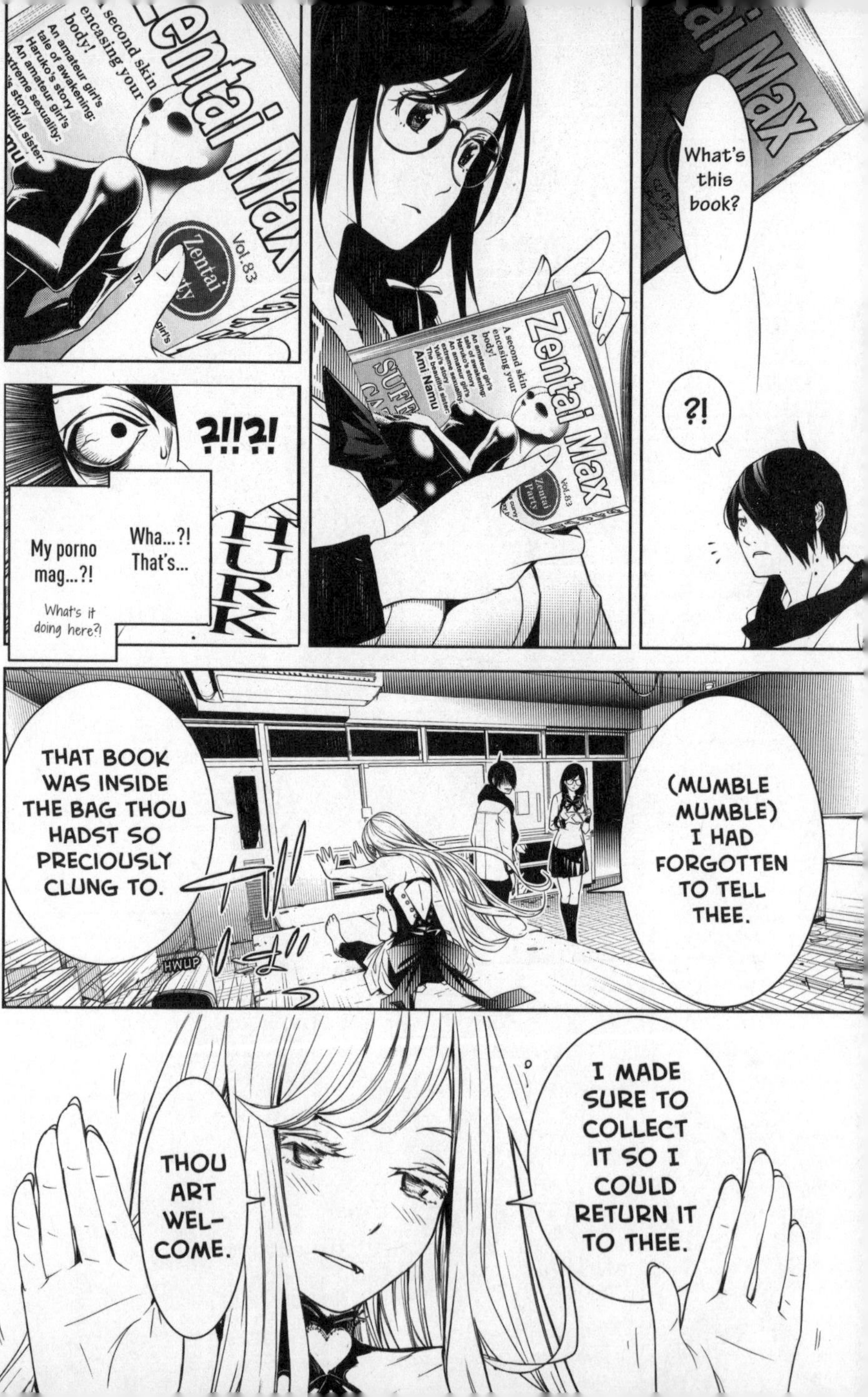
Zentai Max
What's this book?
?!
Zentai Max
A second skin encasing your body!
An amateur girl's tale of awakening: Haruko's story
An amateur girl's extreme sexuality: Yuki's story
The beautiful sister: Ami Namu
Vol.83
Zentai Party
?!!?!
HURK
Wha...?! That's...
My porno mag...?!
What's it doing here?!
(MUMBLE MUMBLE) I HAD FORGOTTEN TO TELL THEE.
THAT BOOK WAS INSIDE THE BAG THOU HADST SO PRECIOUSLY CLUNG TO.
HWUP
I MADE SURE TO COLLECT IT SO I COULD RETURN IT TO THEE.
THOU ART WEL-COME.

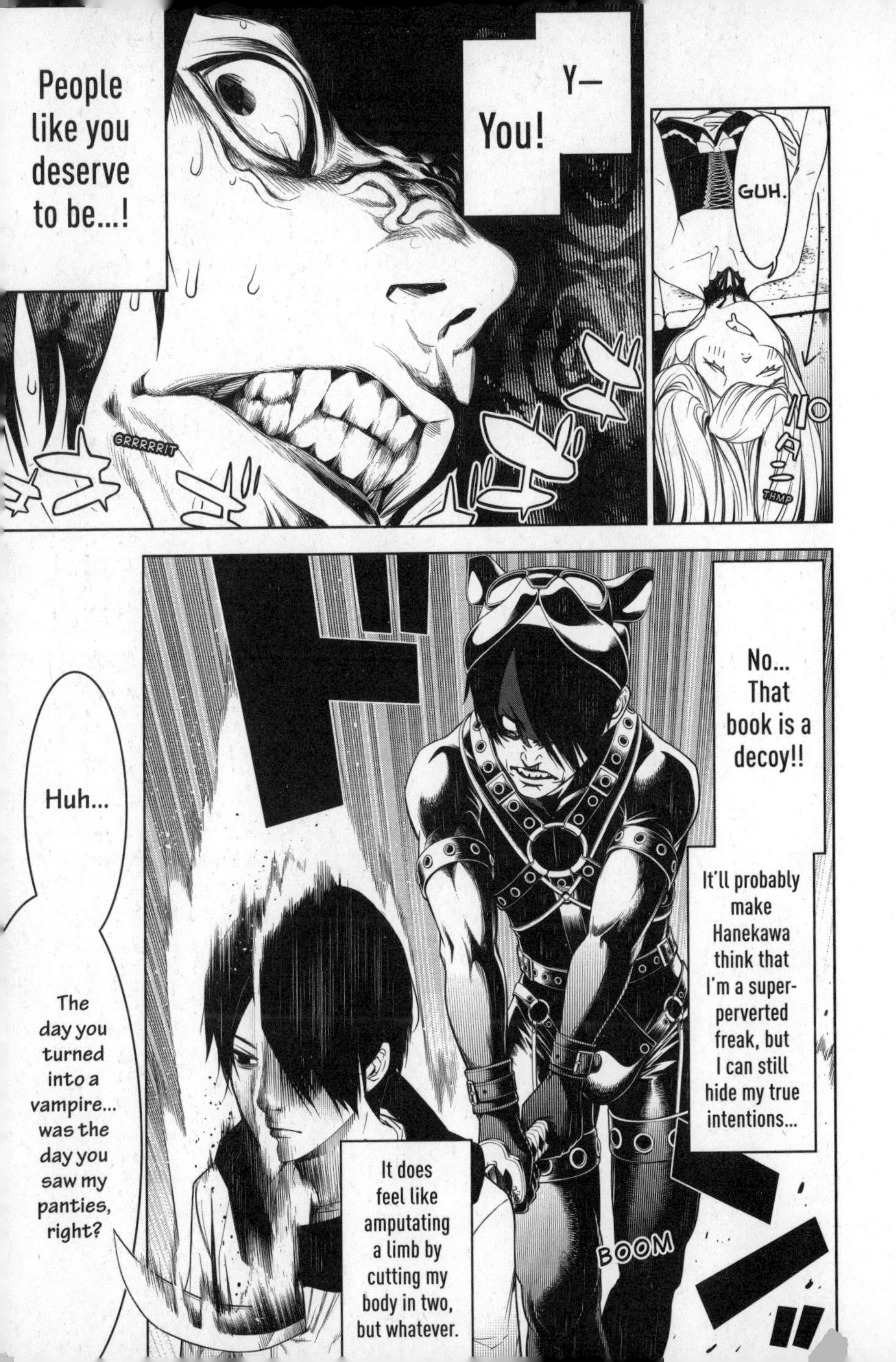
GUH.
THMP
Y— You!
People like you deserve to be...!
GRRRRRIT
No... That book is a decoy!!
It'll probably make Hanekawa think that I'm a super-perverted freak, but I can still hide my true intentions...
BOOM
It does feel like amputating a limb by cutting my body in two, but whatever.
Huh...
The day you turned into a vampire... was the day you saw my panties, right?

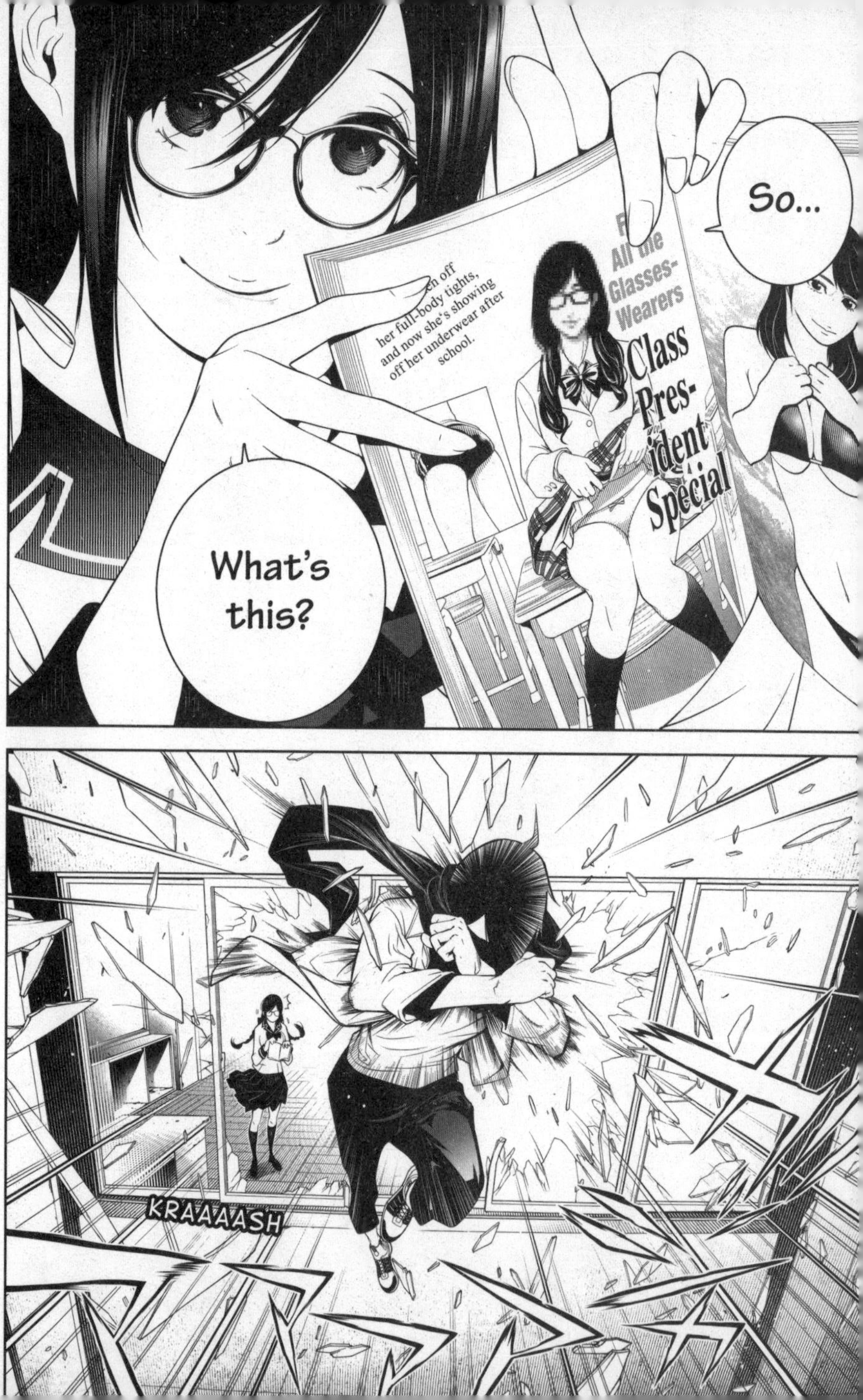
So...
All the Glasses-Wearers
Class President Special
her full-body tights, and now she's showing off her underwear after school.
What's this?
KRAAAASH

BAKEMONOGATARI

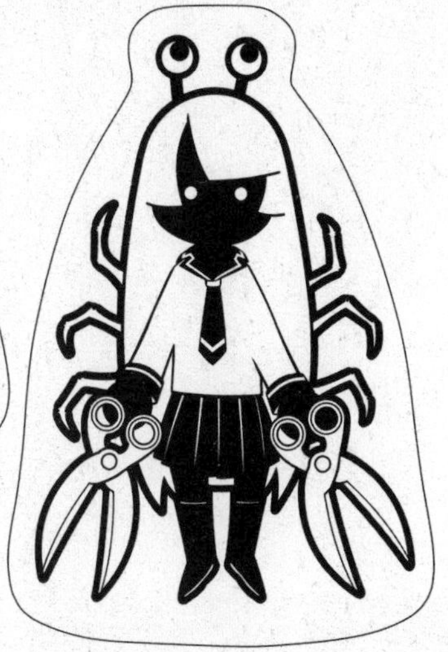
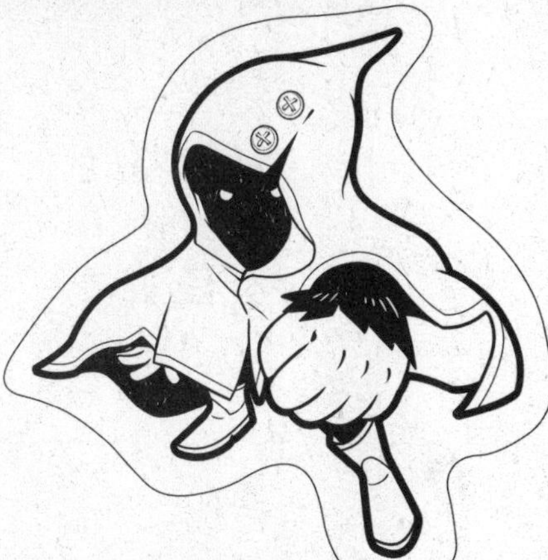
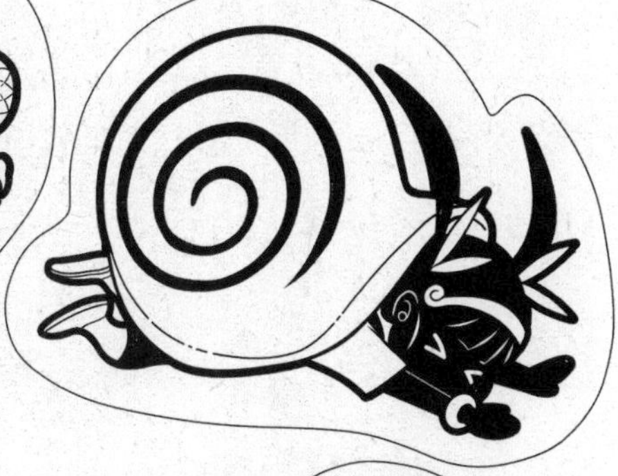
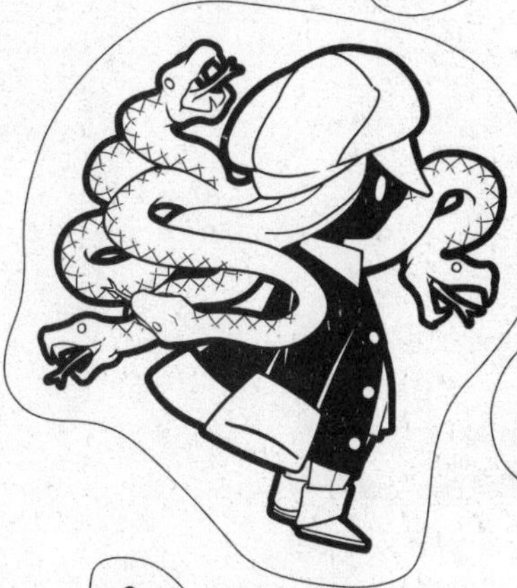
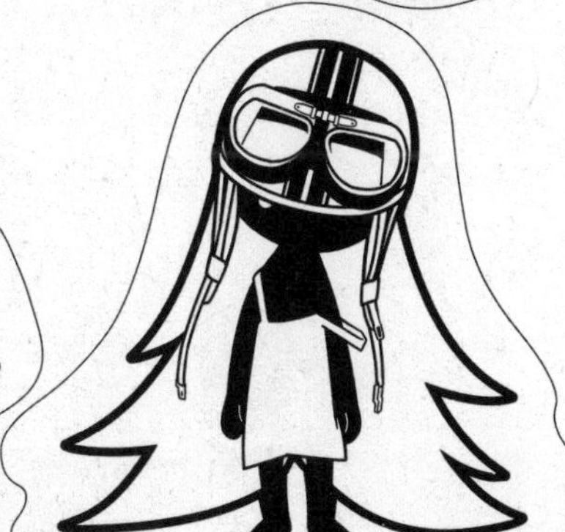
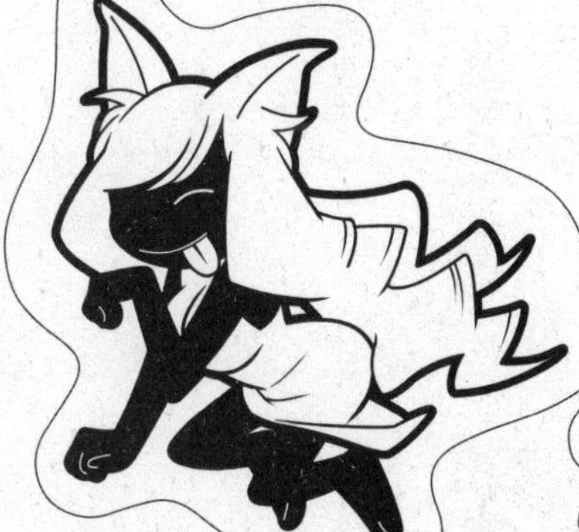

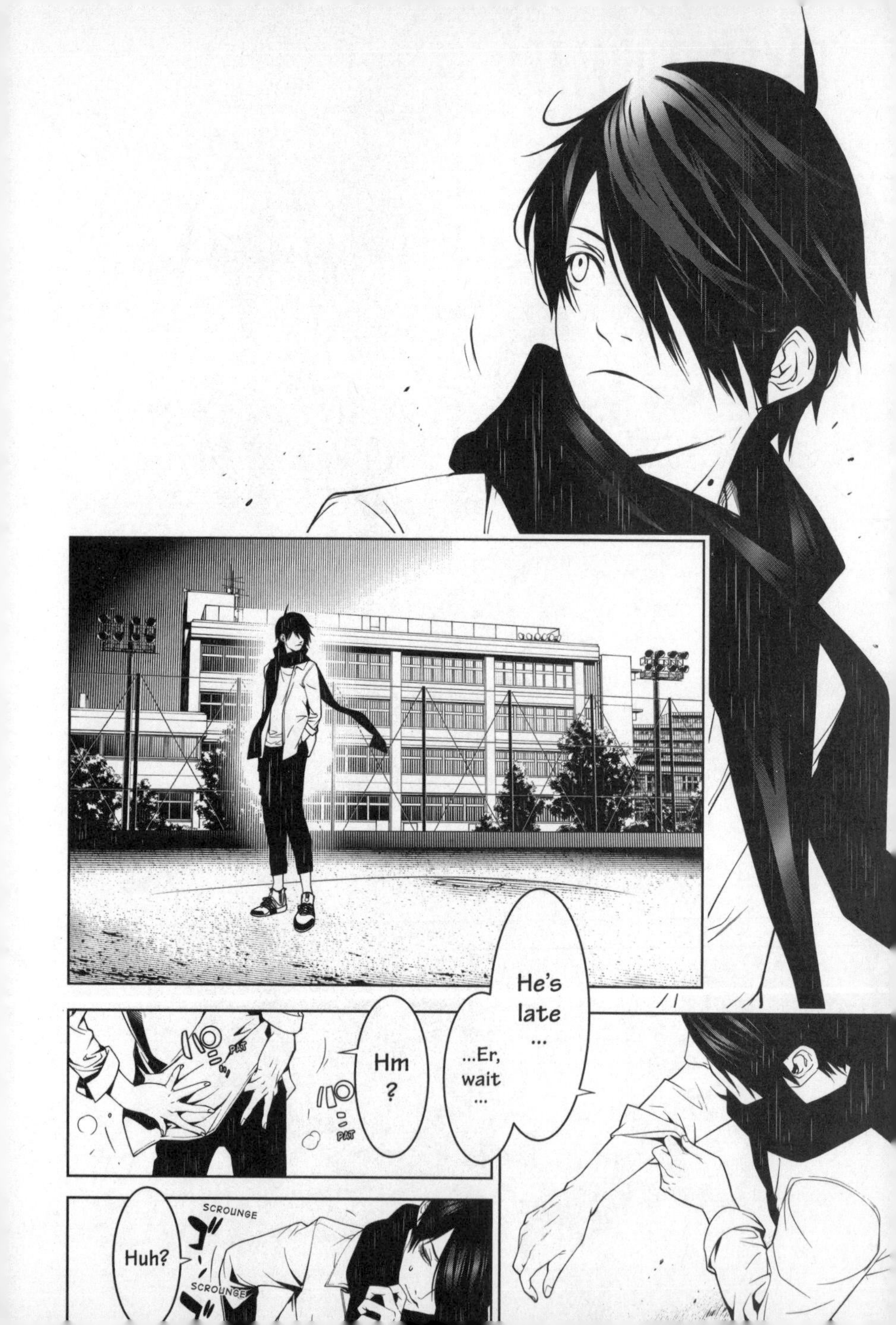
He's late ...
...Er, wait ...
Hm ?
PAT
PAT
SCROUNGE
Huh?
SCROUNGE

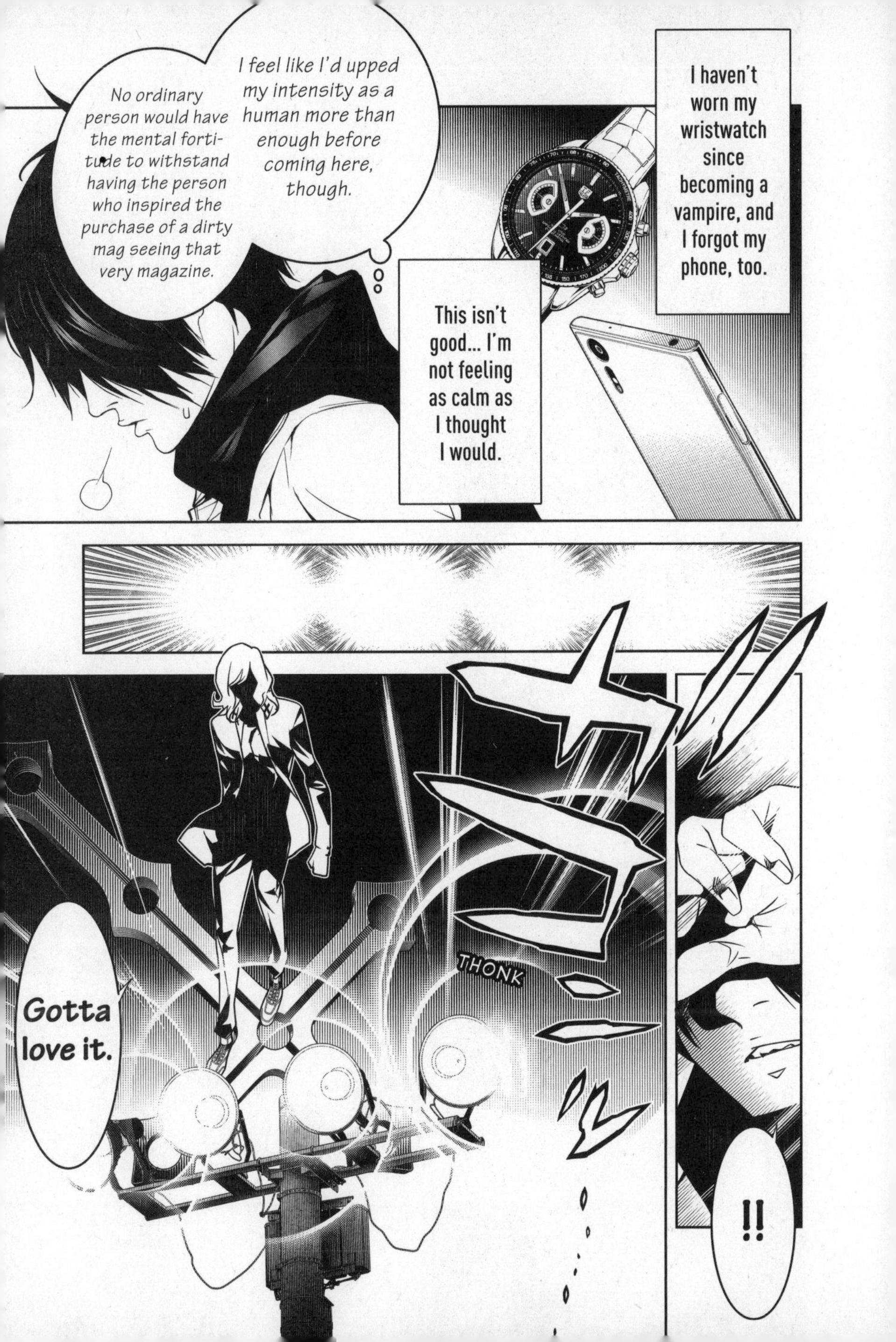

I haven't worn my wristwatch since becoming a vampire, and I forgot my phone, too.
This isn't good... I'm not feeling as calm as I thought I would.
I feel like I'd upped my intensity as a human more than enough before coming here, though.
No ordinary person would have the mental forti-tude to withstand having the person who inspired the purchase of a dirty mag seeing that very magazine.
!!
THONK
Gotta love it.

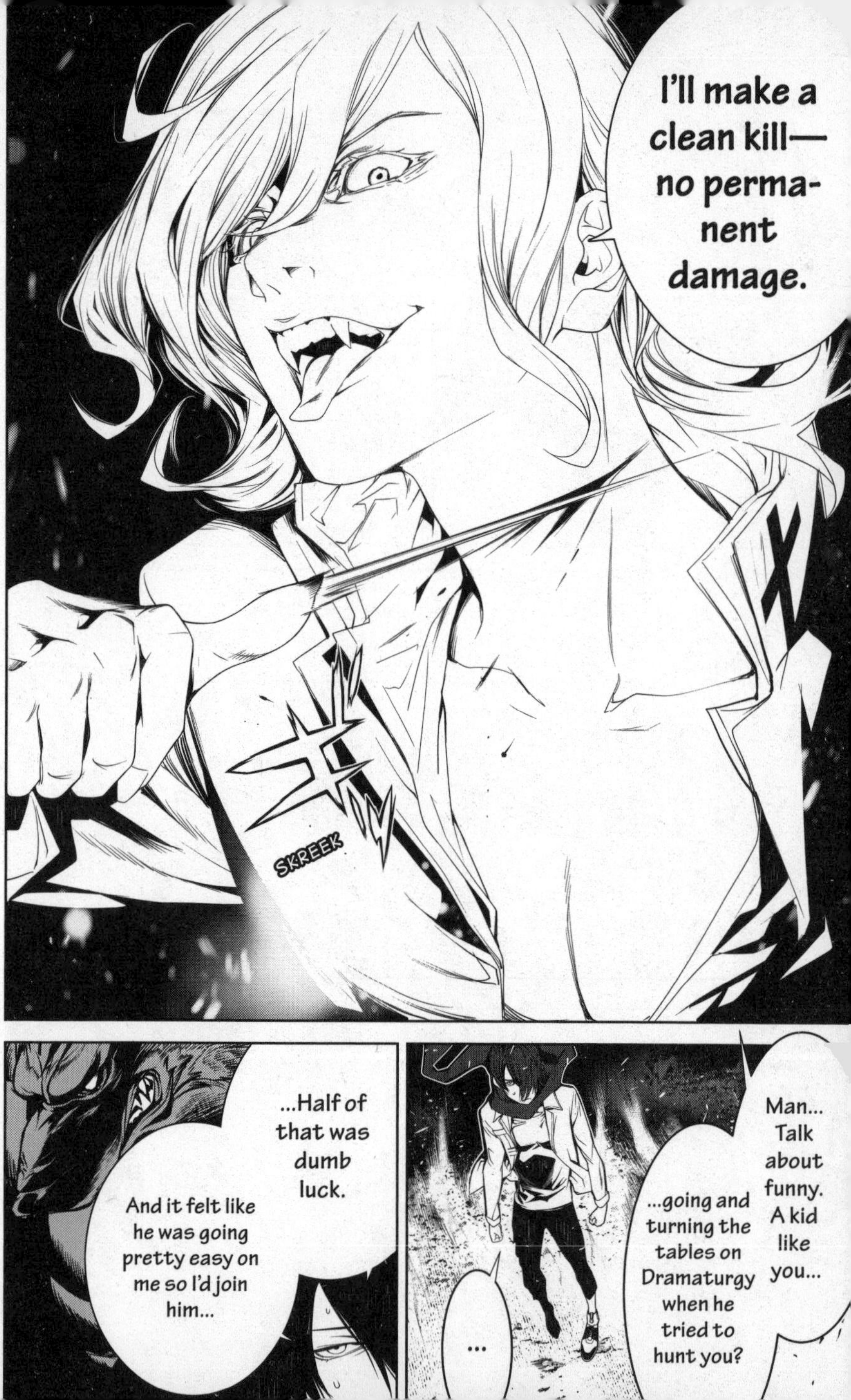
I'll make a clean kill—no permanent damage.
SKREEK
Man... Talk about funny. A kid like you...
...going and turning the tables on Dramaturgy when he tried to hunt you?
...
...Half of that was dumb luck.
And it felt like he was going pretty easy on me so I'd join him...

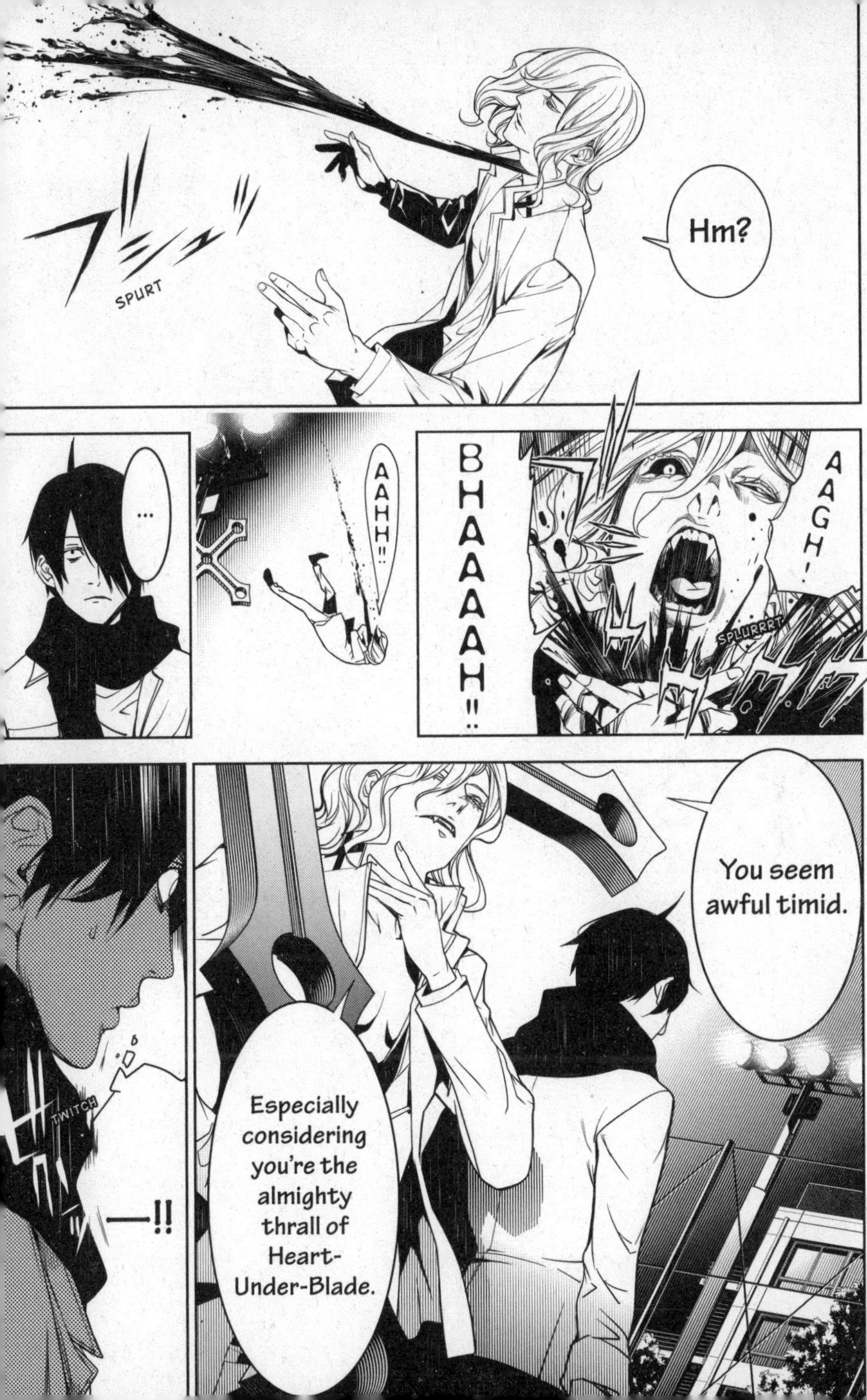
Hm?
SPURT
AAGH!
BHAAAAAH!!
SPLURRRT
AAHH!!
...
You seem awful timid.
Especially considering you're the almighty thrall of Heart-Under-Blade.
TWITCH
—!!

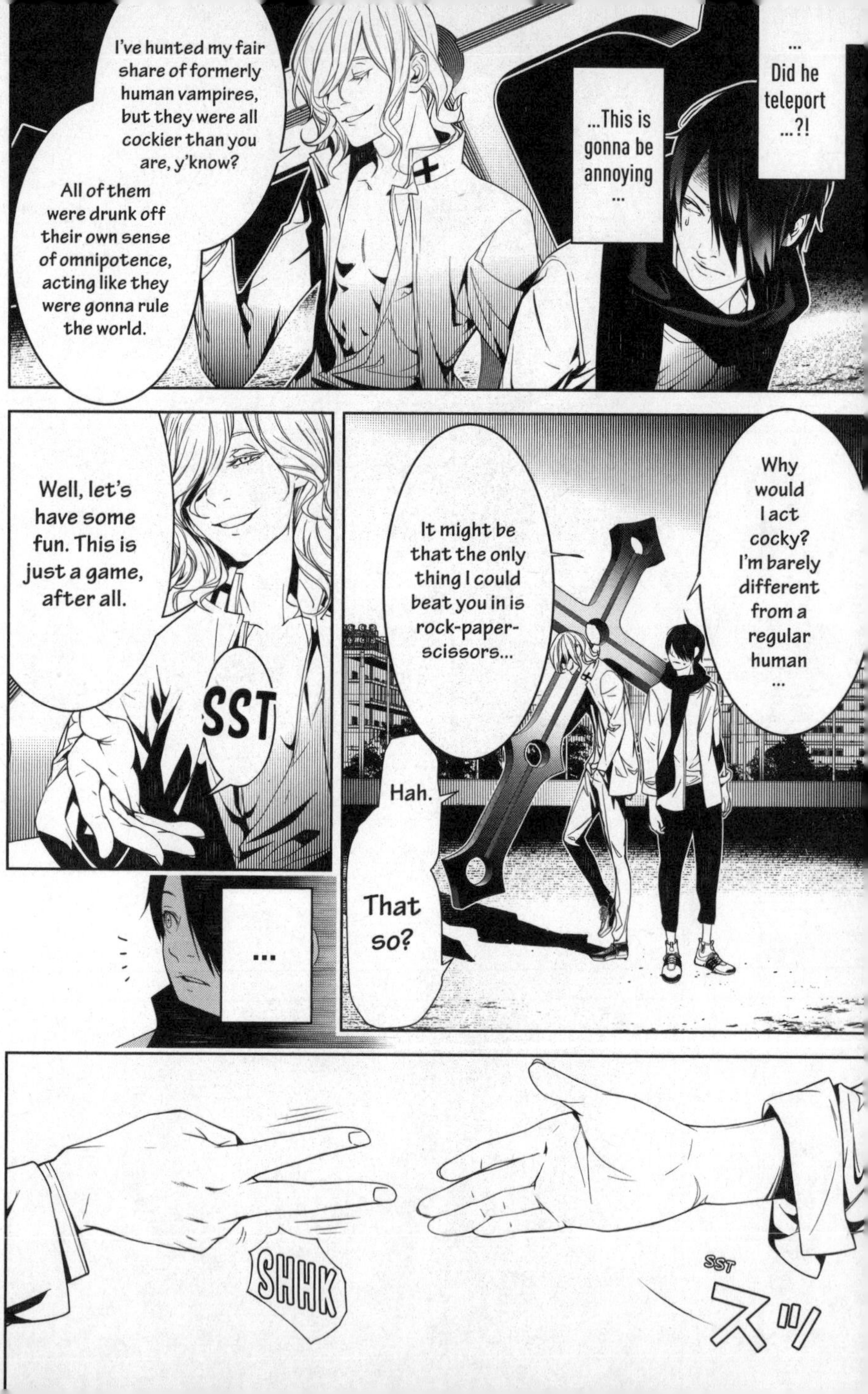

... Did he teleport ...?!
...This is gonna be annoying ...
I've hunted my fair share of formerly human vampires, but they were all cockier than you are, y'know?
All of them were drunk off their own sense of omnipotence, acting like they were gonna rule the world.
Why would I act cocky? I'm barely different from a regular human ...
It might be that the only thing I could beat you in is rock-paper-scissors...
Hah.
That so?
Well, let's have some fun. This is just a game, after all.
SST
...
SST
スッ
SHHK

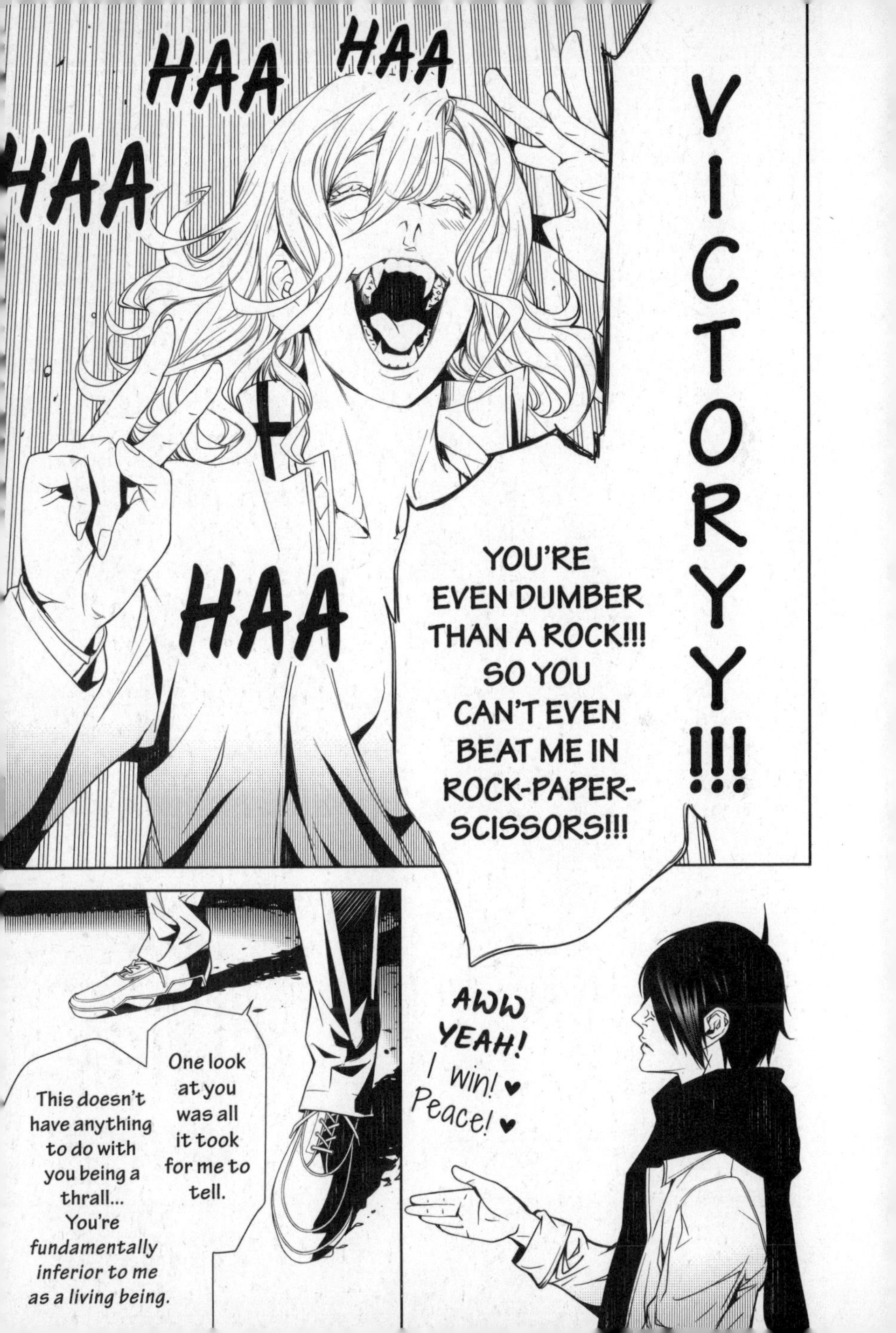
HAA HAA
HAA
VICTORY!!!
YOU'RE EVEN DUMBER THAN A ROCK!!! SO YOU CAN'T EVEN BEAT ME IN ROCK-PAPER-SCISSORS!!!
HAA
AWW YEAH!
I win! ♥ Peace! ♥
One look at you was all it took for me to tell.
This doesn't have anything to do with you being a thrall... You're fundamentally inferior to me as a living being.

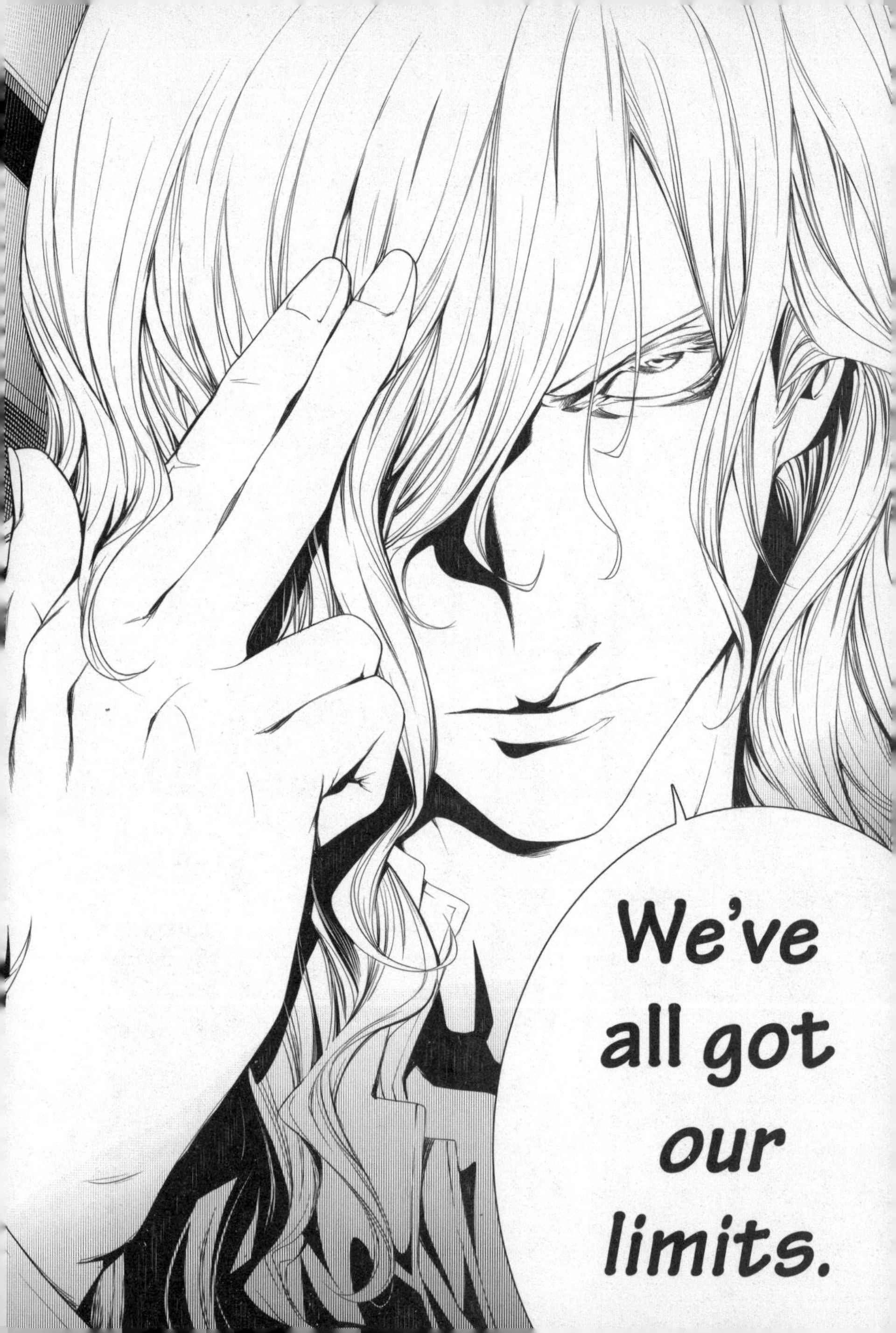
We've all got our limits.

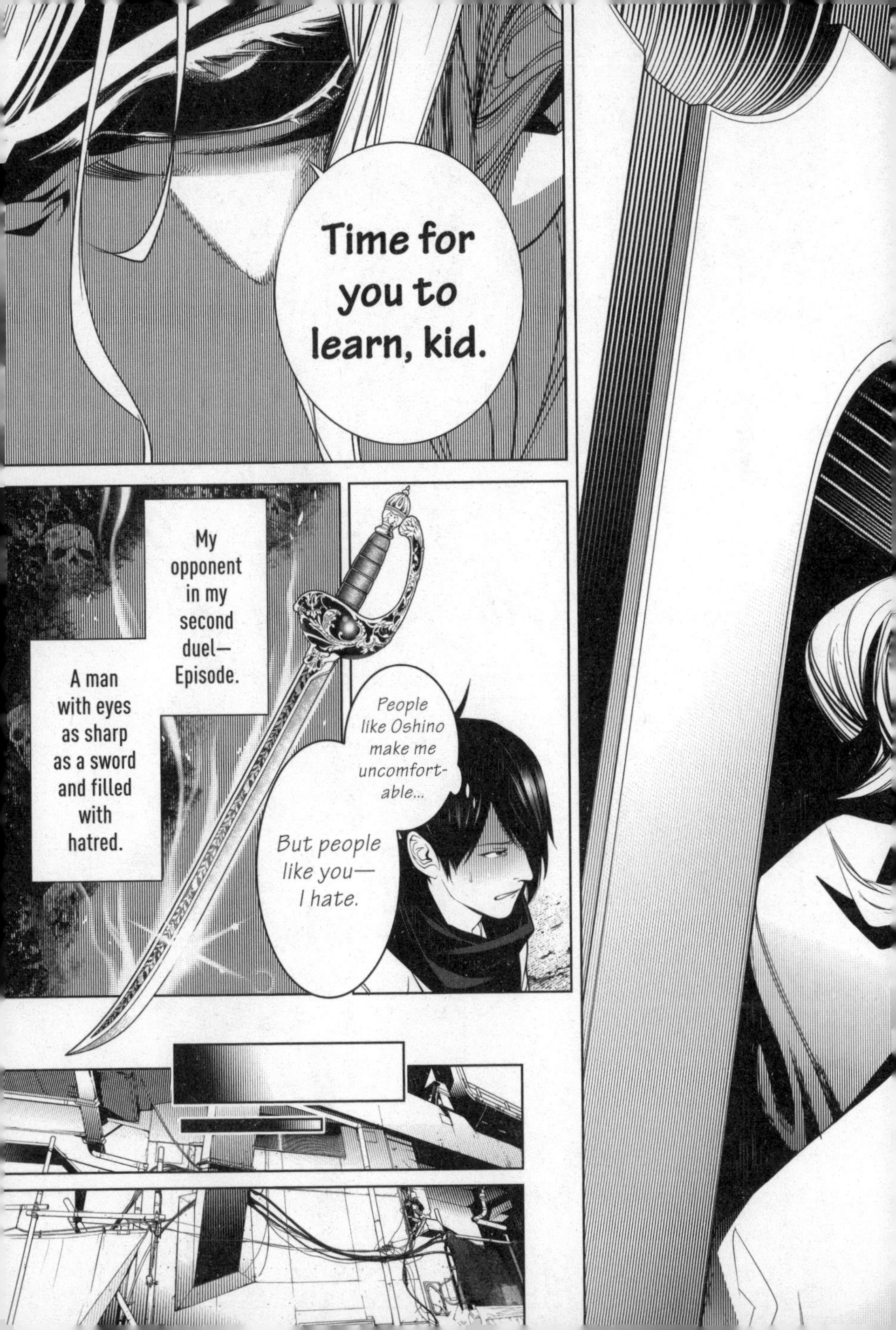
Time for you to learn, kid.
People like Oshino make me uncomfortable...
But people like you—I hate.
My opponent in my second duel—Episode.
A man with eyes as sharp as a sword and filled with hatred.

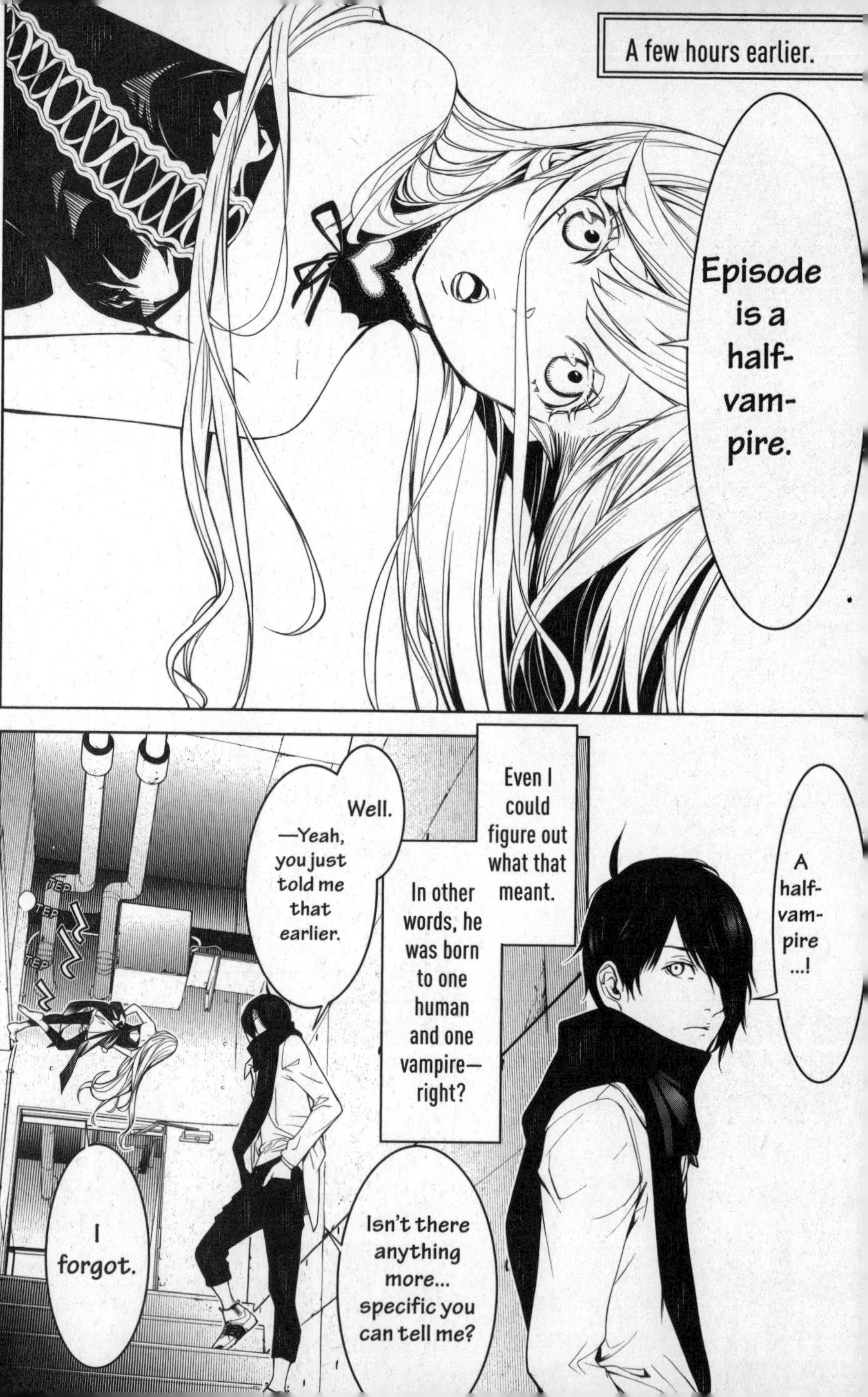
A few hours earlier.
Episode is a half-vampire.
A half-vampire...!
Even I could figure out what that meant.
In other words, he was born to one human and one vampire—right?
Well. —Yeah, you just told me that earlier.
TEP TEP TEP
Isn't there anything more... specific you can tell me?
I forgot.

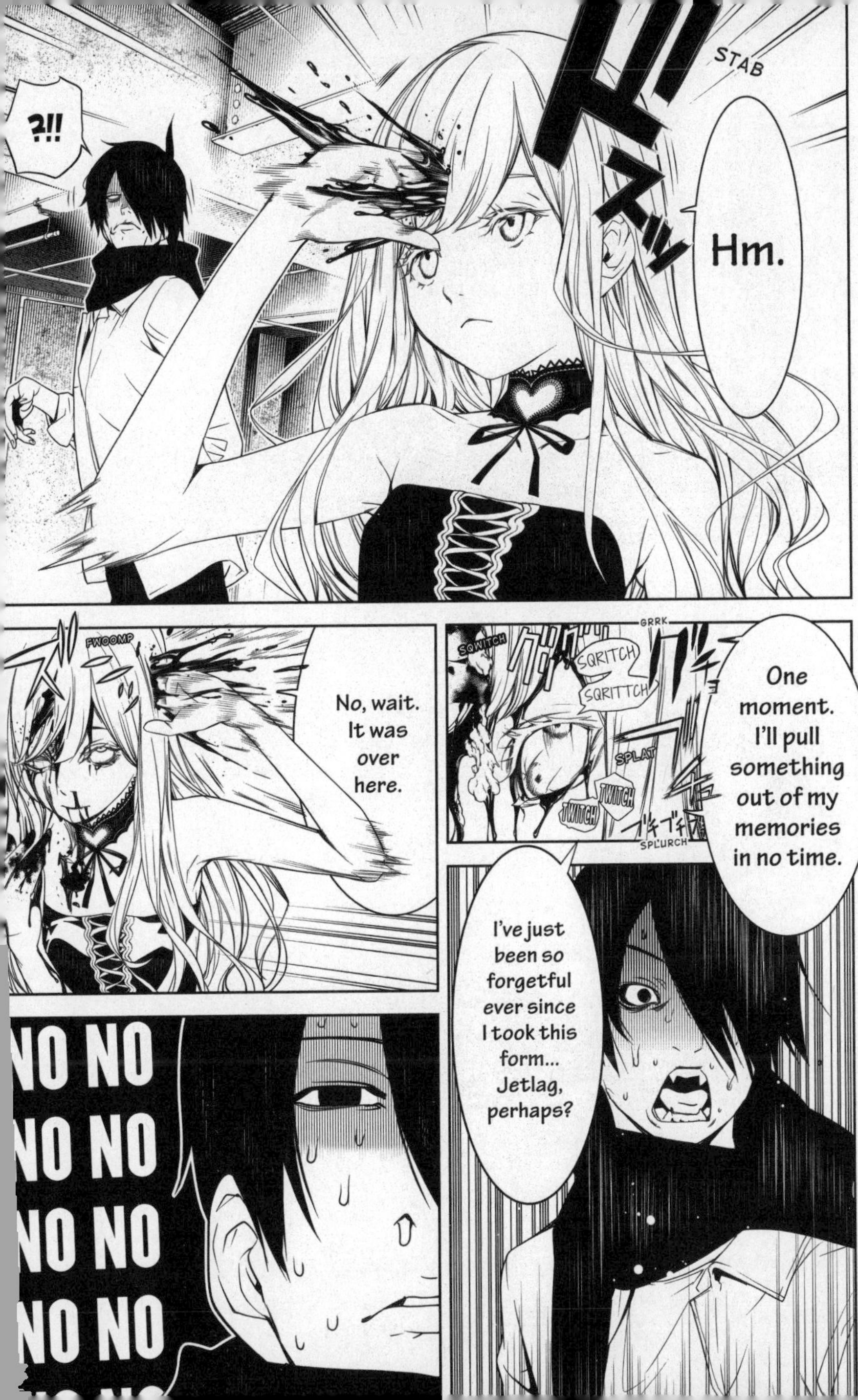
STAB
Hm.
?!!
GRRK
SQRITCH
SQRITTCH
SQWITCH
SPLAT
TWITCH
TWITCH
SPLURCH
One moment. I'll pull something out of my memories in no time.
FWOOMP
No, wait. It was over here.
I've just been so forgetful ever since I took this form... Jetlag, perhaps?
NO NO
NO NO
NO NO
NO NO

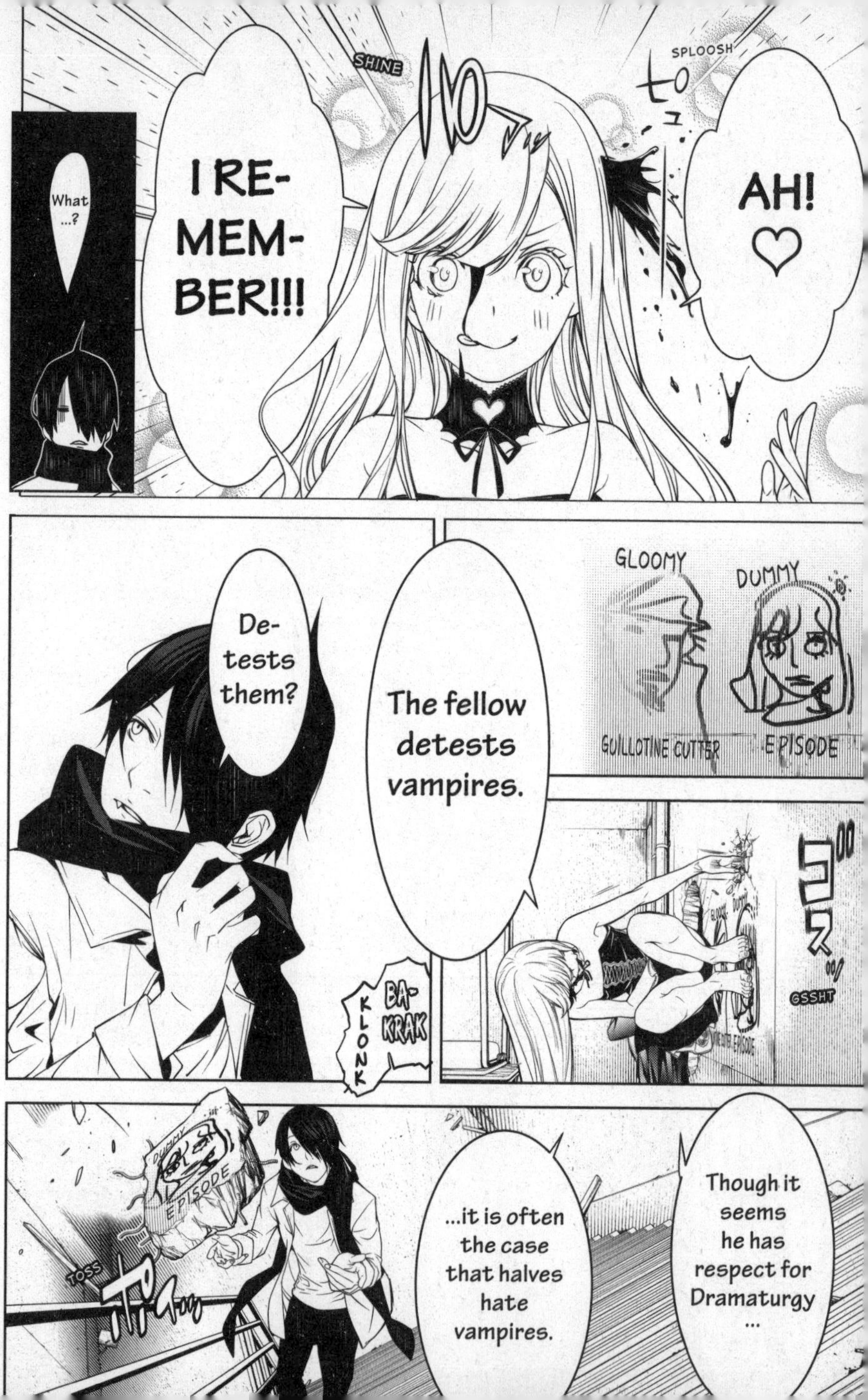
SPLOOSH
AH! ♡
SHINE
I RE-MEM-BER!!!
What ...?
GLOOMY
DUMMY
GUILLOTINE CUTTER
EPISODE
GSSHT
BA-KRAK
KLONK
The fellow detests vampires.
De-tests them?
Though it seems he has respect for Dramaturgy ...
...it is often the case that halves hate vampires.
DUMMY
EPISODE
TOSS

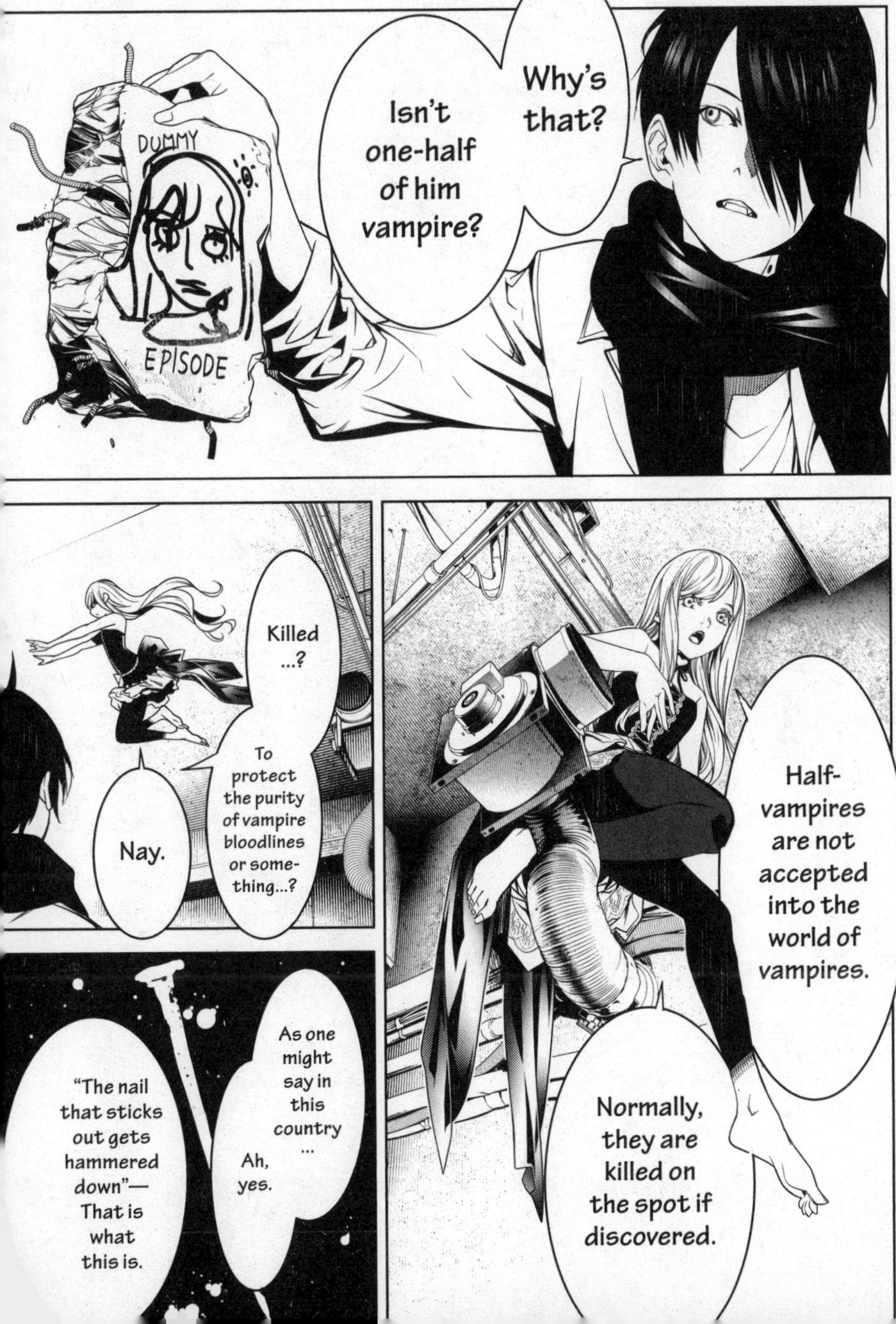
Why's that?
Isn't one-half of him vampire?
DUMMY
EPISODE
Half-vampires are not accepted into the world of vampires.
Normally, they are killed on the spot if discovered.
Killed ...?
To protect the purity of vampire bloodlines or some-thing...?
Nay.
As one might say in this country ...
Ah, yes.
"The nail that sticks out gets hammered down"— That is what this is.

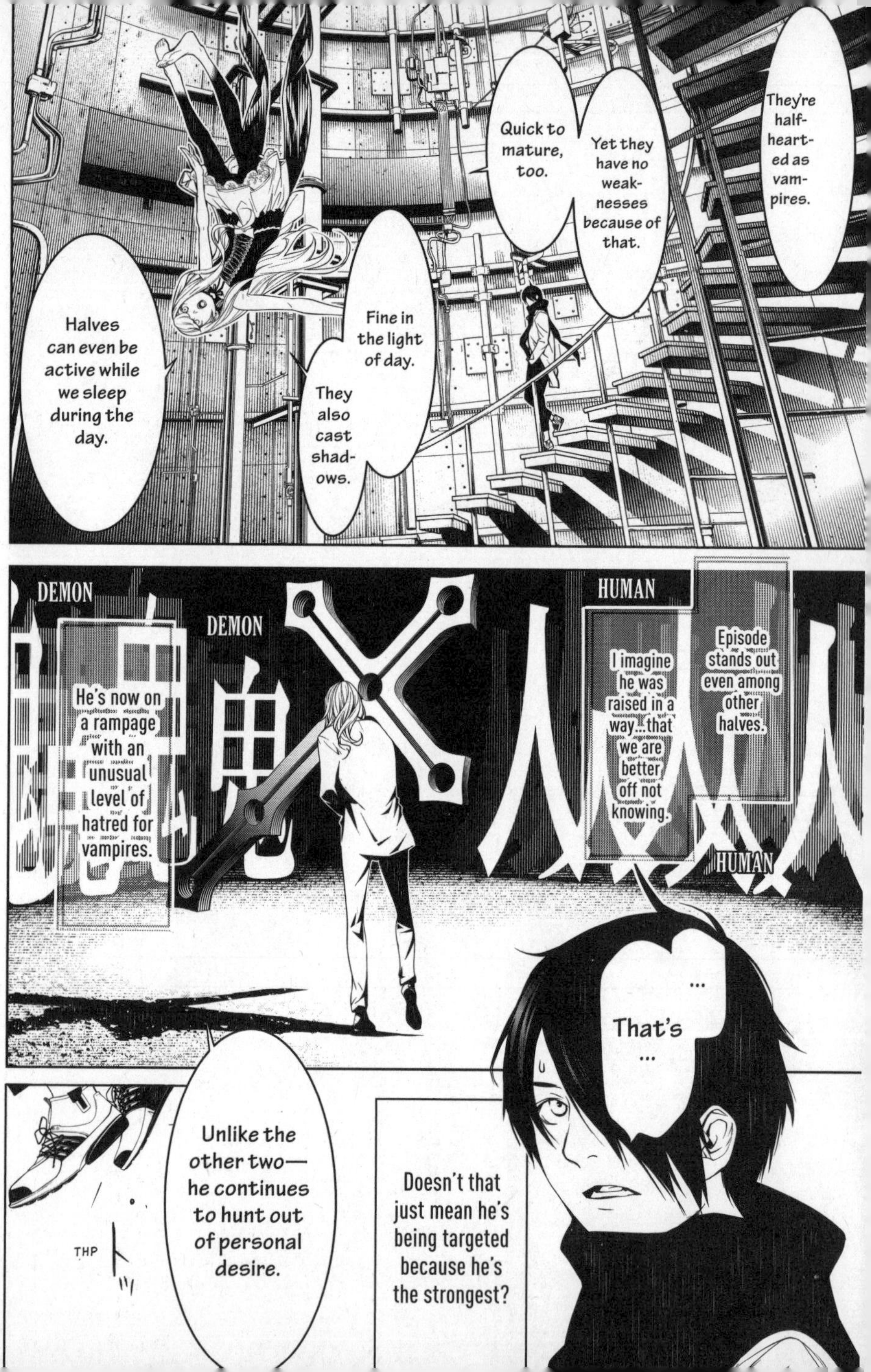
They're half-hearted as vampires.
Yet they have no weaknesses because of that.
Quick to mature, too.
Fine in the light of day.
They also cast shadows.
Halves can even be active while we sleep during the day.
HUMAN
HUMAN
Episode stands out even among other halves.
I imagine he was raised in a way...that we are better off not knowing.
DEMON
DEMON
He's now on a rampage with an unusual level of hatred for vampires.
Unlike the other two—he continues to hunt out of personal desire.
THP
... That's ...
Doesn't that just mean he's being targeted because he's the strongest?

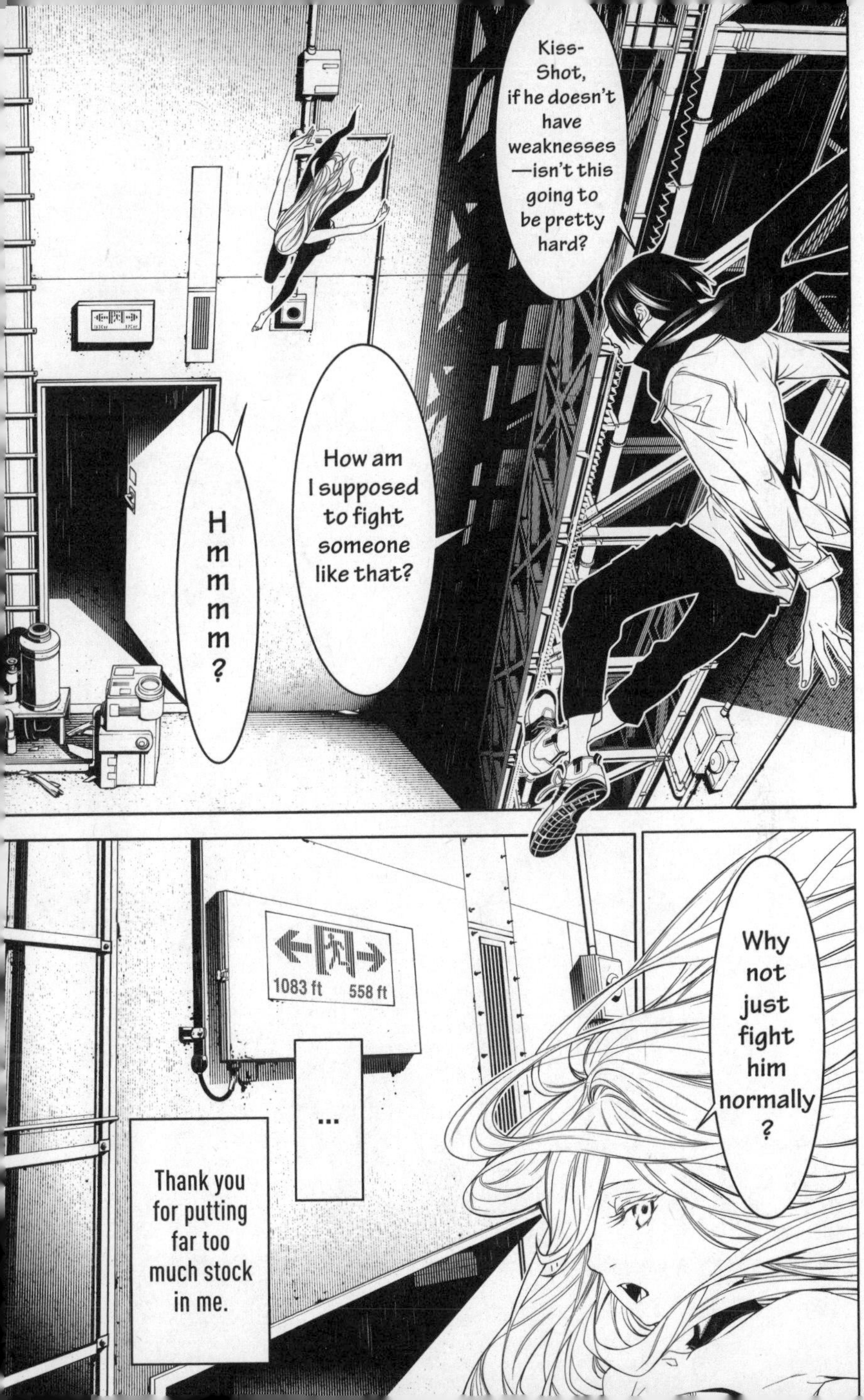
Kiss-Shot, if he doesn't have weaknesses—isn't this going to be pretty hard?
How am I supposed to fight someone like that?
Hmmmm?
Why not just fight him normally?
1083 ft 558 ft
...
Thank you for putting far too much stock in me.

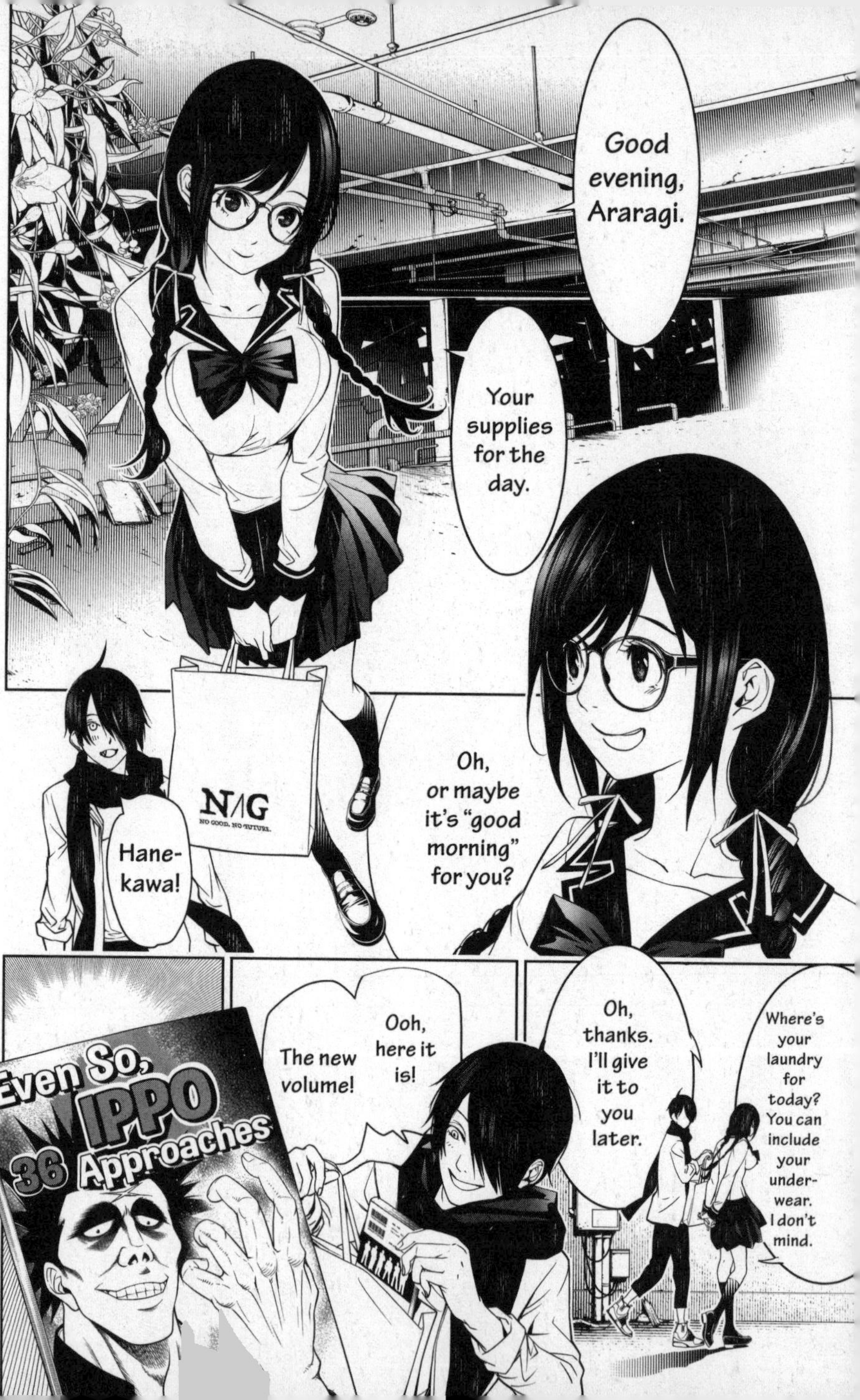
Good evening, Araragi.
Your supplies for the day.
N/G
NO GOOD, NO FUTURE.
Oh, or maybe it's "good morning" for you?
Hane-kawa!
Where's your laundry for today? You can include your under-wear. I don't mind.
Oh, thanks. I'll give it to you later.
Ooh, here it is!
The new volume!
Even So, IPPO 36 Approaches

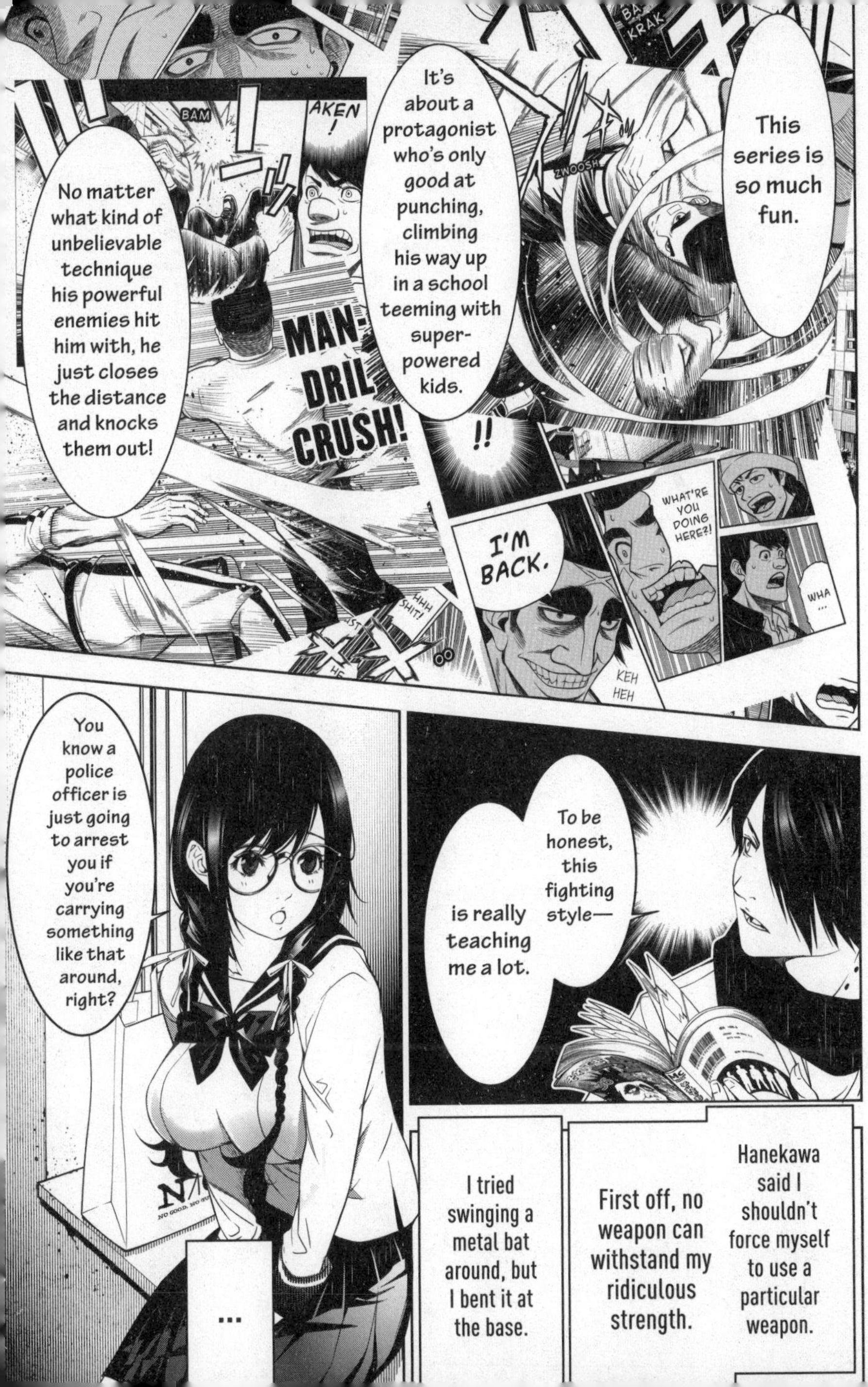
BA KRAK
This series is so much fun.
ZWOOSH
It's about a protagonist who's only good at punching, climbing his way up in a school teeming with super-powered kids.
AKEN!
BAM
No matter what kind of unbelievable technique his powerful enemies hit him with, he just closes the distance and knocks them out!
MAN-DRIL CRUSH!
!!
WHAT'RE YOU DOING HERE?!
WHA...
I'M BACK.
KEH HEH
HHH SHIT!
To be honest, this fighting style—
is really teaching me a lot.
You know a police officer is just going to arrest you if you're carrying something like that around, right?
Hanekawa said I shouldn't force myself to use a particular weapon.
First off, no weapon can withstand my ridiculous strength.
I tried swinging a metal bat around, but I bent it at the base.
...

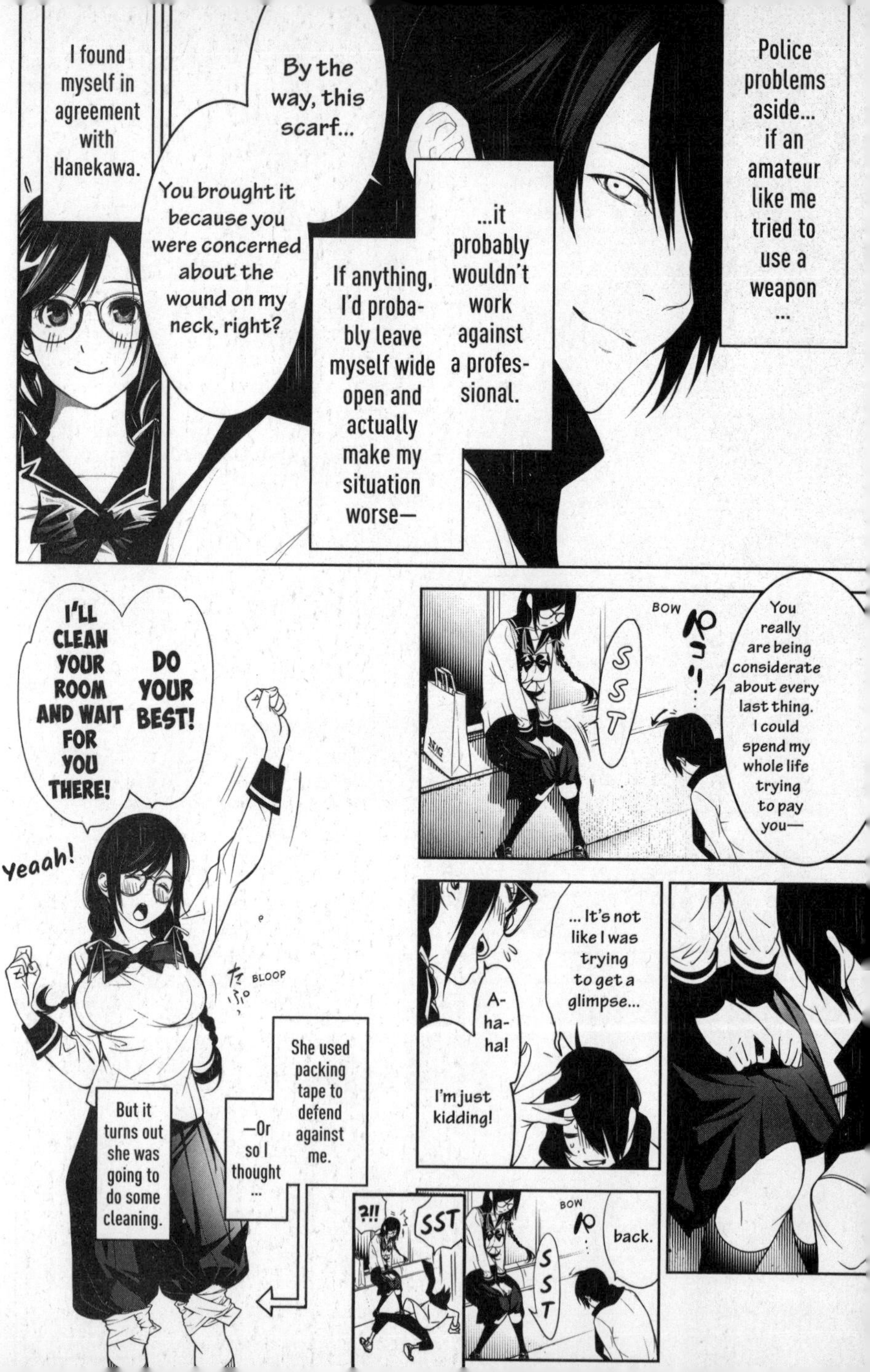
Police problems aside... if an amateur like me tried to use a weapon ...
...it probably wouldn't work against a profes-sional.
If anything, I'd proba-bly leave myself wide open and actually make my situation worse—
By the way, this scarf...
You brought it because you were concerned about the wound on my neck, right?
I found myself in agreement with Hanekawa.
You really are being considerate about every last thing. I could spend my whole life trying to pay you—
BOW
SST
... It's not like I was trying to get a glimpse...
A-ha-ha!
I'm just kidding!
back.
BOW
SST
SST
?!!
DO YOUR BEST!
I'LL CLEAN YOUR ROOM AND WAIT FOR YOU THERE!
Yeaah!
BLOOP
She used packing tape to defend against me.
—Or so I thought ...
But it turns out she was going to do some cleaning.

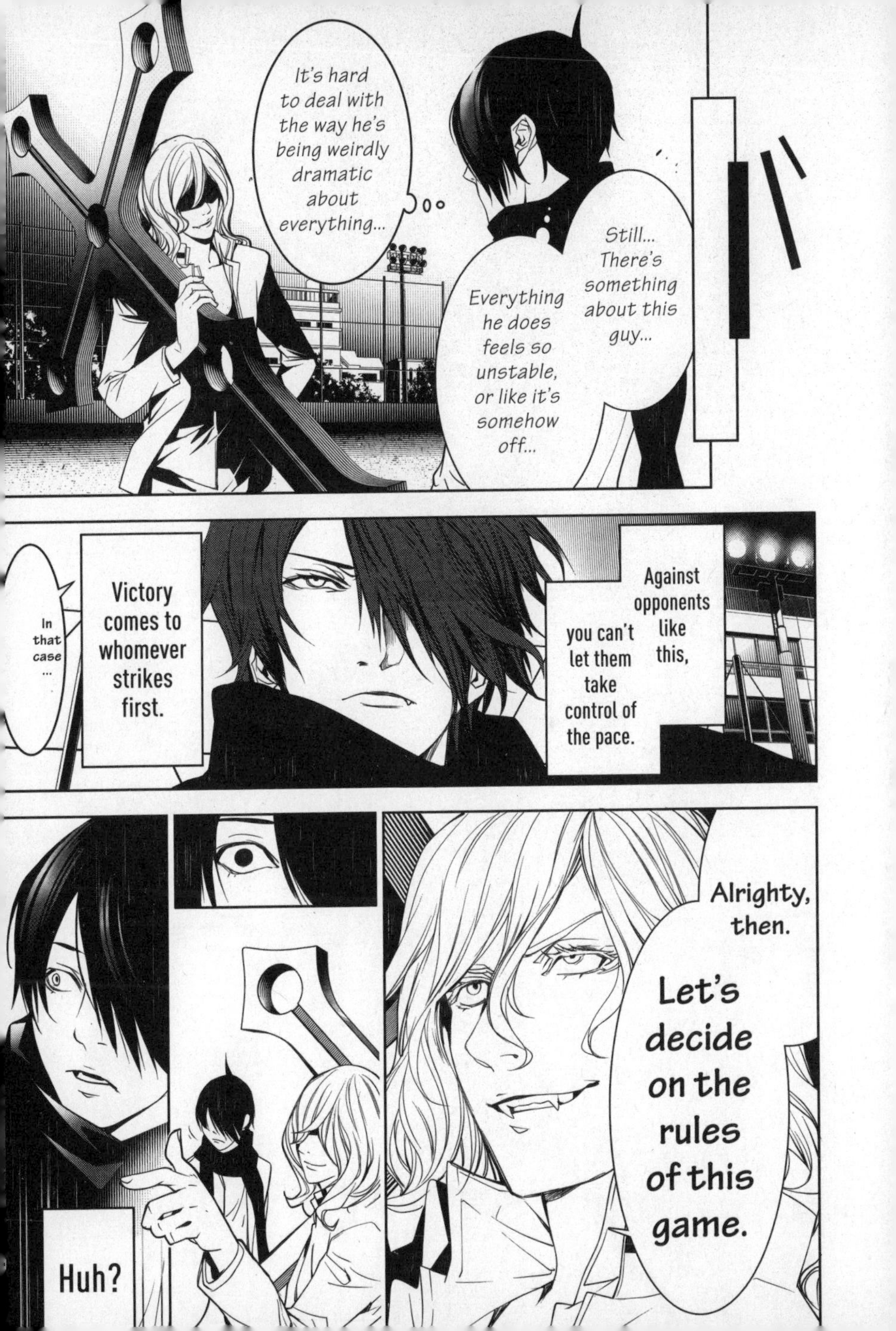
Still... There's something about this guy...
Everything he does feels so unstable, or like it's somehow off...
It's hard to deal with the way he's being weirdly dramatic about everything...
Against opponents like this,
you can't let them take control of the pace.
Victory comes to whomever strikes first.
In that case...
Alrighty, then.
Let's decide on the rules of this game.
Huh?

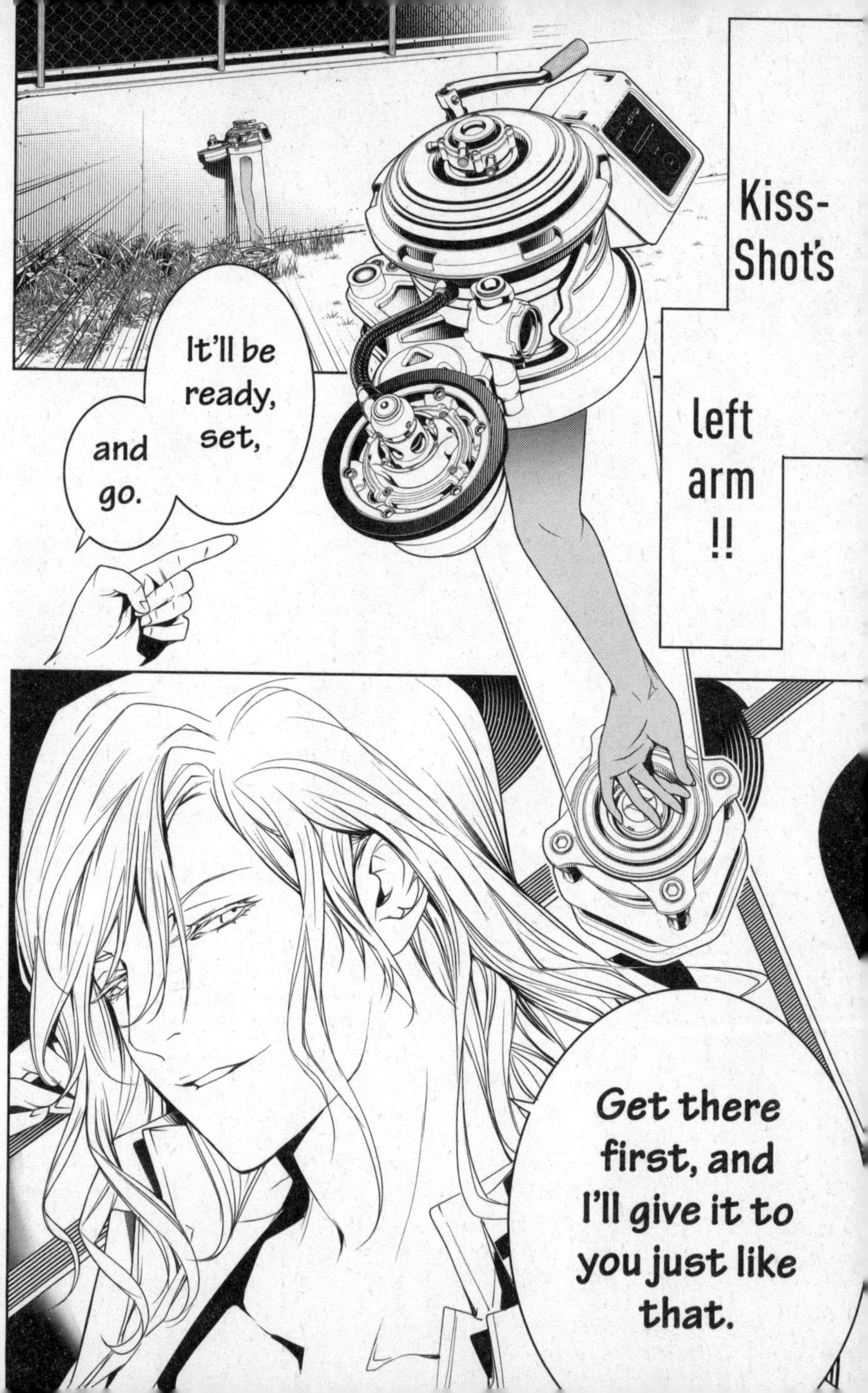
Kiss-Shot's
left arm!!
It'll be ready, set, and go.
Get there first, and I'll give it to you just like that.

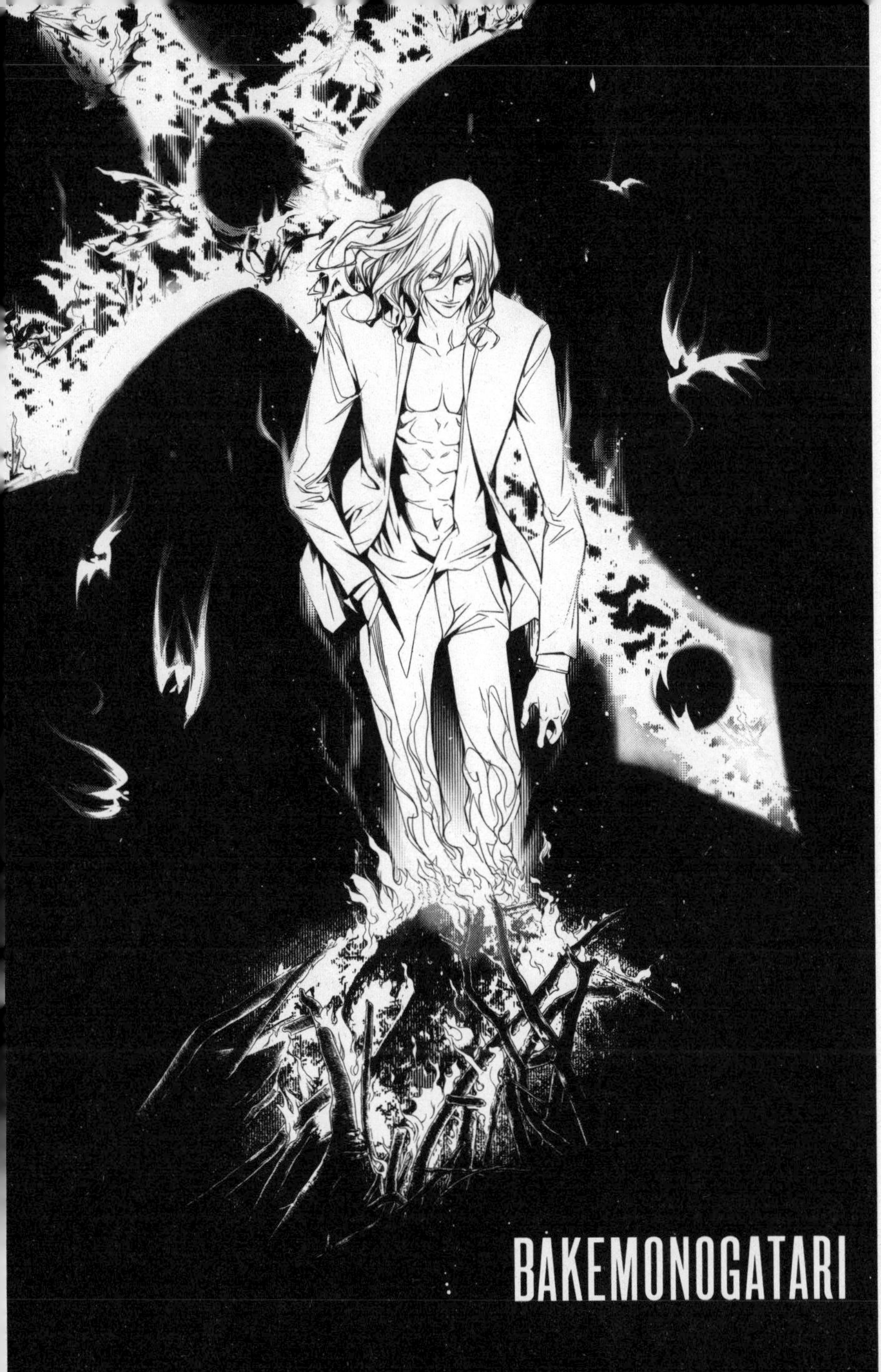
BAKEMONOGATARI

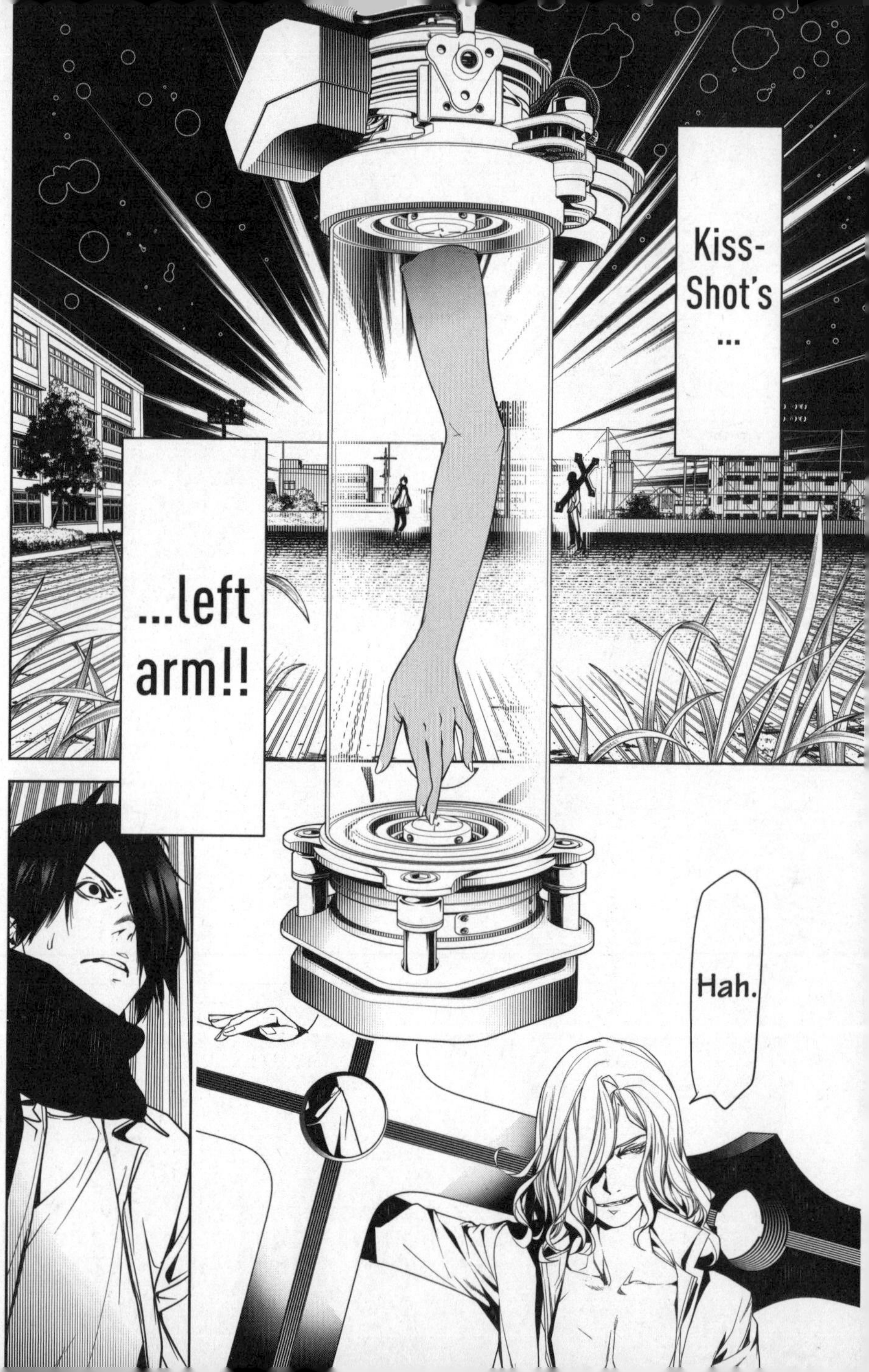
Kiss-Shot's ...
...left arm!!
Hah.

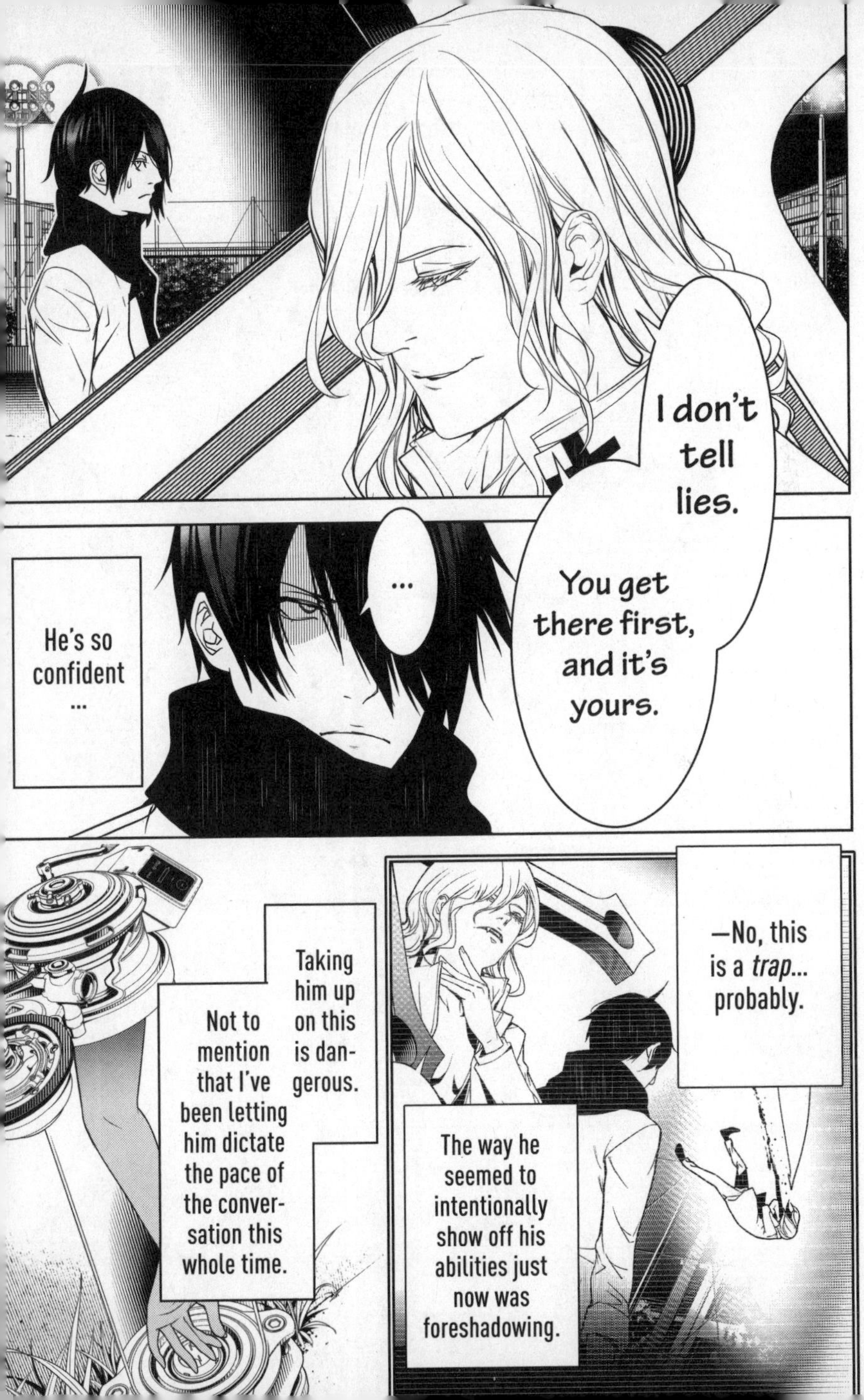
I don't tell lies.
You get there first, and it's yours.
...
He's so confident ...
—No, this is a *trap*... probably.
The way he seemed to intentionally show off his abilities just now was foreshadowing.
Taking him up on this is dan-gerous.
Not to mention that I've been letting him dictate the pace of the conver-sation this whole time.

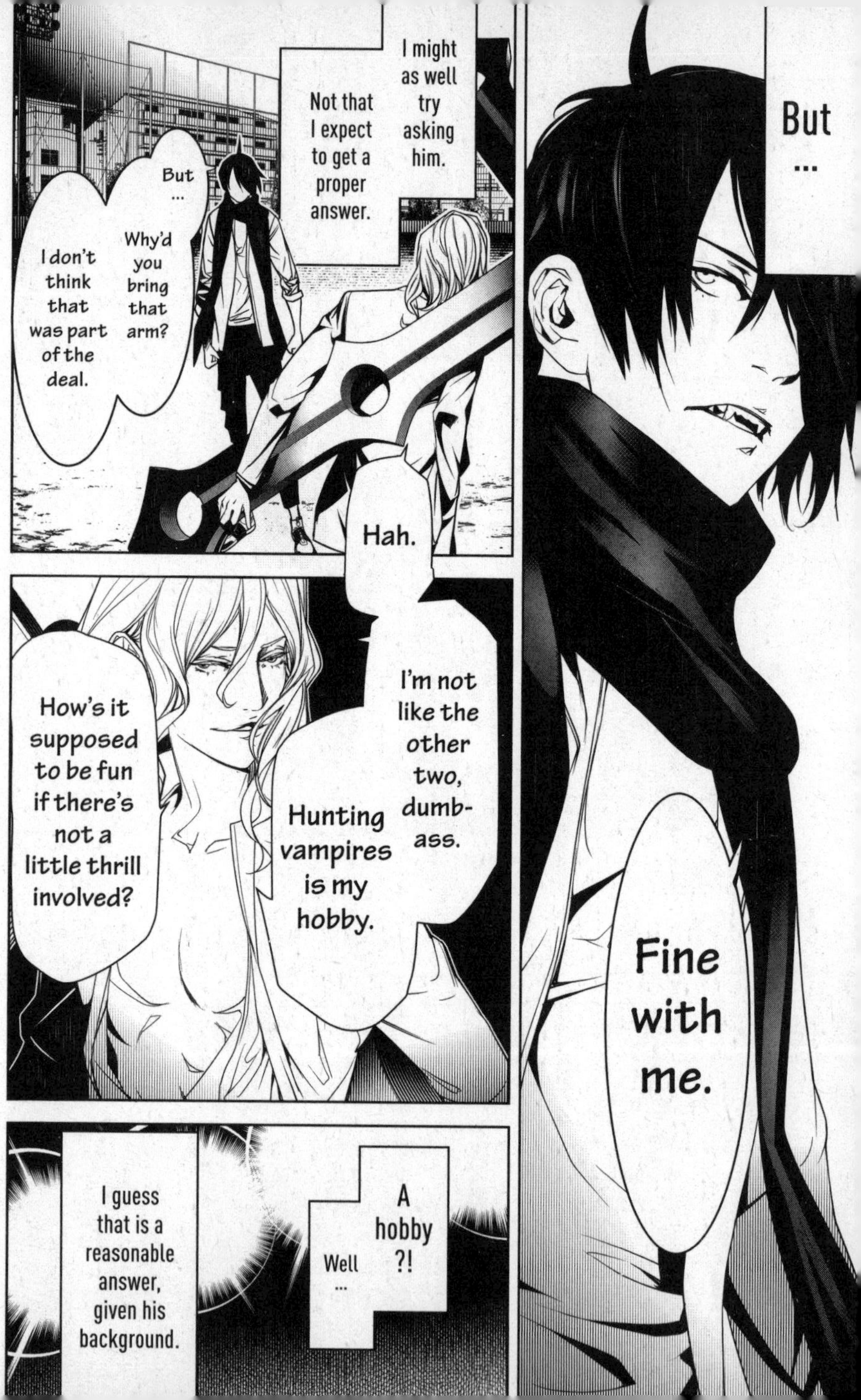
But ...
Fine with me.
I might as well try asking him.
Not that I expect to get a proper answer.
But ...
Why'd you bring that arm?
I don't think that was part of the deal.
Hah.
I'm not like the other two, dumbass.
Hunting vampires is my hobby.
How's it supposed to be fun if there's not a little thrill involved?
A hobby ?!
Well ...
I guess that is a reasonable answer, given his background.

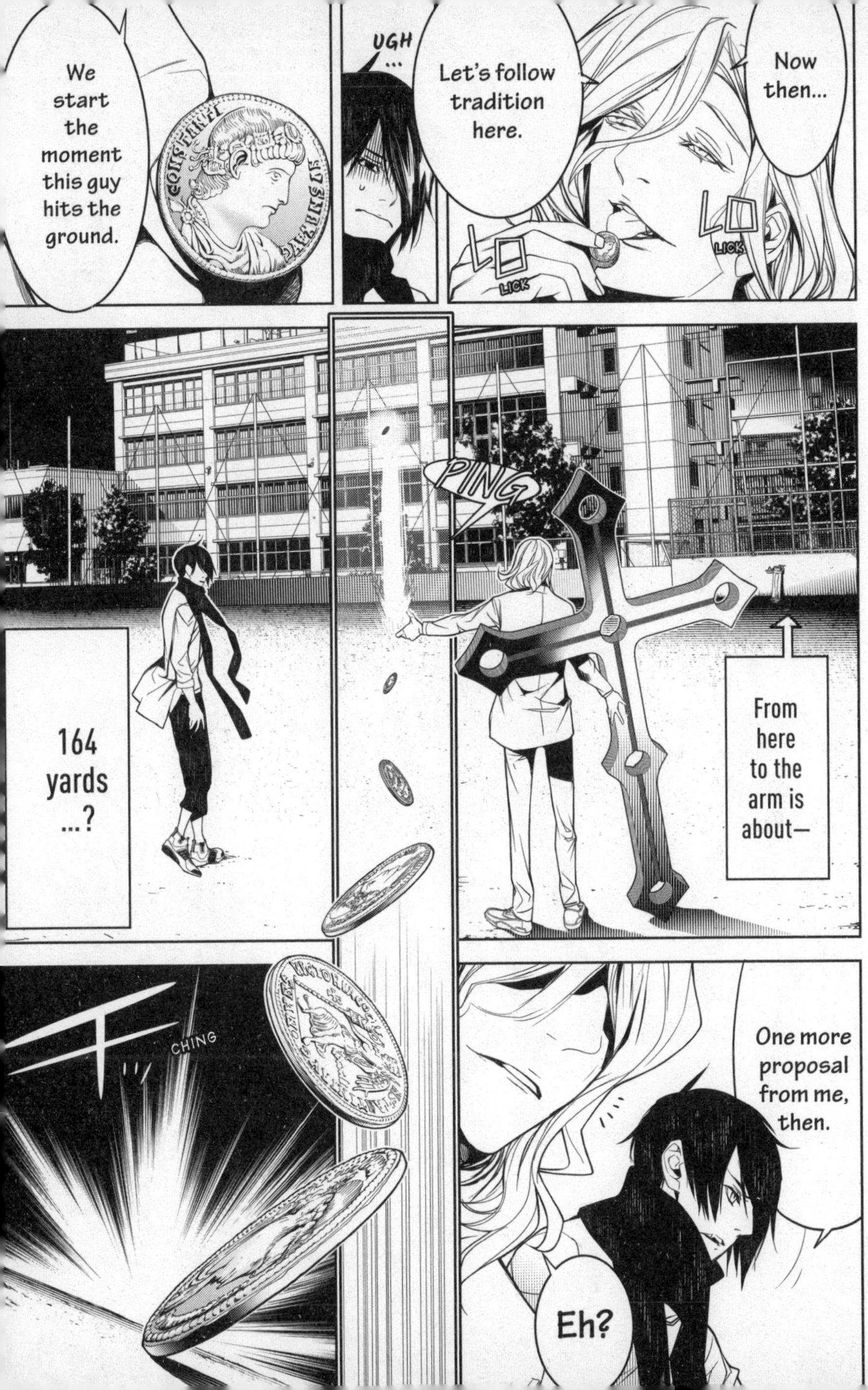
Now then...
LO
LICK
LO
LICK
Let's follow tradition here.
UGH ...
We start the moment this guy hits the ground.
PING
From here to the arm is about—
164 yards ...?
One more proposal from me, then.
Eh?
CHING

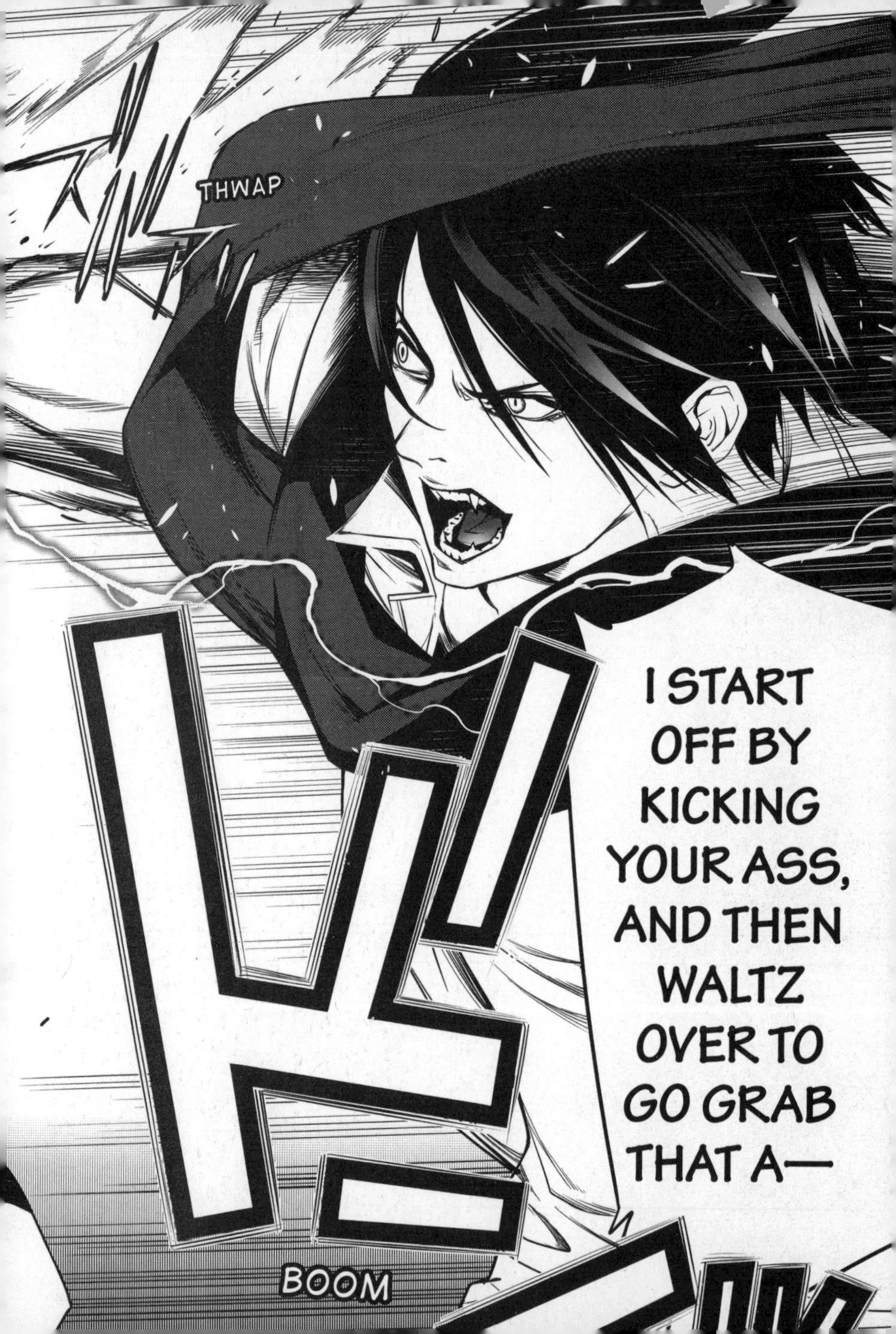
THWAP
I START OFF BY KICKING YOUR ASS, AND THEN WALTZ OVER TO GO GRAB THAT A—
BOOM

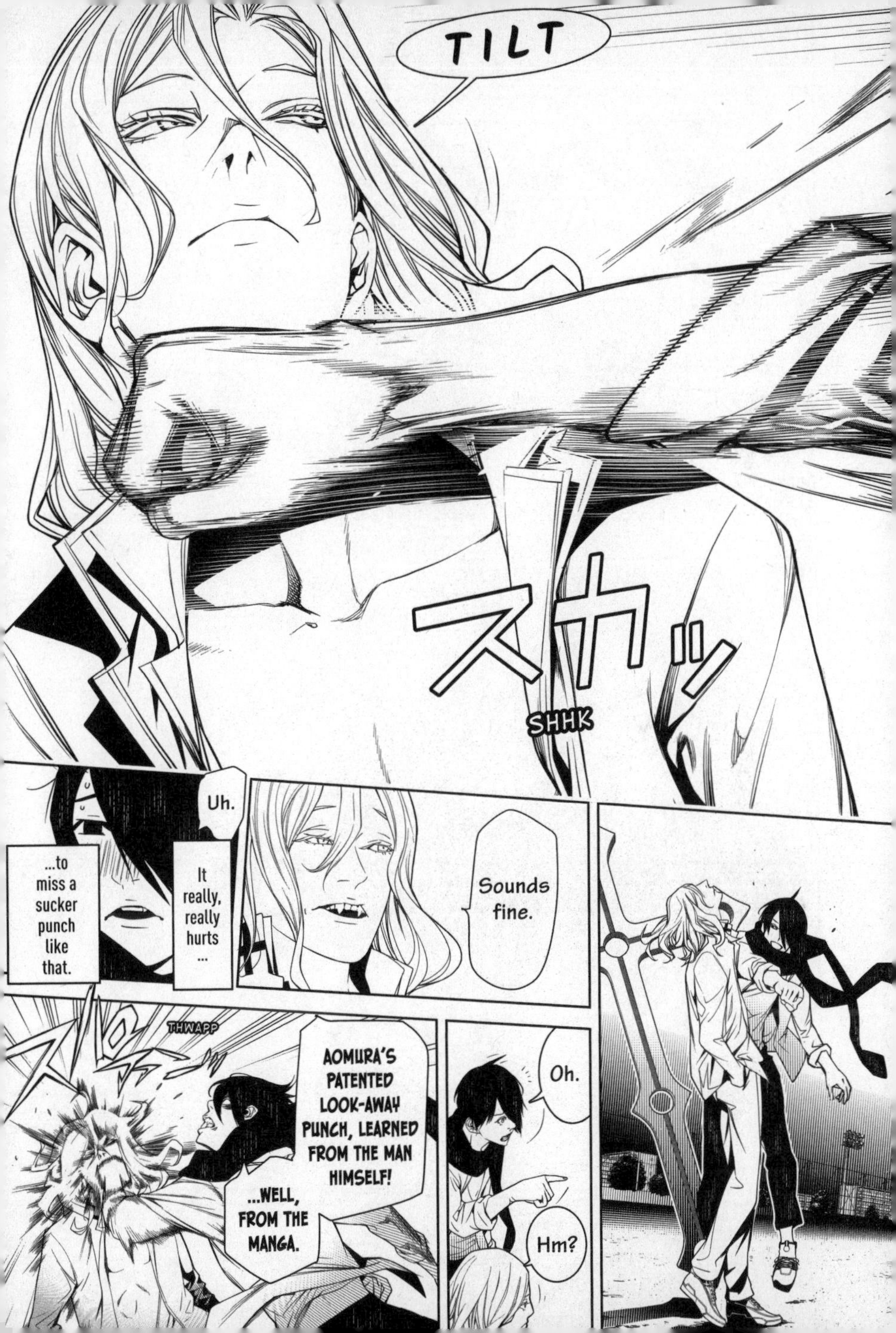
TILT
スカッ
SHHK
Sounds fine.
Uh.
It really, really hurts...
...to miss a sucker punch like that.
Oh.
Hm?
THWAPP
AOMURA'S PATENTED LOOK-AWAY PUNCH, LEARNED FROM THE MAN HIMSELF!
...WELL, FROM THE MANGA.

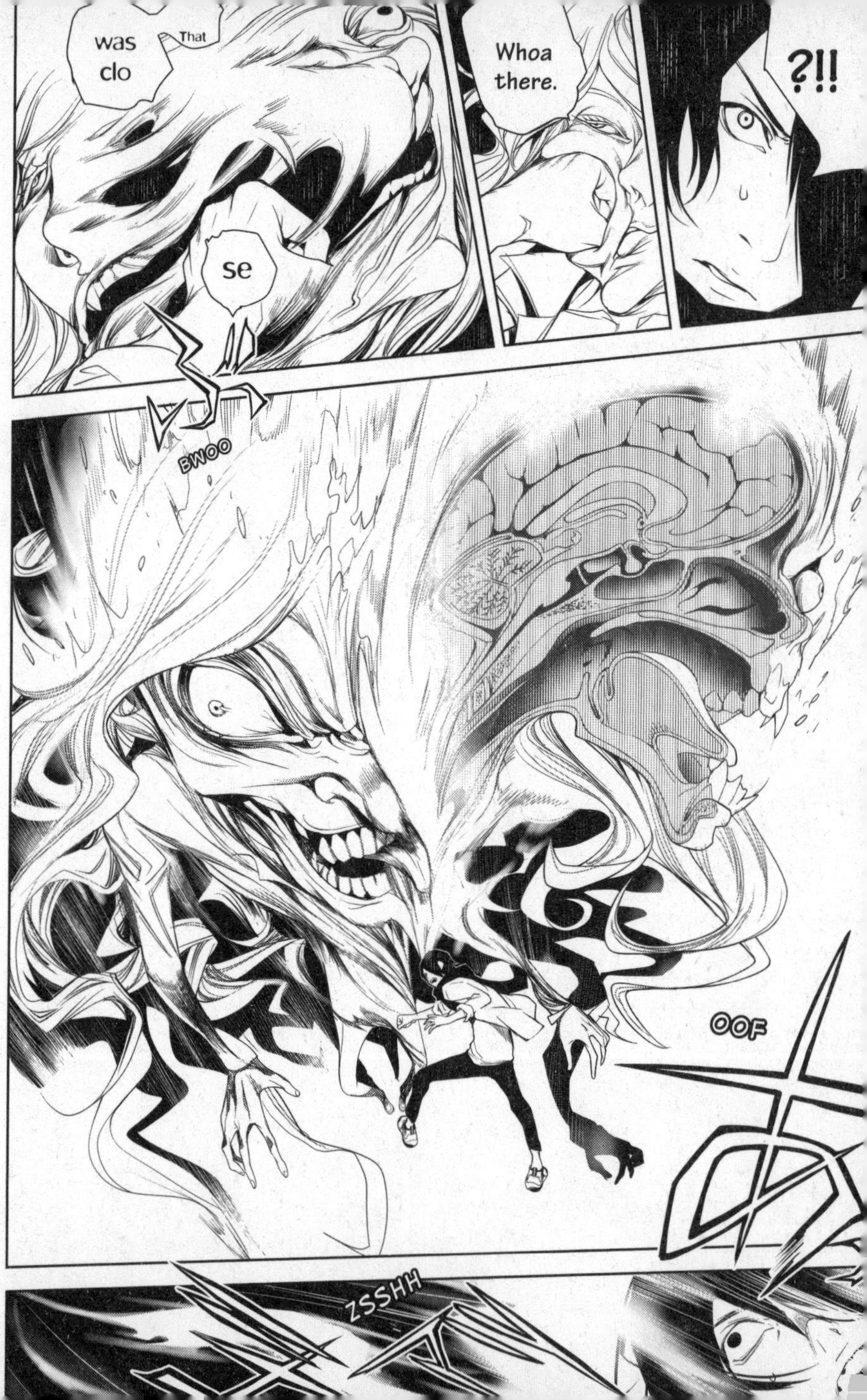
?!!
Whoa there.
That was clo
se
BWOO
OOF
ZSSHH

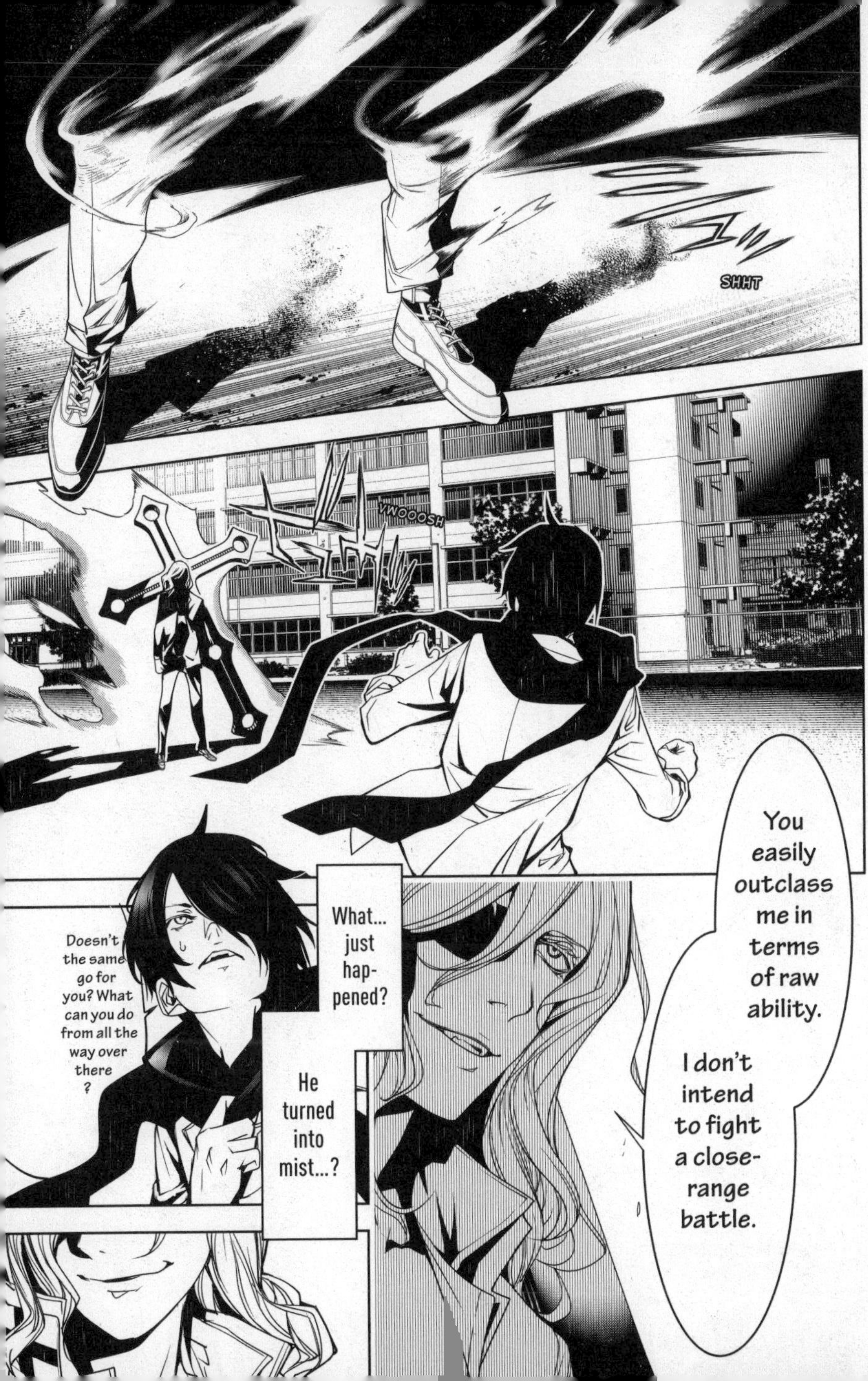
SHHT
VWOOOSH
You easily outclass me in terms of raw ability.
I don't intend to fight a close-range battle.
What... just hap-pened?
He turned into mist...?
Doesn't the same go for you? What can you do from all the way over there?

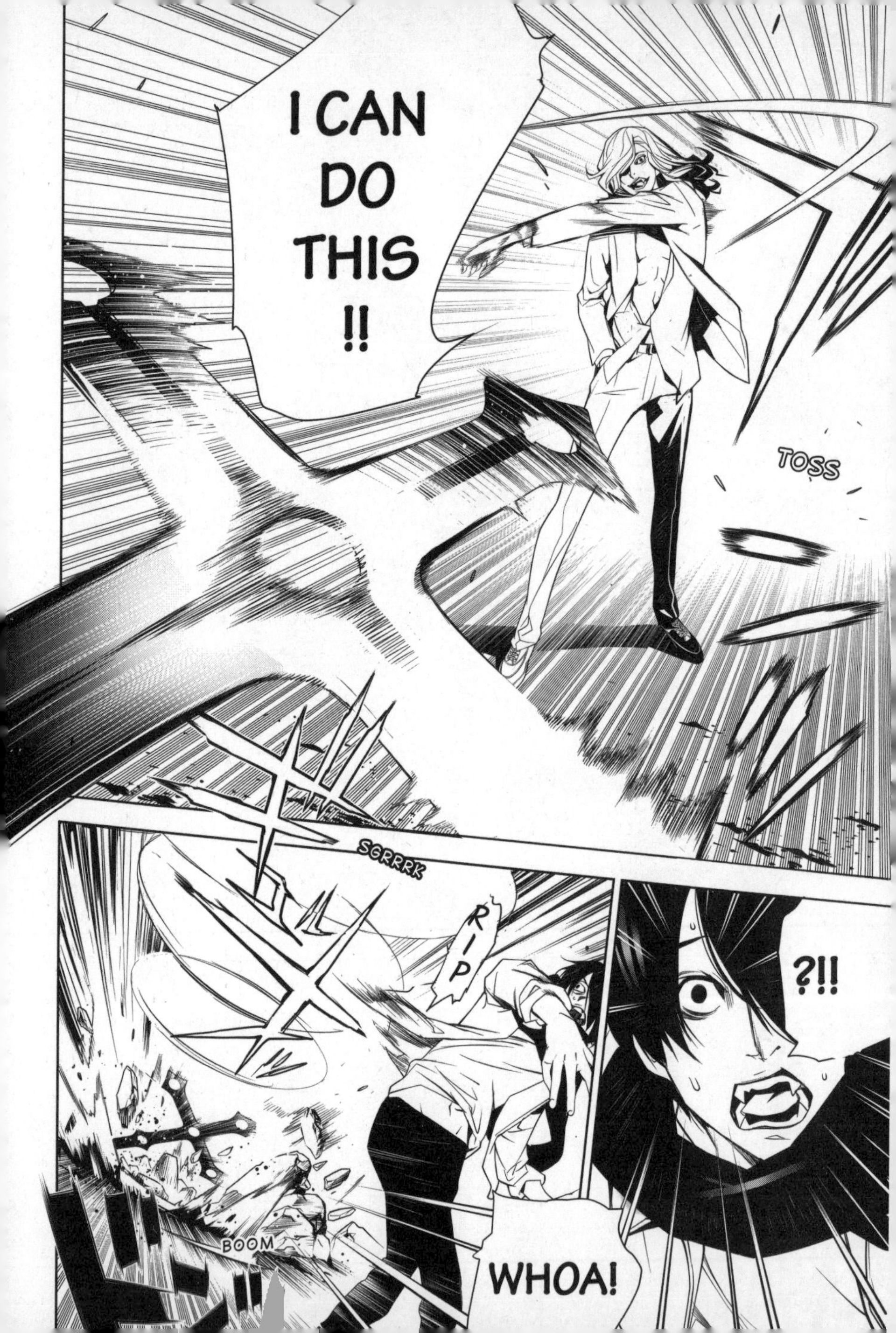
I CAN DO THIS !!
TOSS
?!!
WHOA!
SGRRRK
RIP
BOOM

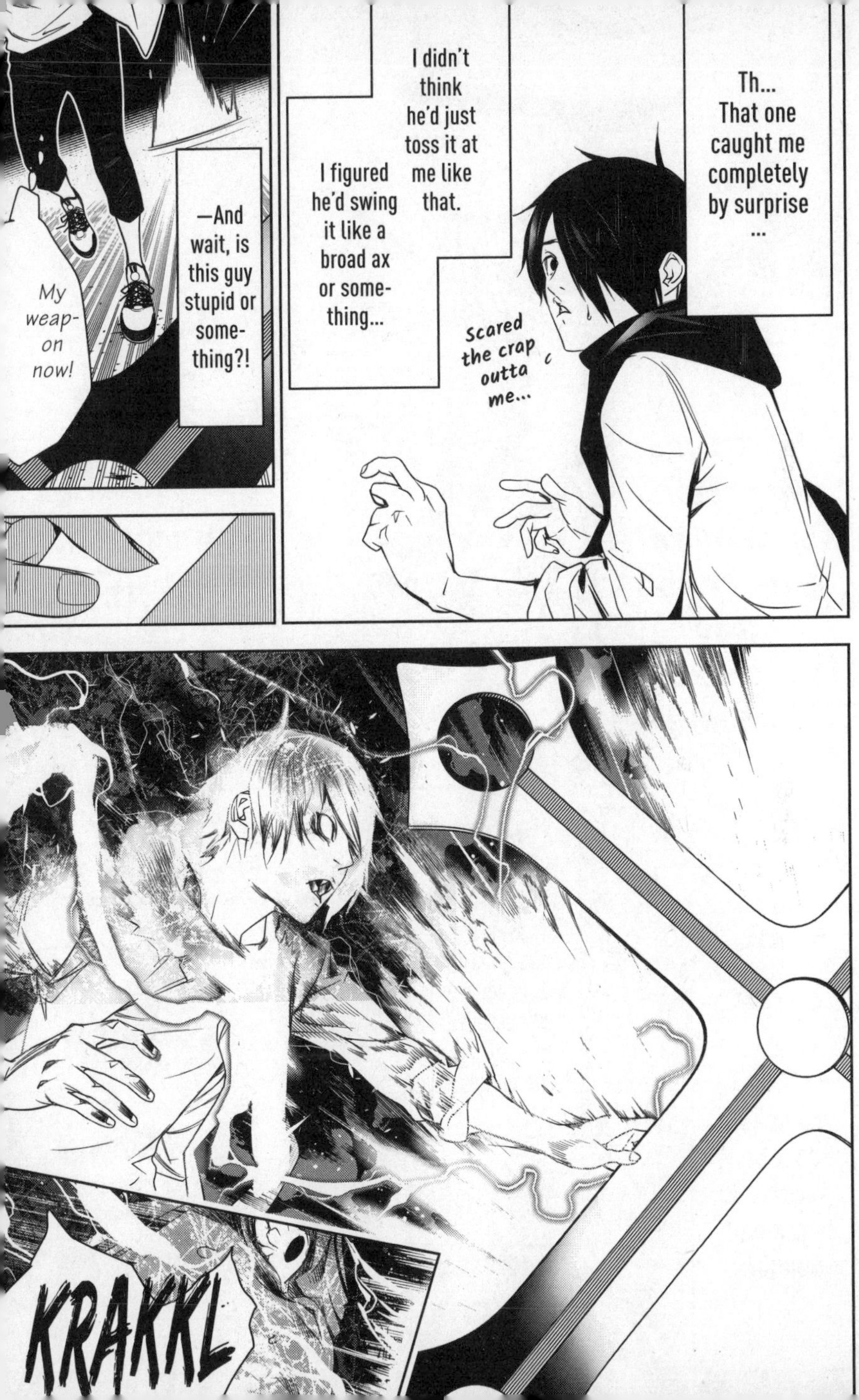
Th... That one caught me completely by surprise ...
I didn't think he'd just toss it at me like that.
I figured he'd swing it like a broad ax or something...
Scared the crap outta me...
—And wait, is this guy stupid or something?!
My weap-on now!
KRAKKL

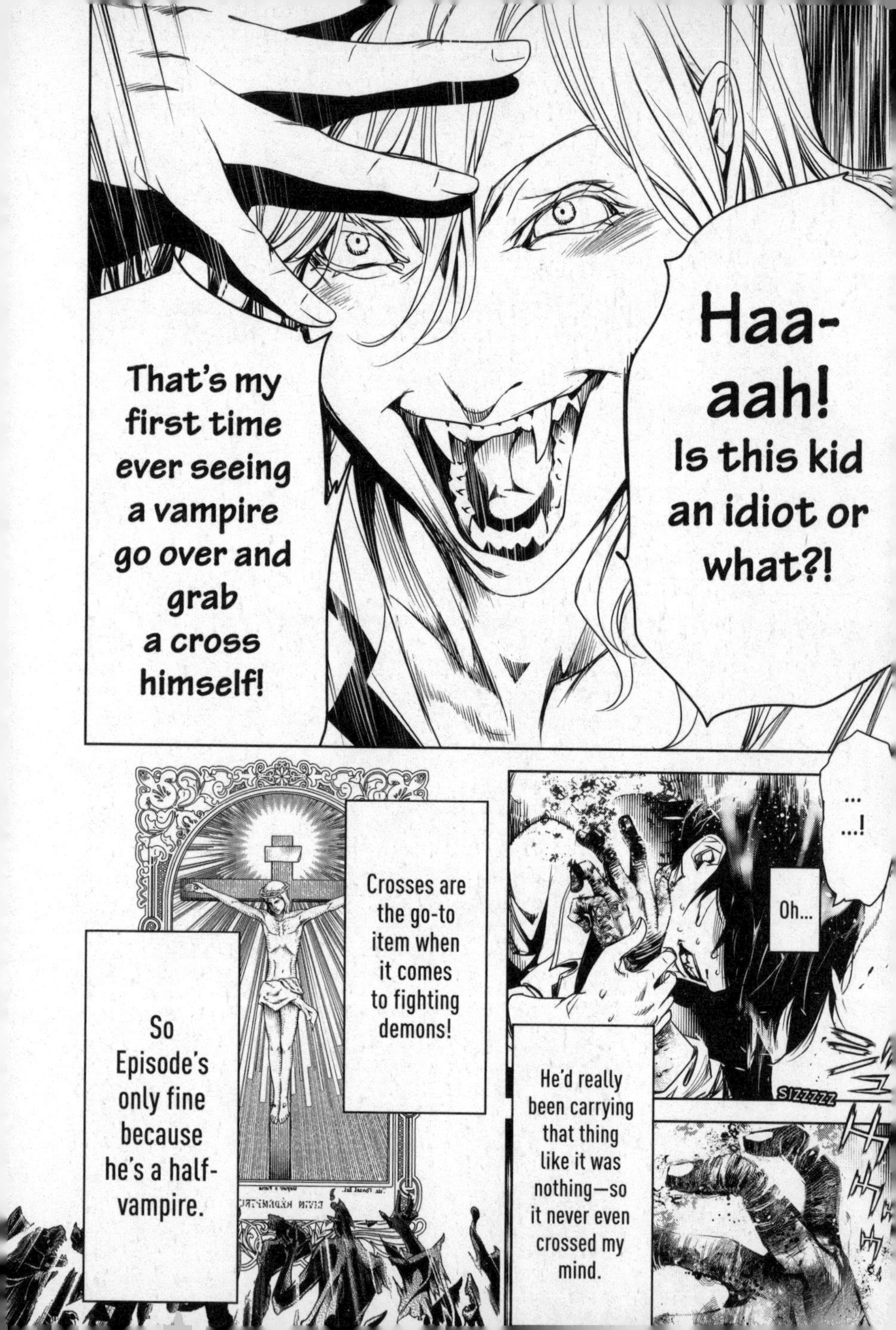
Haaa-aah! Is this kid an idiot or what?!
That's my first time ever seeing a vampire go over and grab a cross himself!
...
...!
Oh...
SIZZZZZ
He'd really been carrying that thing like it was nothing—so it never even crossed my mind.
Crosses are the go-to item when it comes to fighting demons!
So Episode's only fine because he's a half-vampire.

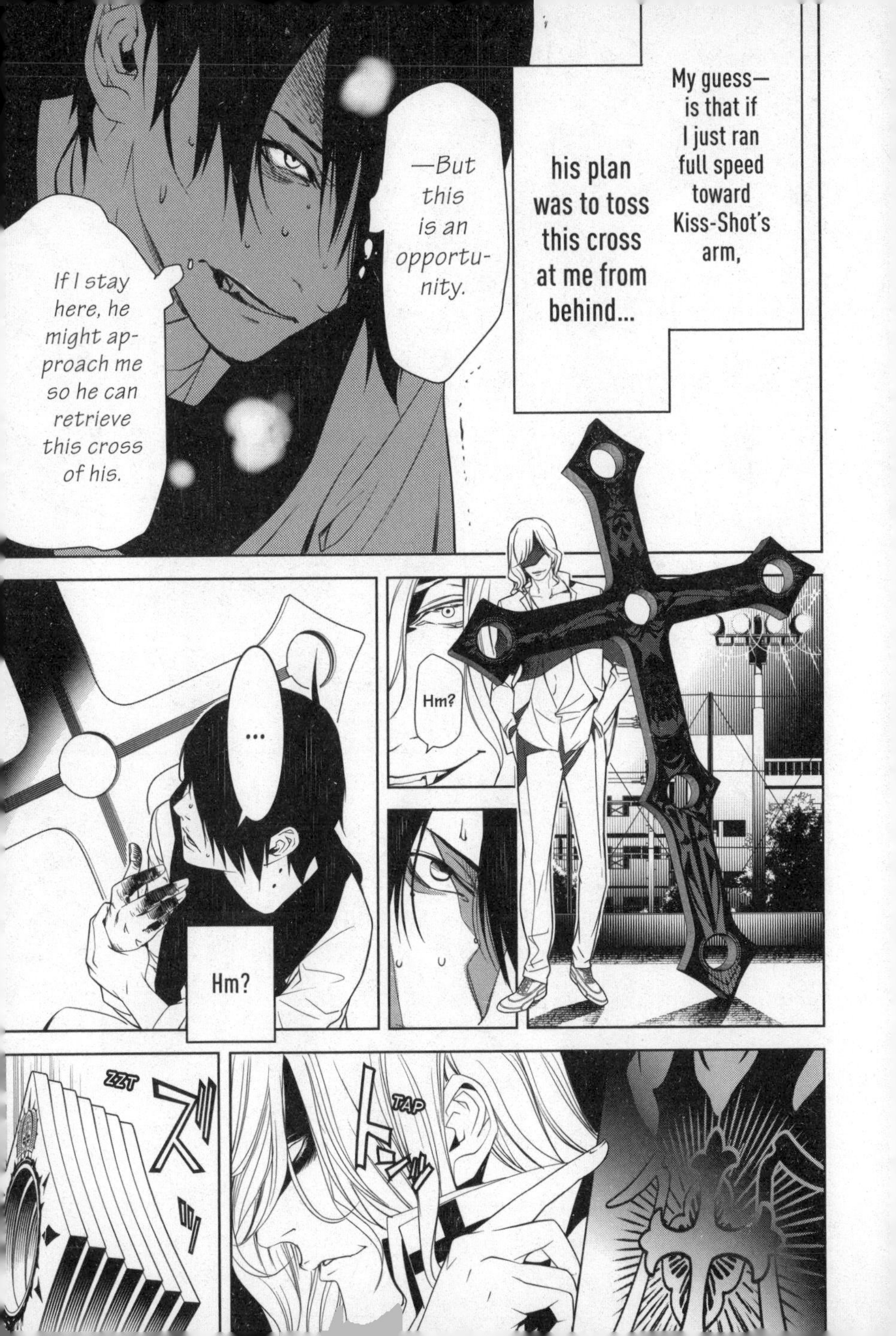
My guess— is that if I just ran full speed toward Kiss-Shot's arm,
his plan was to toss this cross at me from behind...
—But this is an opportunity.
If I stay here, he might approach me so he can retrieve this cross of his.
Hm?
...
Hm?
TAP
ZZT

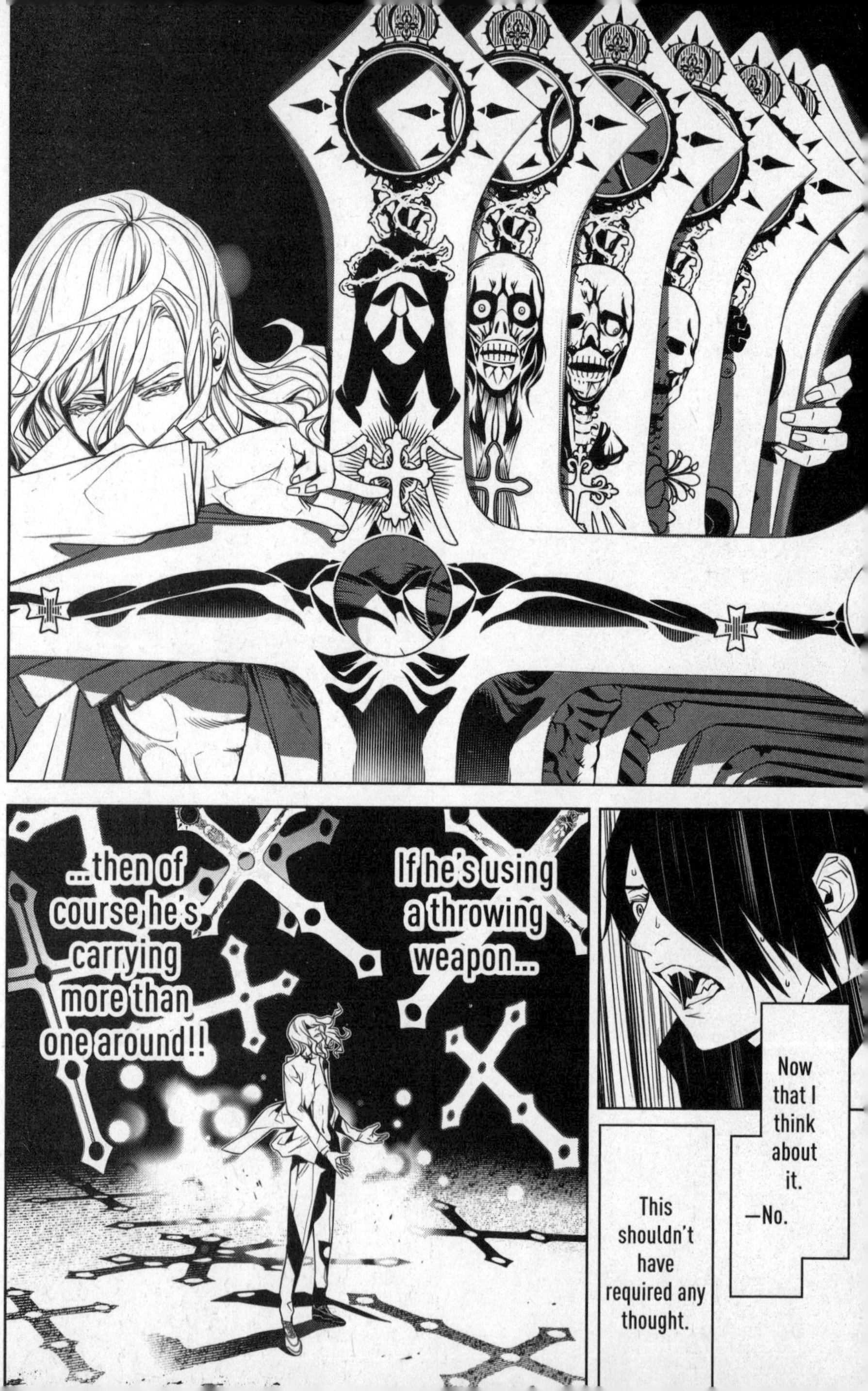
Now that I think about it.
—No.
This shouldn't have required any thought.
If he's using a throwing weapon...
...then of course he's carrying more than one around!!

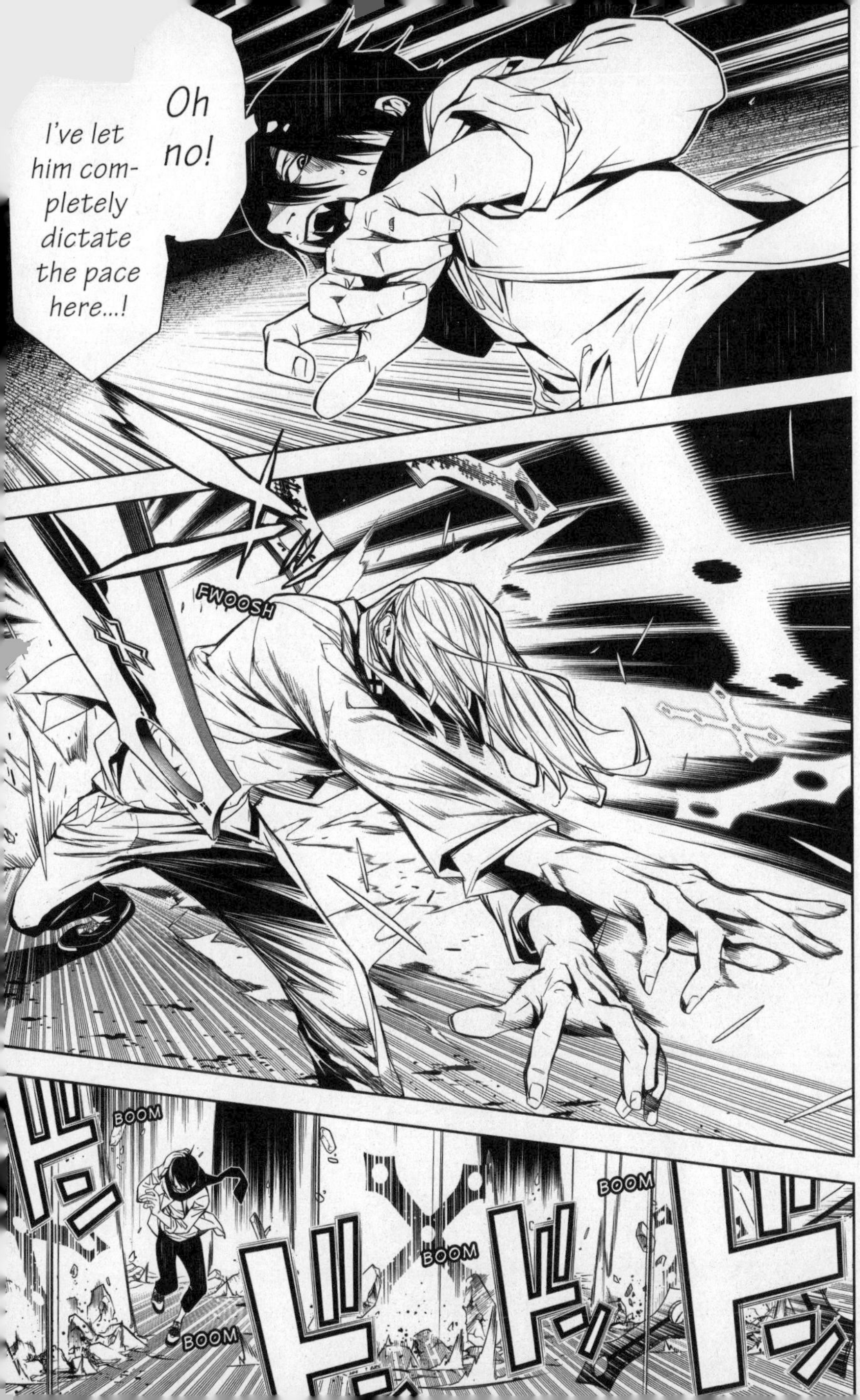
Oh no!
I've let him com-pletely dictate the pace here...!
FWOOSH
BOOM
BOOM
BOOM
BOOM

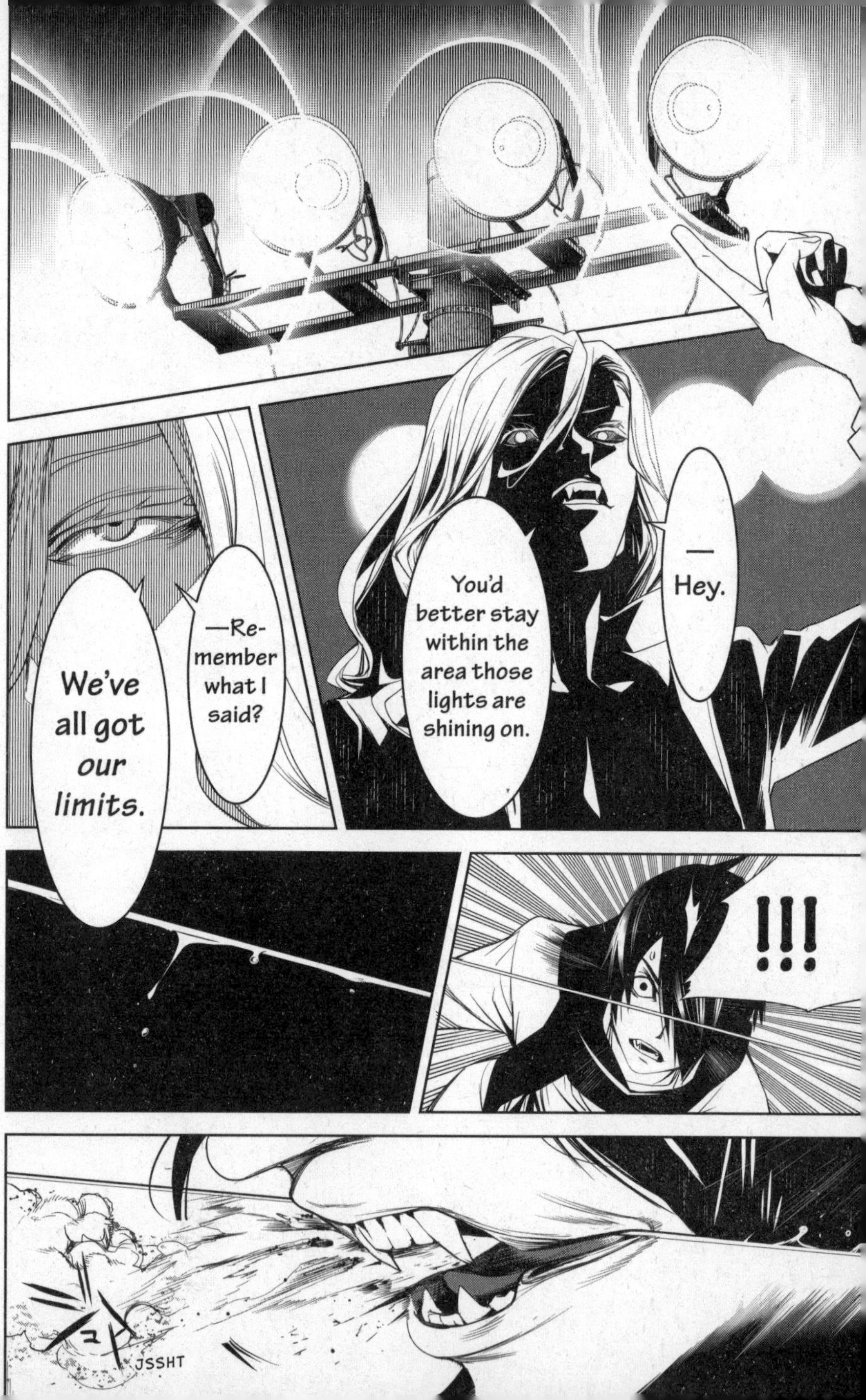
—Hey.
You'd better stay within the area those lights are shining on.
—Re-member what I said?
We've all got our limits.
!!!
JSSHT

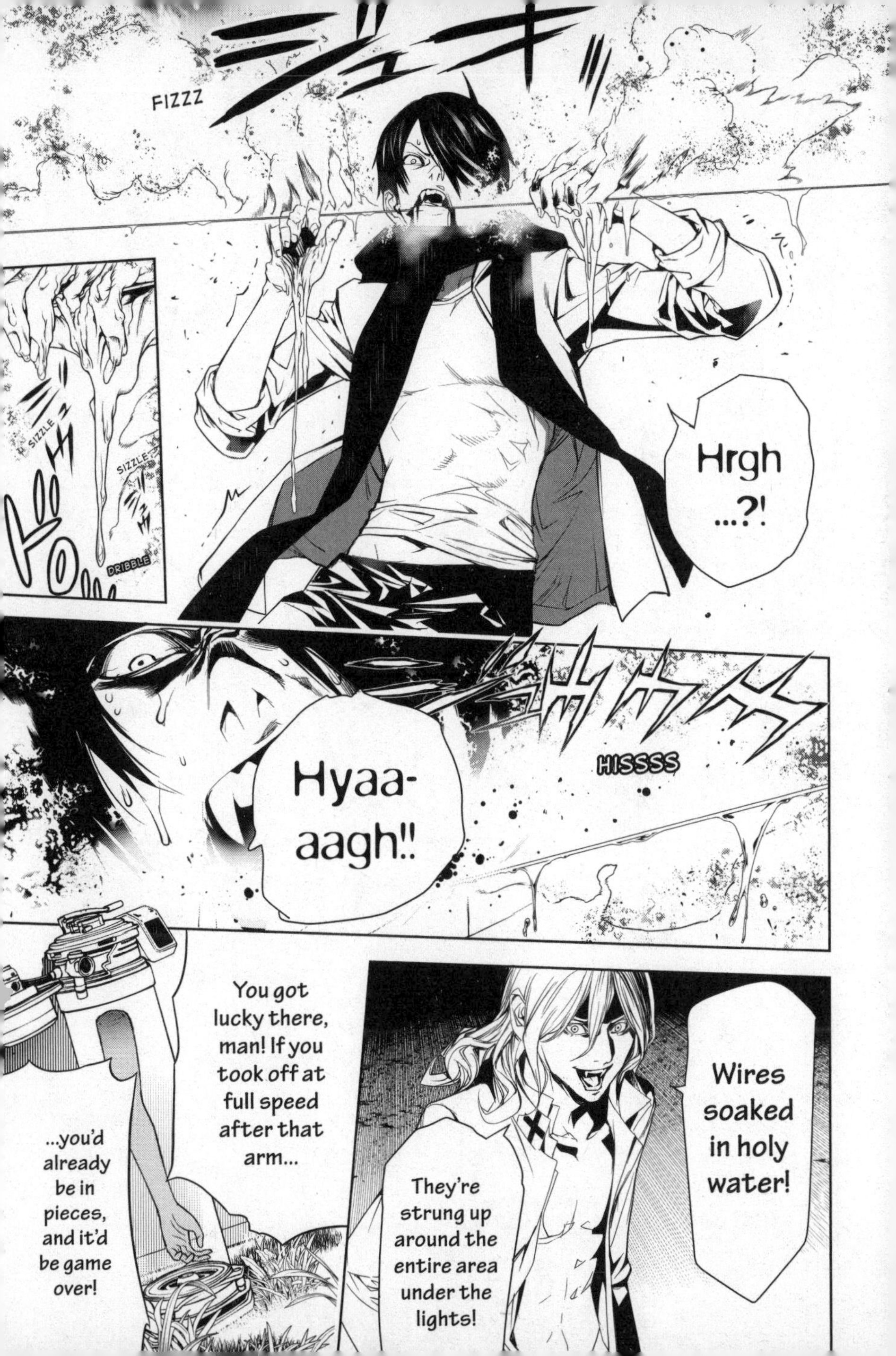
FIZZZ
Hrgh ...?!
SIZZLE
SIZZLE
DRIBBLE
HISSSS
Hyaa-aagh!!
Wires soaked in holy water!
They're strung up around the entire area under the lights!
You got lucky there, man! If you took off at full speed after that arm...
...you'd already be in pieces, and it'd be game over!

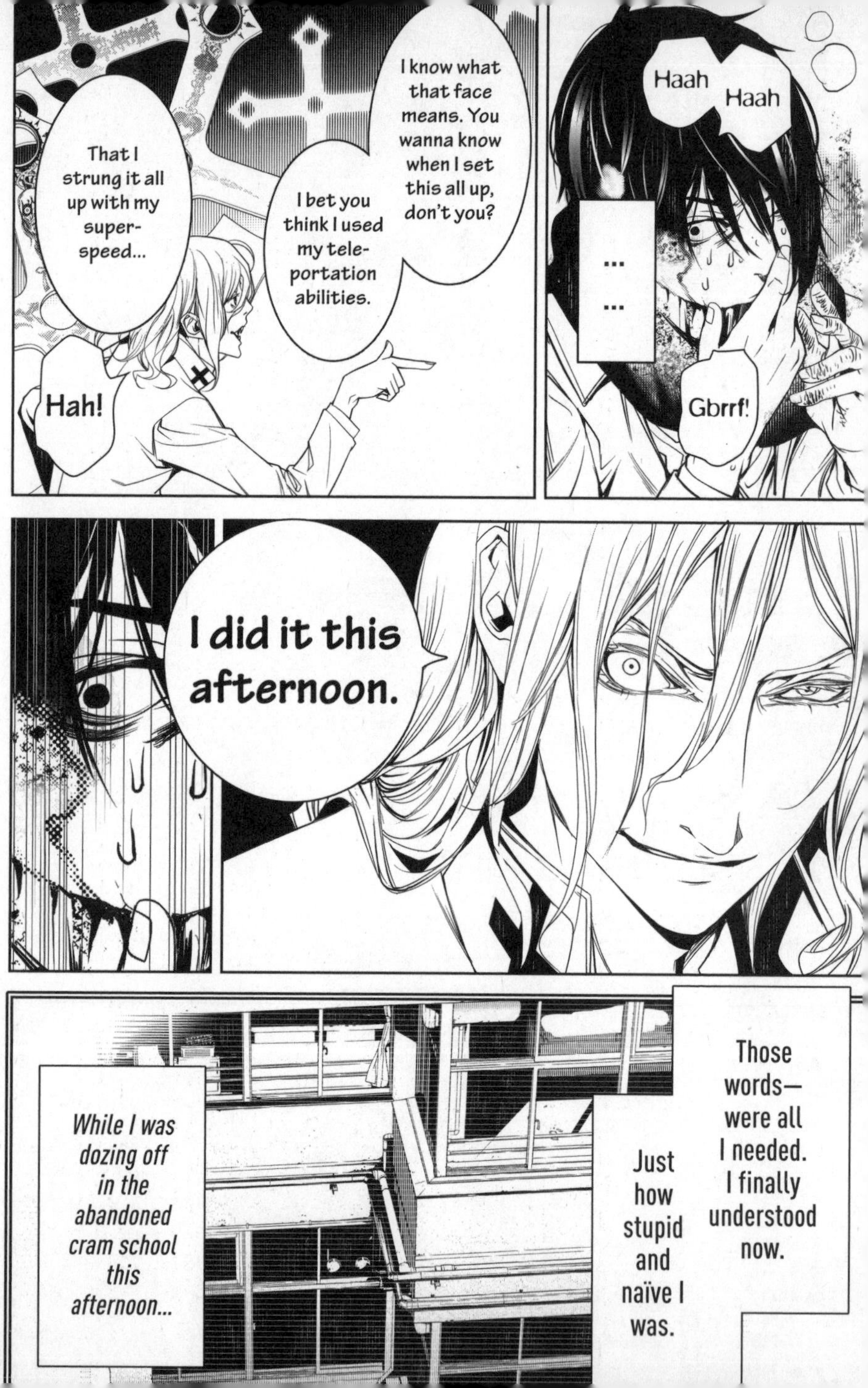
Haah Haah
...
...
Gbrrf!
I know what that face means. You wanna know when I set this all up, don't you?
I bet you think I used my teleportation abilities.
That I strung it all up with my super-speed...
Hah!
I did it this afternoon.
Those words—were all I needed. I finally understood now.
Just how stupid and naïve I was.
While I was dozing off in the abandoned cram school this afternoon...

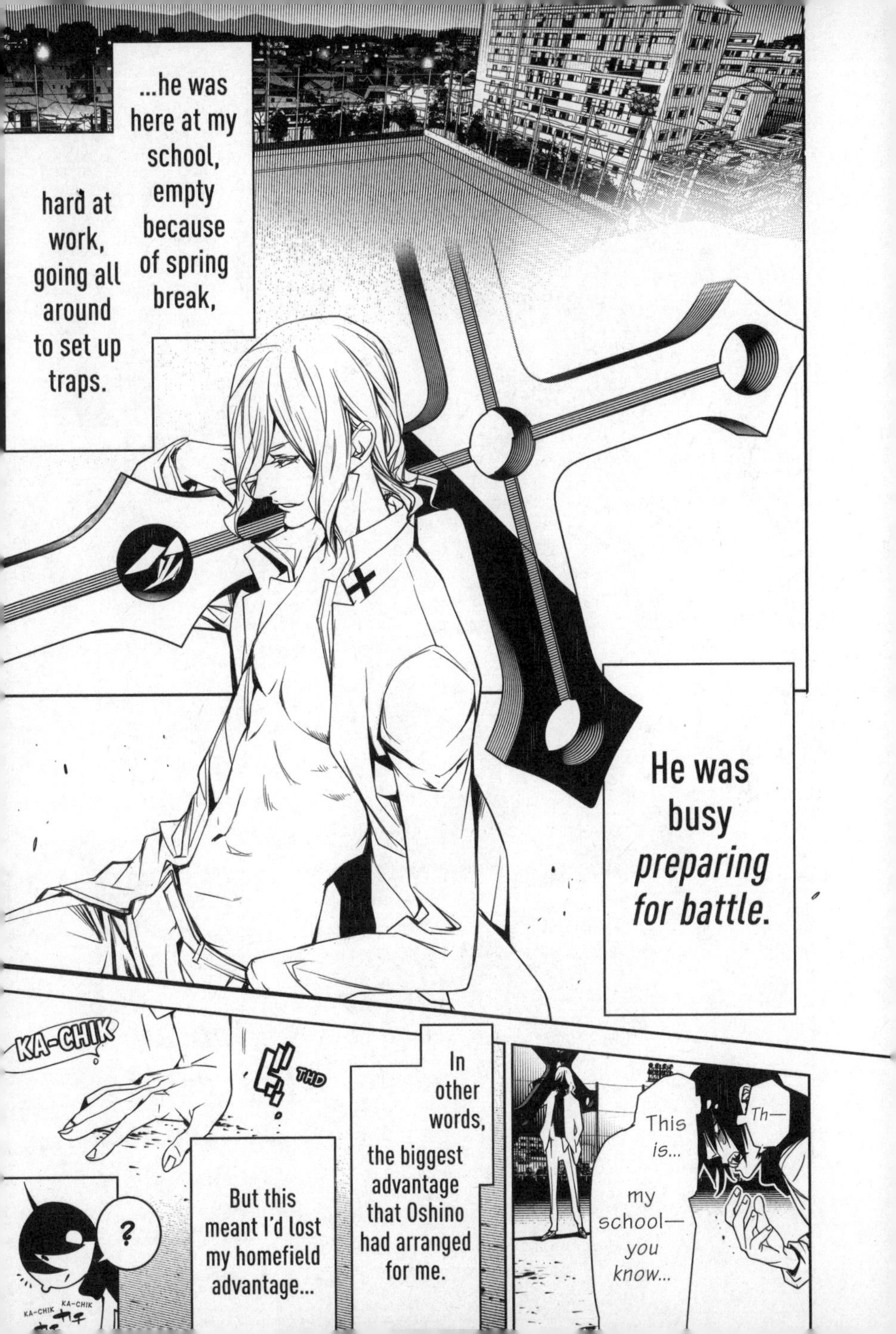
...he was here at my school, empty because of spring break,
hard at work, going all around to set up traps.
He was busy *preparing for battle.*
Th—
This is... my school— you know...
In other words, the biggest advantage that Oshino had arranged for me.
But this meant I'd lost my homefield advantage...
THD
KA-CHIK
?
KA-CHIK KA-CHIK

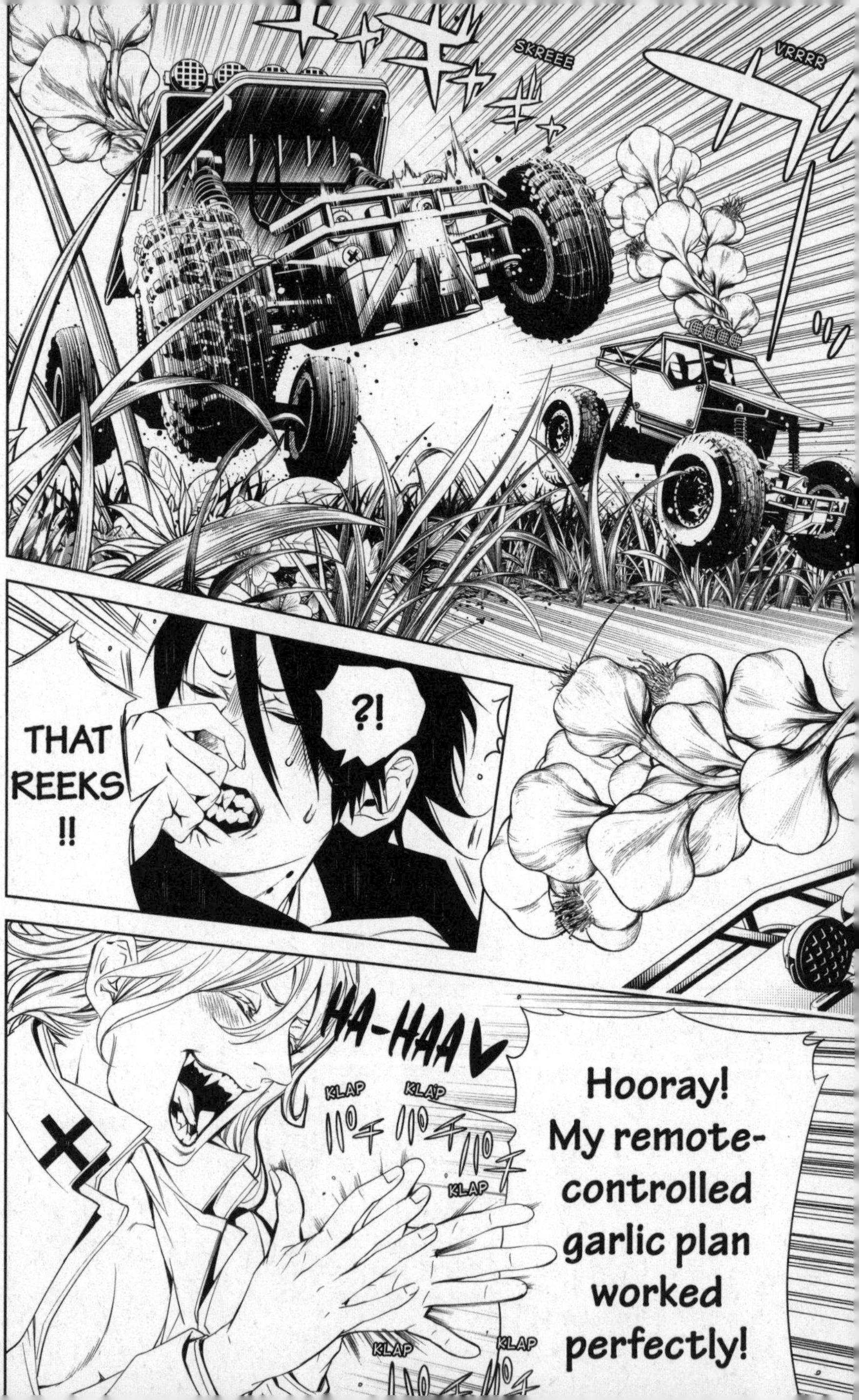
VRRRR
SKREEE
?!
THAT REEKS !!
HA-HAA
Hooray! My remote-controlled garlic plan worked perfectly!
KLAP
KLAP
KLAP
KLAP
KLAP

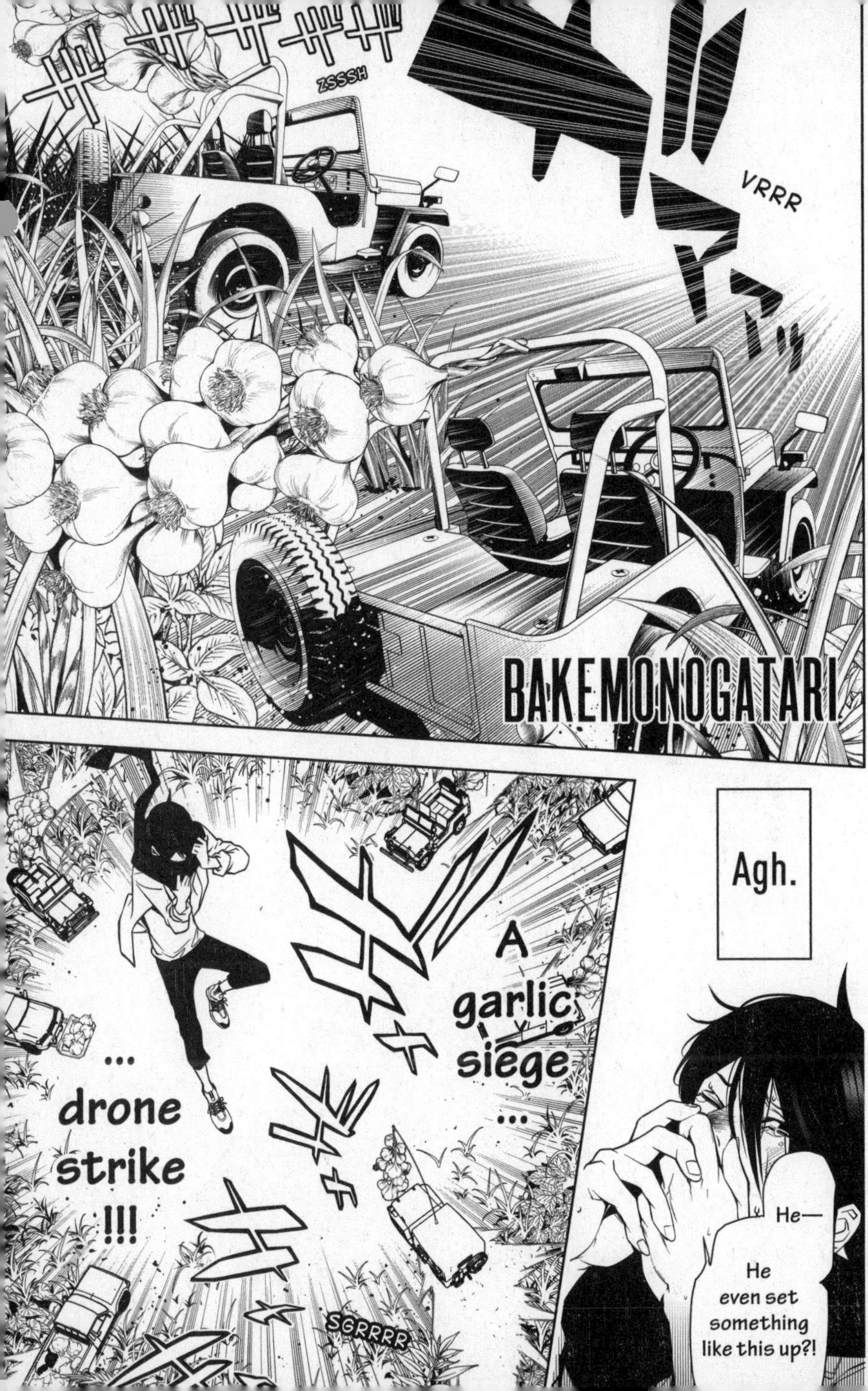
VRRR
ZSSSH
BAKEMONOGATARI
Agh.
He—
He even set something like this up?!
A garlic siege ...
... drone strike !!!
SGRRRR

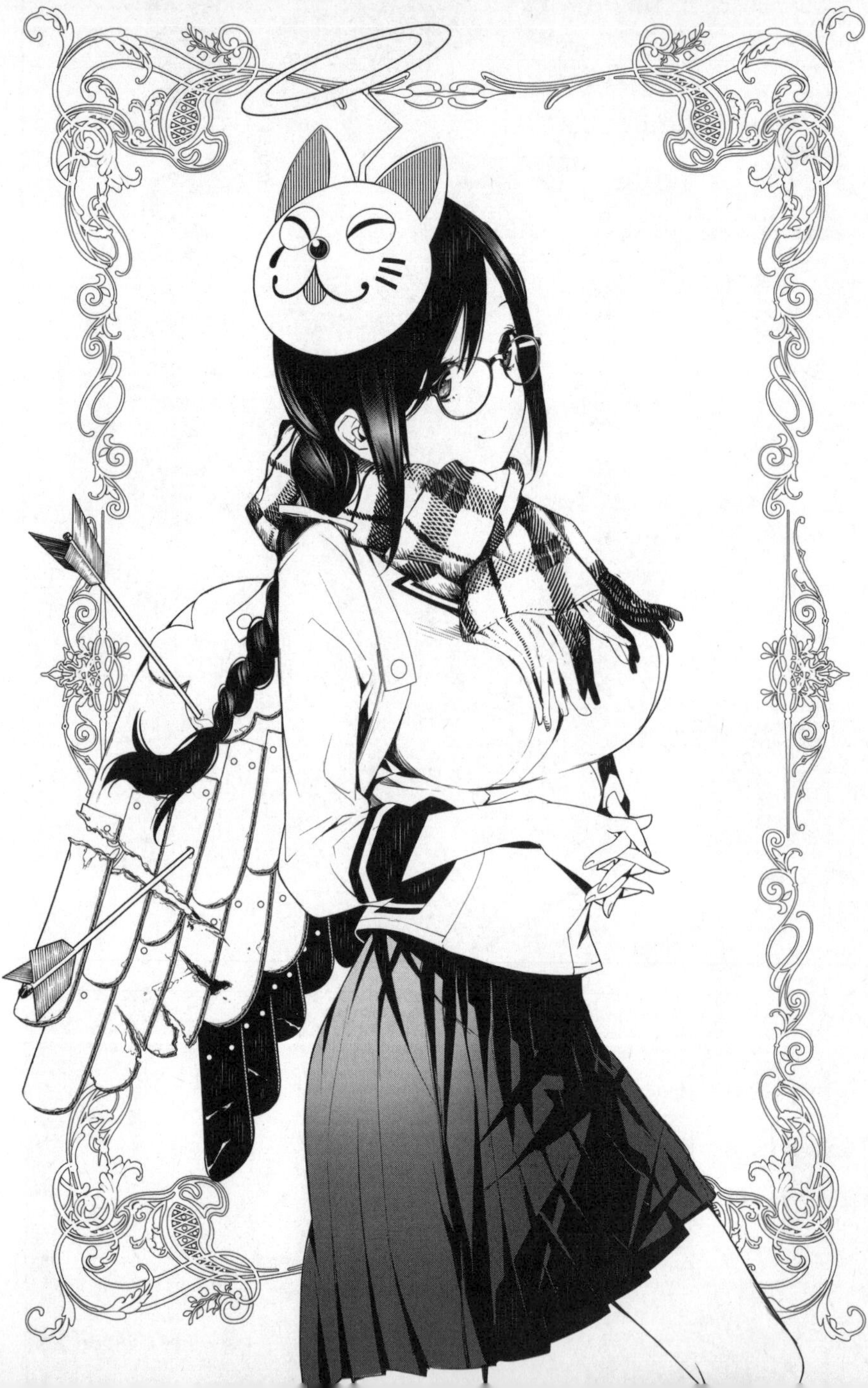

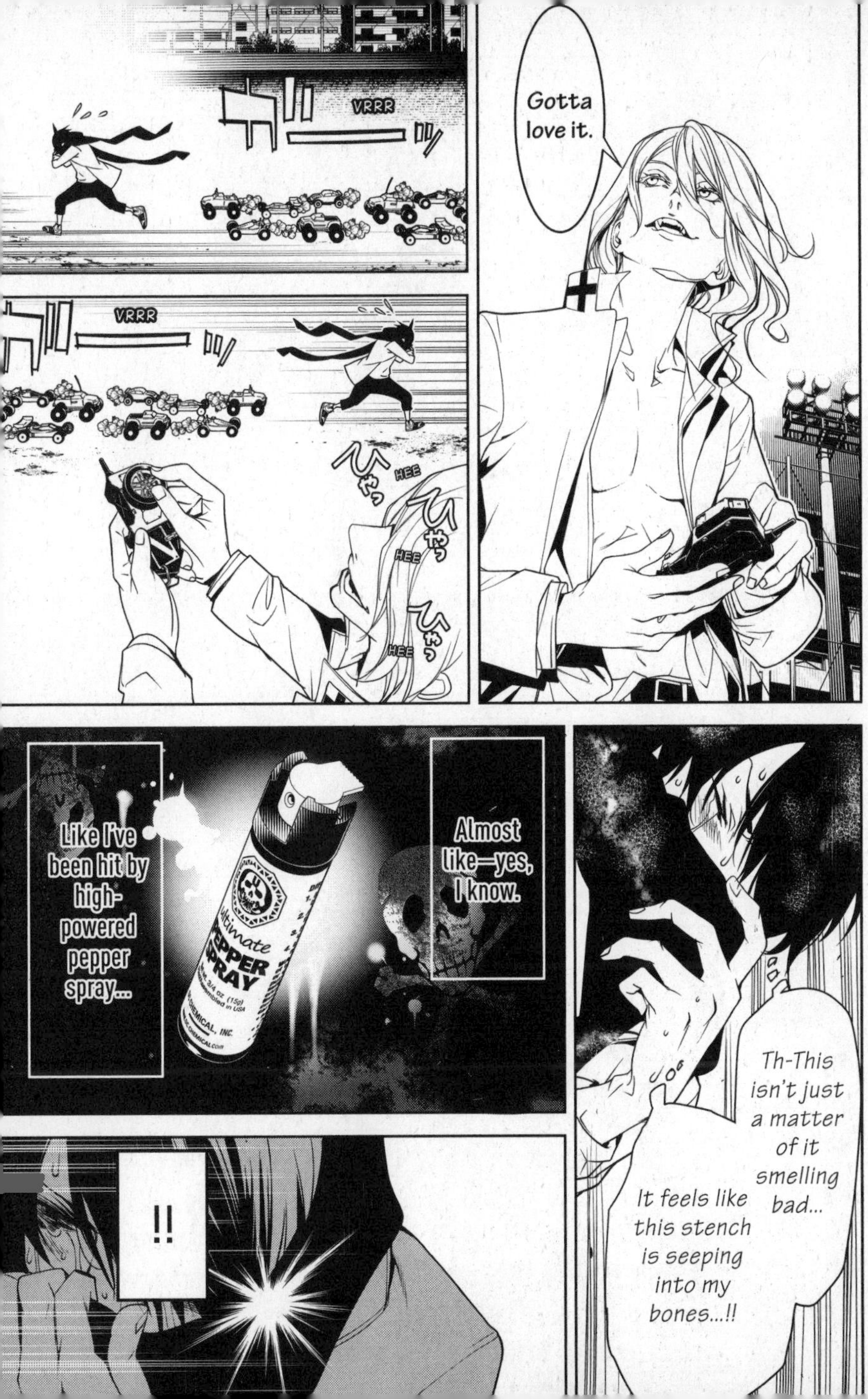
Gotta love it.
VRRR
VRRR
HEE
HEE
HEE
Th-This isn't just a matter of it smelling bad...
It feels like this stench is seeping into my bones...!!
Almost like—yes, I know.
Like I've been hit by high-powered pepper spray...
ultimate PEPPER SPRAY
!!

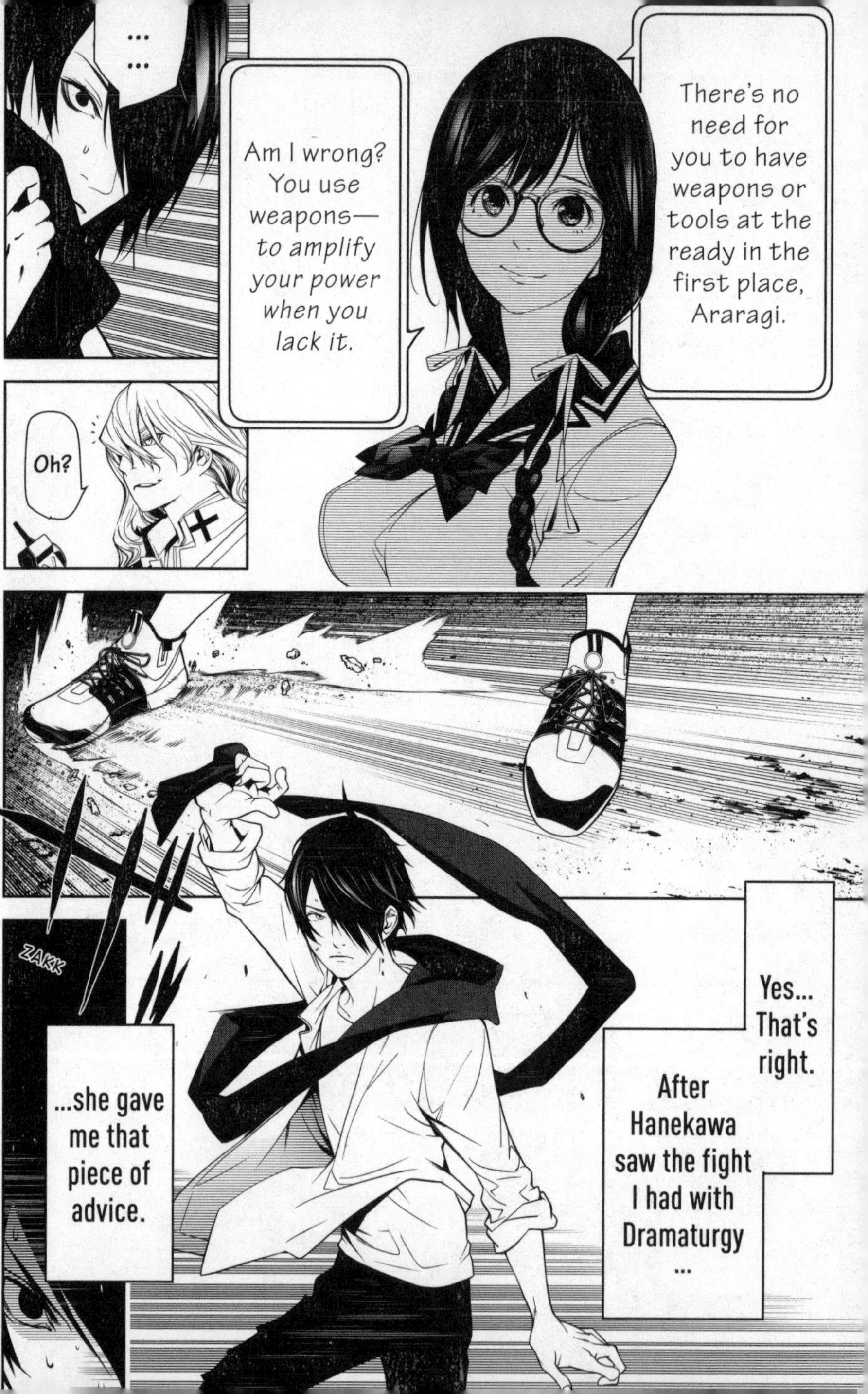
There's no need for you to have weapons or tools at the ready in the first place, Araragi.
Am I wrong? You use weapons—to amplify your power when you lack it.
... ...
Oh?
Yes... That's right.
After Hanekawa saw the fight I had with Dramaturgy ...
...she gave me that piece of advice.
ZAKK

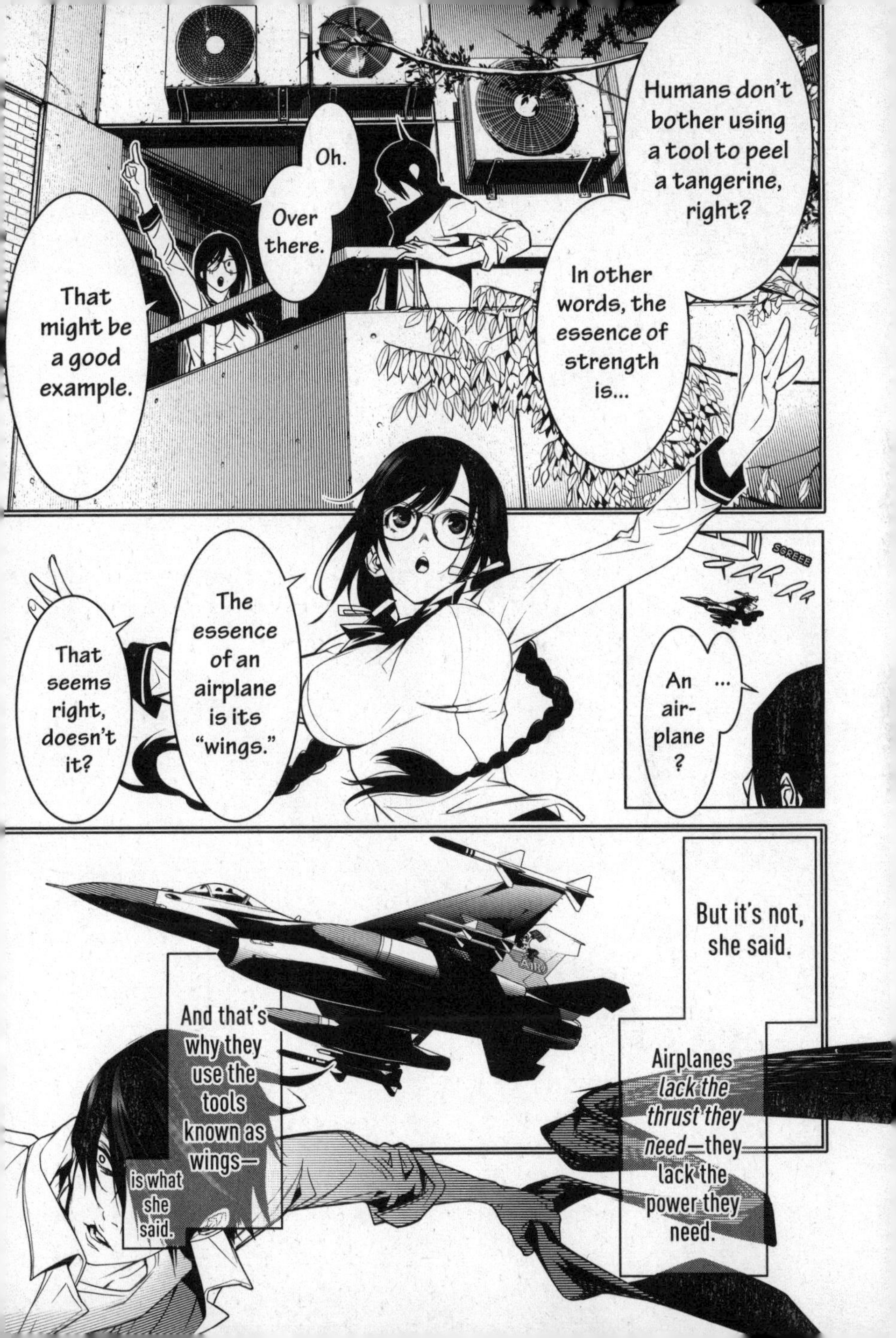
Humans don't bother using a tool to peel a tangerine, right?
In other words, the essence of strength is...
Oh.
Over there.
That might be a good example.
SCREEE
An airplane ...?
The essence of an airplane is its "wings."
That seems right, doesn't it?
But it's not, she said.
Airplanes *lack the thrust they need*—they lack the power they need.
And that's why they use the tools known as wings—
is what she said.

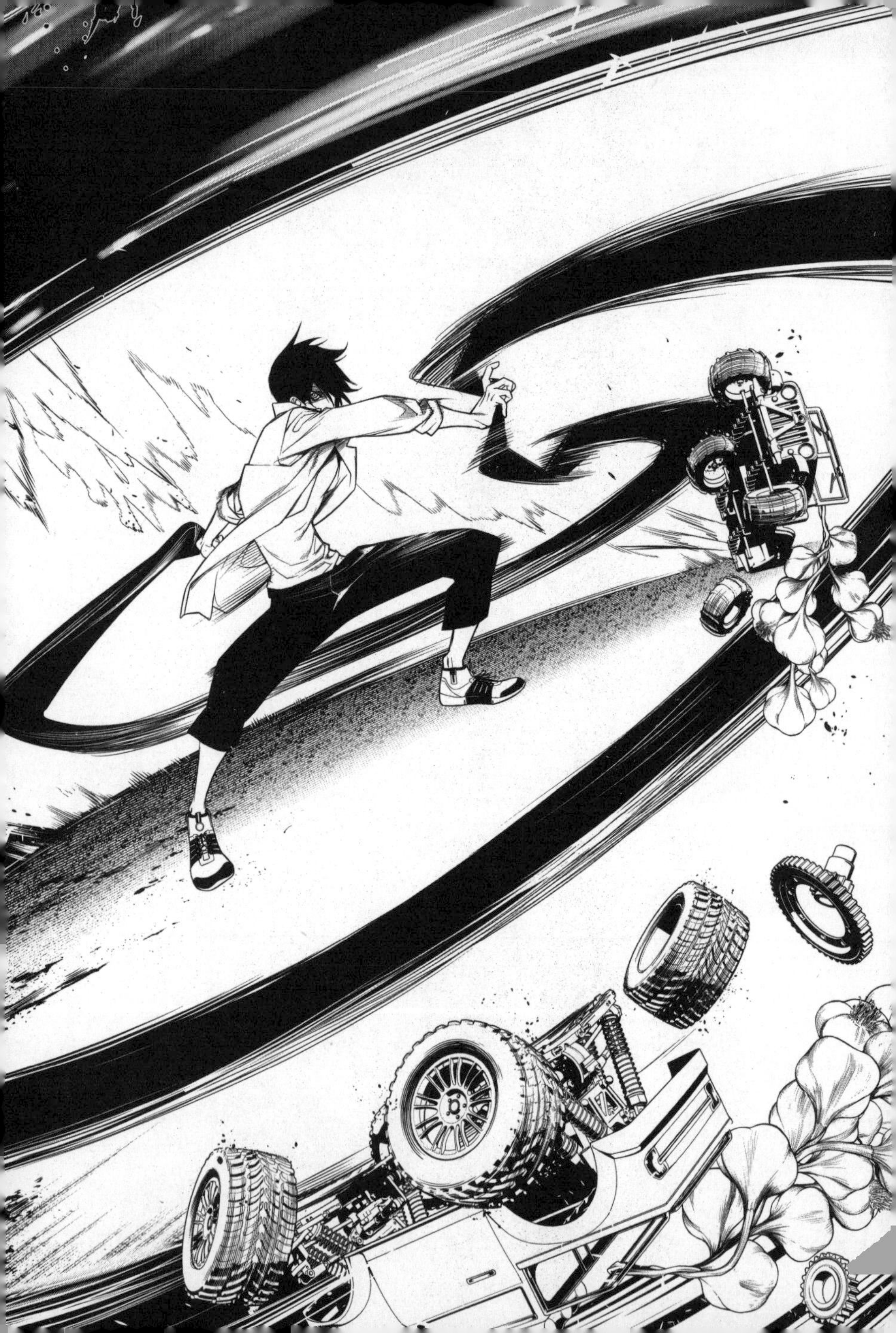

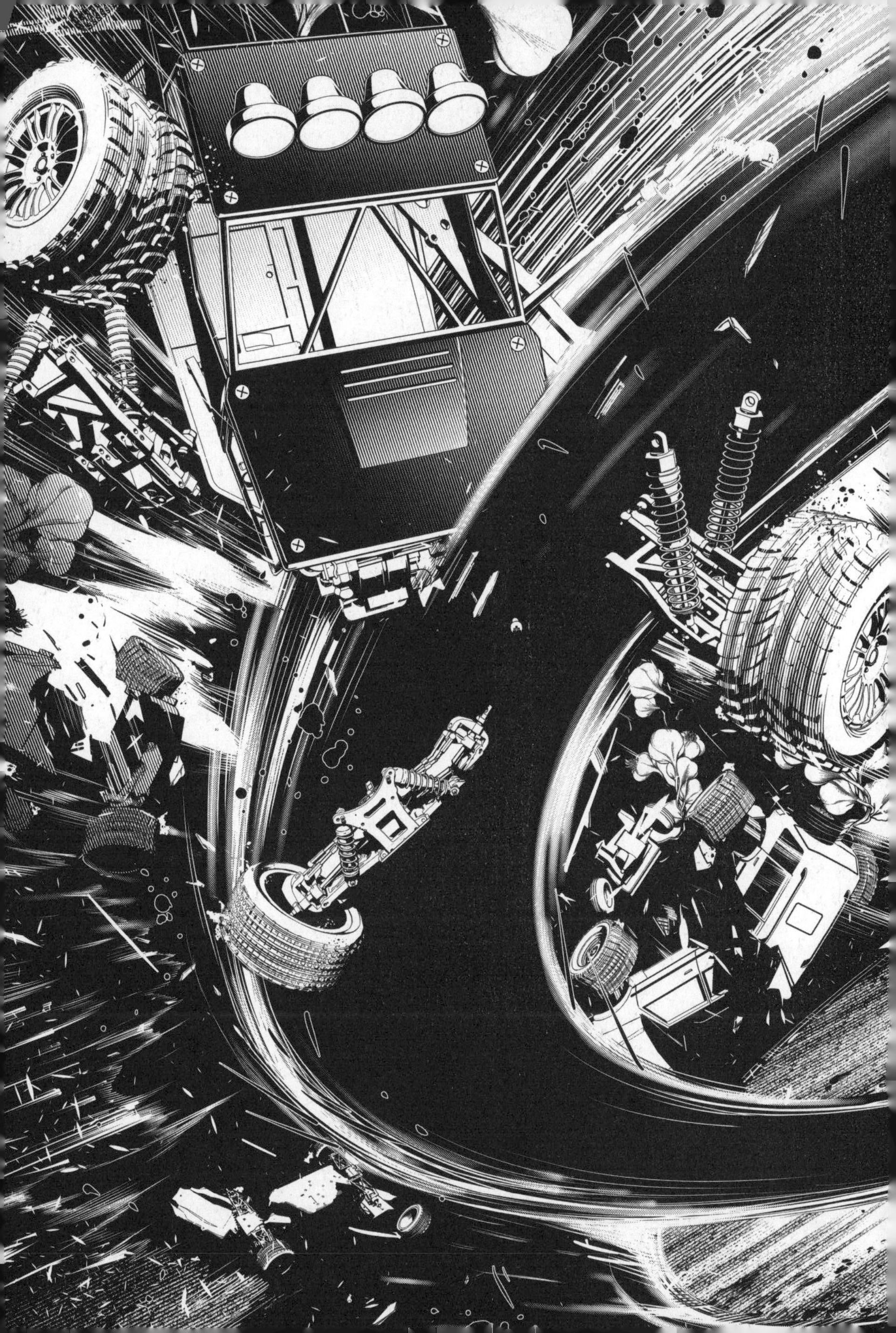

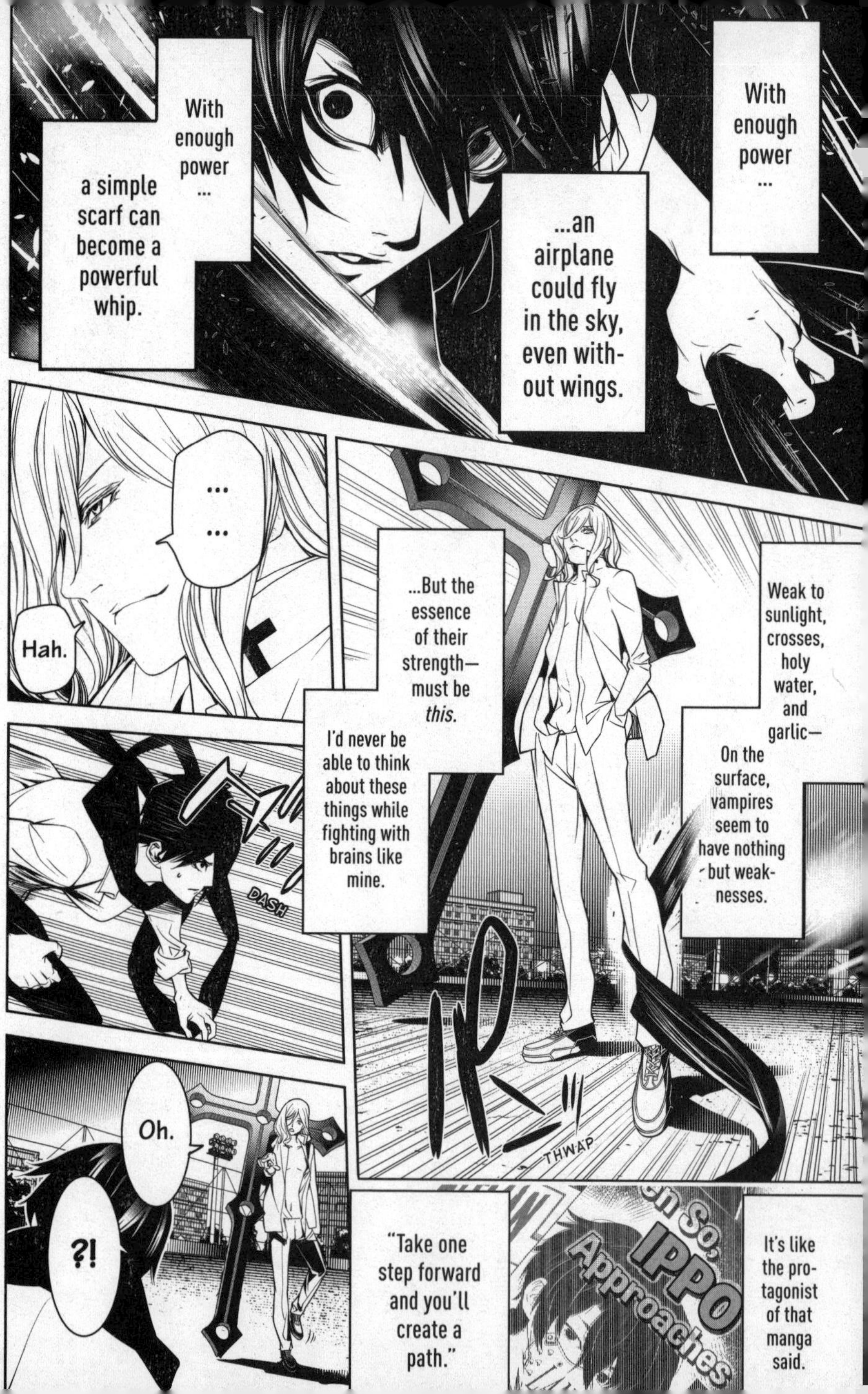
With enough power ...
...an airplane could fly in the sky, even with-out wings.
With enough power ...
a simple scarf can become a powerful whip.
Weak to sunlight, crosses, holy water, and garlic—
On the surface, vampires seem to have nothing but weak-nesses.
...But the essence of their strength—must be *this.*
I'd never be able to think about these things while fighting with brains like mine.
THWAP
...
...
Hah.
DASH
It's like the pro-tagonist of that manga said.
IPPO
Approaches
"Take one step forward and you'll create a path."
Oh.
?!

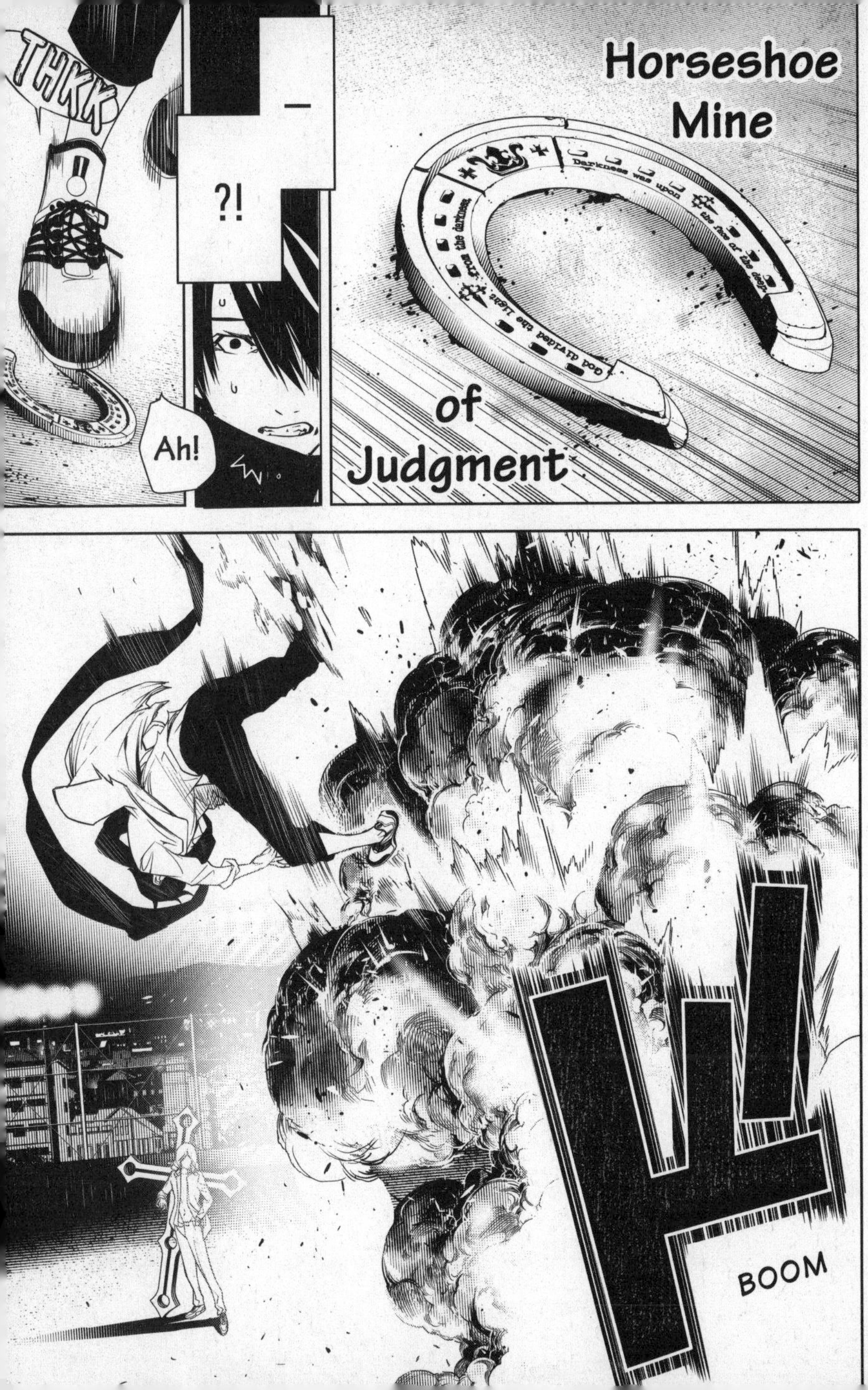
Horseshoe Mine
of
Judgment
Darkness was upon the face of the deep.
God divided the Light from the darkness.
—
?!
Ah!
THKK
BOOM

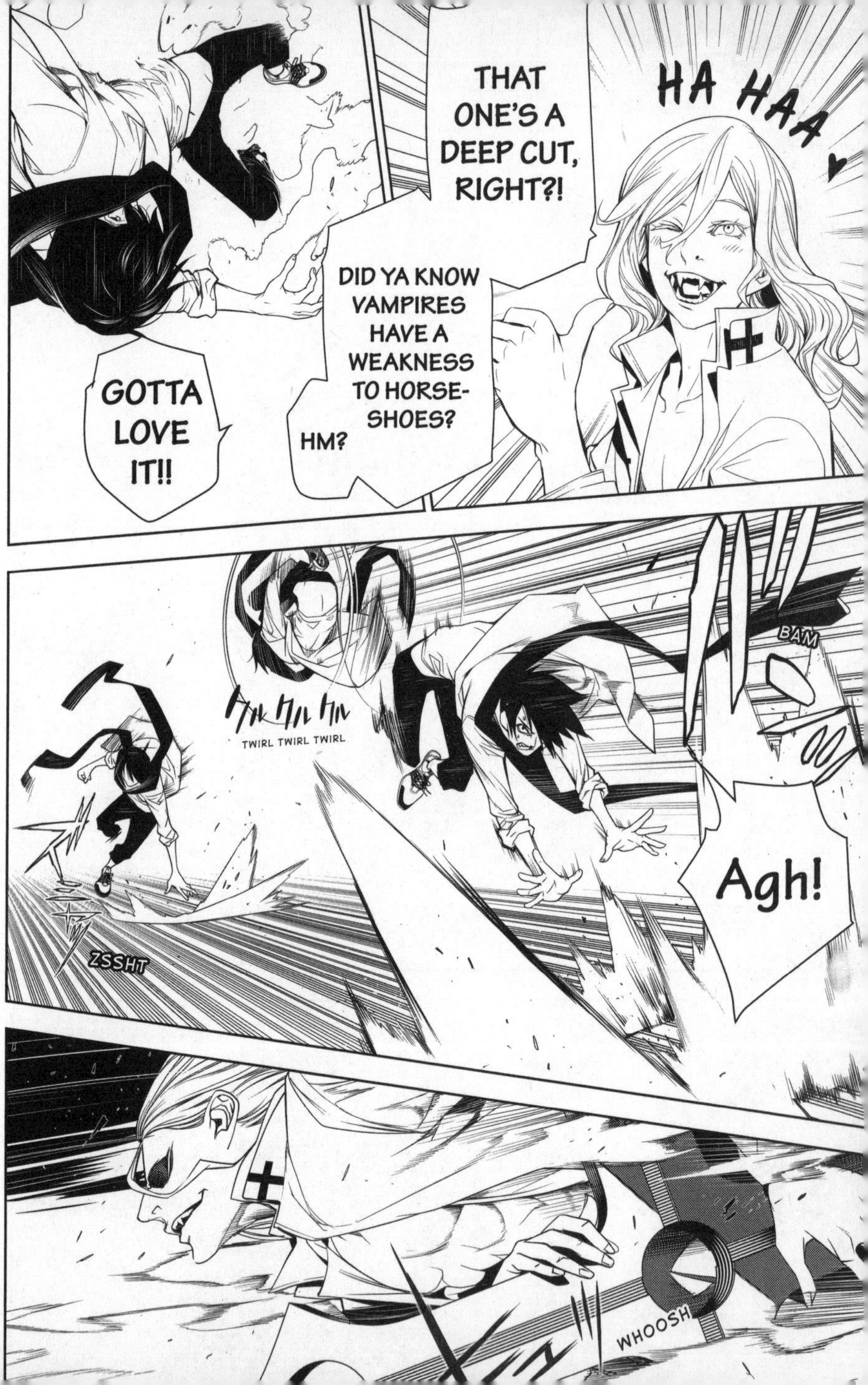
HA HAA ♥
THAT ONE'S A DEEP CUT, RIGHT?!
DID YA KNOW VAMPIRES HAVE A WEAKNESS TO HORSE-SHOES?
HM?
GOTTA LOVE IT!!
BAM
Agh!
TWIRL TWIRL TWIRL
ZSSHT
WHOOSH

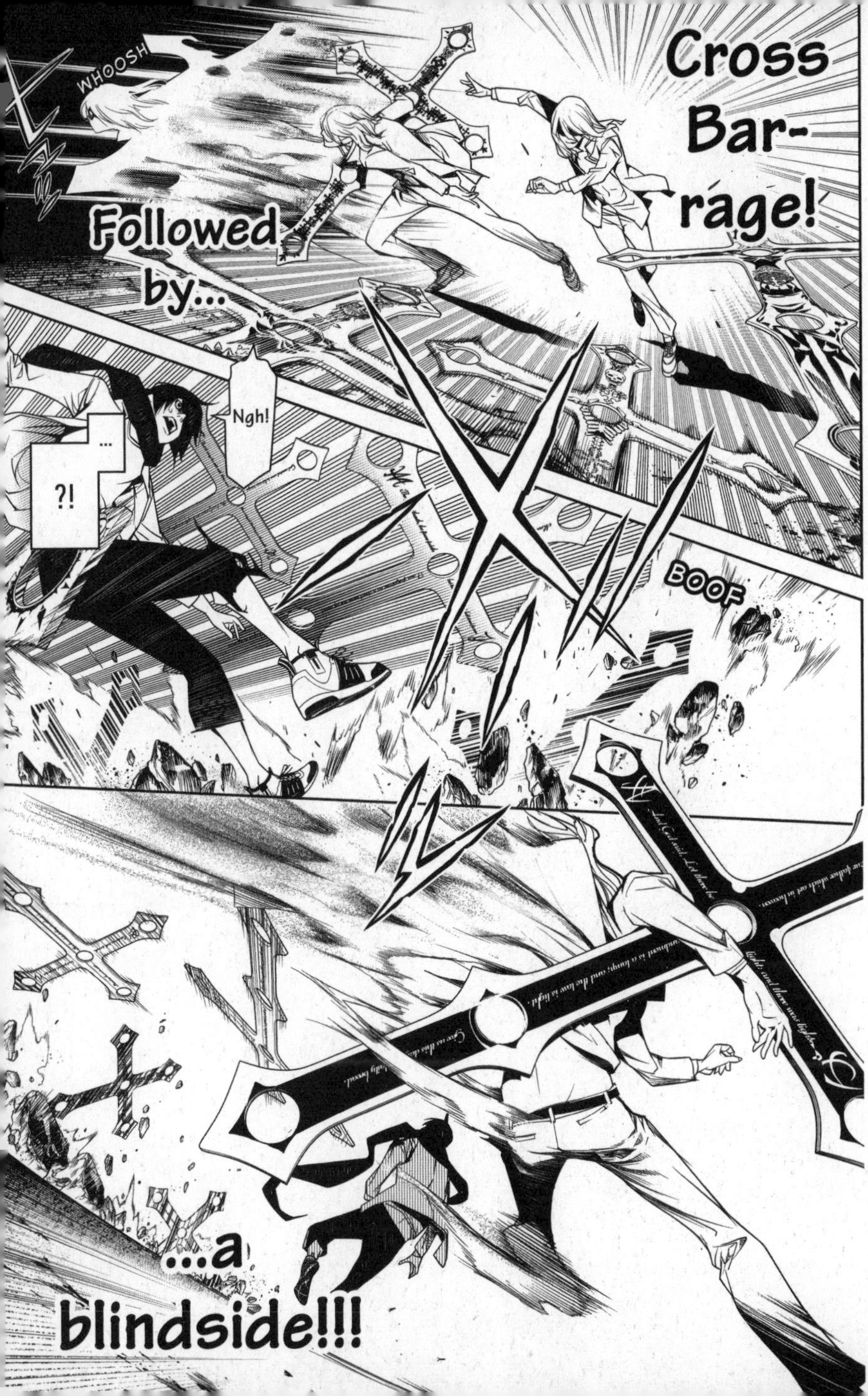
Cross Barrage!
WHOOSH
Followed by...
BOOF
Ngh!
...
?!
...a blindside!!!

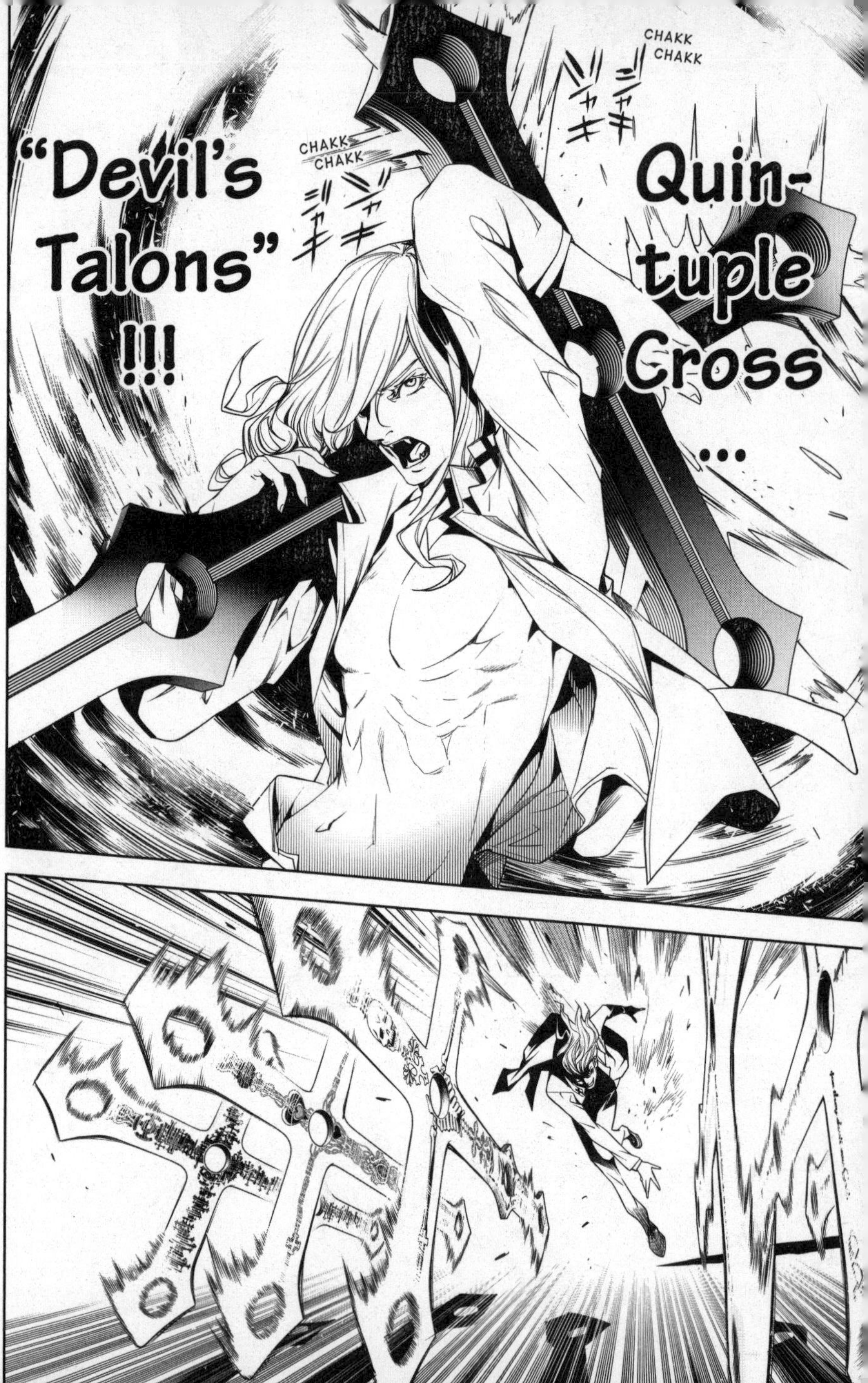
CHAKK CHAKK
Quin-tuple Cross…
CHAKK CHAKK
"Devil's Talons"!!!

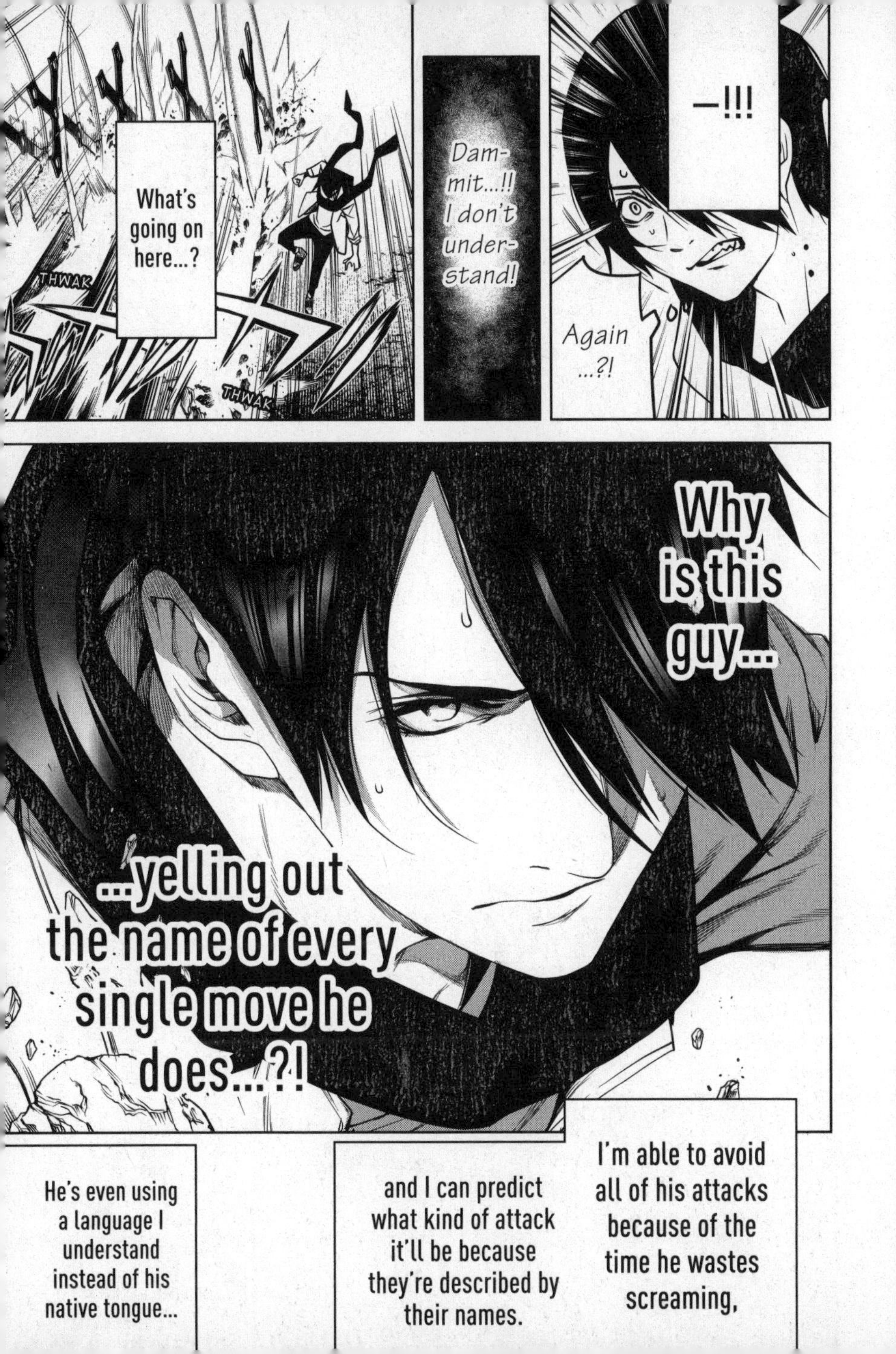
—!!!
Again ...?!
Dam-mit...!! I don't under-stand!
What's going on here...?
THWAK
THWAK
Why is this guy...
...yelling out the name of every single move he does...?!
I'm able to avoid all of his attacks because of the time he wastes screaming,
and I can predict what kind of attack it'll be because they're described by their names.
He's even using a language I understand instead of his native tongue...

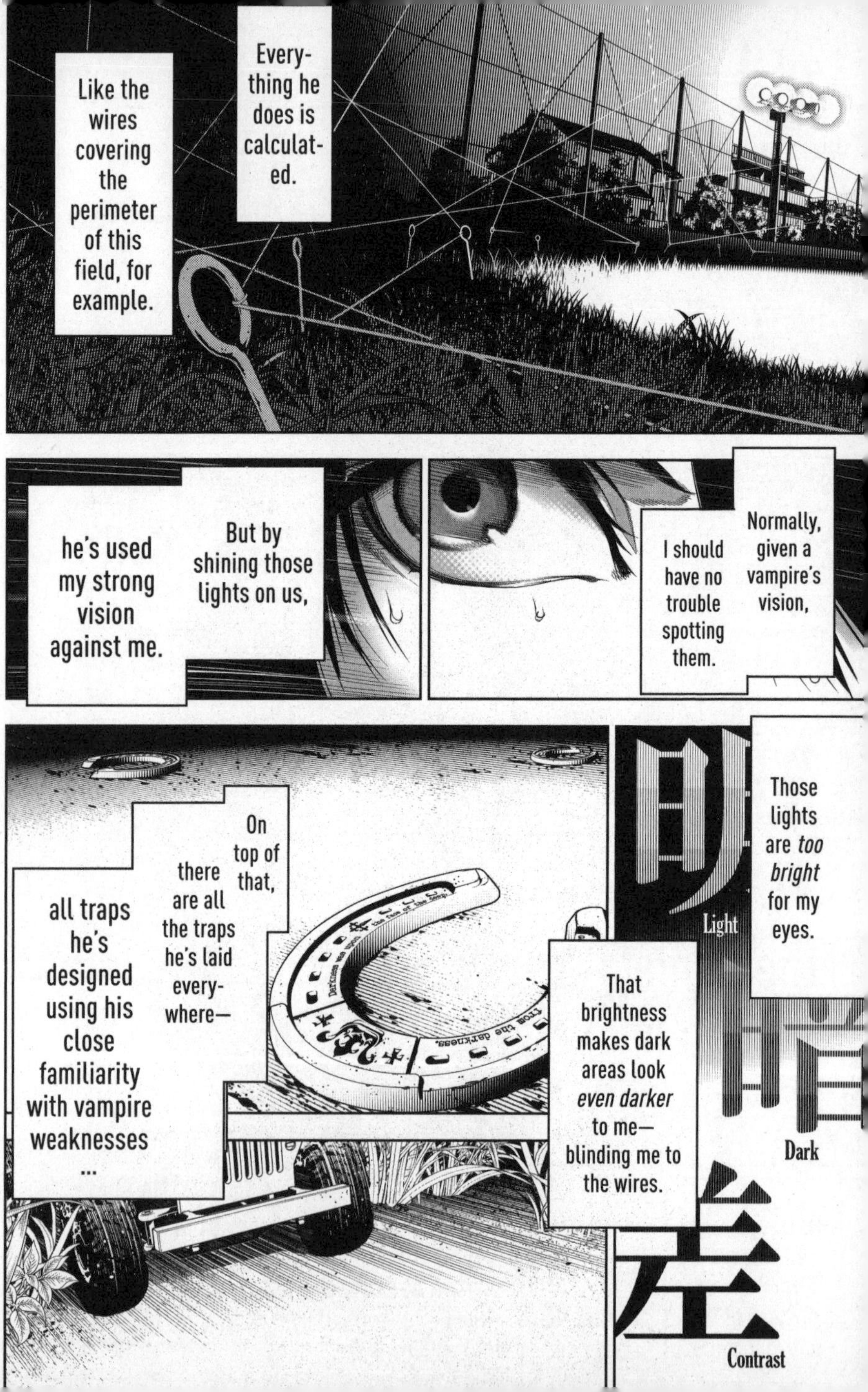
Every-thing he does is calculat-ed.
Like the wires covering the perimeter of this field, for example.
Normally, given a vampire's vision,
I should have no trouble spotting them.
But by shining those lights on us,
he's used my strong vision against me.
明暗差
Light
Dark
Contrast
Those lights are *too bright* for my eyes.
That brightness makes dark areas look *even darker* to me—blinding me to the wires.
On top of that,
there are all the traps he's laid every-where—
all traps he's designed using his close familiarity with vampire weaknesses...

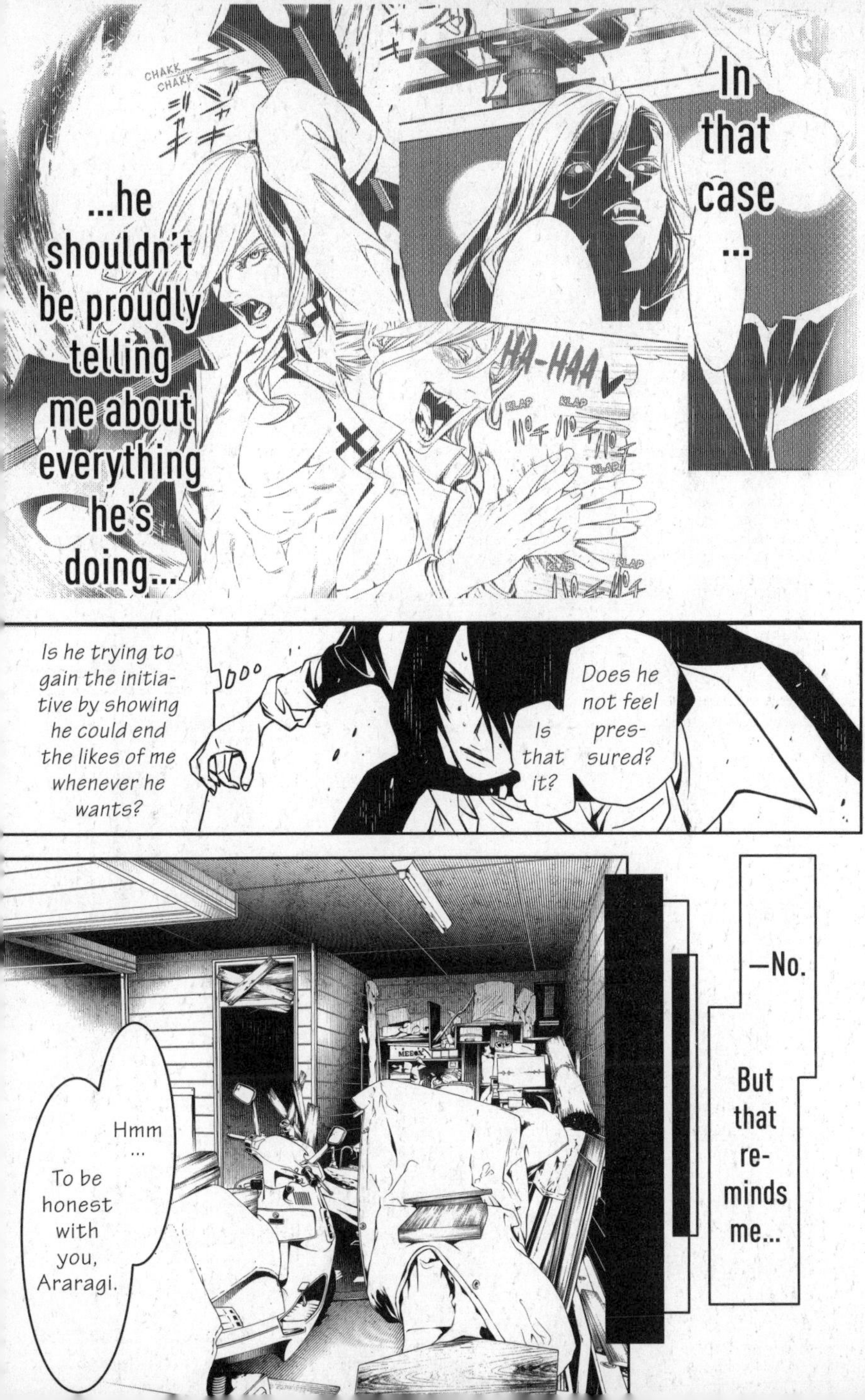
In that case ...
CHAKK CHAKK
...he shouldn't be proudly telling me about everything he's doing...
HA-HAA
KLAP KLAP KLAP
KLAP KLAP
Does he not feel pres-sured?
Is that it?
Is he trying to gain the initia-tive by showing he could end the likes of me whenever he wants?
—No.
But that re-minds me...
Hmm ... To be honest with you, Araragi.

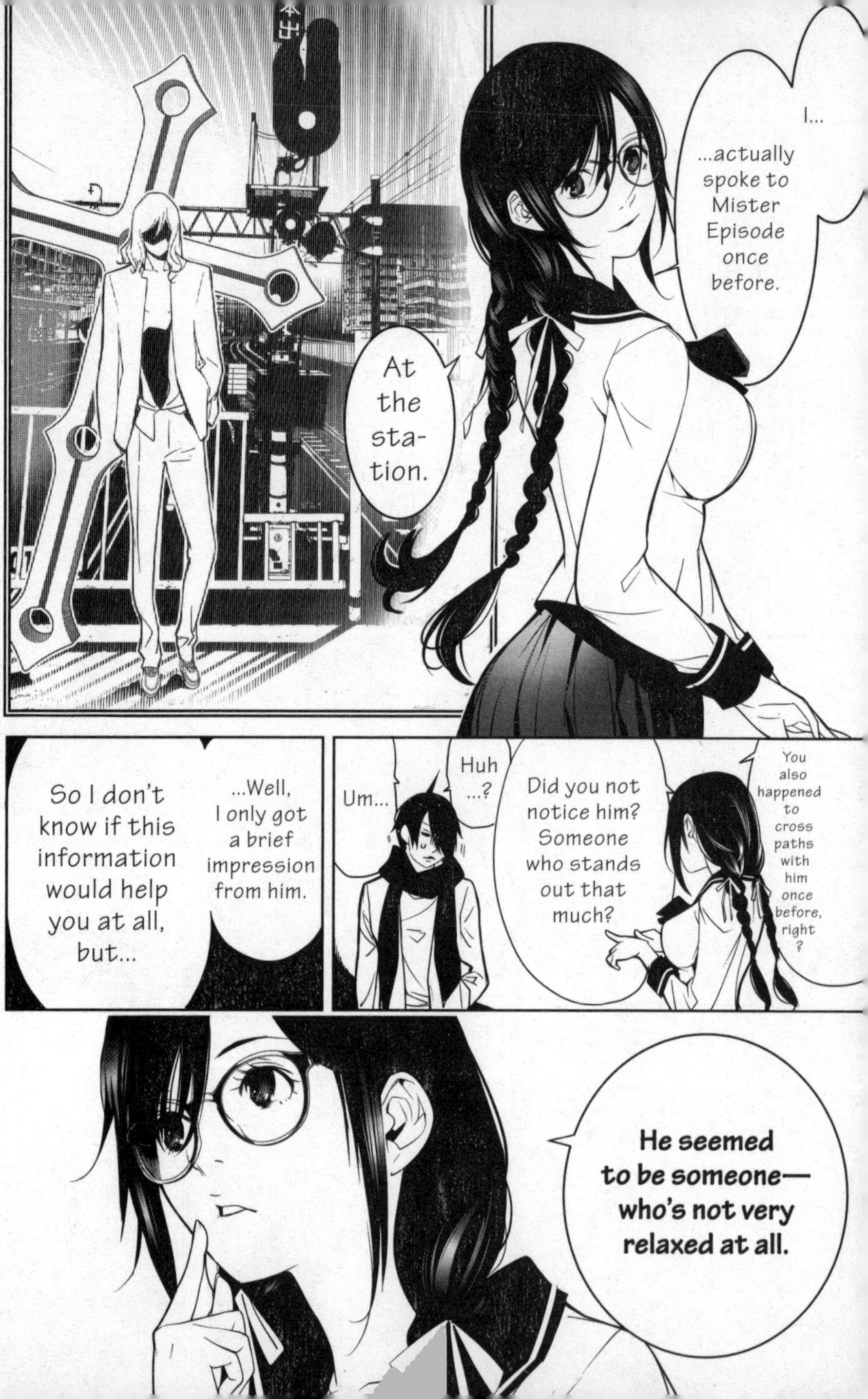

I...
...actually spoke to Mister Episode once before.
At the station.
You also happened to cross paths with him once before, right?
Did you not notice him? Someone who stands out that much?
Huh ...?
Um...
...Well, I only got a brief impression from him.
So I don't know if this information would help you at all, but...
He seemed to be someone—who's not very relaxed at all.

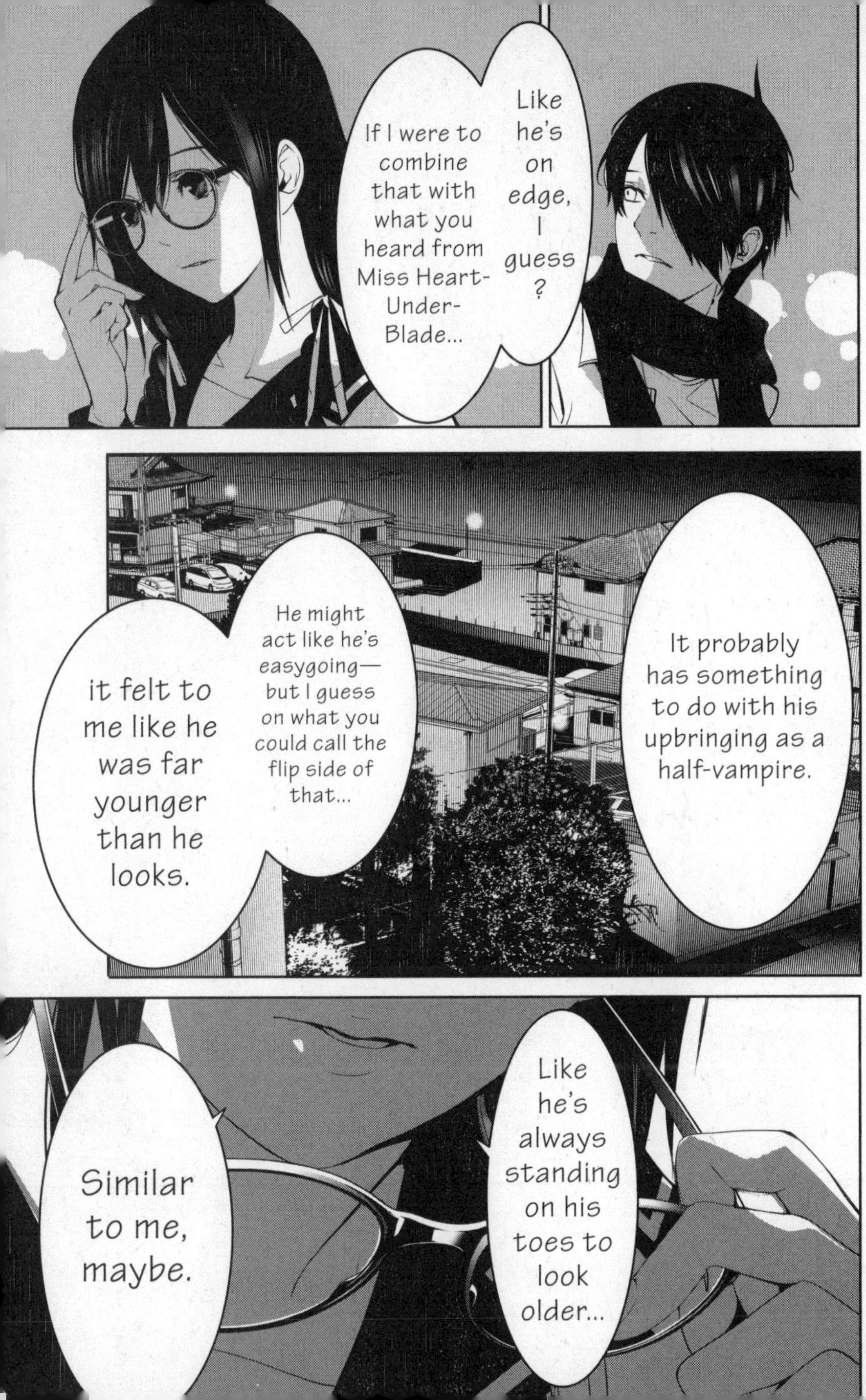
Like he's on edge, I guess?
If I were to combine that with what you heard from Miss Heart-Under-Blade...
It probably has something to do with his upbringing as a half-vampire.
He might act like he's easygoing—but I guess on what you could call the flip side of that...
it felt to me like he was far younger than he looks.
Like he's always standing on his toes to look older...
Similar to me, maybe.

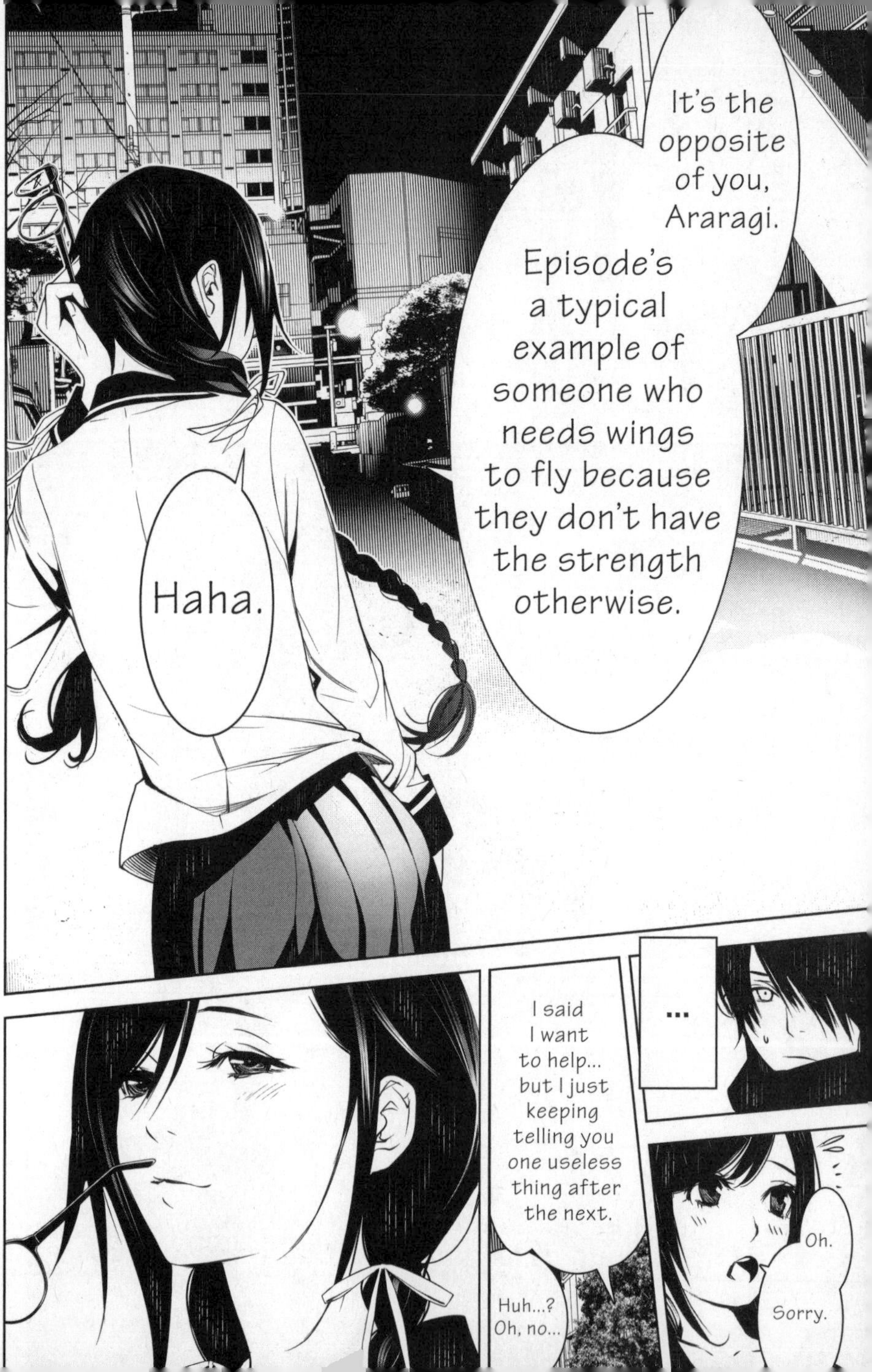
It's the opposite of you, Araragi.
Episode's a typical example of someone who needs wings to fly because they don't have the strength otherwise.
Haha.
...
Oh.
Sorry.
I said I want to help... but I just keeping telling you one useless thing after the next.
Huh...? Oh, no...

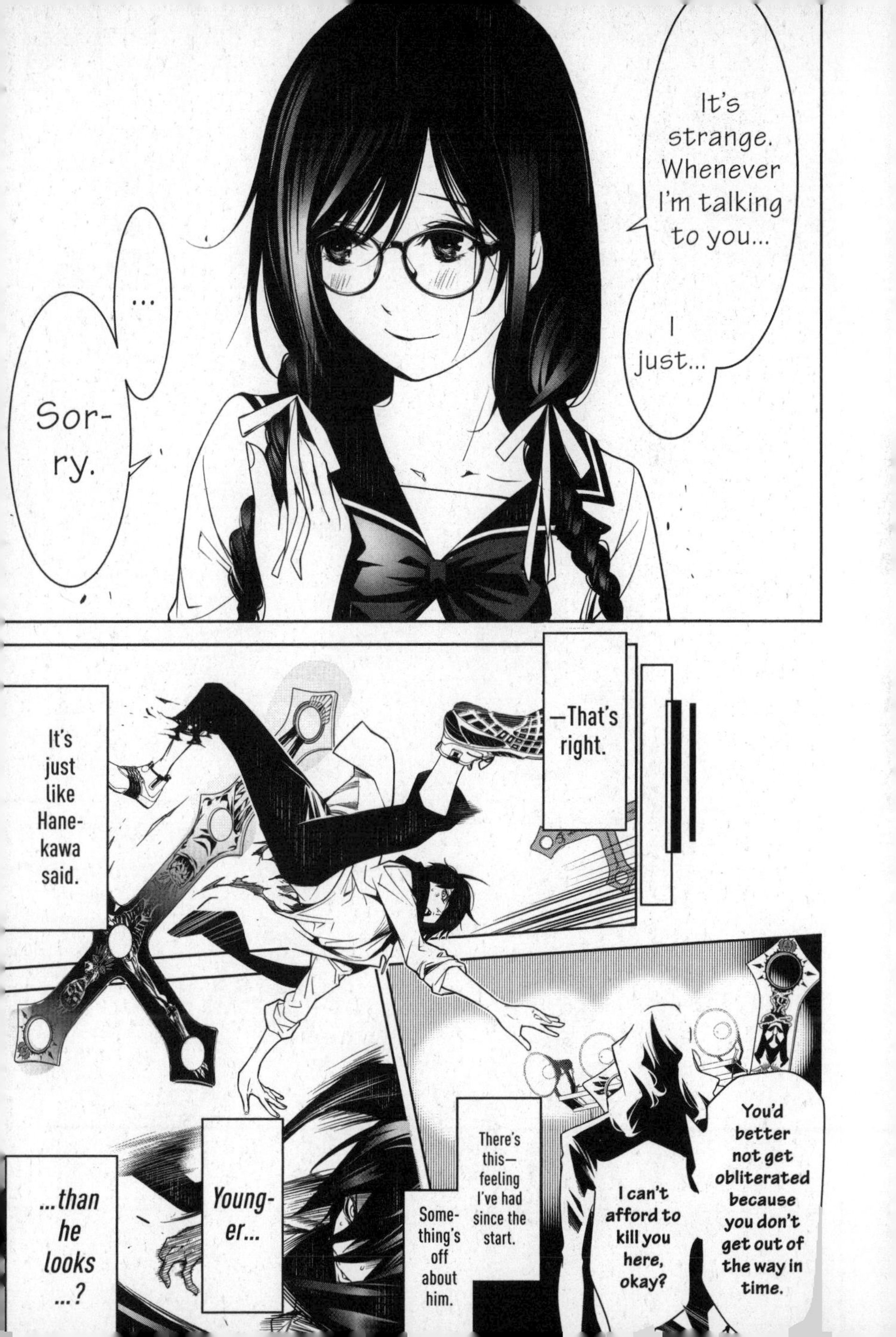
It's strange. Whenever I'm talking to you...
I just...
...
Sorry.
—That's right.
It's just like Hanekawa said.
You'd better not get obliterated because you don't get out of the way in time.
I can't afford to kill you here, okay?
There's this—feeling I've had since the start.
Something's off about him.
Younger...
...than he looks ...?

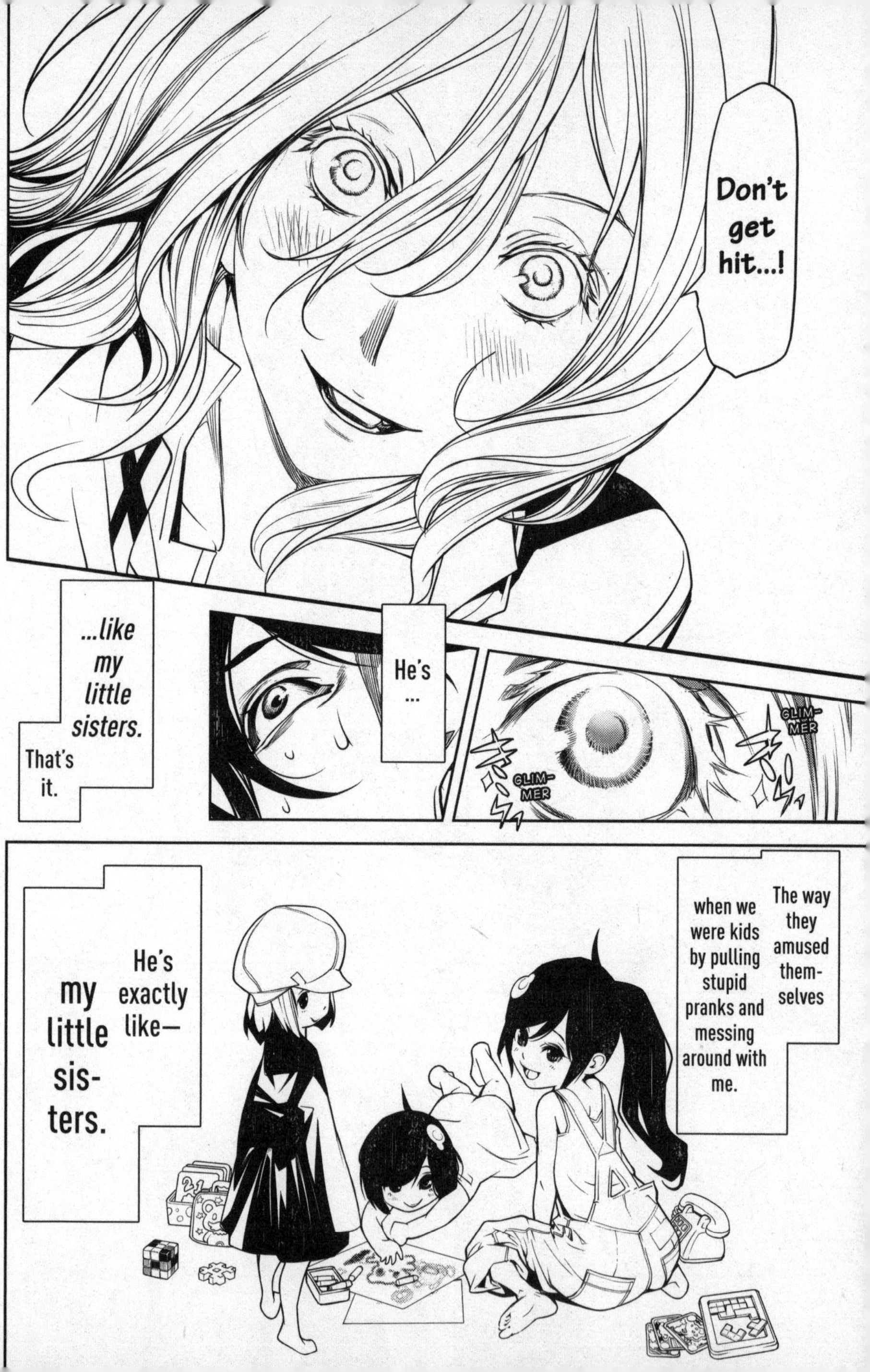
Don't get hit...!
GLIM-MER
GLIM-MER
He's ...
...like my little sisters.
That's it.
The way they amused them-selves
when we were kids by pulling stupid pranks and messing around with me.
He's exactly like—
my little sis-ters.

BAKEMONOGATARI

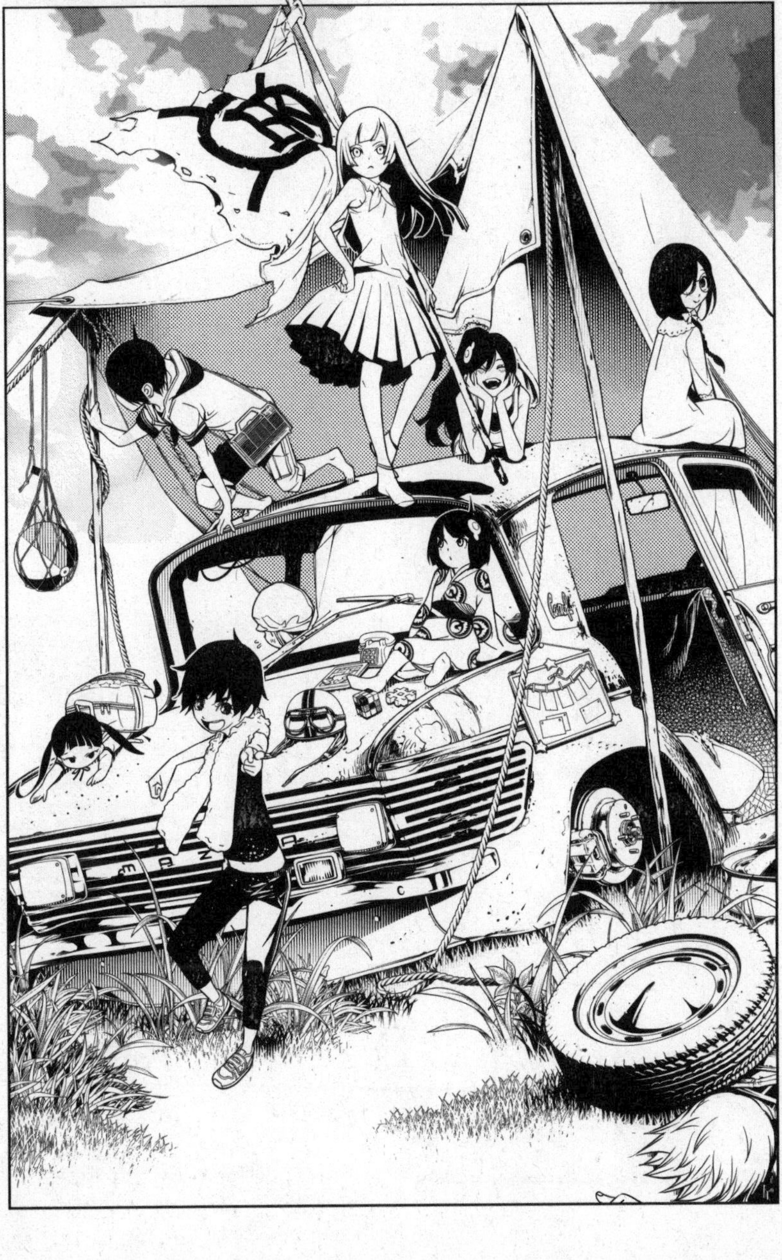

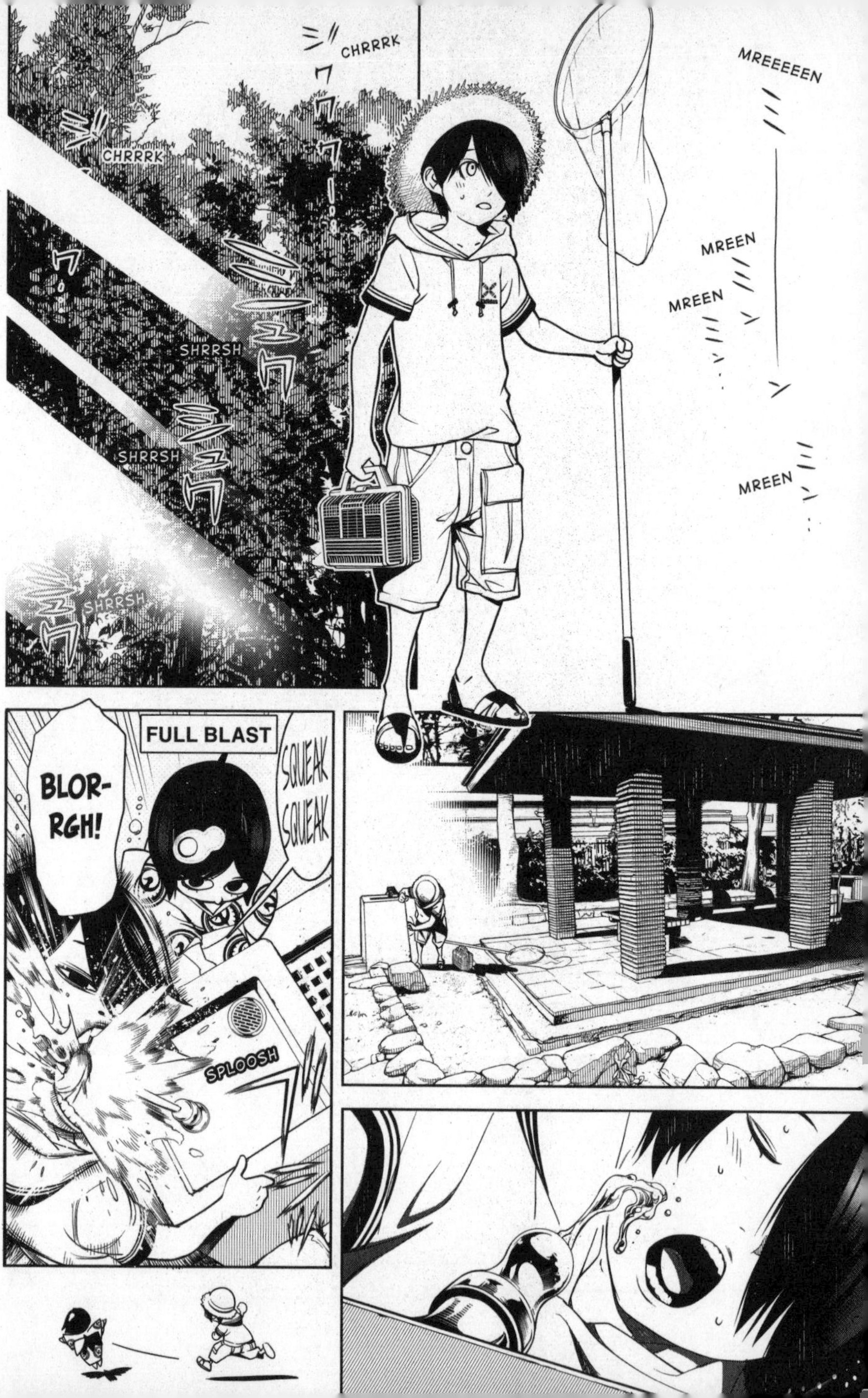
MREEEEEN
MREEN
MREEN
MREEN
CHRRRK
CHRRRK
SHRRSH
SHRRSH
SHRRSH
SQUEAK SQUEAK
FULL BLAST
BLOR-RGH!
SPLOOSH

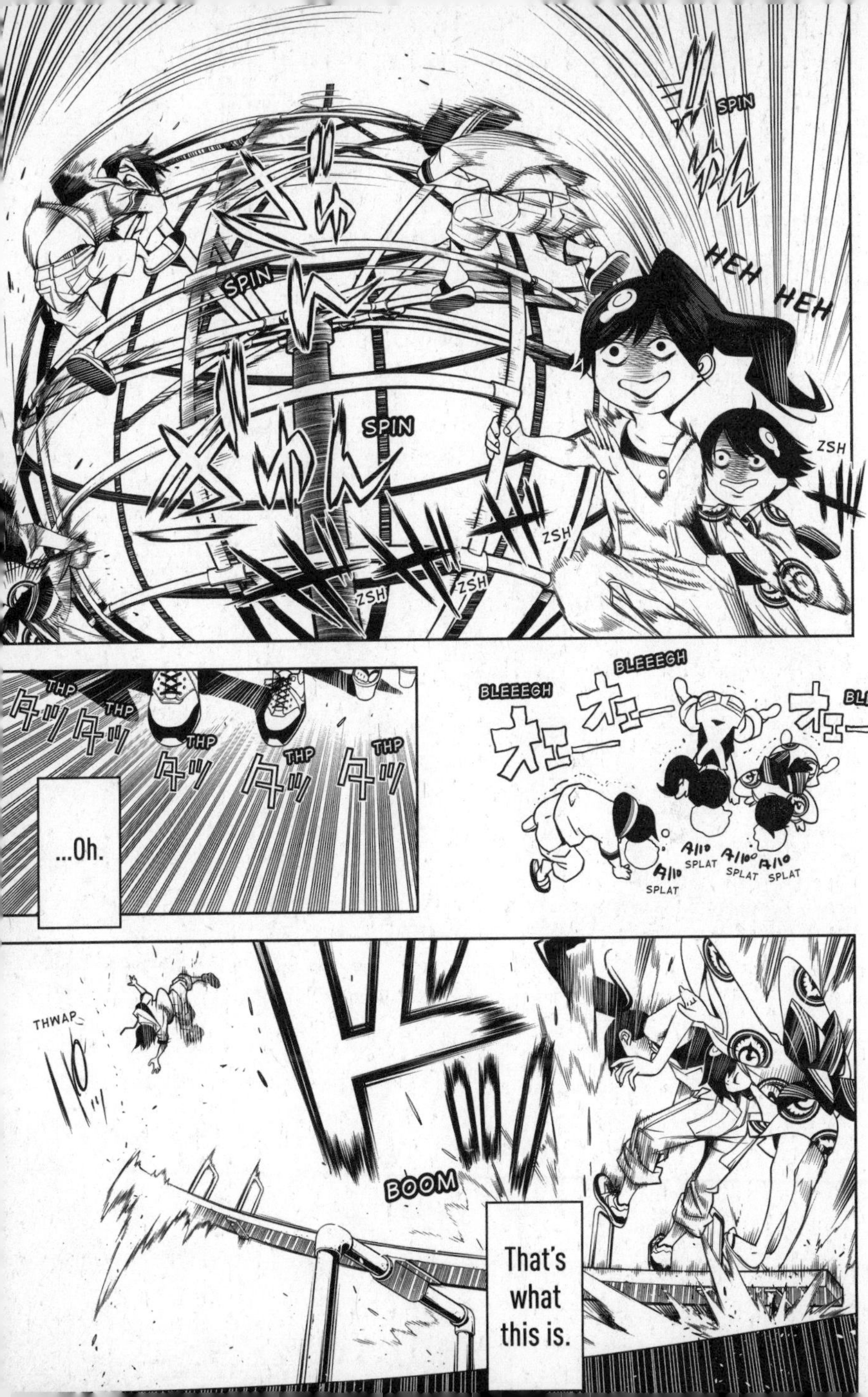
SPIN
HEH HEH
ZSH
SPIN
SPIN
ZSH
ZSH
ZSH
BLEEEGH
BLEEEGH
BLEEEGH
SPLAT
SPLAT
SPLAT
SPLAT
THP
THP
THP
THP
THP
...Oh.
BOOM
THWAP
That's what this is.

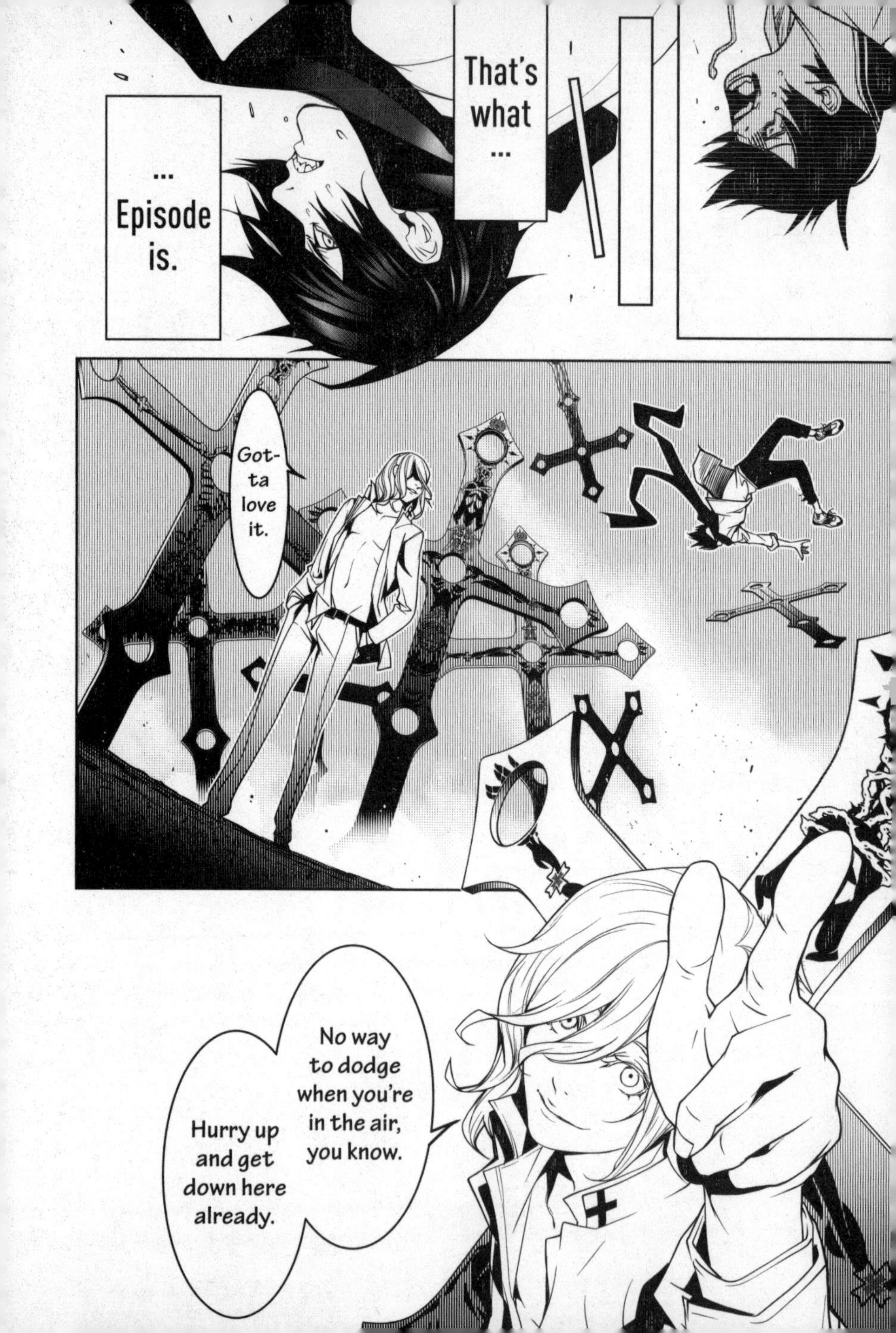
That's what ...
... Episode is.
Got-ta love it.
No way to dodge when you're in the air, you know.
Hurry up and get down here already.

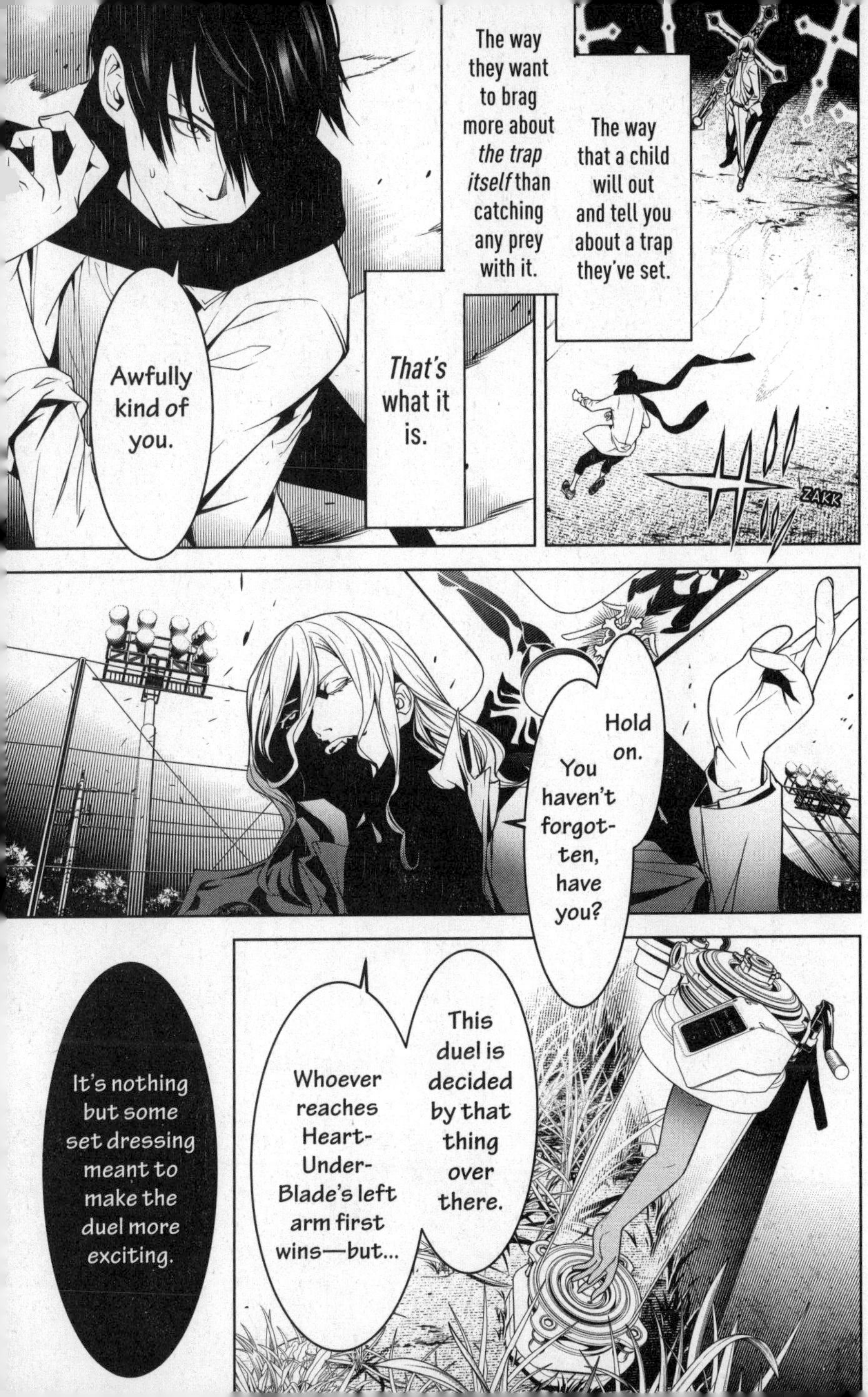
The way that a child will out and tell you about a trap they've set.
ZAKK
The way they want to brag more about *the trap itself* than catching any prey with it.
That's what it is.
Awfully kind of you.
Hold on. You haven't forgot-ten, have you?
This duel is decided by that thing over there.
Whoever reaches Heart-Under-Blade's left arm first wins—but...
It's nothing but some set dressing meant to make the duel more exciting.

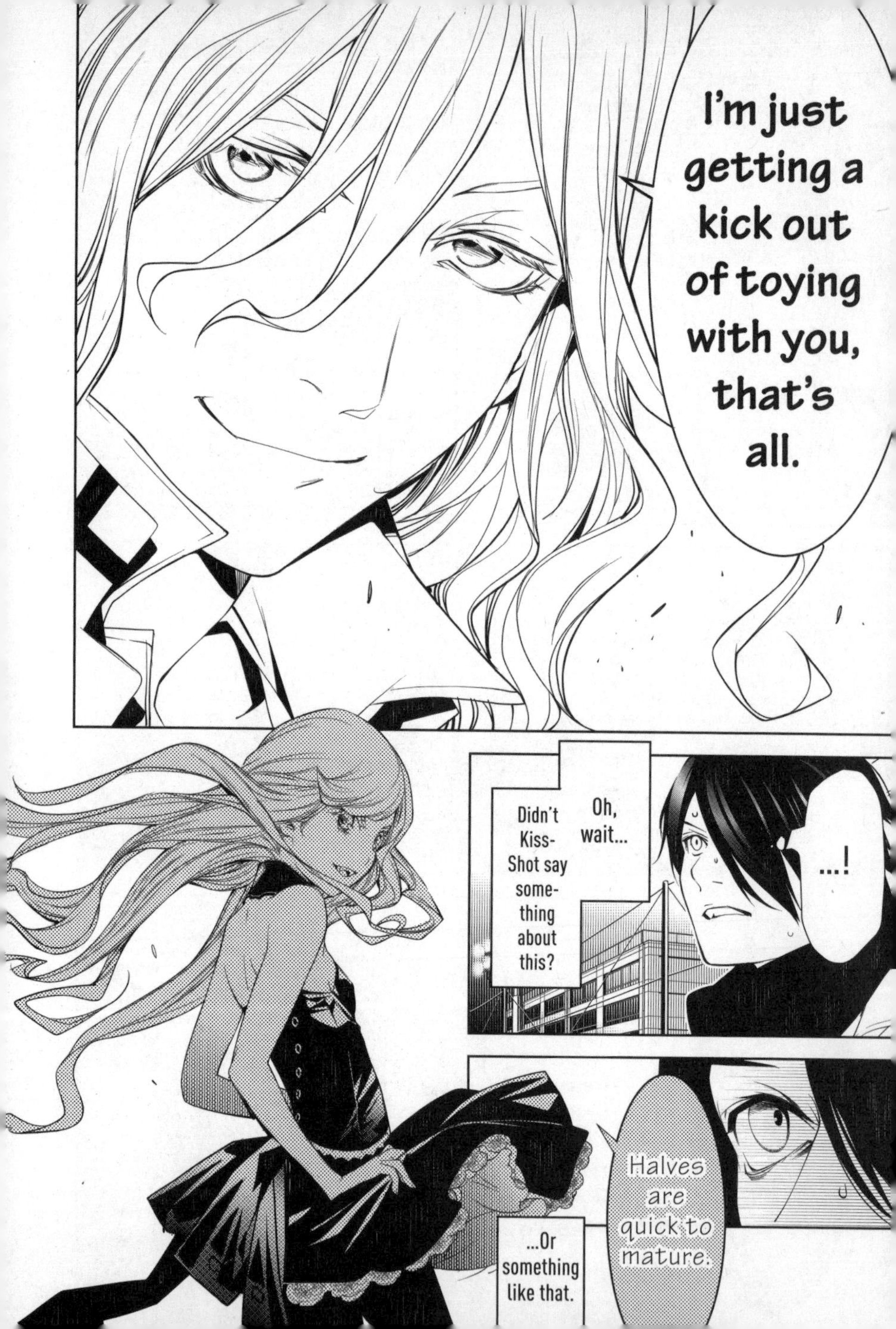
I'm just getting a kick out of toying with you, that's all.
...!
Oh, wait...
Didn't Kiss-Shot say some-thing about this?
Halves are quick to mature.
...Or something like that.

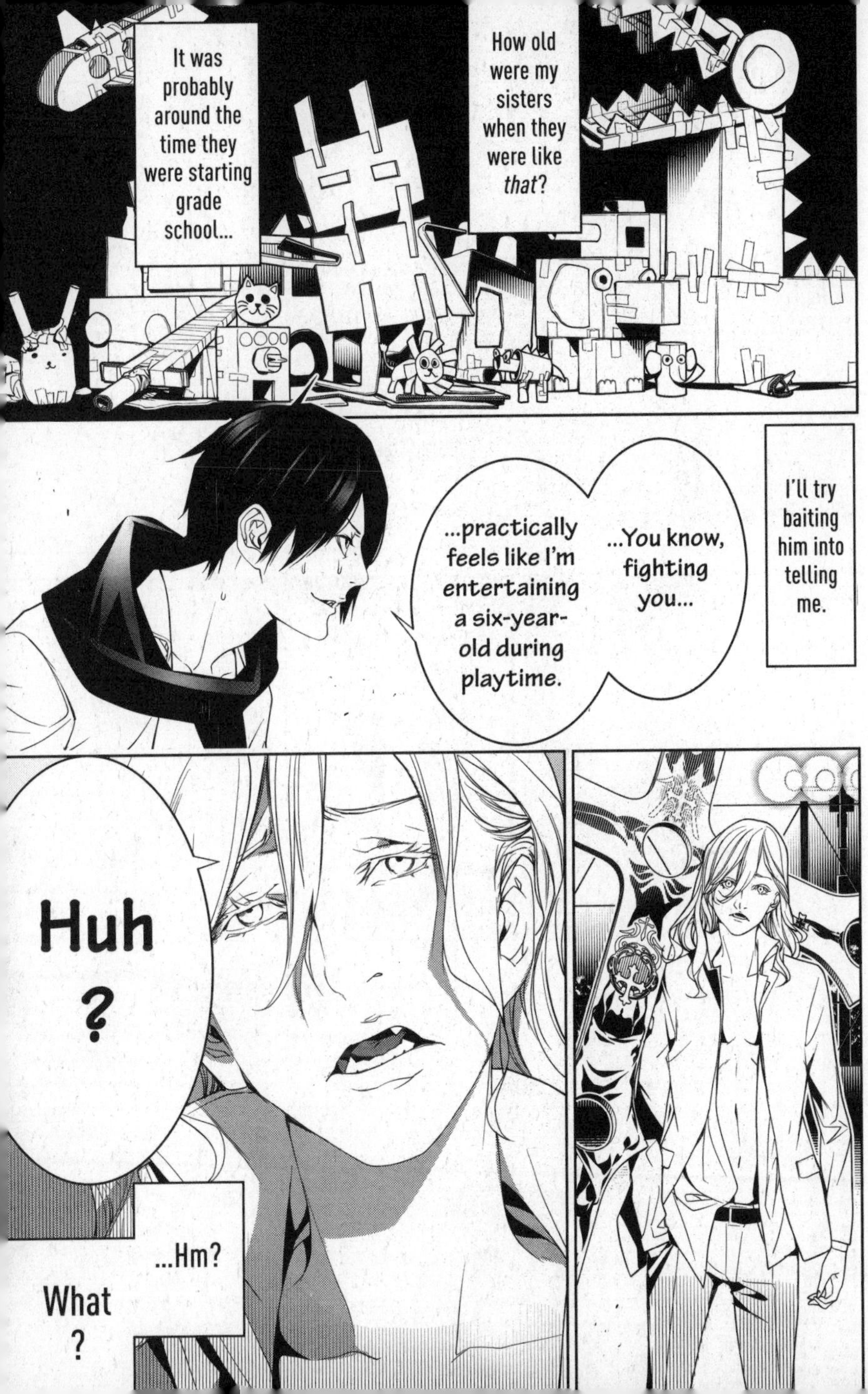
How old were my sisters when they were like *that*?
It was probably around the time they were starting grade school...
I'll try baiting him into telling me.
...You know, fighting you...
...practically feels like I'm entertaining a six-year-old during playtime.
Huh?
...Hm?
What?

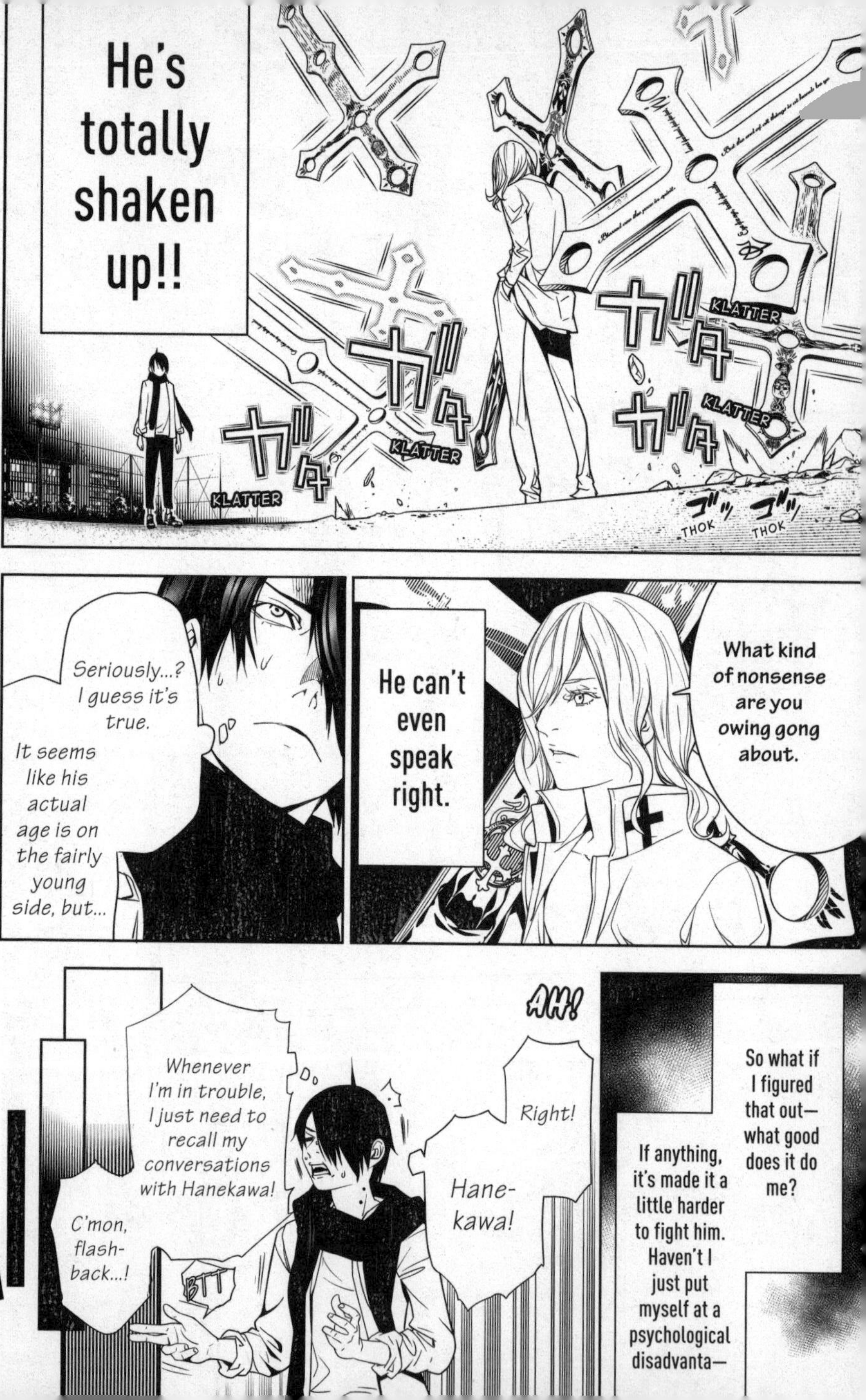
KLATTER
KLATTER
KLATTER
KLATTER
THOK
THOK
He's totally shaken up!!
What kind of nonsense are you owing gong about.
He can't even speak right.
Seriously...? I guess it's true.
It seems like his actual age is on the fairly young side, but...
So what if I figured that out—what good does it do me?
If anything, it's made it a little harder to fight him. Haven't I just put myself at a psychological disadvanta—
AH!
Right!
Hane-kawa!
Whenever I'm in trouble, I just need to recall my conversations with Hanekawa!
BTT
C'mon, flash-back...!

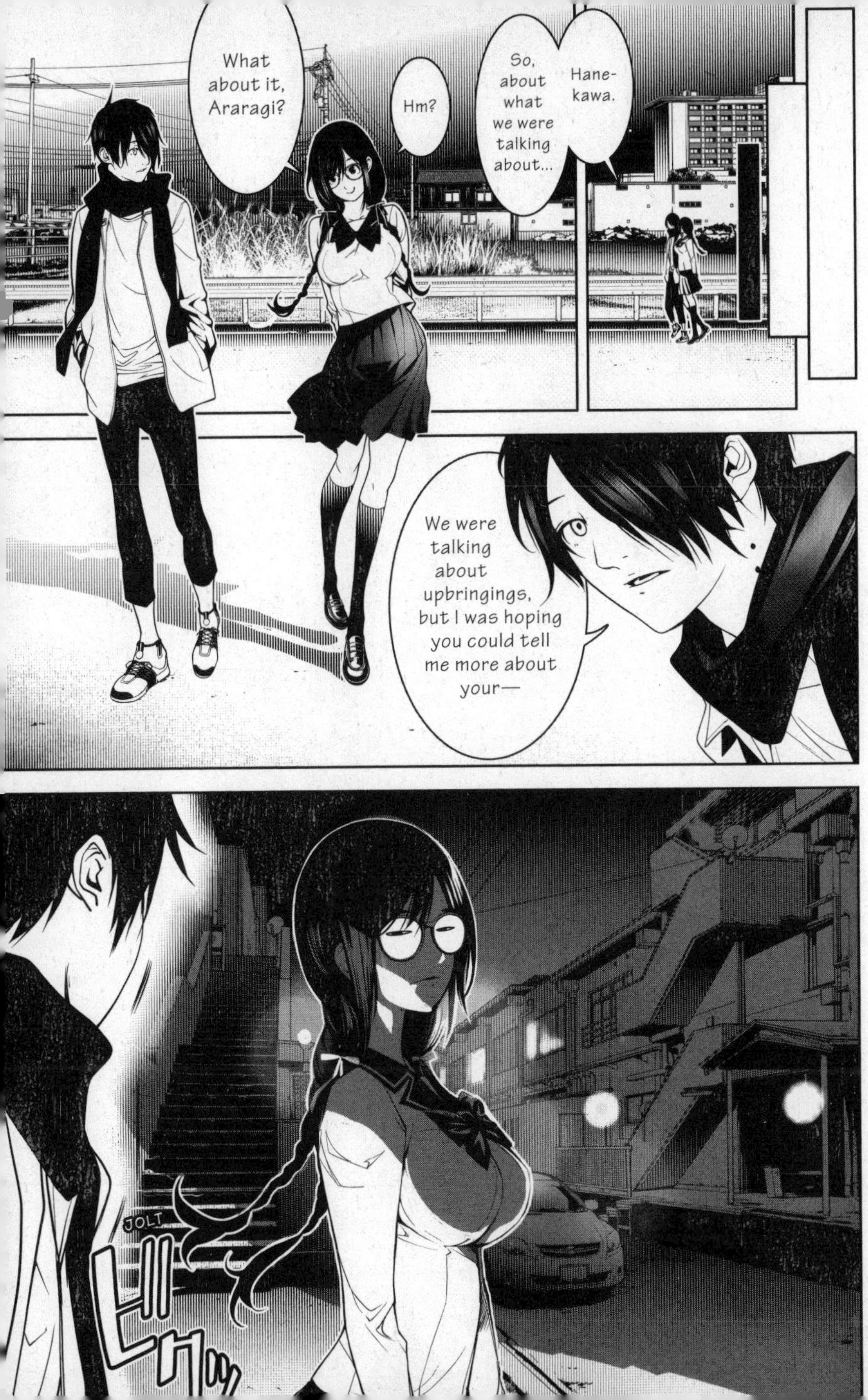
Hane-kawa.
So, about what we were talking about...
Hm?
What about it, Araragi?
We were talking about upbringings, but I was hoping you could tell me more about your—
JOLT

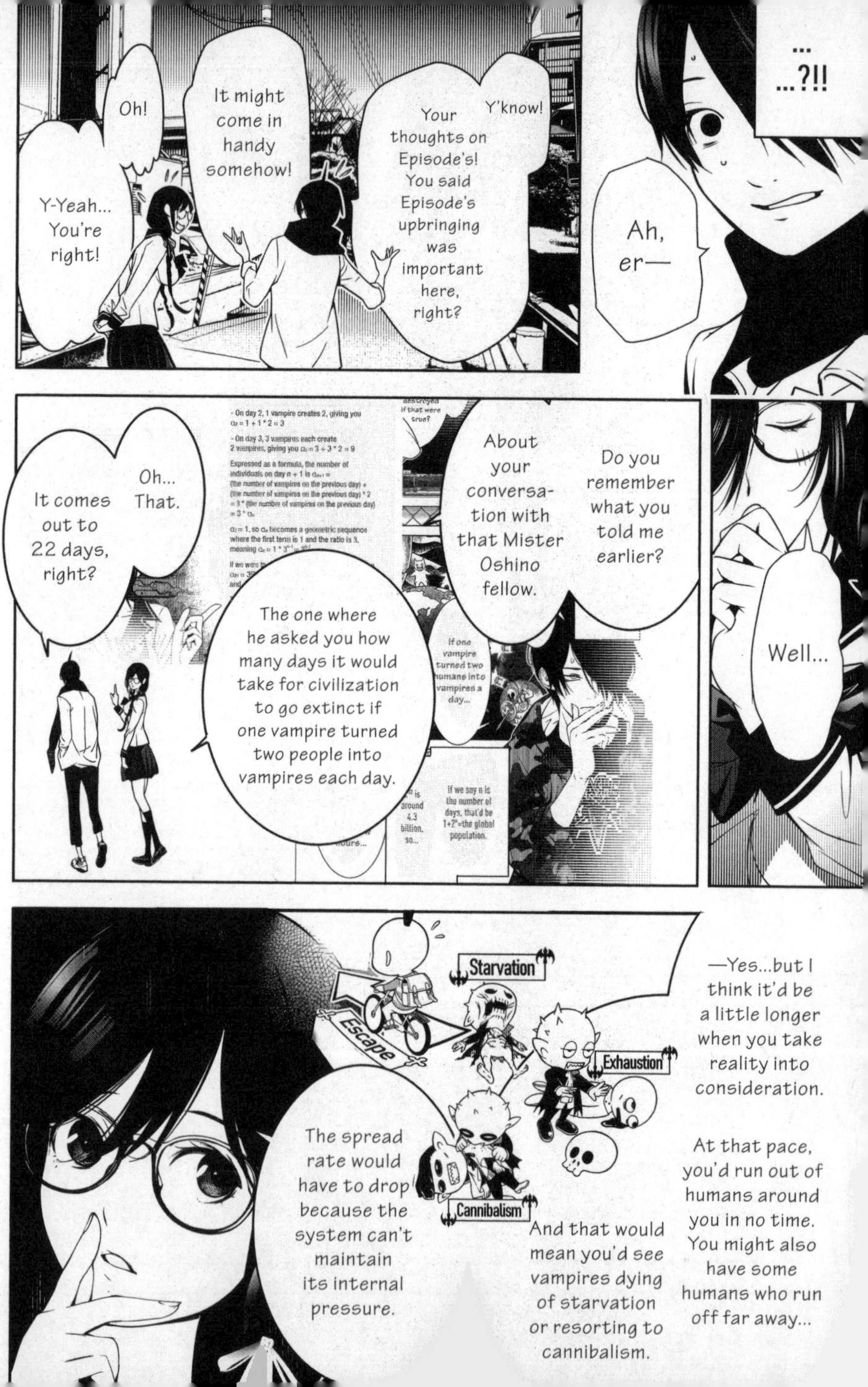
...
...?!!
Ah, er—
Y'know!
Your thoughts on Episode's! You said Episode's upbringing was important here, right?
It might come in handy somehow!
Oh!
Y-Yeah... You're right!
Well...
Do you remember what you told me earlier?
About your conversation with that Mister Oshino fellow.
The one where he asked you how many days it would take for civilization to go extinct if one vampire turned two people into vampires each day.
If one vampire turned two humans into vampires a day...
If we say n is the number of days, that'd be 1+2ⁿ=the global population.
Oh... That.
It comes out to 22 days, right?
—Yes...but I think it'd be a little longer when you take reality into consideration.
At that pace, you'd run out of humans around you in no time. You might also have some humans who run off far away...
Starvation
Escape
Exhaustion
Cannibalism
The spread rate would have to drop because the system can't maintain its internal pressure.
And that would mean you'd see vampires dying of starvation or resorting to cannibalism.

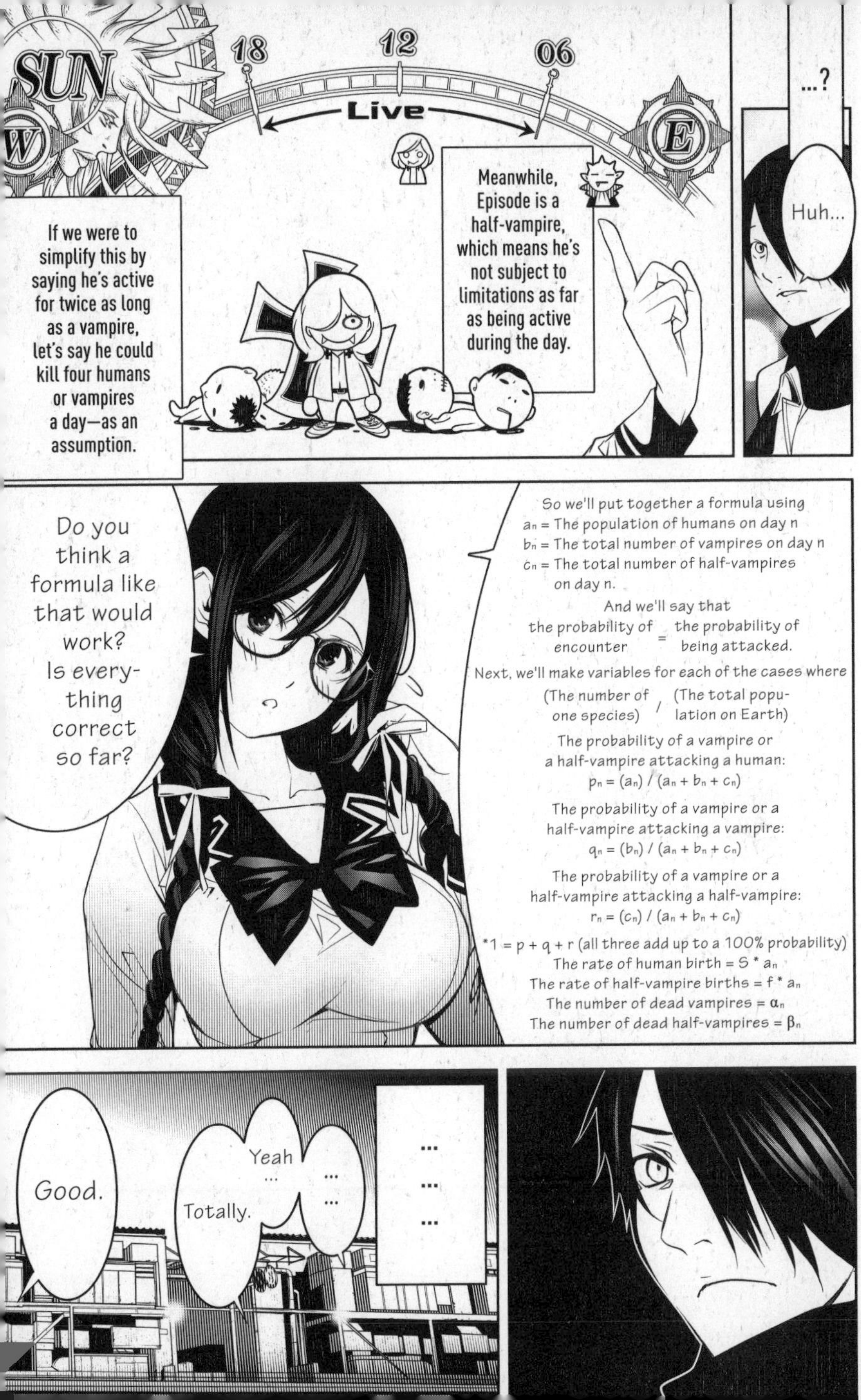
...?
Huh...
SUN
18
12
06
Live
W
E
Meanwhile, Episode is a half-vampire, which means he's not subject to limitations as far as being active during the day.
If we were to simplify this by saying he's active for twice as long as a vampire, let's say he could kill four humans or vampires a day—as an assumption.
So we'll put together a formula using
a_n = The population of humans on day n
b_n = The total number of vampires on day n
c_n = The total number of half-vampires on day n.
And we'll say that
the probability of encounter = the probability of being attacked.
Next, we'll make variables for each of the cases where
(The number of one species) / (The total population on Earth)
The probability of a vampire or a half-vampire attacking a human:
$p_n = (a_n) / (a_n + b_n + c_n)$
The probability of a vampire or a half-vampire attacking a vampire:
$q_n = (b_n) / (a_n + b_n + c_n)$
The probability of a vampire or a half-vampire attacking a half-vampire:
$r_n = (c_n) / (a_n + b_n + c_n)$
*1 = p + q + r (all three add up to a 100% probability)
The rate of human birth = $S * a_n$
The rate of half-vampire births = $f * a_n$
The number of dead vampires = α_n
The number of dead half-vampires = β_n
Do you think a formula like that would work? Is everything correct so far?
... ...
Yeah ... ... Totally.
Good.

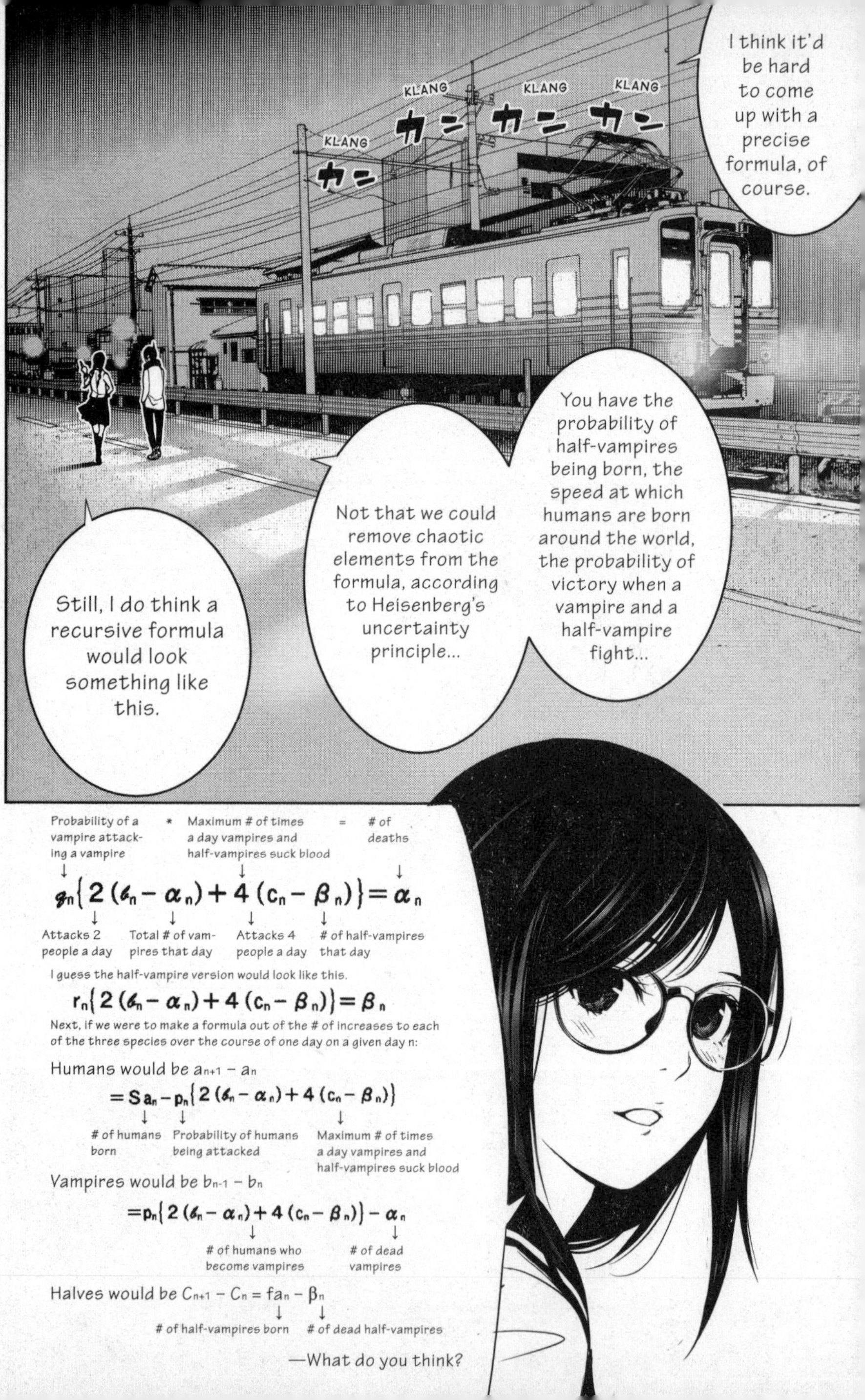
I think it'd be hard to come up with a precise formula, of course.
KLANG
KLANG
KLANG
KLANG
You have the probability of half-vampires being born, the speed at which humans are born around the world, the probability of victory when a vampire and a half-vampire fight...
Not that we could remove chaotic elements from the formula, according to Heisenberg's uncertainty principle...
Still, I do think a recursive formula would look something like this.
Probability of a vampire attacking a vampire * Maximum # of times a day vampires and half-vampires suck blood = # of deaths
$g_n\{2(b_n-\alpha_n)+4(c_n-\beta_n)\}=\alpha_n$
Attacks 2 people a day
Total # of vampires that day
Attacks 4 people a day
# of half-vampires that day
I guess the half-vampire version would look like this.
$r_n\{2(b_n-\alpha_n)+4(c_n-\beta_n)\}=\beta_n$
Next, if we were to make a formula out of the # of increases to each of the three species over the course of one day on a given day n:
Humans would be $a_{n+1}-a_n$
$=Sa_n-p_n\{2(b_n-\alpha_n)+4(c_n-\beta_n)\}$
# of humans born
Probability of humans being attacked
Maximum # of times a day vampires and half-vampires suck blood
Vampires would be $b_{n-1}-b_n$
$=p_n\{2(b_n-\alpha_n)+4(c_n-\beta_n)\}-\alpha_n$
# of humans who become vampires
# of dead vampires
Halves would be $C_{n+1}-C_n=fa_n-\beta_n$
# of half-vampires born
# of dead half-vampires
—What do you think?

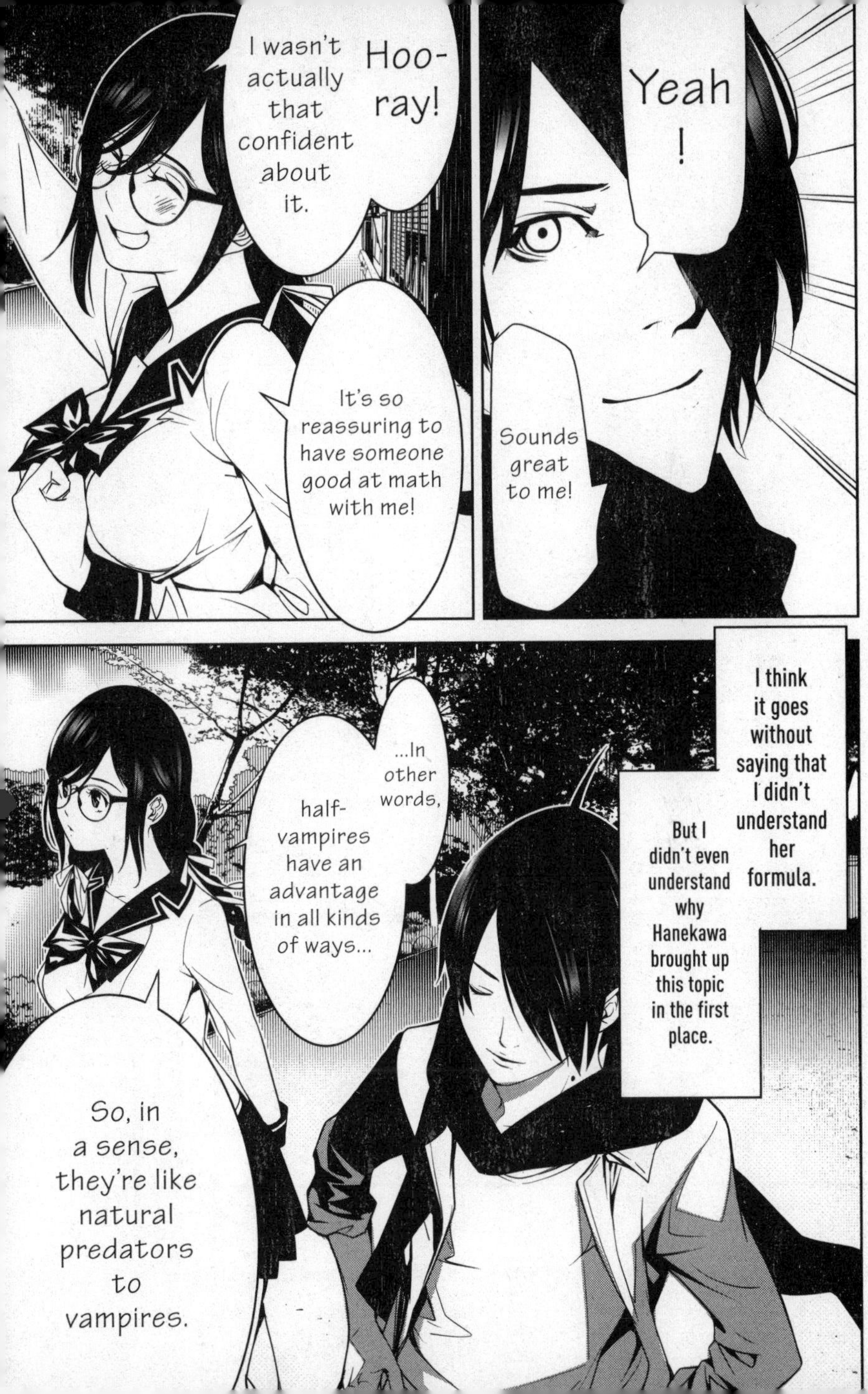
Yeah!
Sounds great to me!
Hooray!
I wasn't actually that confident about it.
It's so reassuring to have someone good at math with me!
I think it goes without saying that I didn't understand her formula.
But I didn't even understand why Hanekawa brought up this topic in the first place.
...In other words, half-vampires have an advantage in all kinds of ways...
So, in a sense, they're like natural predators to vampires.

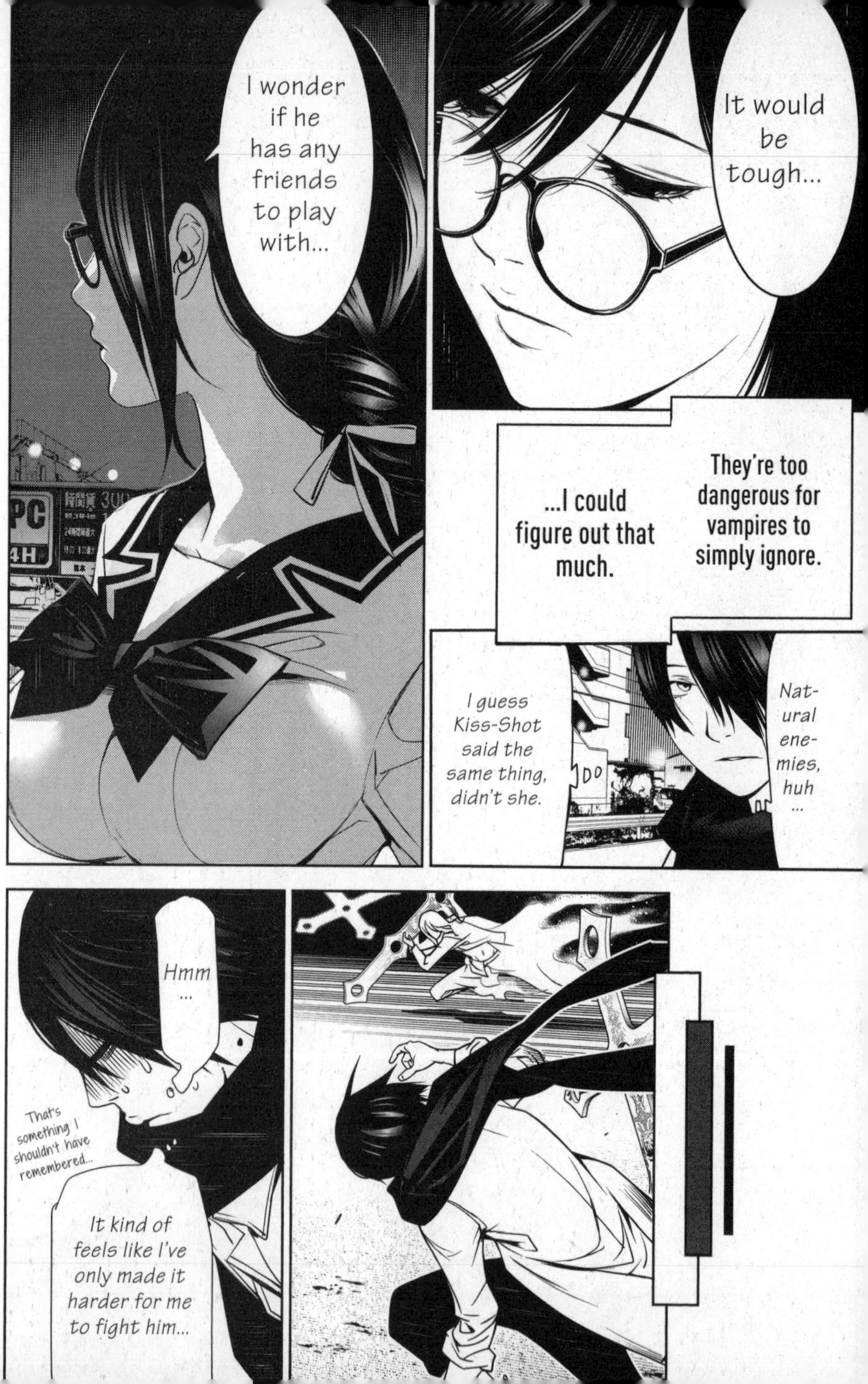
It would be tough...
They're too dangerous for vampires to simply ignore.
...I could figure out that much.
Natural enemies, huh...
DO
I guess Kiss-Shot said the same thing, didn't she.
I wonder if he has any friends to play with...
Hmm...
That's something I shouldn't have remembered...
It kind of feels like I've only made it harder for me to fight him...

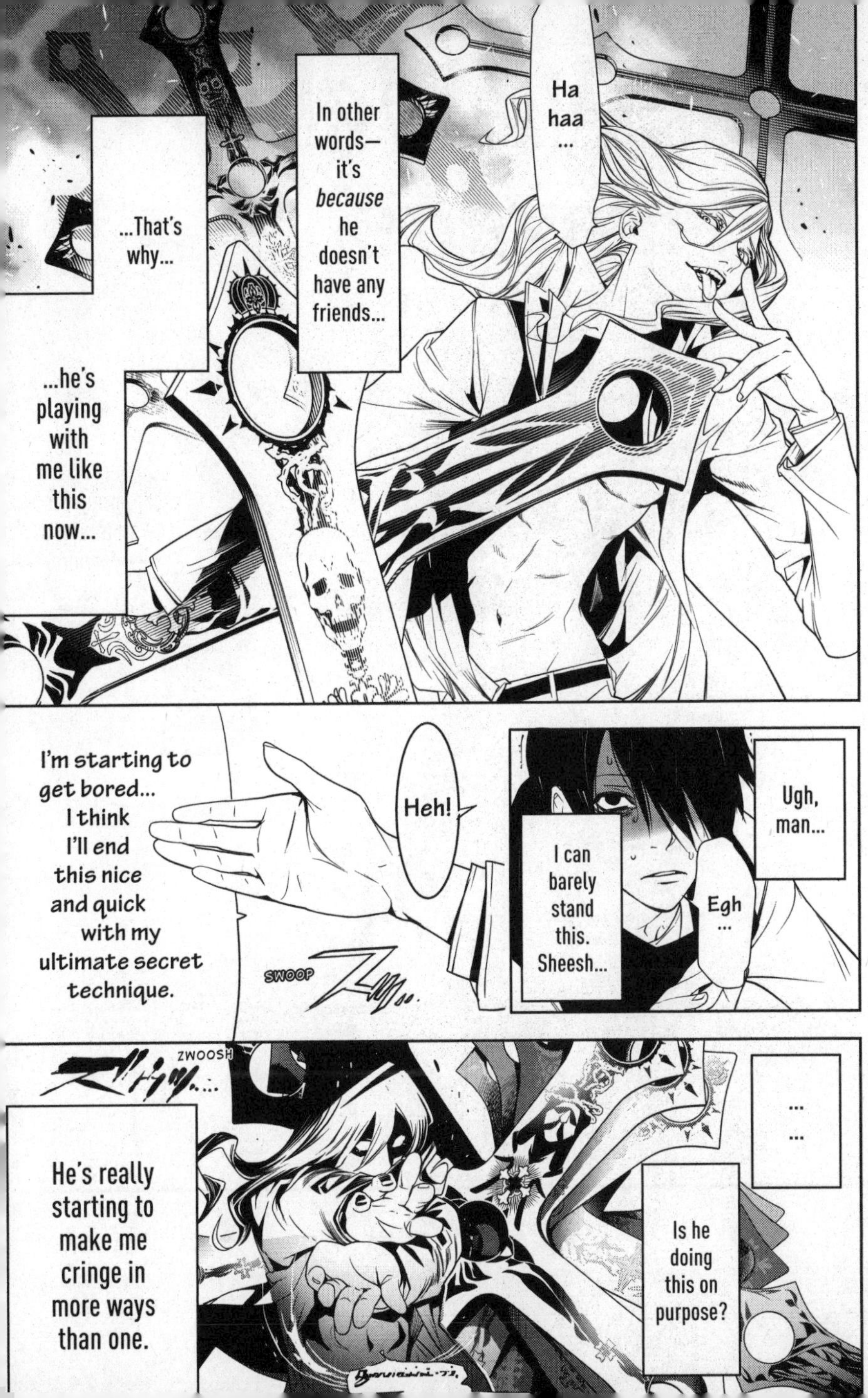
Ha haa ...
In other words— it's *because* he doesn't have any friends...
...That's why...
...he's playing with me like this now...
Ugh, man...
Egh ...
I can barely stand this. Sheesh...
Heh!
I'm starting to get bored... I think I'll end this nice and quick with my ultimate secret technique.
SWOOP
... ...
Is he doing this on purpose?
ZWOOSH
He's really starting to make me cringe in more ways than one.

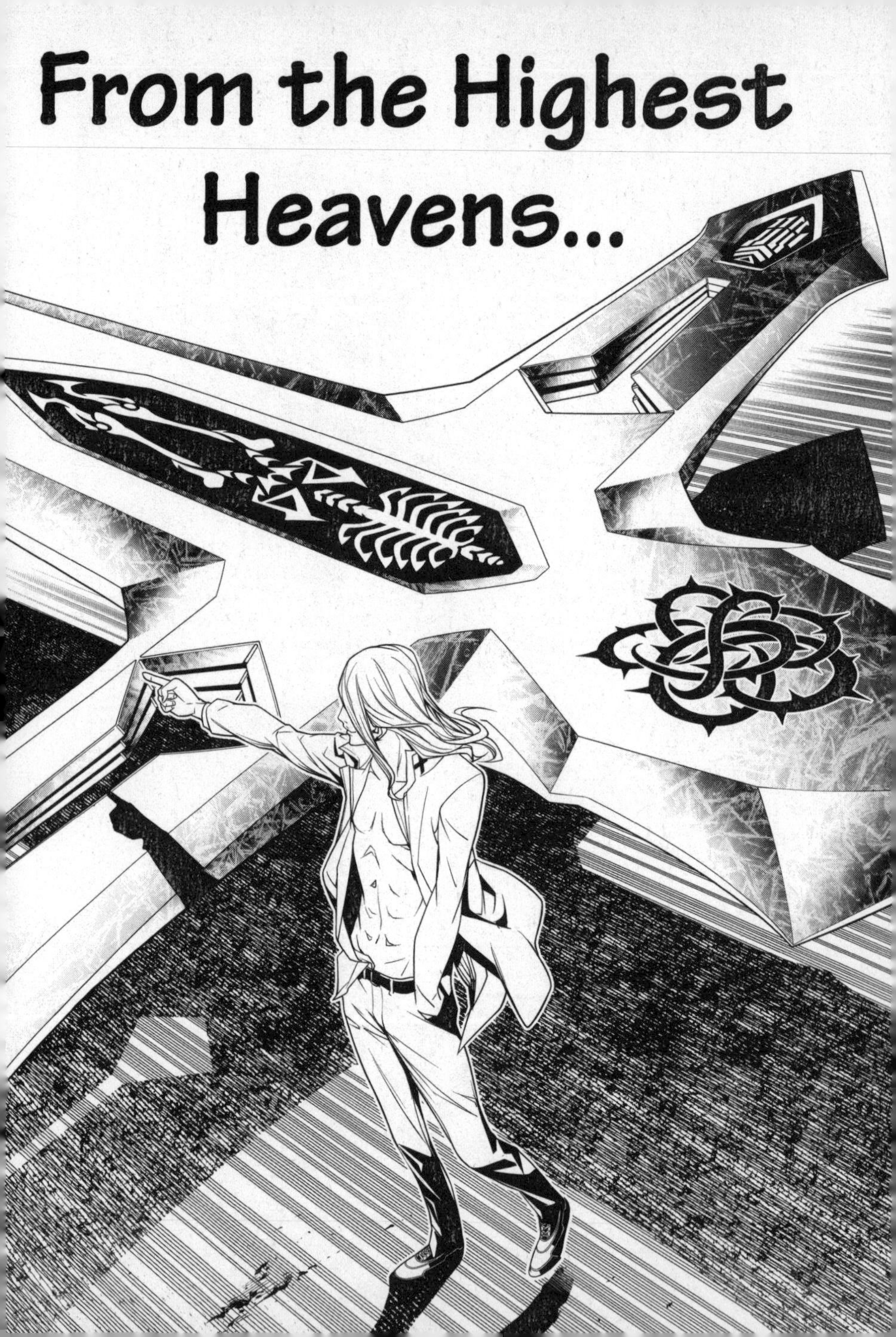
From the Highest Heavens...

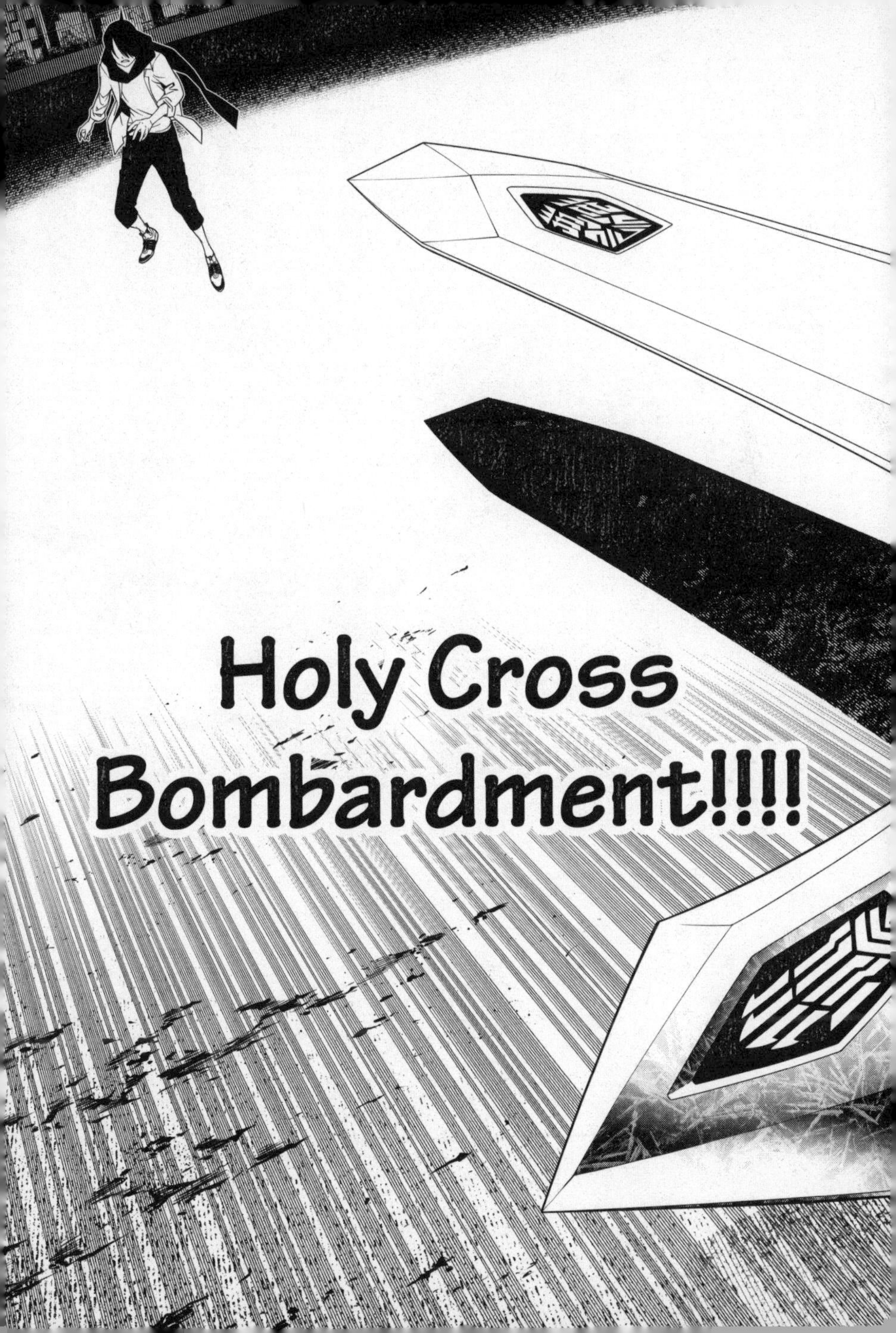
Holy Cross Bombardment!!!!

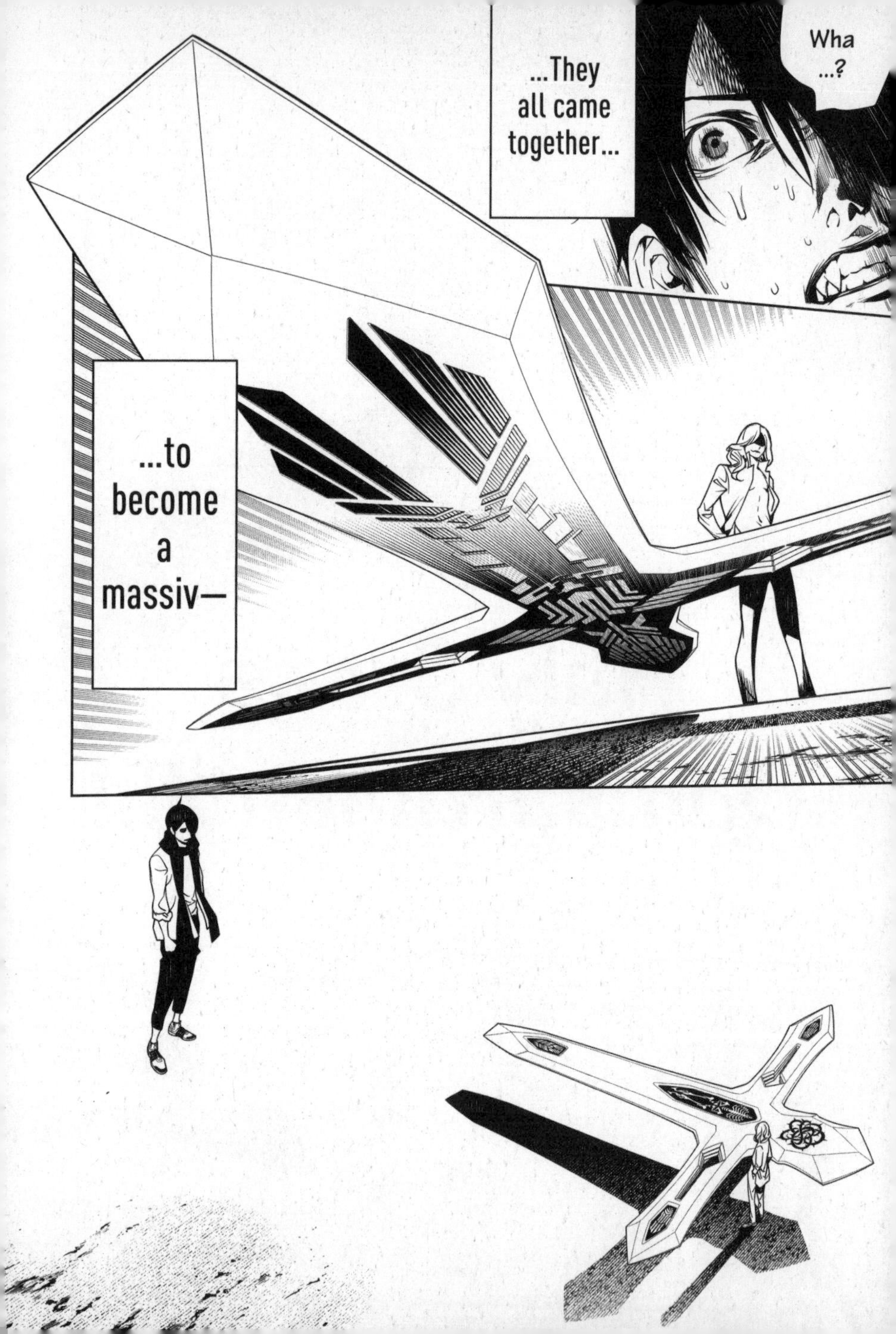
Wha ...?
...They all came together...
...to become a massiv—

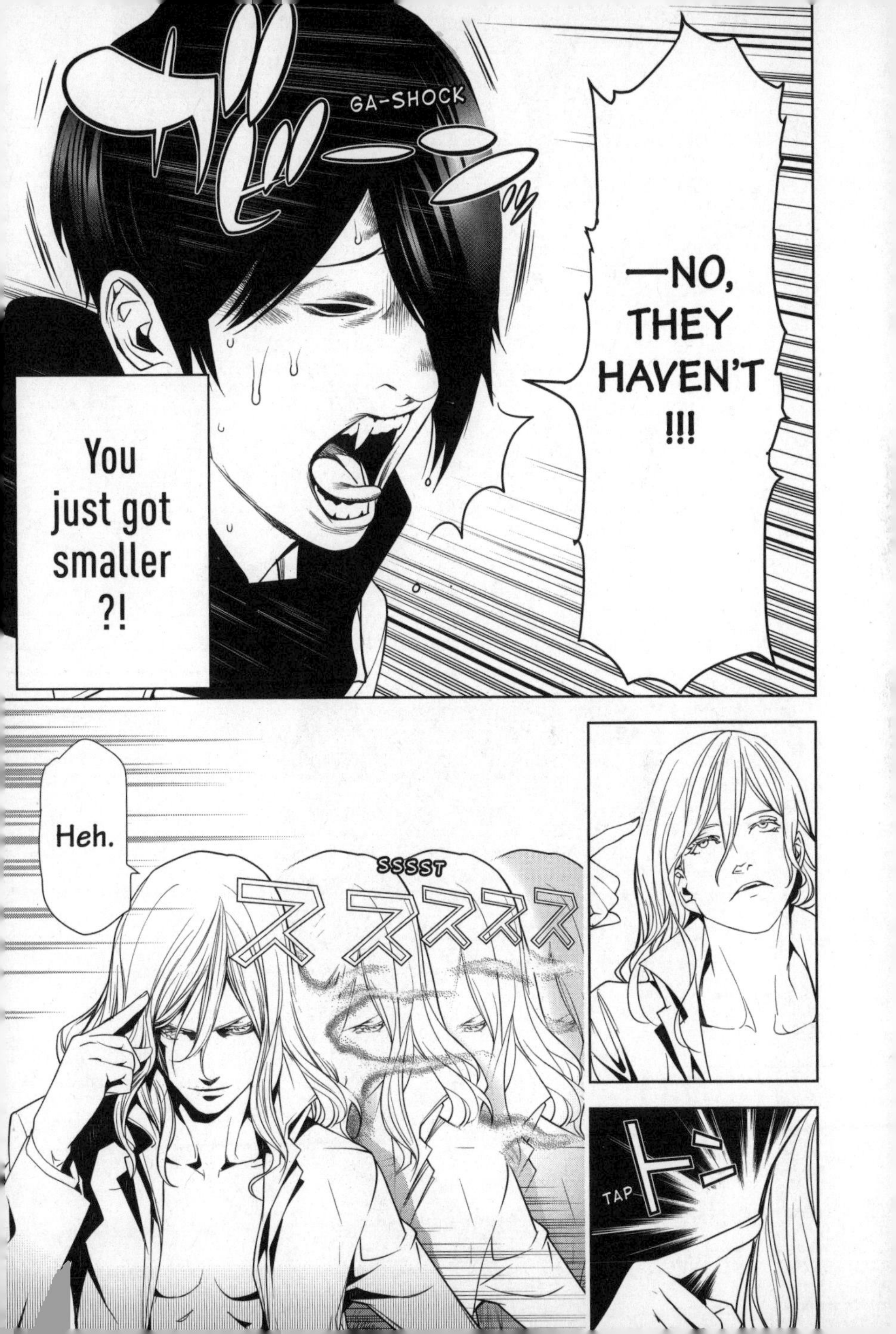
—NO, THEY HAVEN'T !!!
GA-SHOCK
You just got smaller ?!
TAP
SSSST
ススススス
Heh.

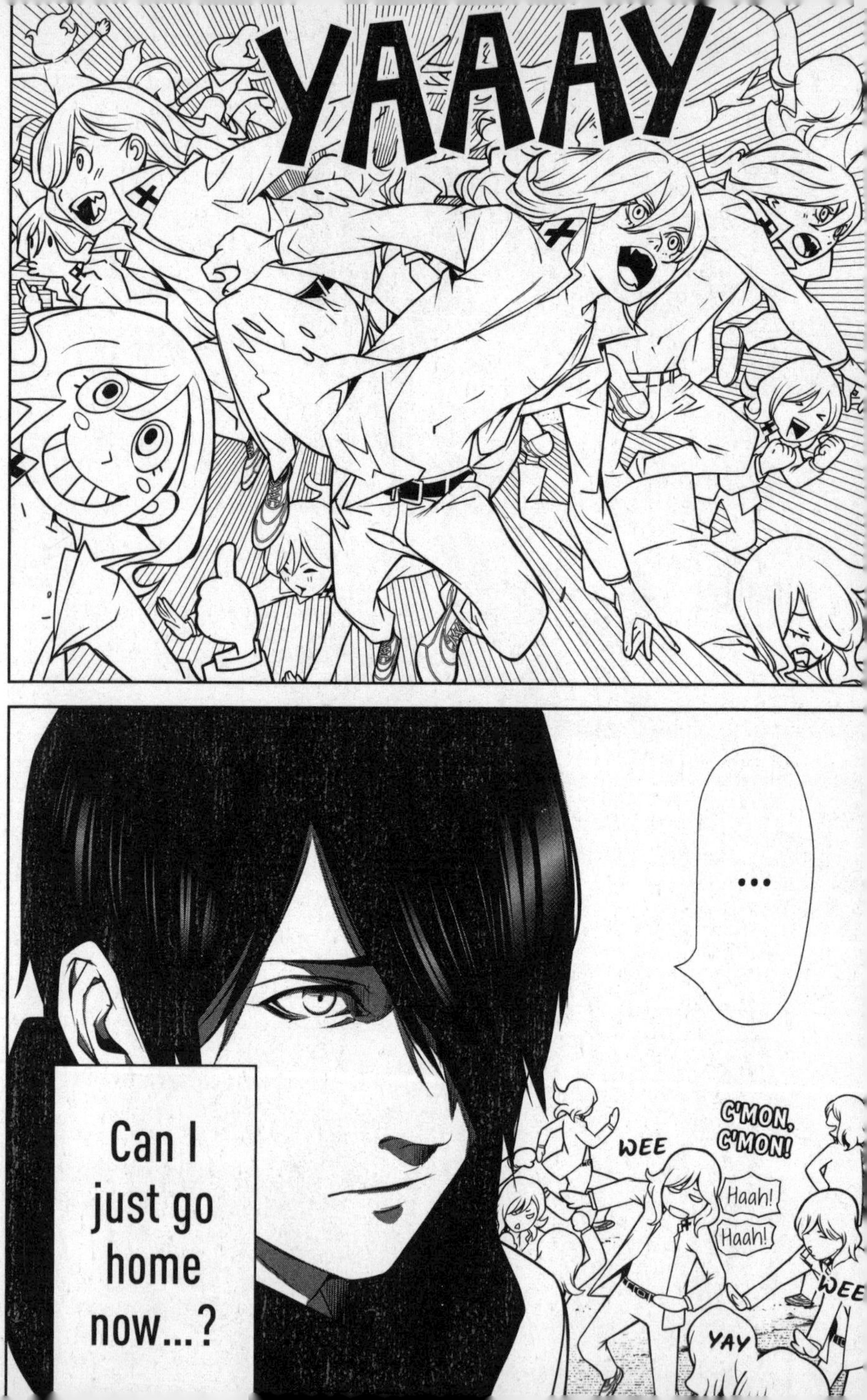
YAAAY
...
C'MON, C'MON!
WEE
Haah!
Haah!
WEE
YAY
Can I just go home now...?

BAKEMONOGATARI

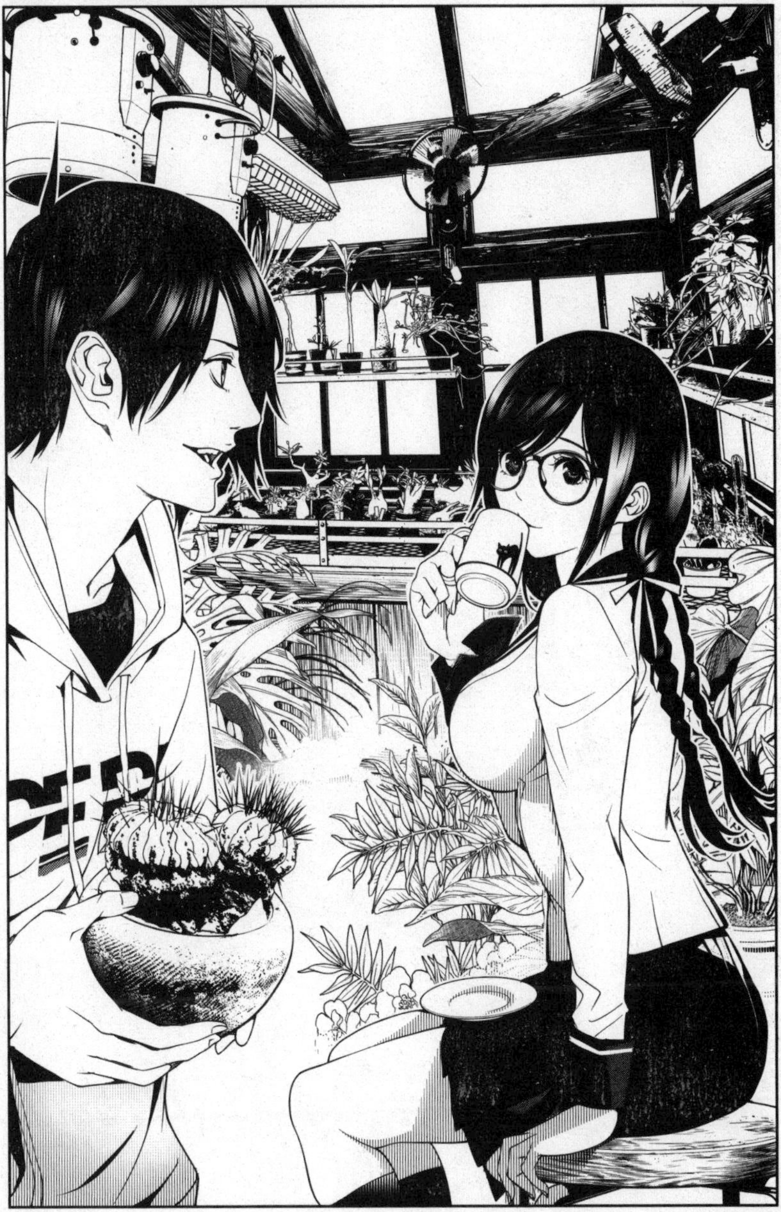

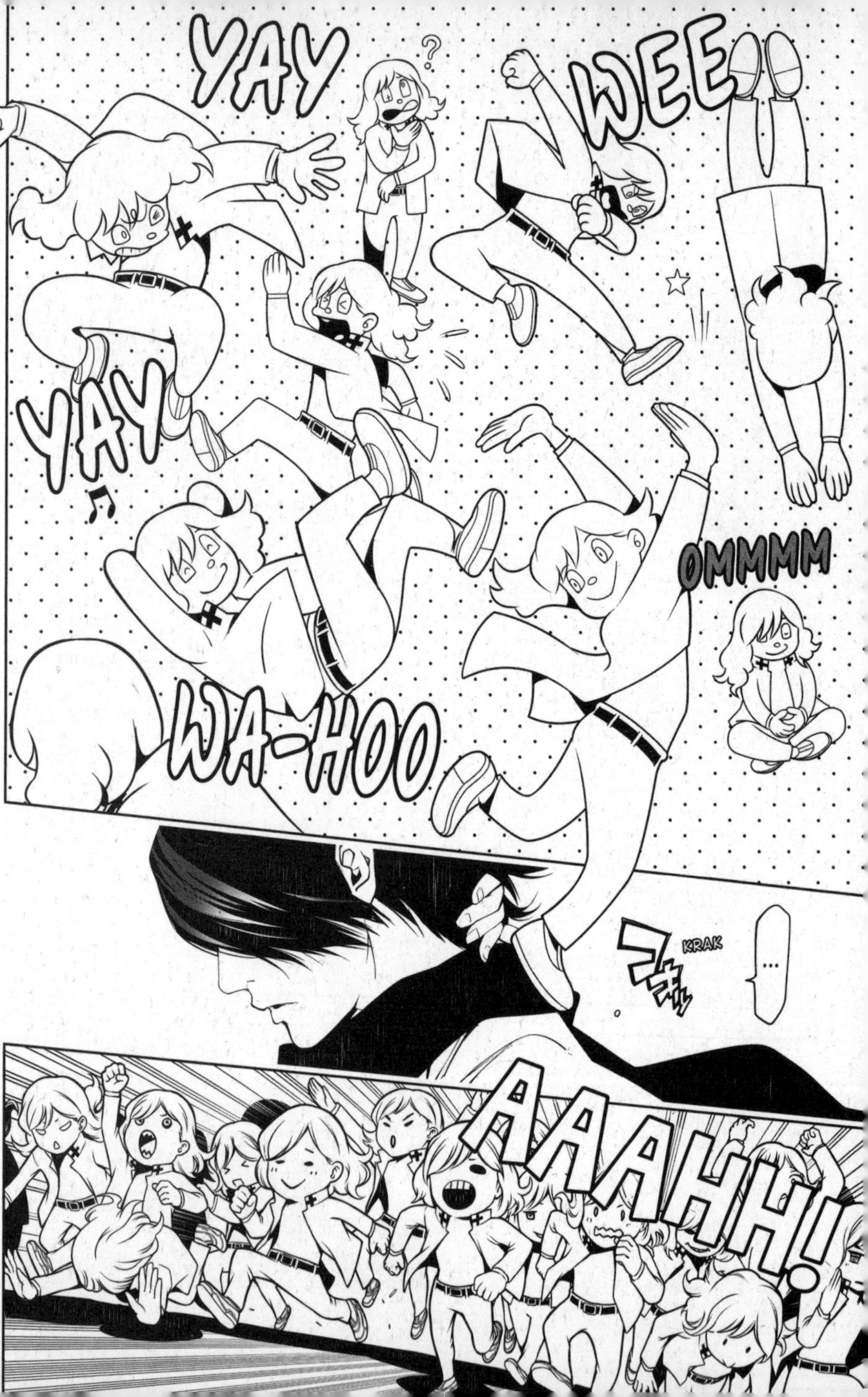
WEE
YAY
OMMMM
YAY
WA-HOO
...
KRAK
AAAAHH!

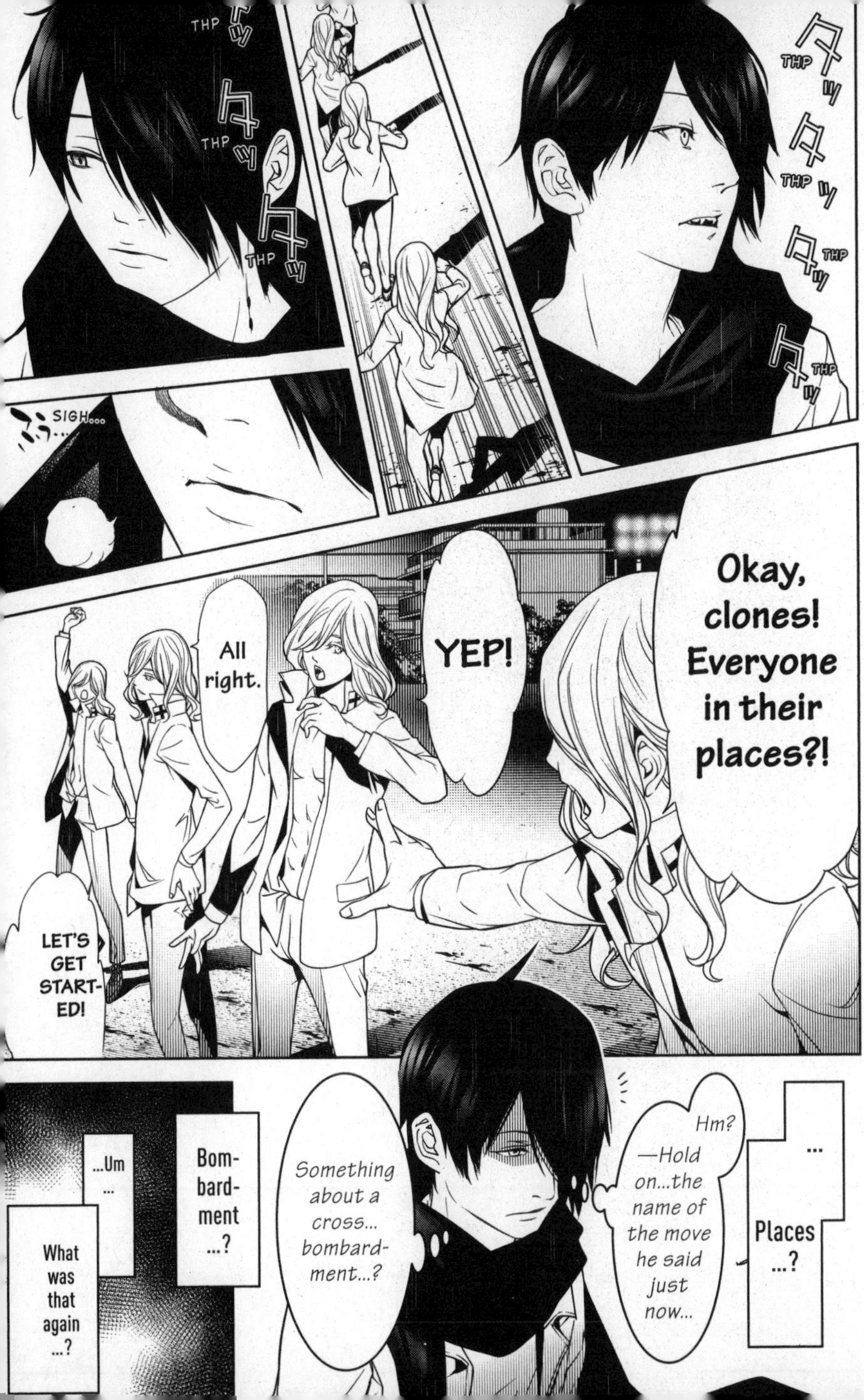
THP
THP
THP
THP
THP
THP
THP
THP
SIGH...
Okay, clones! Everyone in their places?!
YEP!
All right.
LET'S GET START-ED!
...
Places ...?
Hm? —Hold on...the name of the move he said just now...
Something about a cross... bombard-ment...?
Bom-bard-ment ...?
...Um ...
What was that again ...?

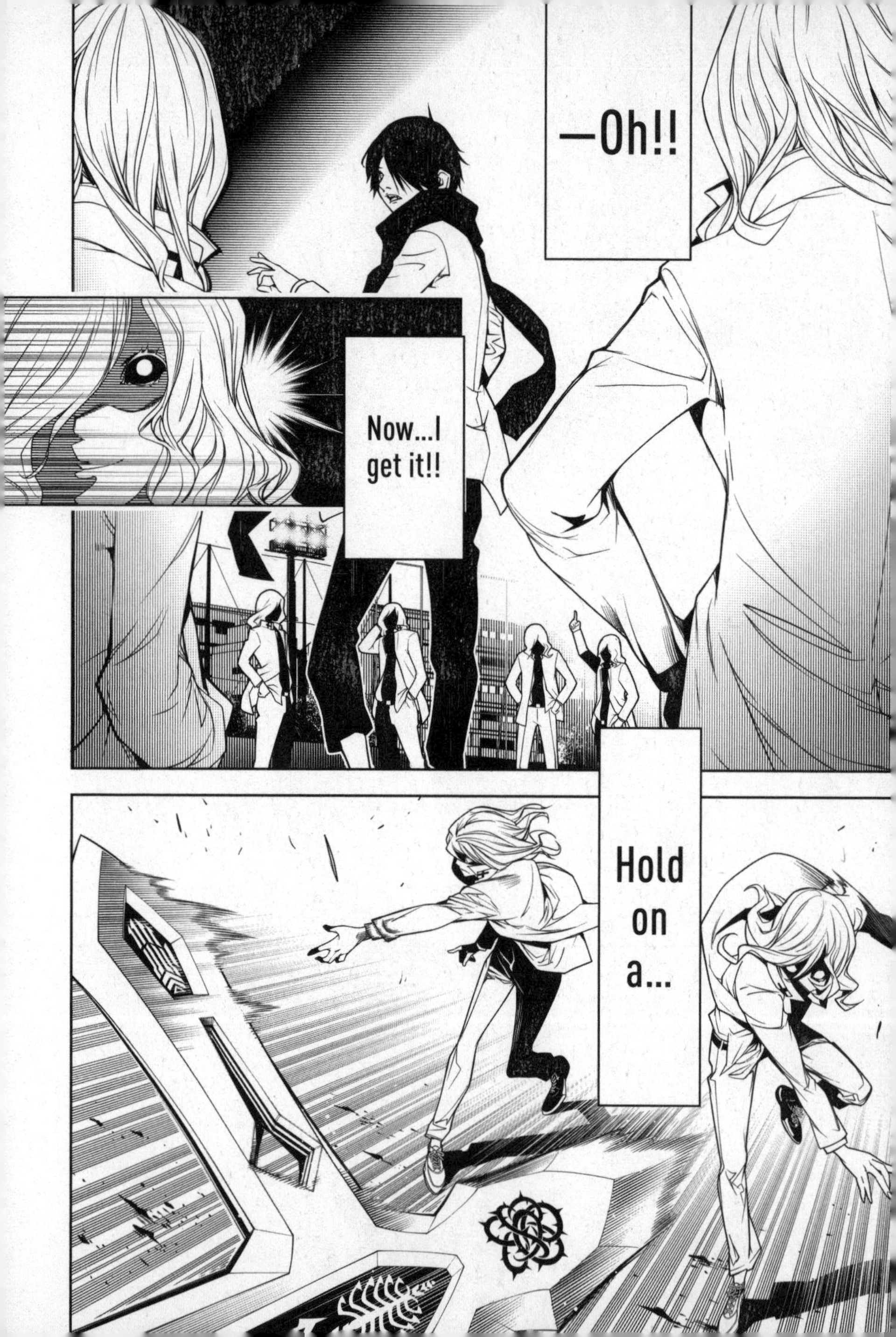
—Oh!!
Now...I get it!!
Hold on a...

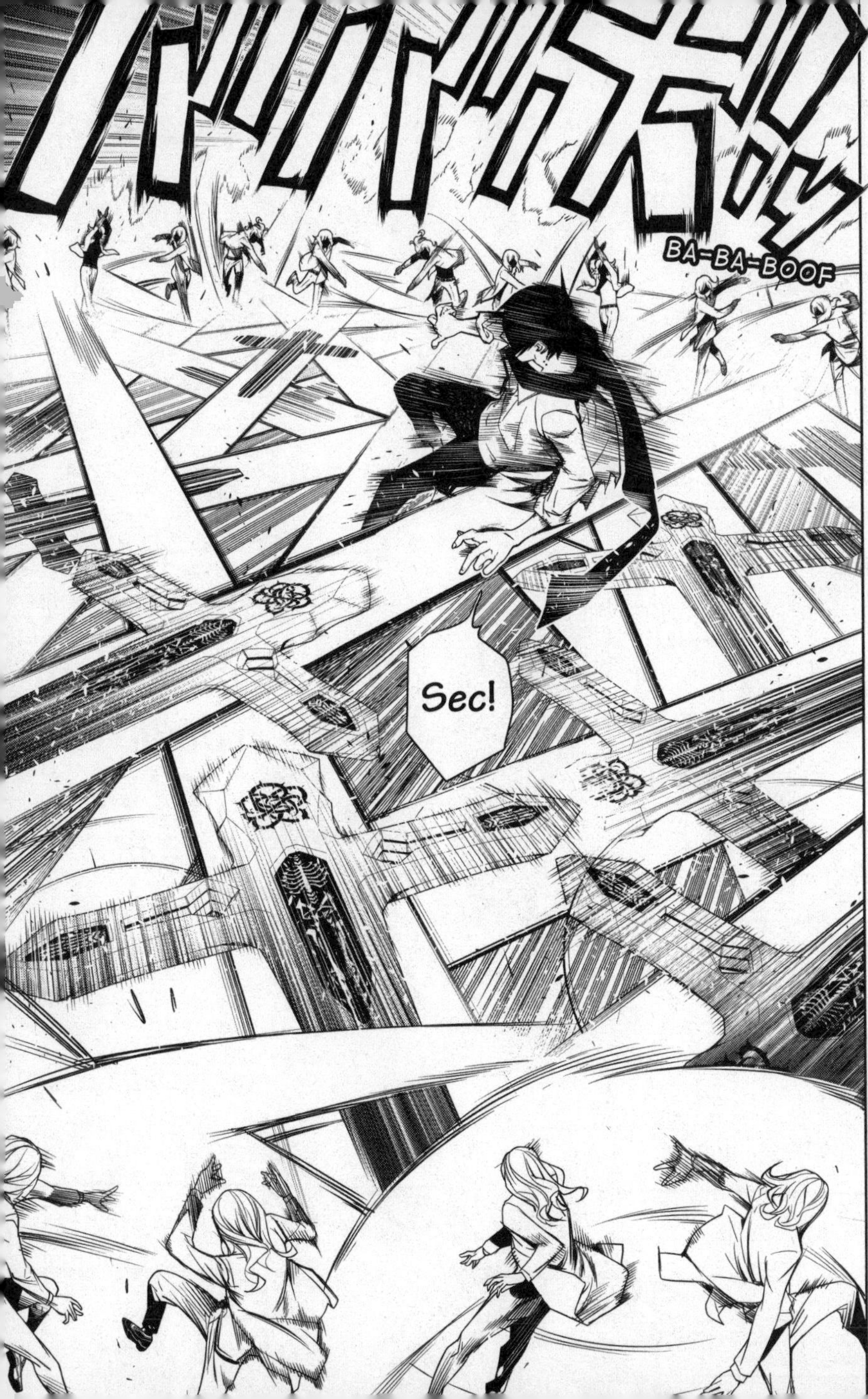
BA-BA-BOOF
Sec!

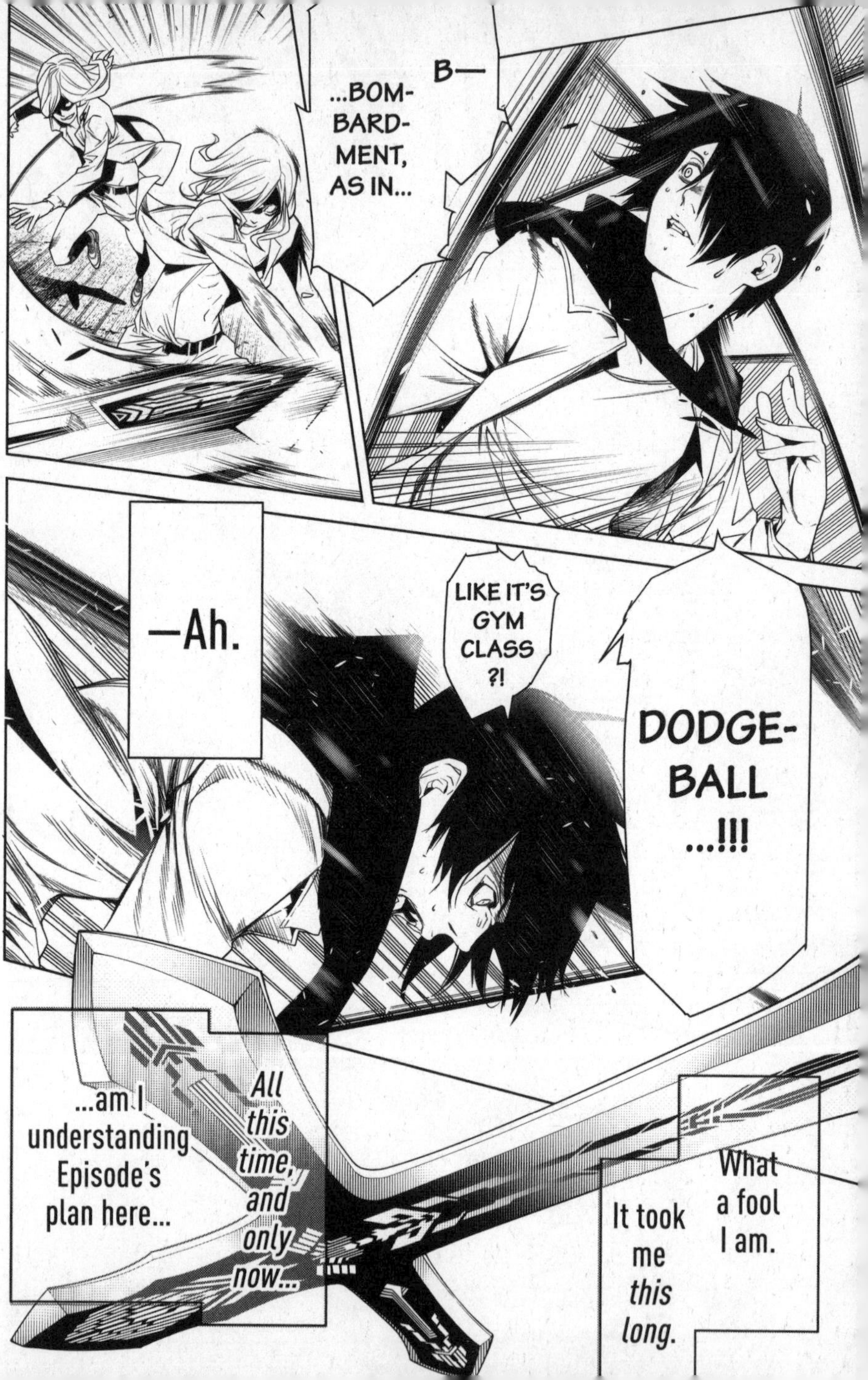
B—
...BOM-BARD-MENT, AS IN...
DODGE-BALL ...!!!
LIKE IT'S GYM CLASS ?!
—Ah.
What a fool I am.
It took me *this* long.
All this time, and only now...
...am I understanding Episode's plan here...

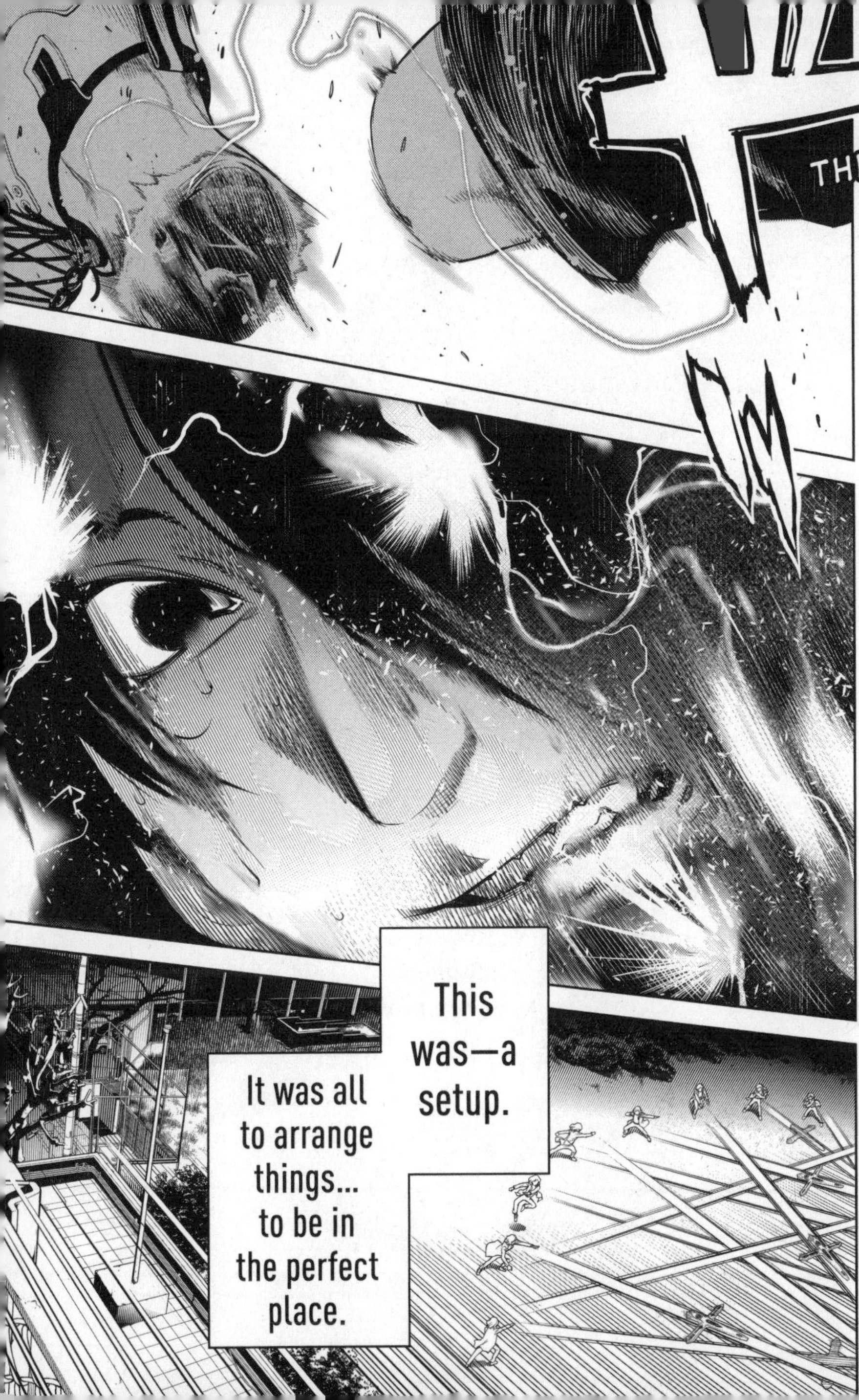
THBP
This was—a setup.
It was all to arrange things... to be in the perfect place.

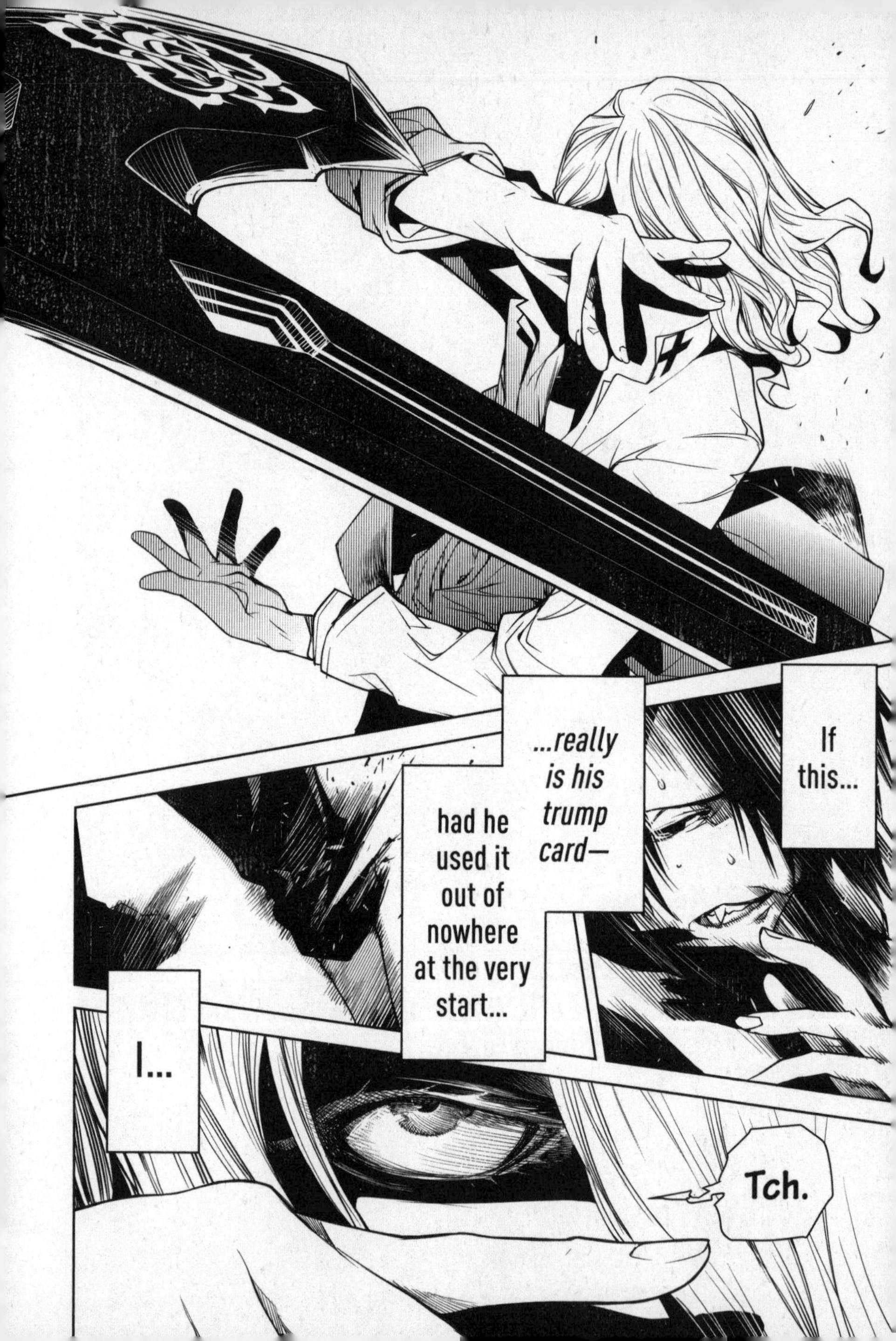
If this...
...really is his trump card—
had he used it out of nowhere at the very start...
I...
Tch.

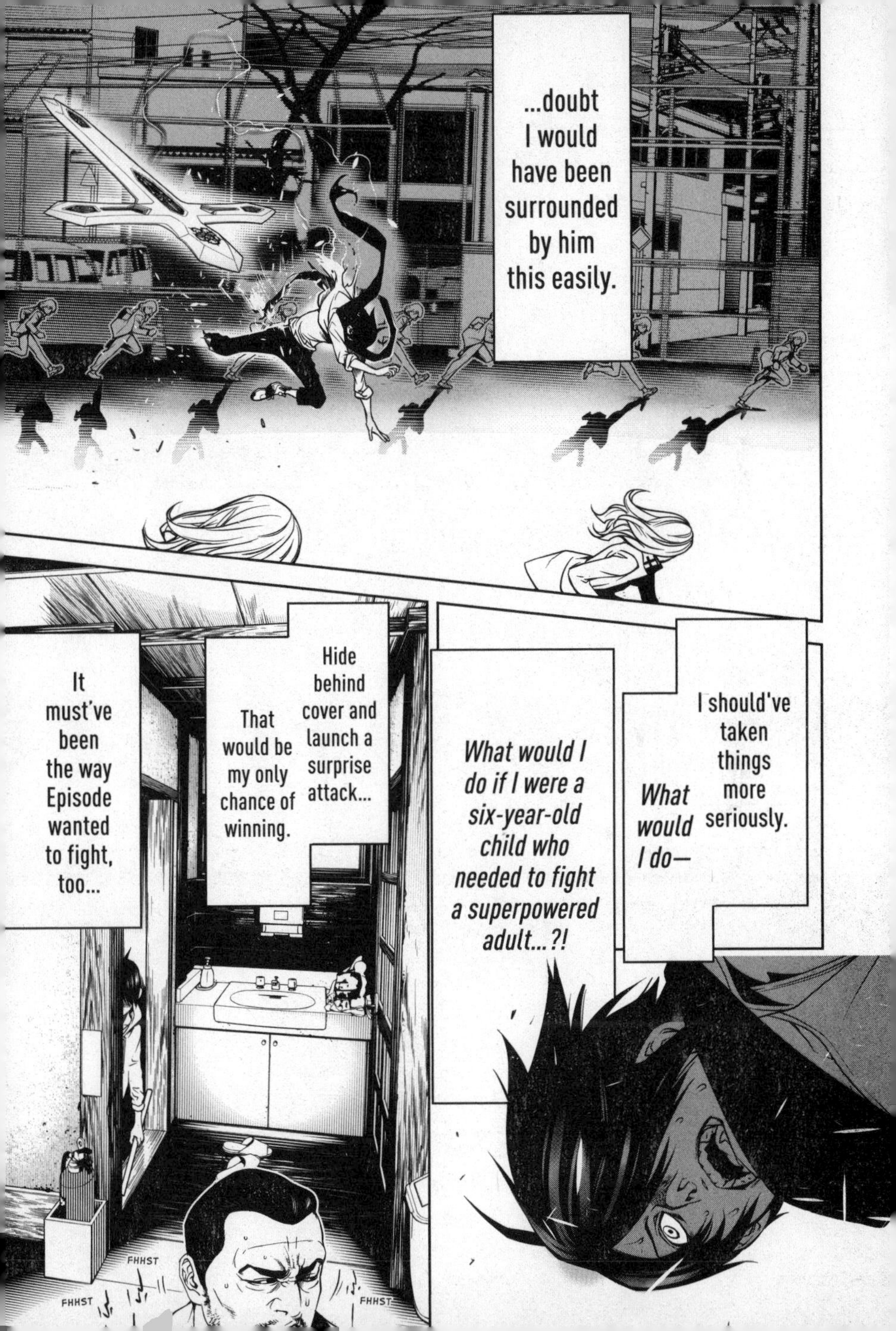
...doubt I would have been surrounded by him this easily.
I should've taken things more seriously.
What would I do—
What would I do if I were a six-year-old child who needed to fight a superpowered adult...?!
Hide behind cover and launch a surprise attack...
That would be my only chance of winning.
It must've been the way Episode wanted to fight, too...
FHHST
FHHST
FHHST

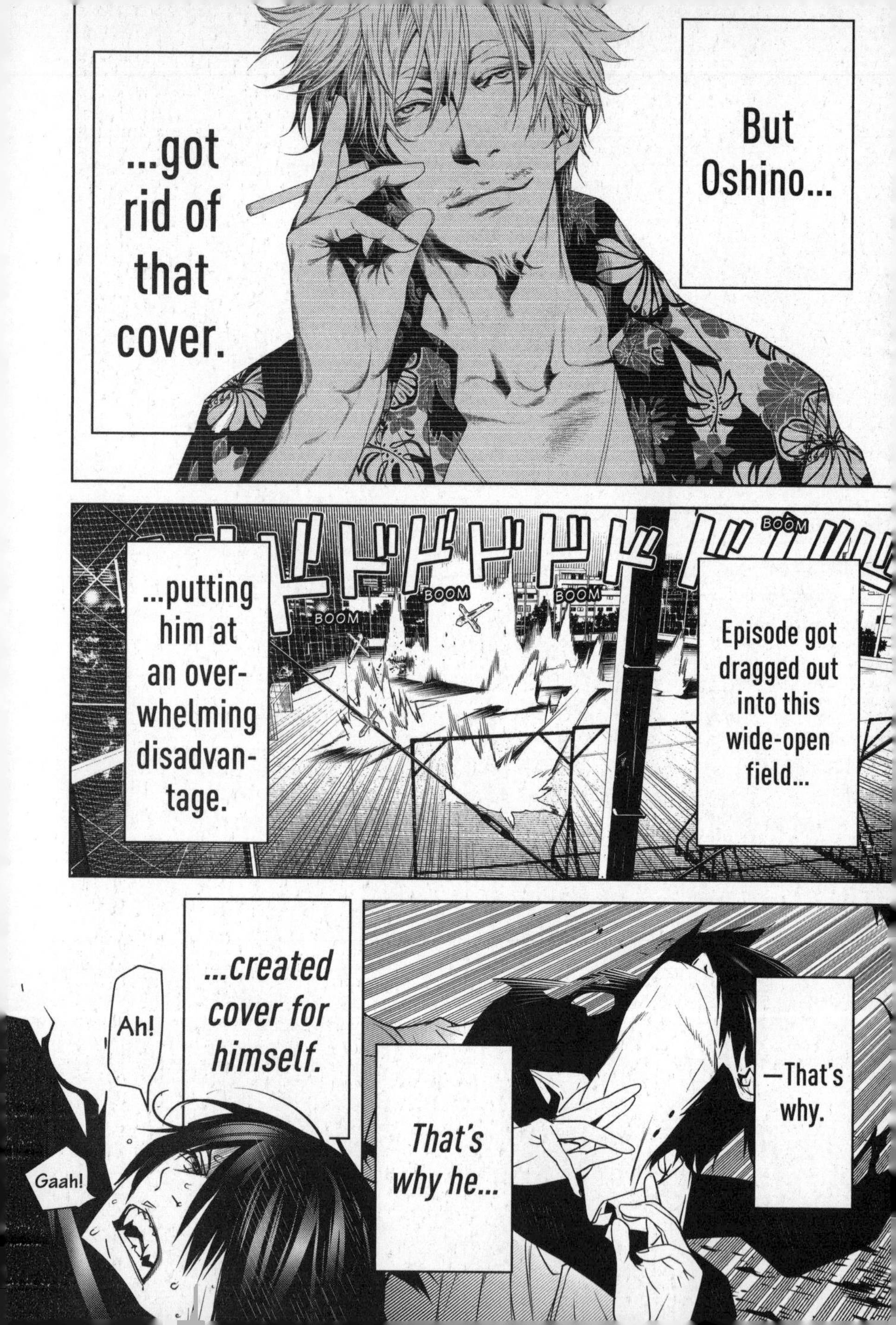
But Oshino...
...got rid of that cover.
BOOM
Episode got dragged out into this wide-open field...
BOOM
BOOM
BOOM
...putting him at an over-whelming disadvan-tage.
—That's why.
That's why he...
...created cover for himself.
Ah!
Gaah!

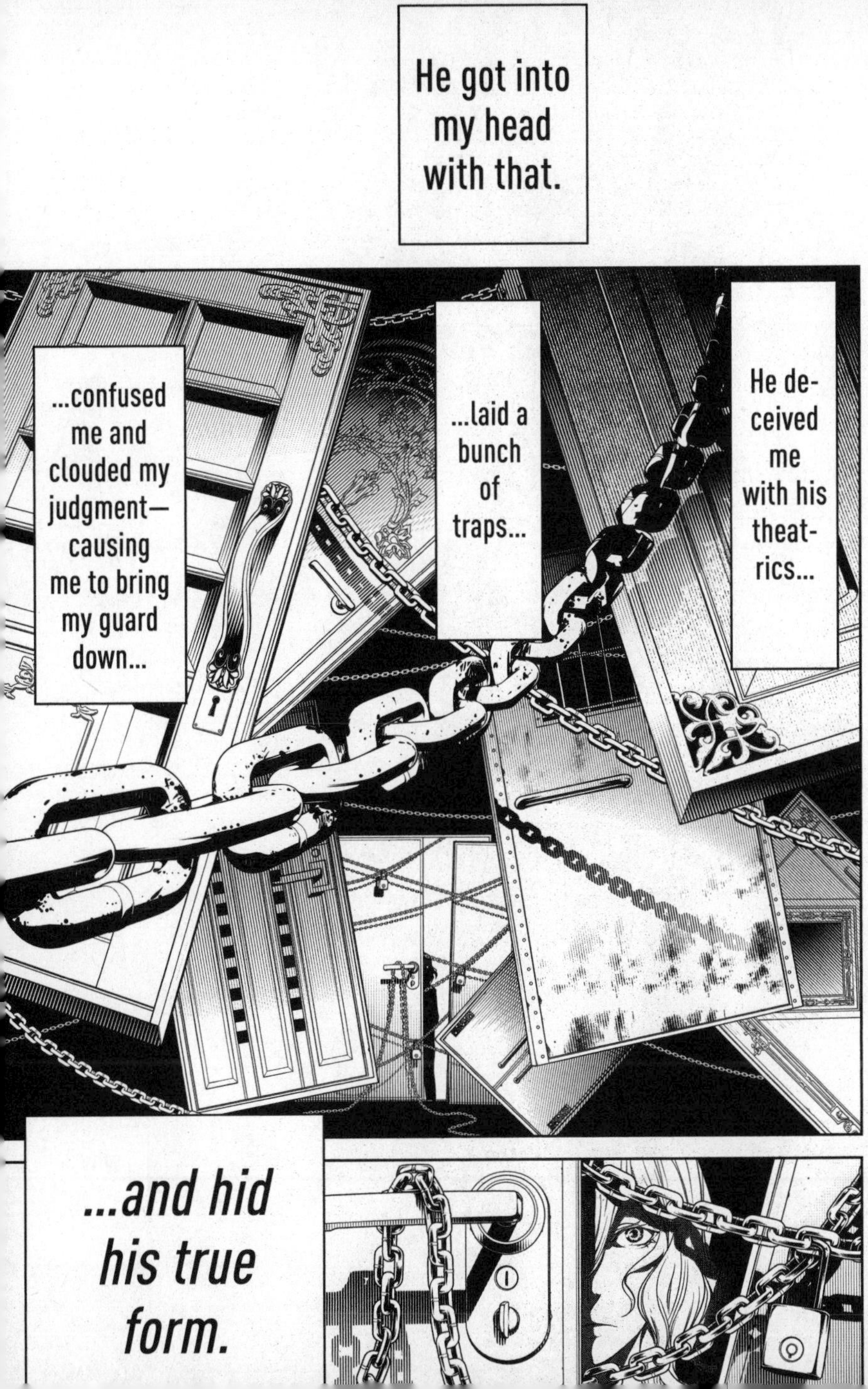
He got into my head with that.
He de-ceived me with his theat-rics...
...laid a bunch of traps...
...confused me and clouded my judgment—causing me to bring my guard down...
...and hid his true form.

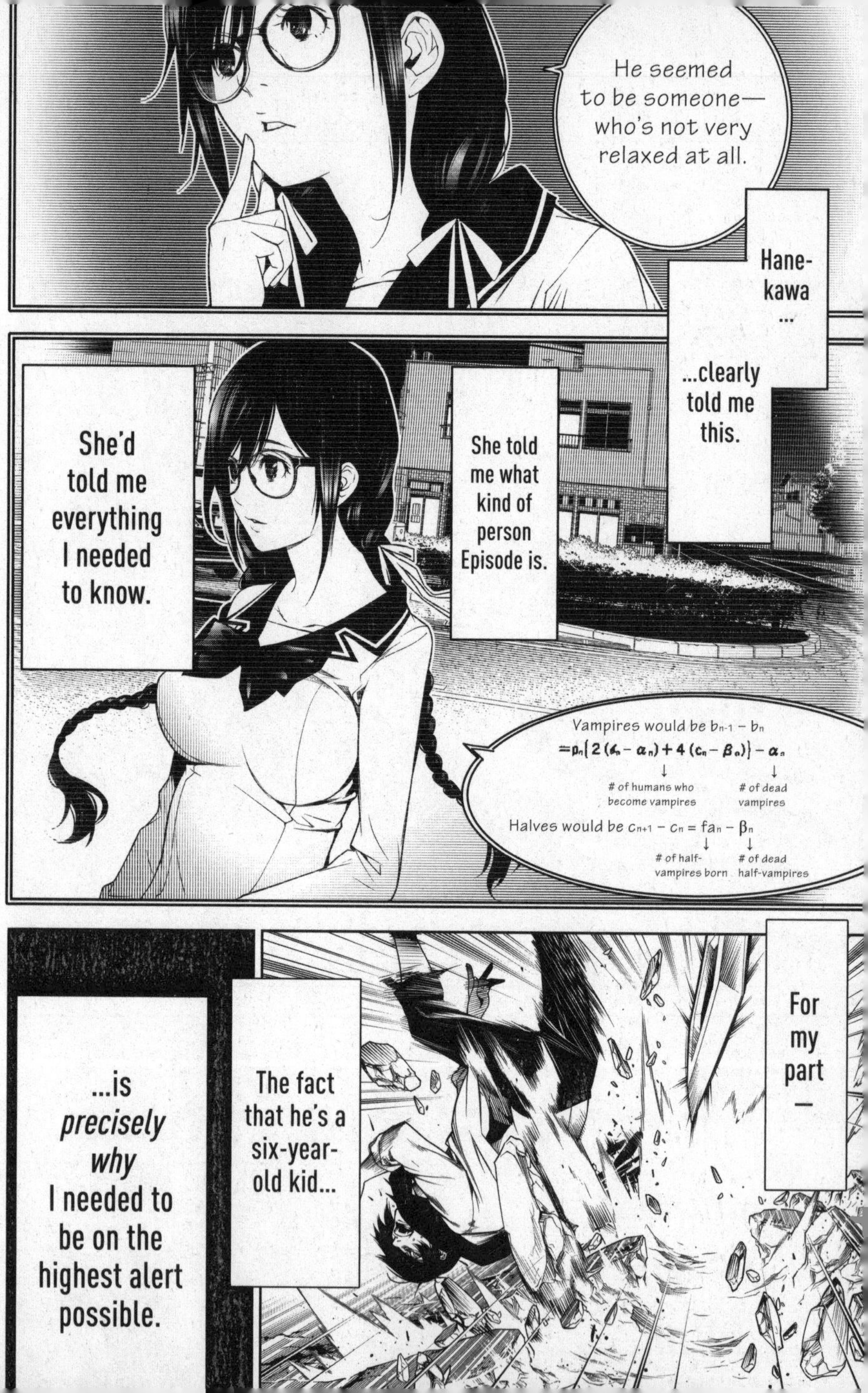
He seemed to be someone— who's not very relaxed at all.
Hane-kawa ... ...clearly told me this.
She told me what kind of person Episode is.
She'd told me everything I needed to know.
Vampires would be $b_{n-1} - b_n$
$= p_n\{2(a_n - \alpha_n) + 4(c_n - \beta_n)\} - \alpha_n$
↓ # of humans who become vampires
↓ # of dead vampires
Halves would be $c_{n+1} - c_n = fa_n - \beta_n$
↓ # of half-vampires born
↓ # of dead half-vampires
For my part—
The fact that he's a six-year-old kid...
...is *precisely why* I needed to be on the highest alert possible.

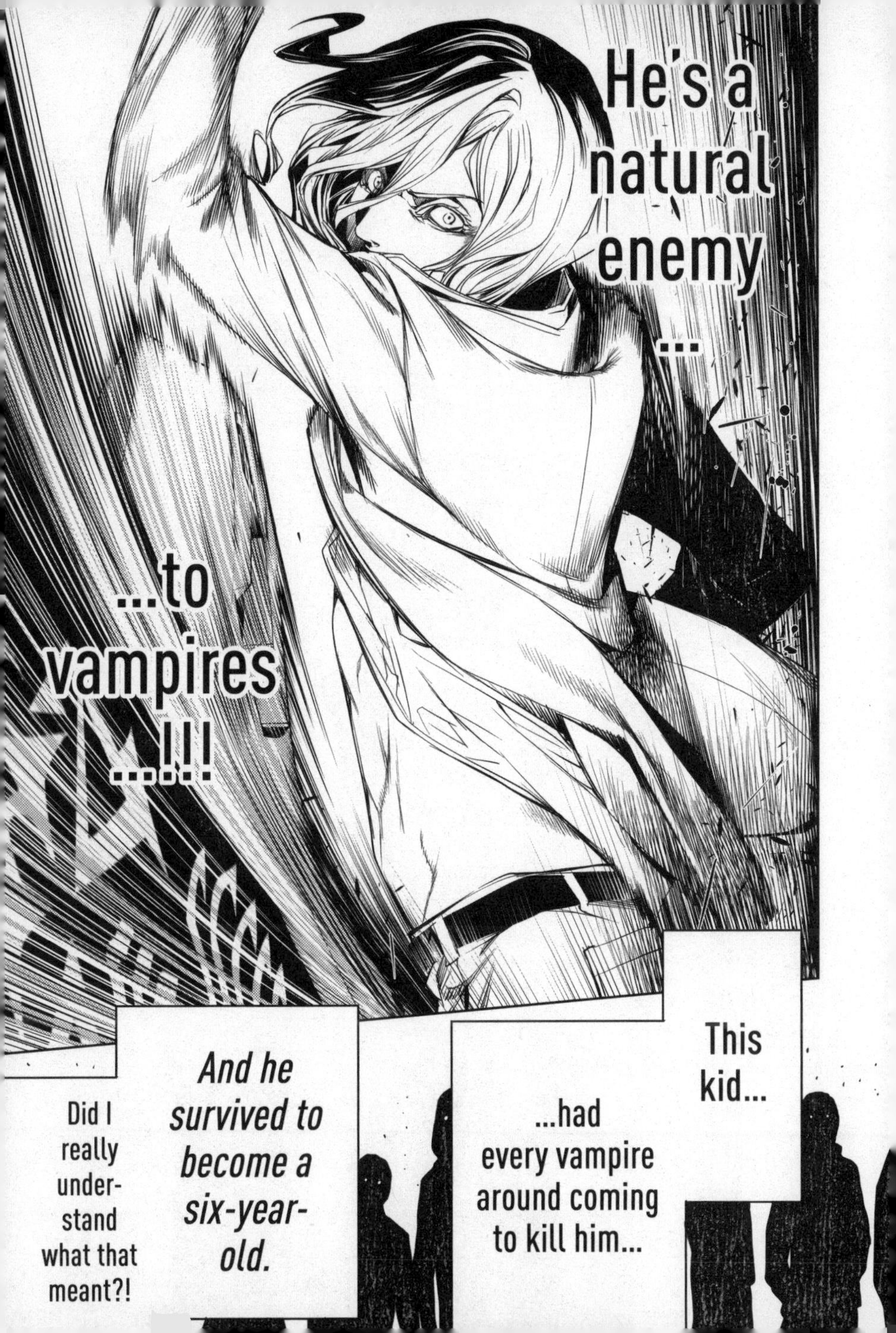
He's a natural enemy...
...to vampires...!!!
This kid...
...had every vampire around coming to kill him...
And he survived to become a six-year-old.
Did I really under-stand what that meant?!

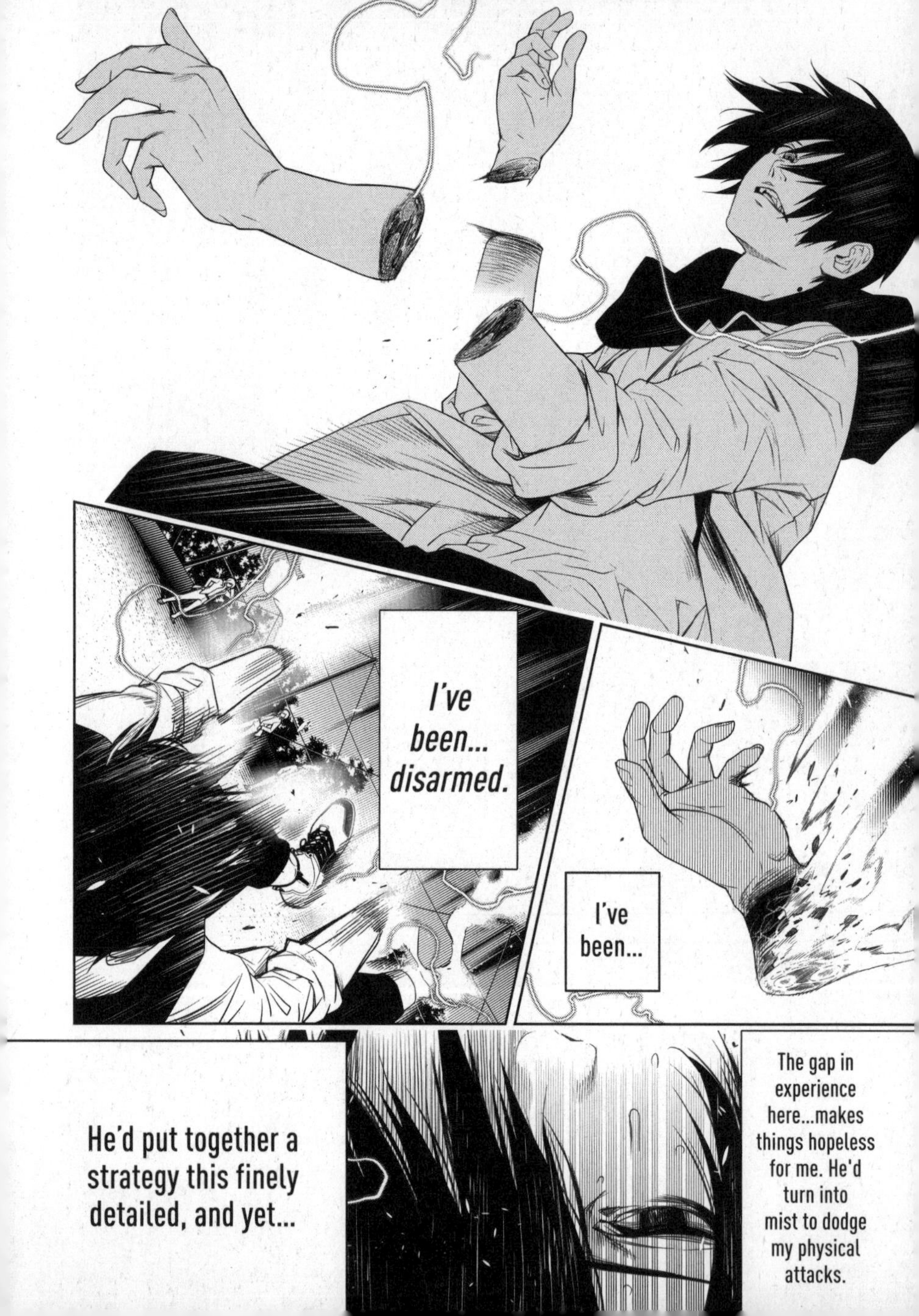
I've been...
I've been... disarmed.
The gap in experience here...makes things hopeless for me. He'd turn into mist to dodge my physical attacks.
He'd put together a strategy this finely detailed, and yet...

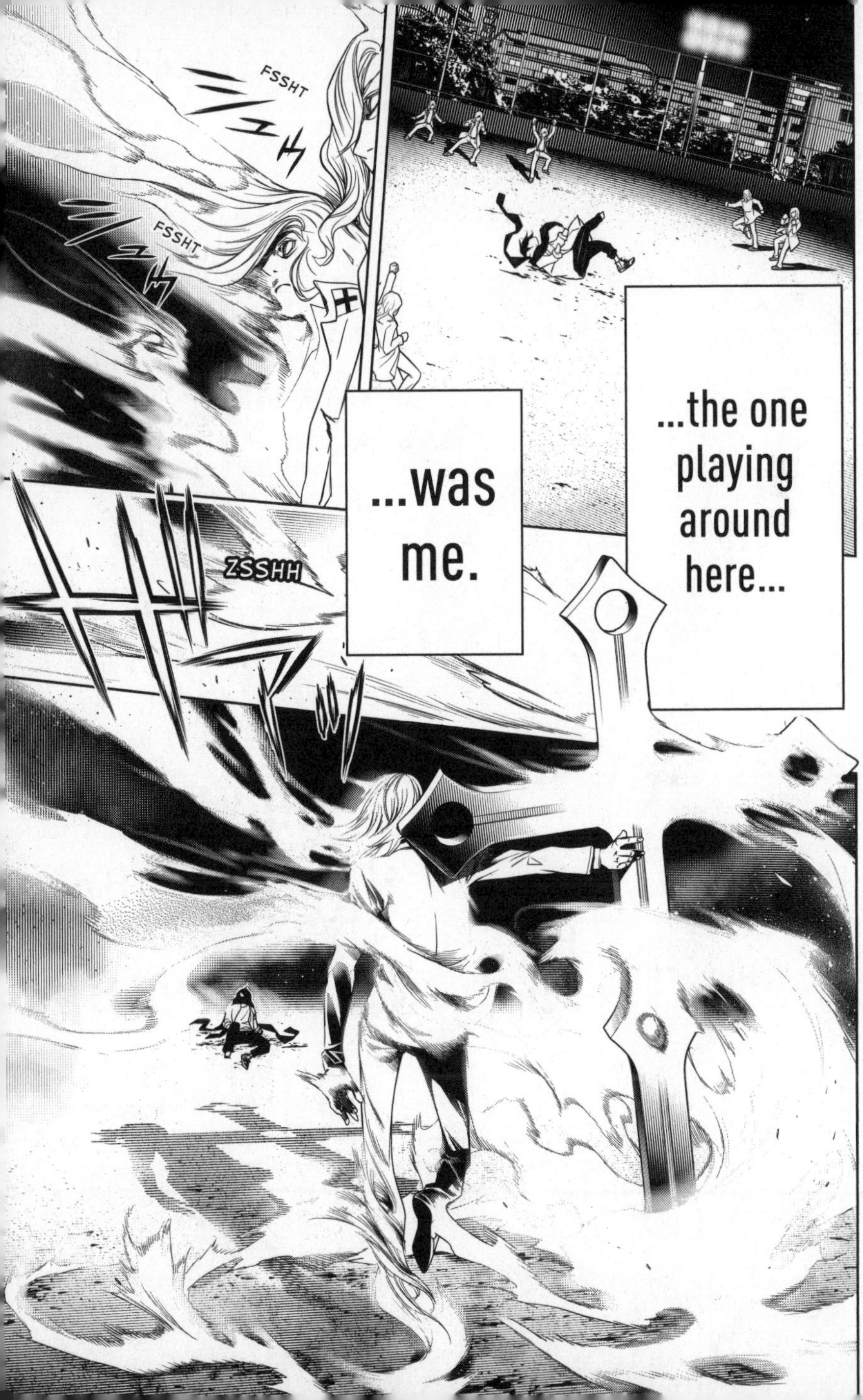
...the one playing around here...
...was me.
FSSHT
FSSHT
ZSSHH

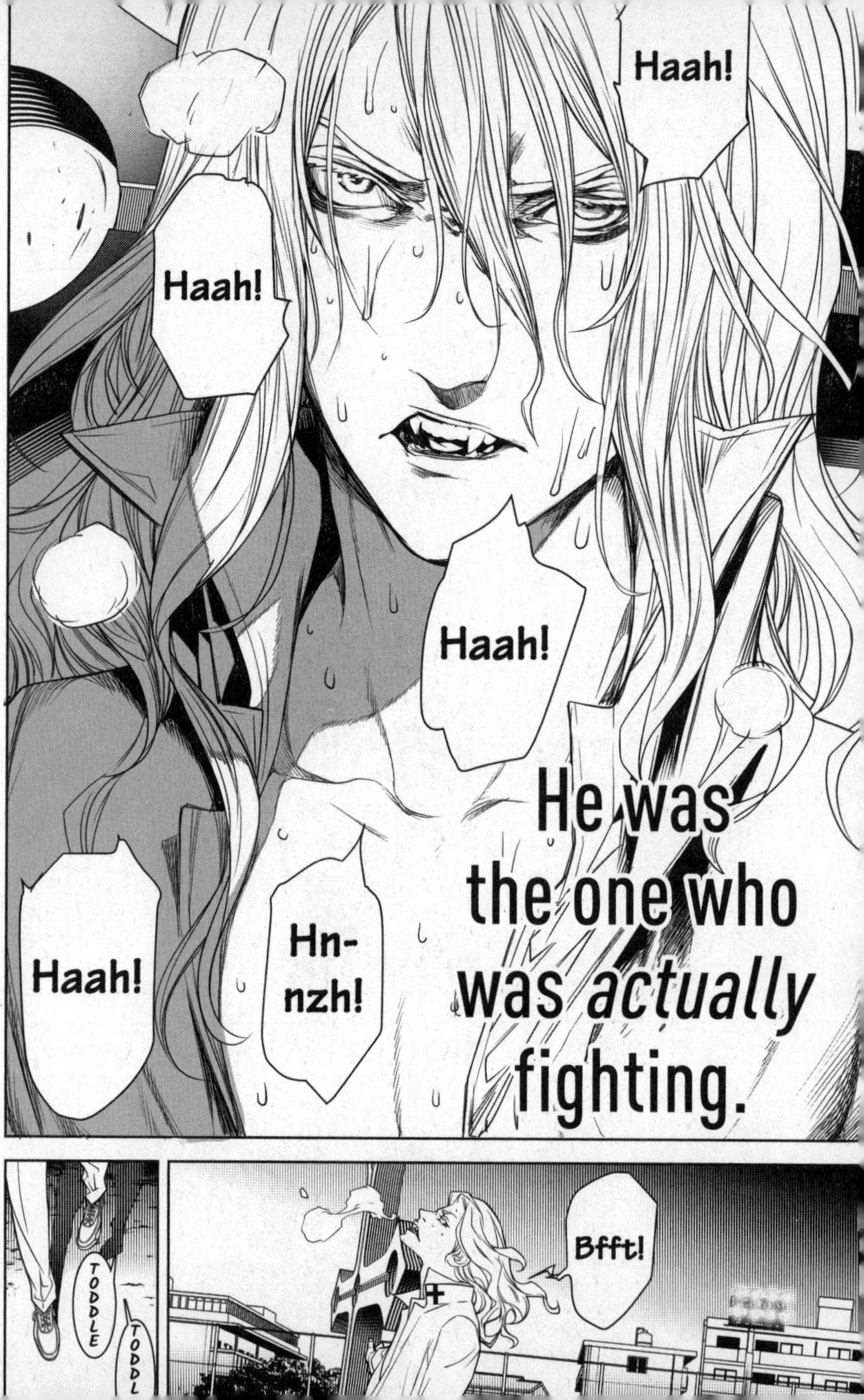
Haah!
Haah!
Haah!
He was the one who was *actually* fighting.
Hn-nzh!
Haah!
Bfft!
TODDLE
TODDL

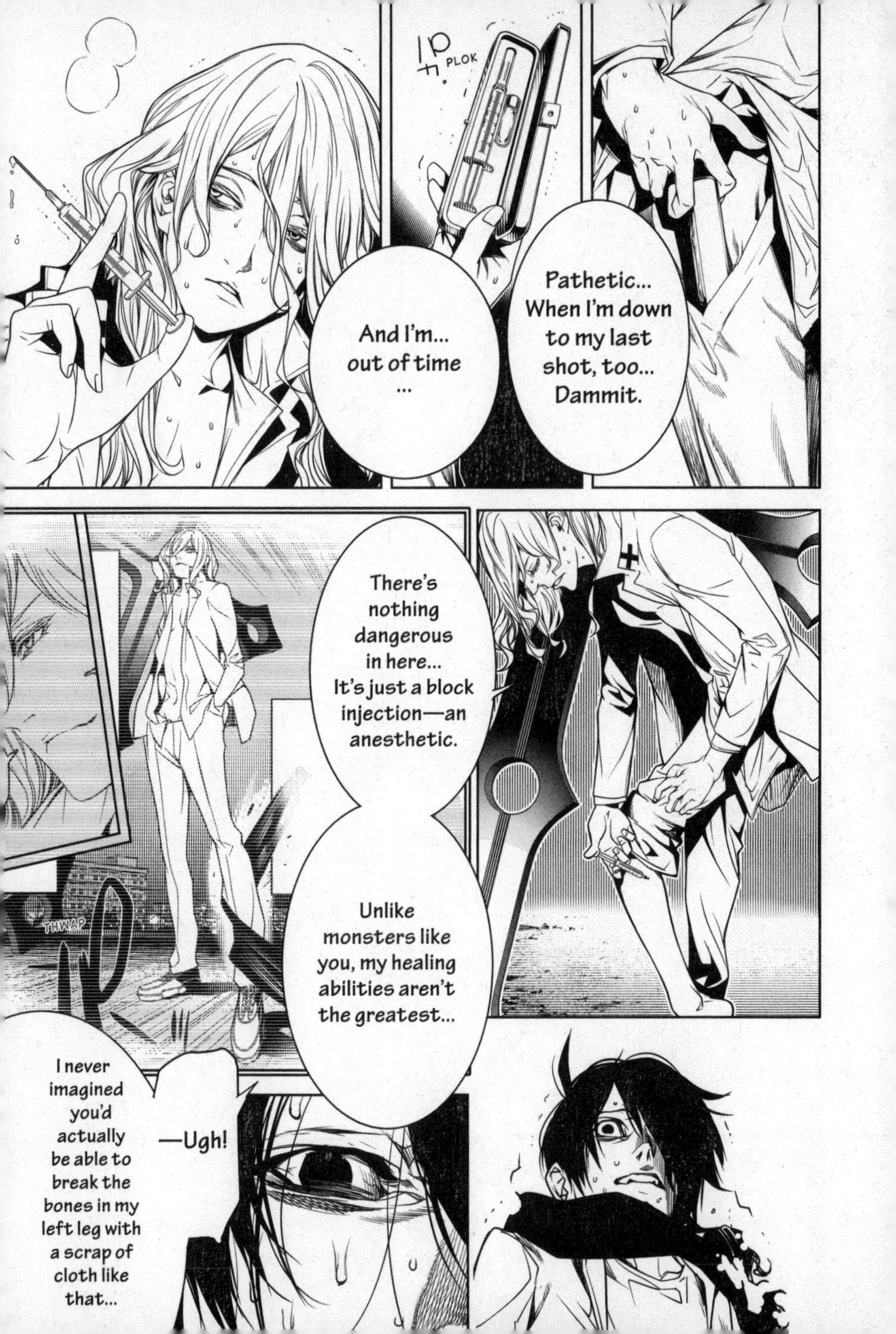
Pathetic... When I'm down to my last shot, too... Dammit.
PLOK
And I'm... out of time ...
There's nothing dangerous in here... It's just a block injection—an anesthetic.
Unlike monsters like you, my healing abilities aren't the greatest...
THWAP
I never imagined you'd actually be able to break the bones in my left leg with a scrap of cloth like that...
—Ugh!

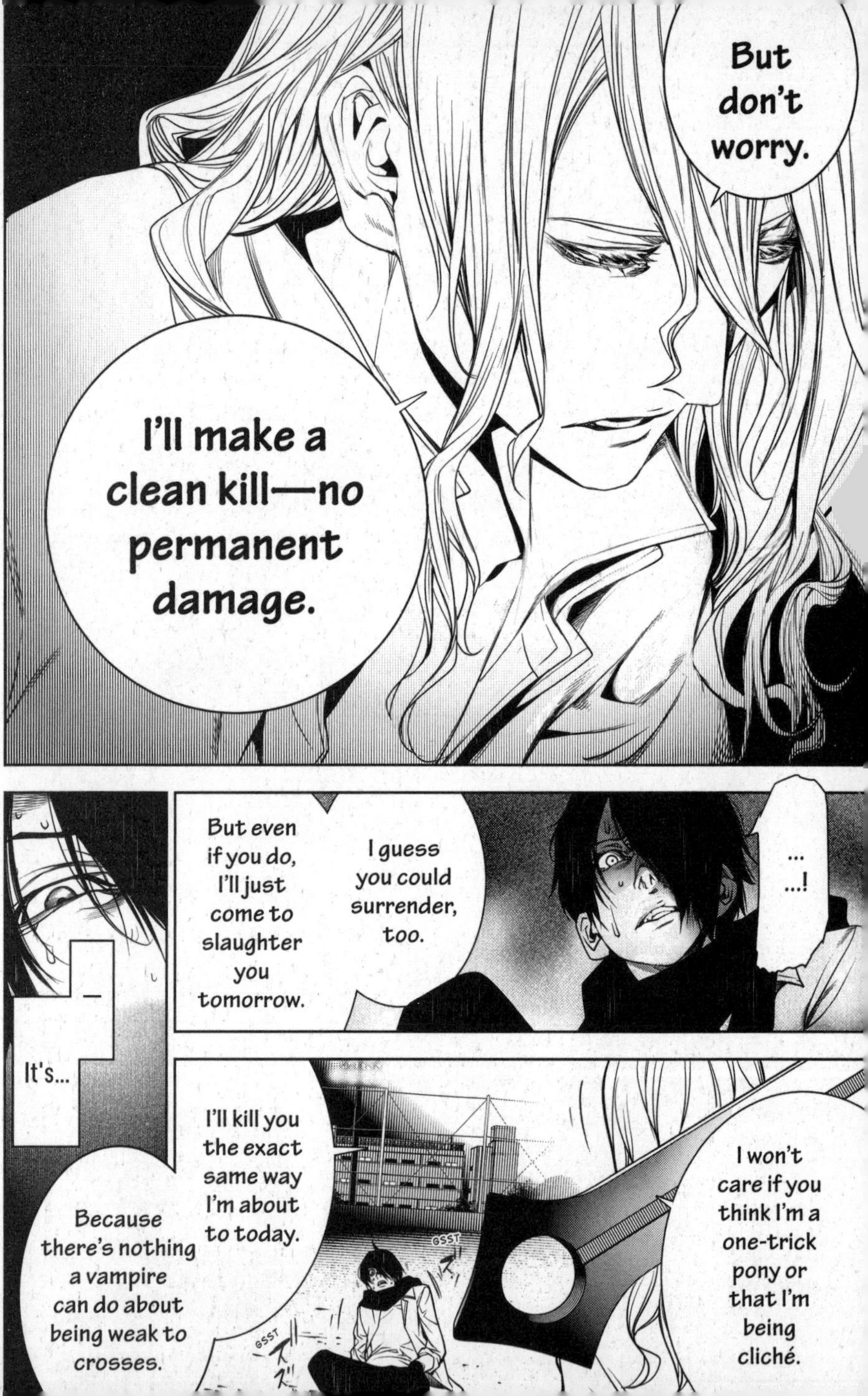
But don't worry.
I'll make a clean kill—no permanent damage.
... ...!
I guess you could surrender, too.
But even if you do, I'll just come to slaughter you tomorrow.
I won't care if you think I'm a one-trick pony or that I'm being cliché.
GSST
I'll kill you the exact same way I'm about to today.
Because there's nothing a vampire can do about being weak to crosses.
GSST
—
It's...

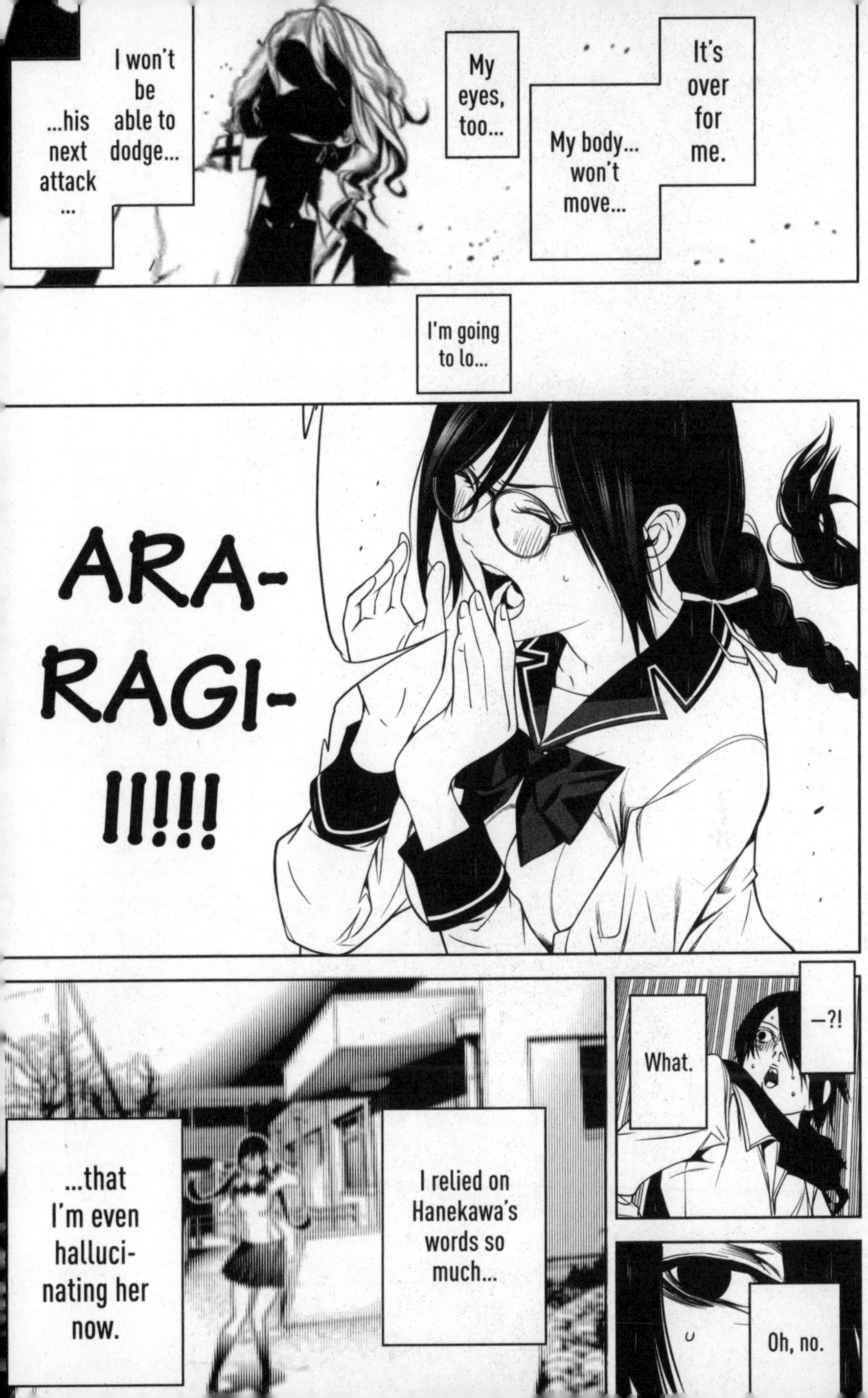
It's over for me.
My body... won't move...
My eyes, too...
I won't be able to dodge...
...his next attack...
I'm going to lo...
ARA-RAGI-IIII!!!
—?!
What.
Oh, no.
I relied on Hanekawa's words so much...
...that I'm even hallucinating her now.

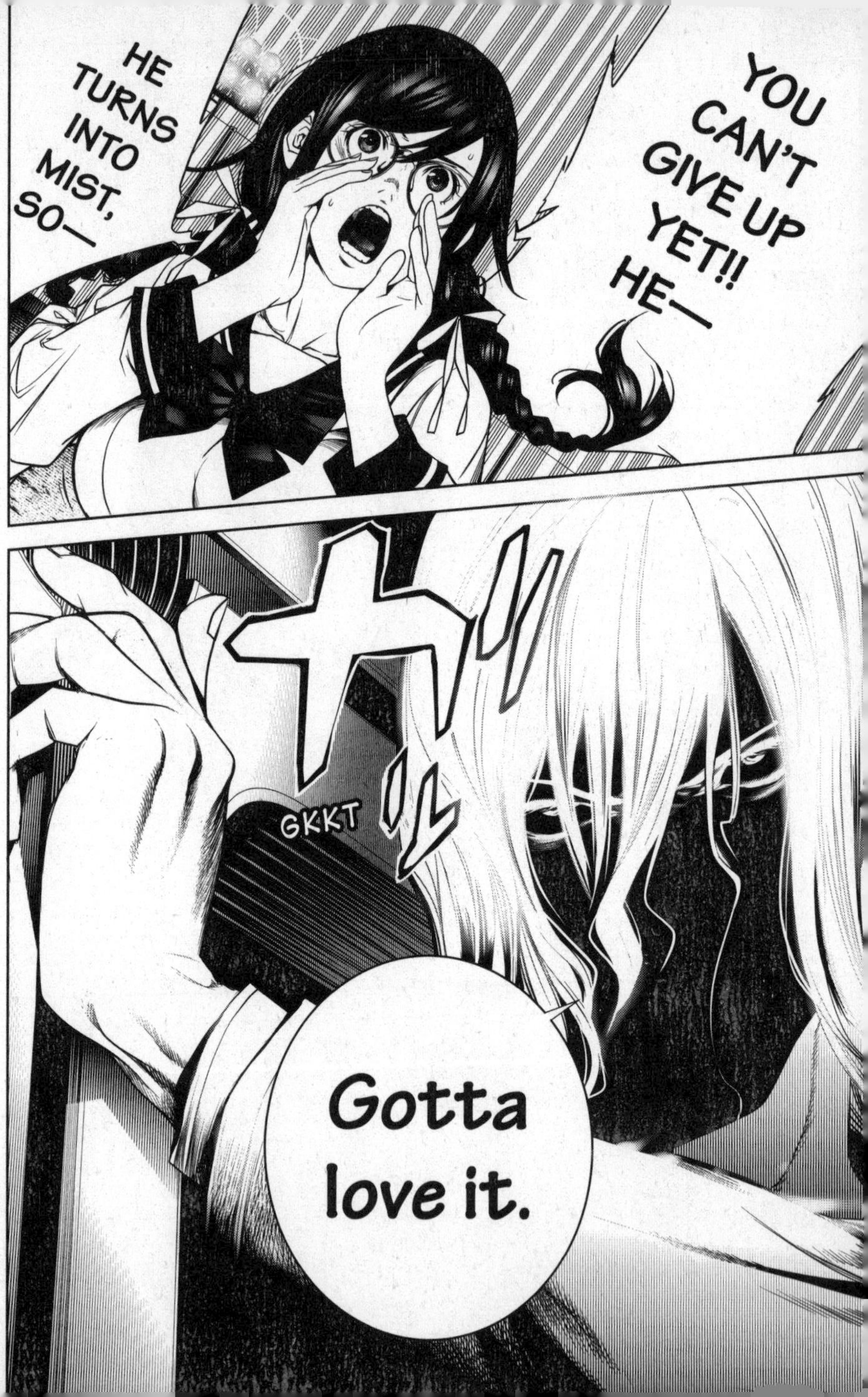
YOU CAN'T GIVE UP YET!! HE—
HE TURNS INTO MIST, SO—
GKKT
Gotta love it.

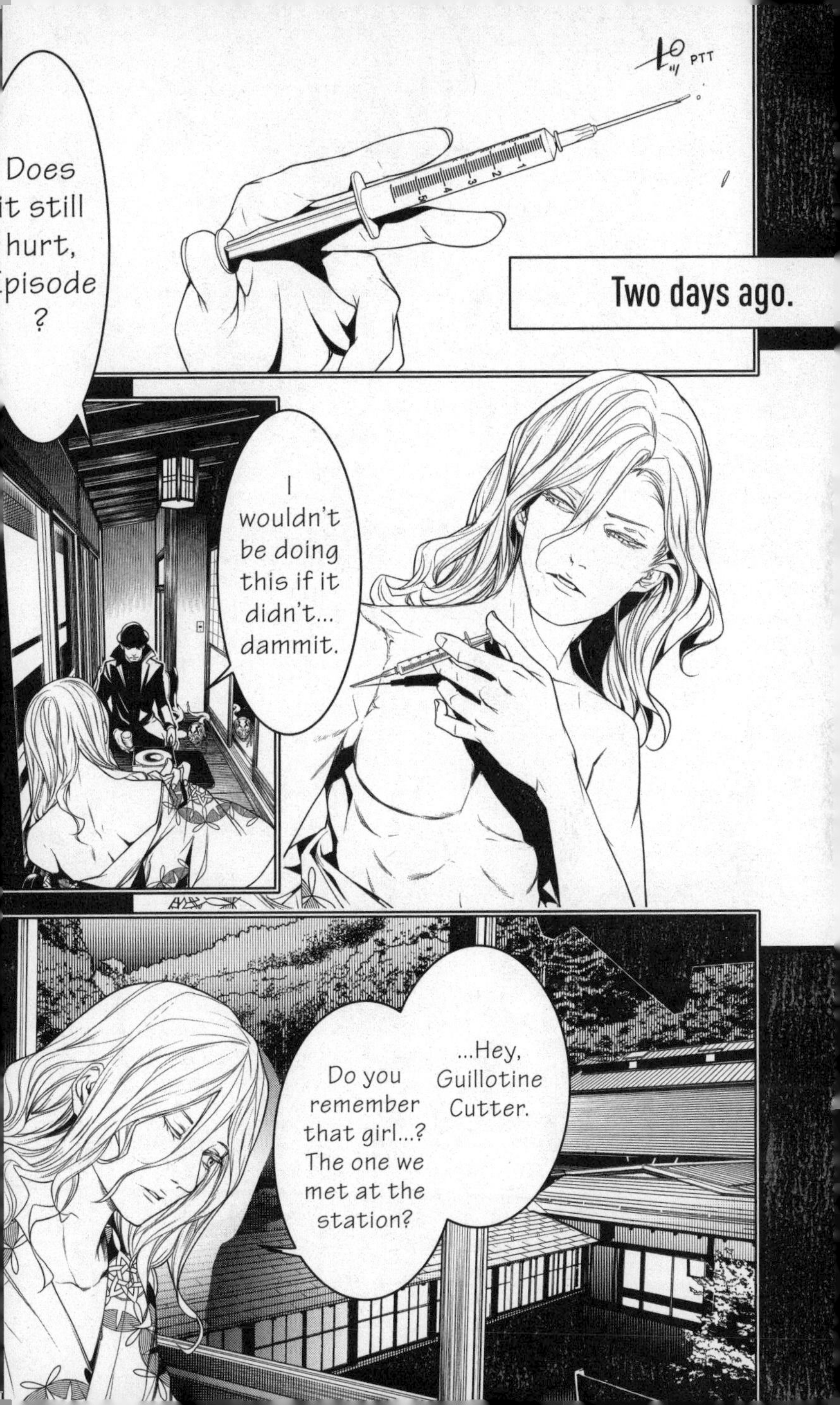
PTT
Two days ago.
Does it still hurt, Episode?
I wouldn't be doing this if it didn't... dammit.
...Hey, Guillotine Cutter.
Do you remember that girl...? The one we met at the station?

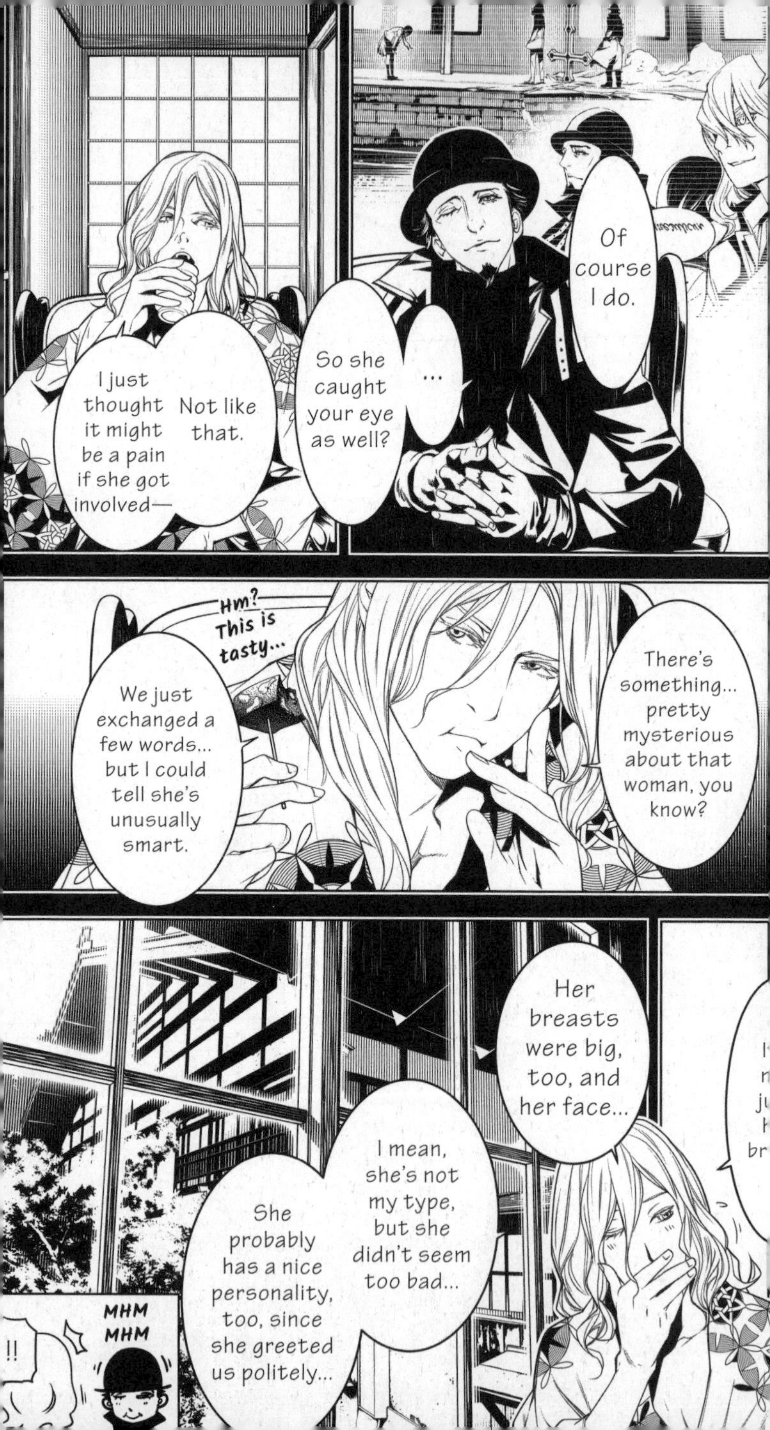
Of course I do.
...
So she caught your eye as well?
Not like that.
I just thought it might be a pain if she got involved—
There's something... pretty mysterious about that woman, you know?
Hm? This is tasty...
We just exchanged a few words... but I could tell she's unusually smart.
Her breasts were big, too, and her face...
I mean, she's not my type, but she didn't seem too bad...
She probably has a nice personality, too, since she greeted us politely...
MHM MHM
!!

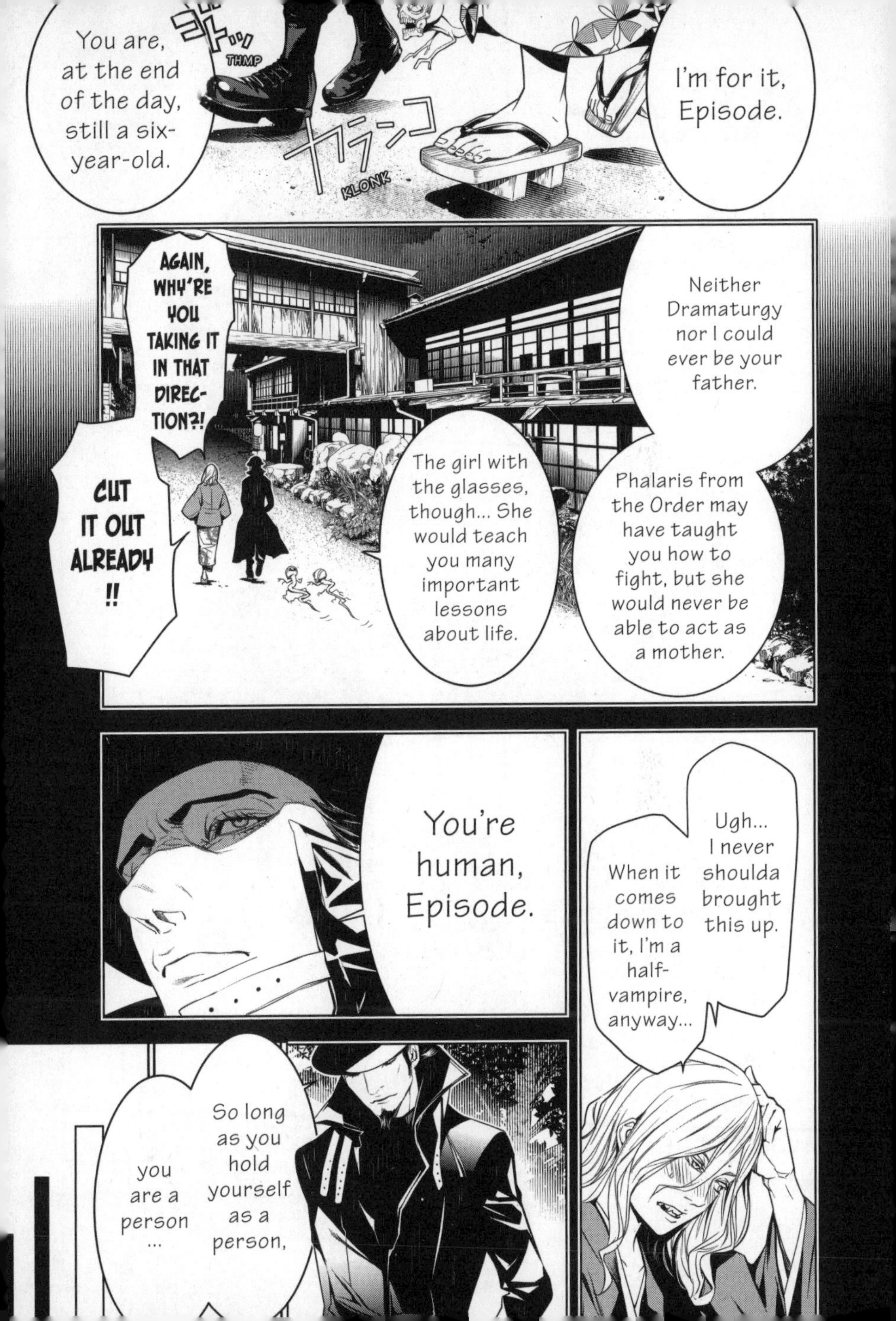
I'm for it, Episode.
KLONK
THMP
You are, at the end of the day, still a six-year-old.
Neither Dramaturgy nor I could ever be your father.
Phalaris from the Order may have taught you how to fight, but she would never be able to act as a mother.
The girl with the glasses, though... She would teach you many important lessons about life.
AGAIN, WHY'RE YOU TAKING IT IN THAT DIRECTION?!
CUT IT OUT ALREADY!!
Ugh... I never shoulda brought this up.
When it comes down to it, I'm a half-vampire, anyway...
You're human, Episode.
So long as you hold yourself as a person,
you are a person...

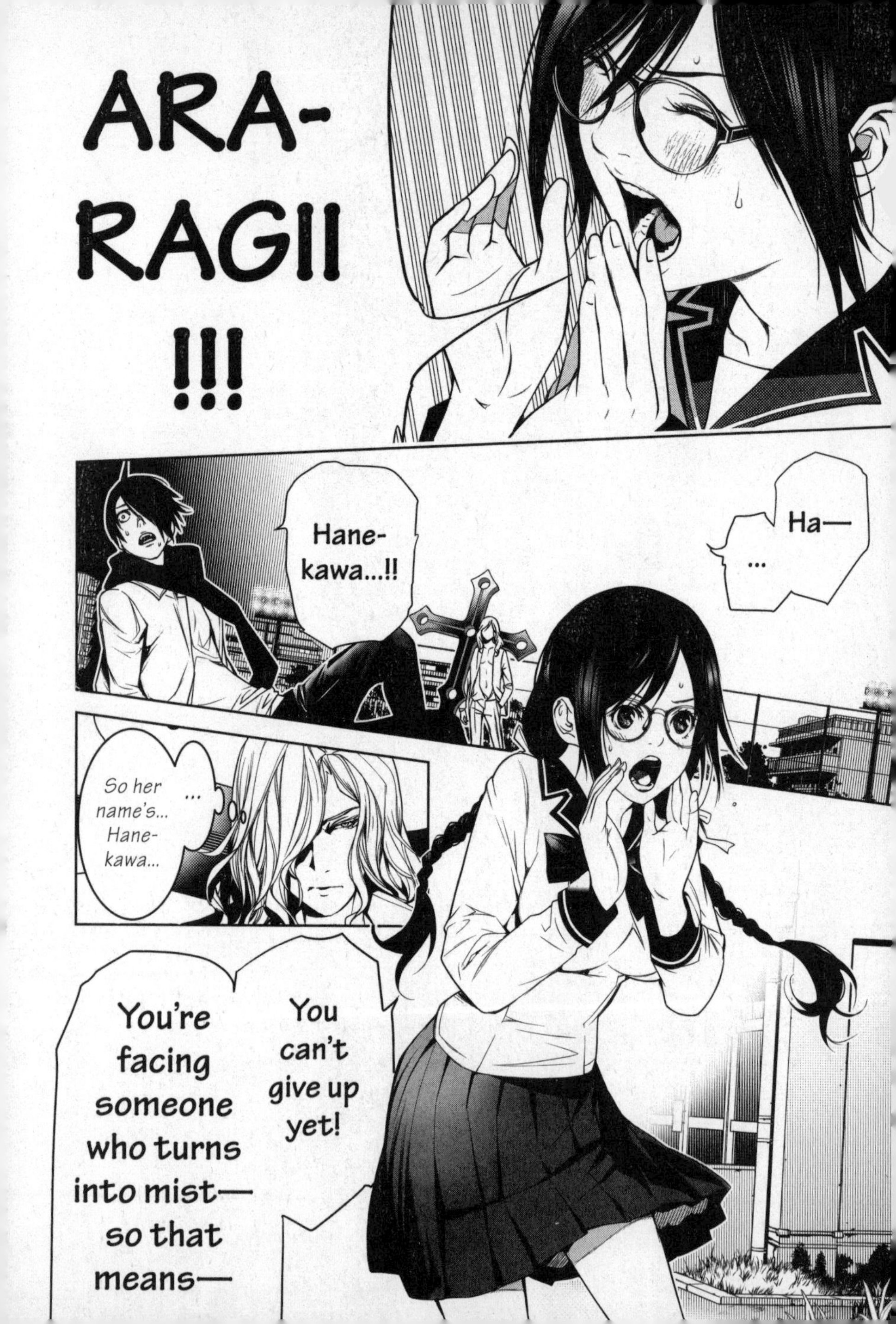
ARA-RAGII!!!
Ha— ...
Hane-kawa...!!
...
So her name's... Hane-kawa...
You can't give up yet!
You're facing someone who turns into mist—so that means—

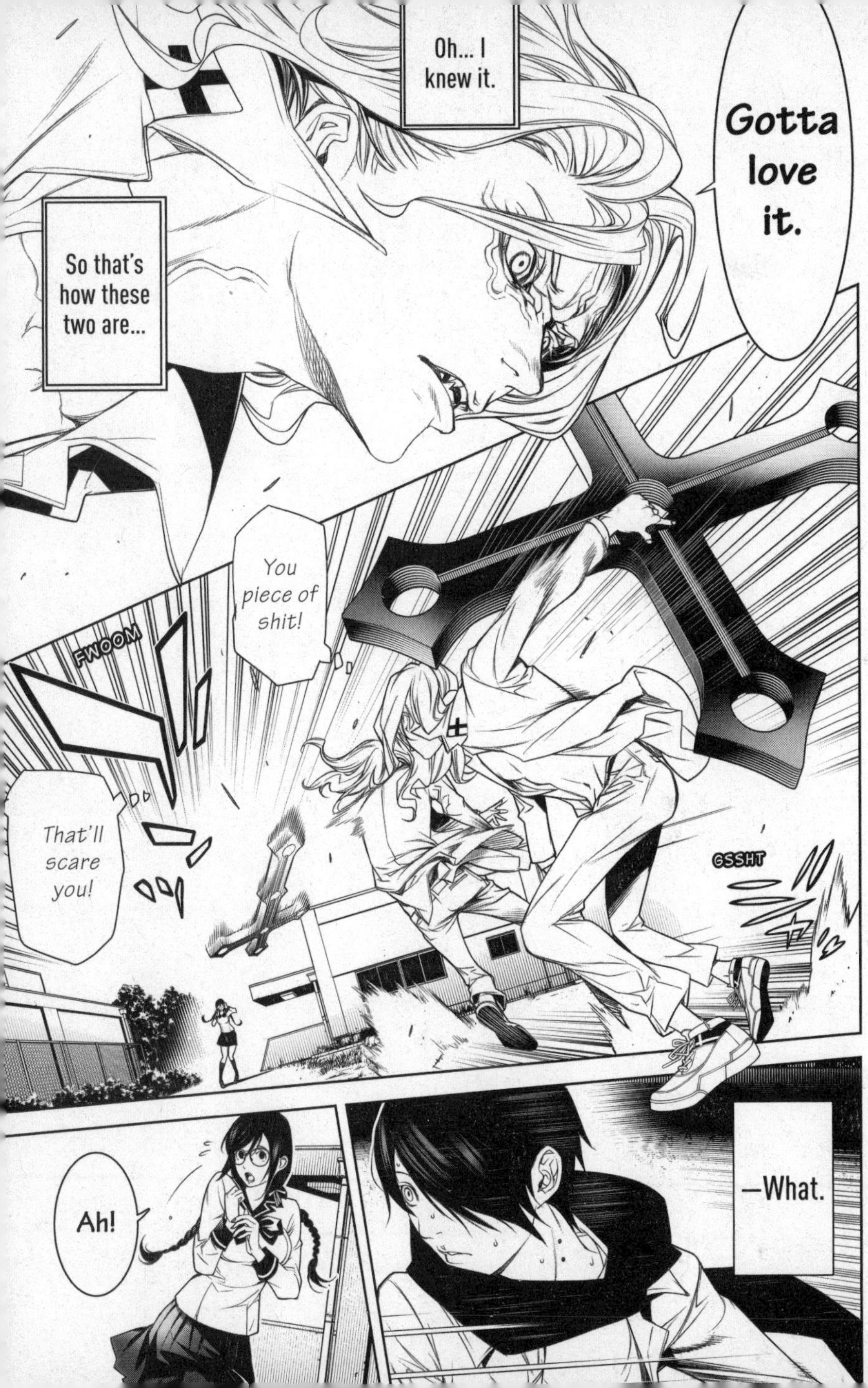
Gotta love it.
Oh... I knew it.
So that's how these two are...
GSSHT
You piece of shit!
FWOOM
That'll scare you!
—What.
Ah!

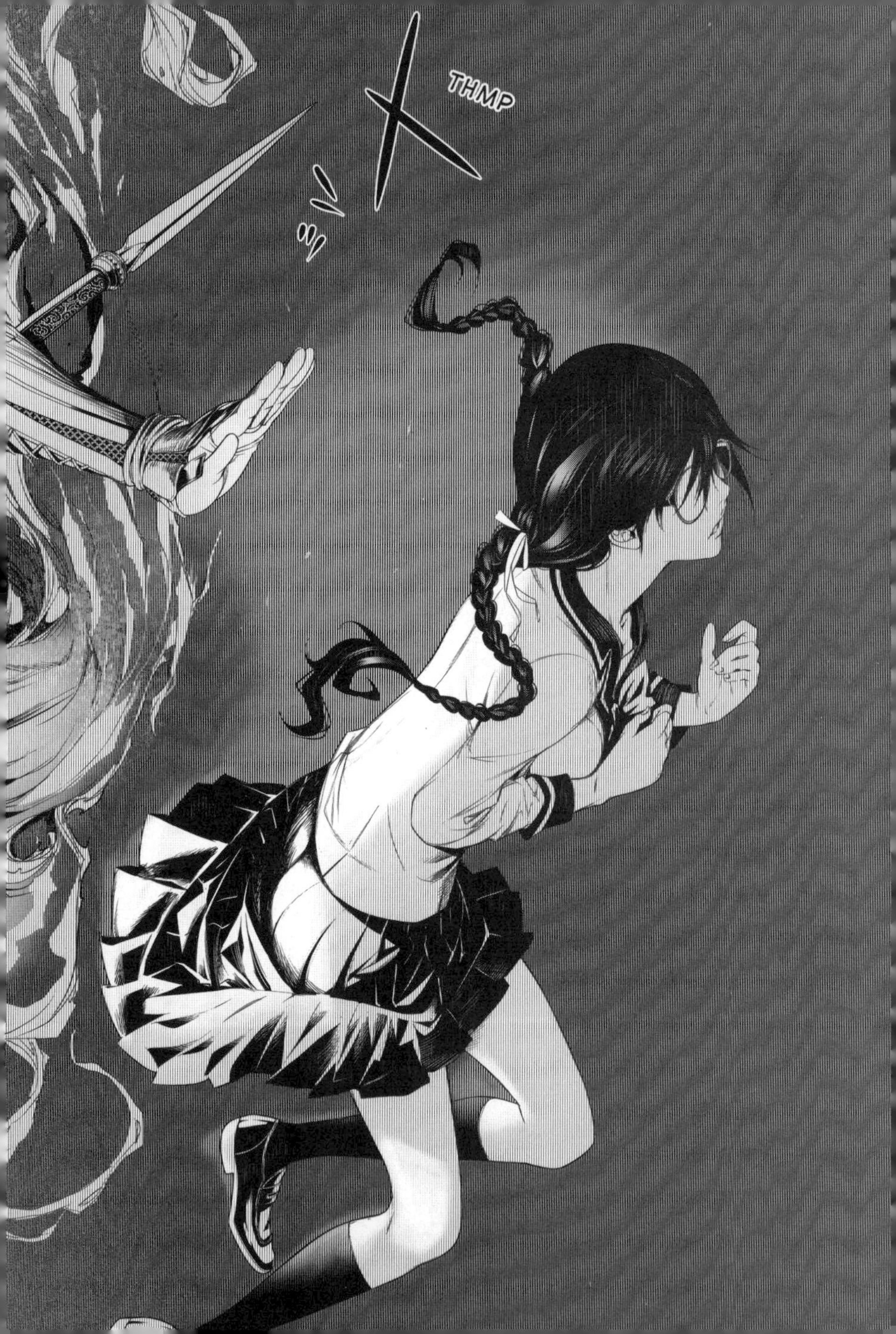
THMP

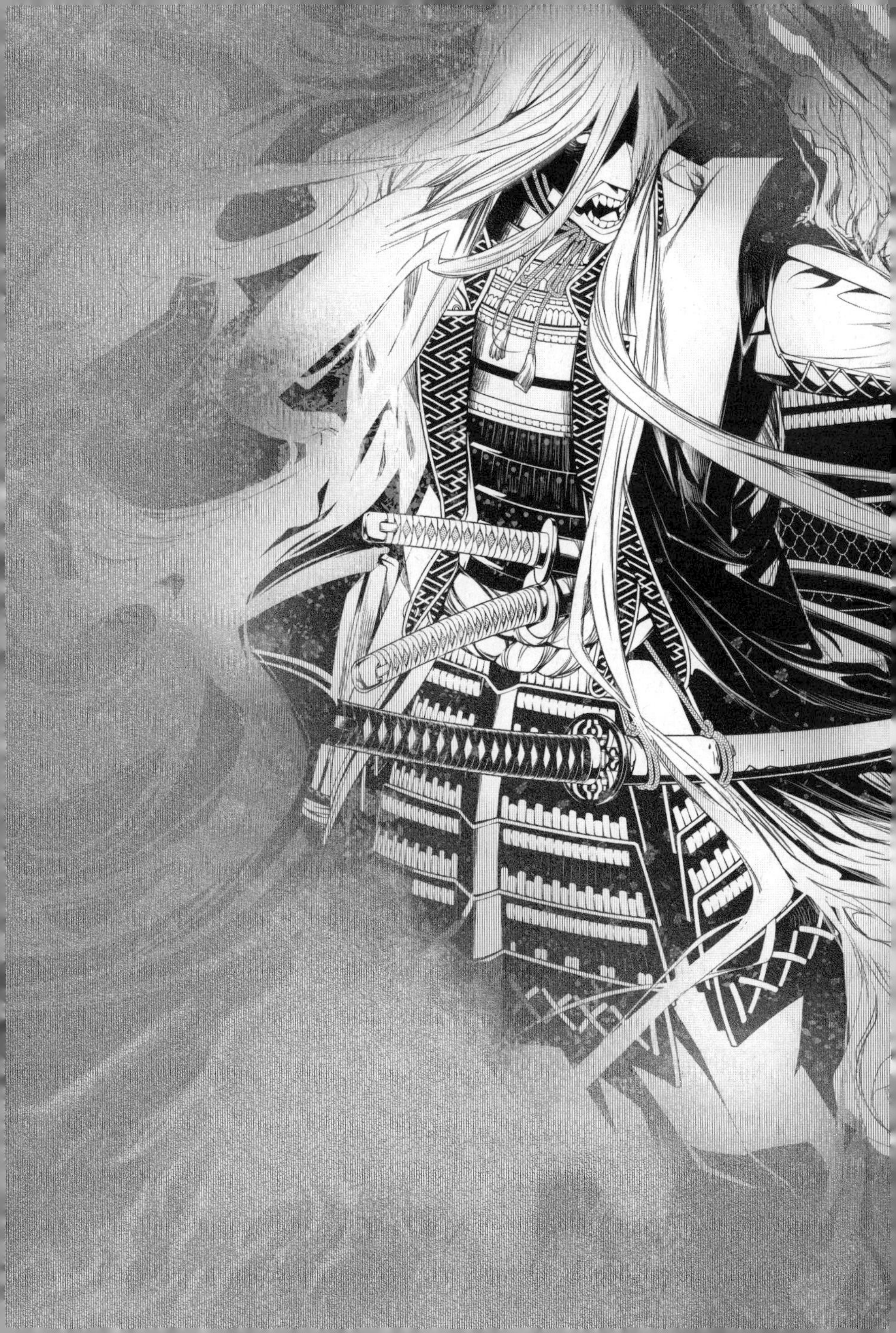

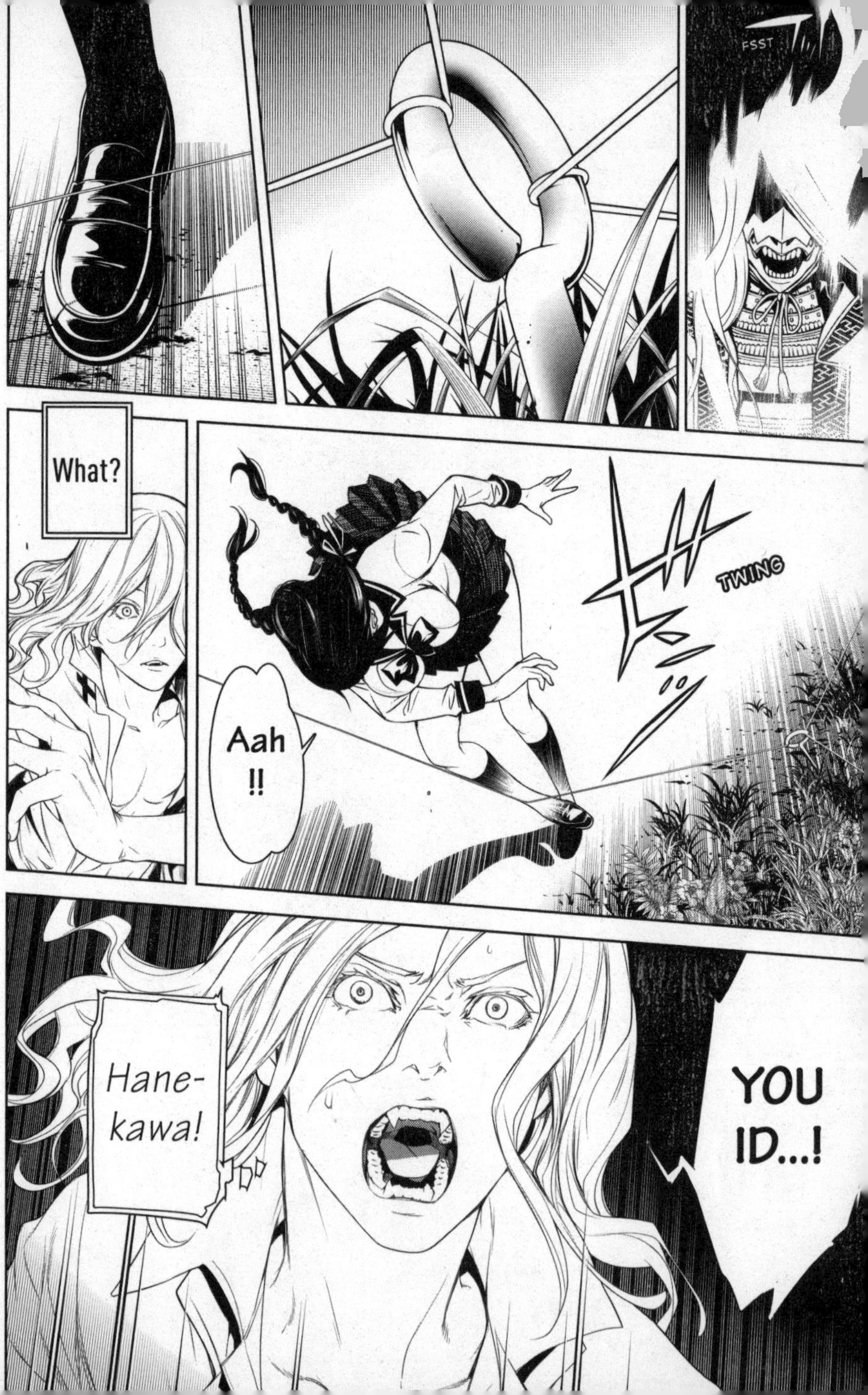
FSST
TWING
Aah !!
What?
YOU ID...!
Hane-kawa!

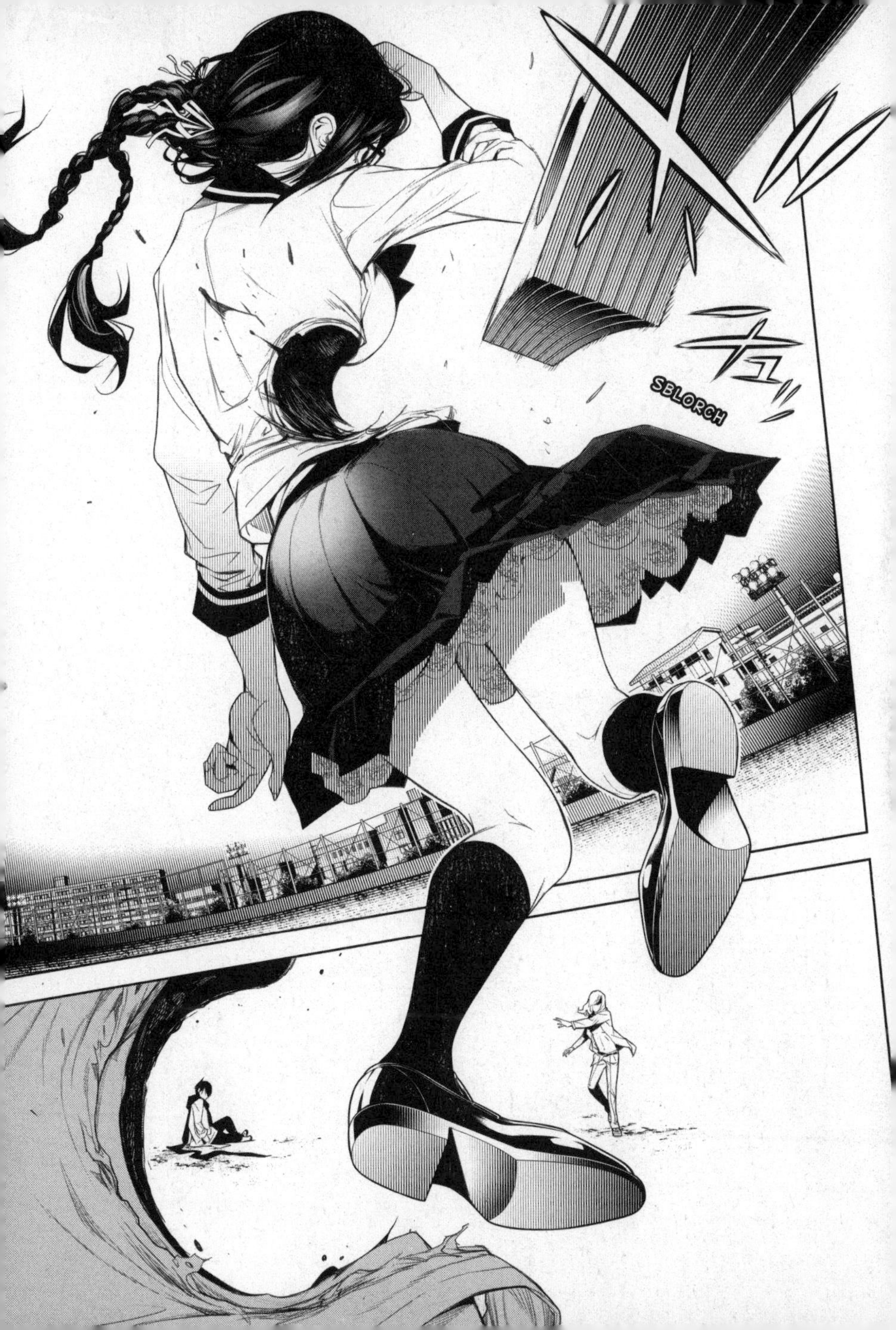
SBLORCH

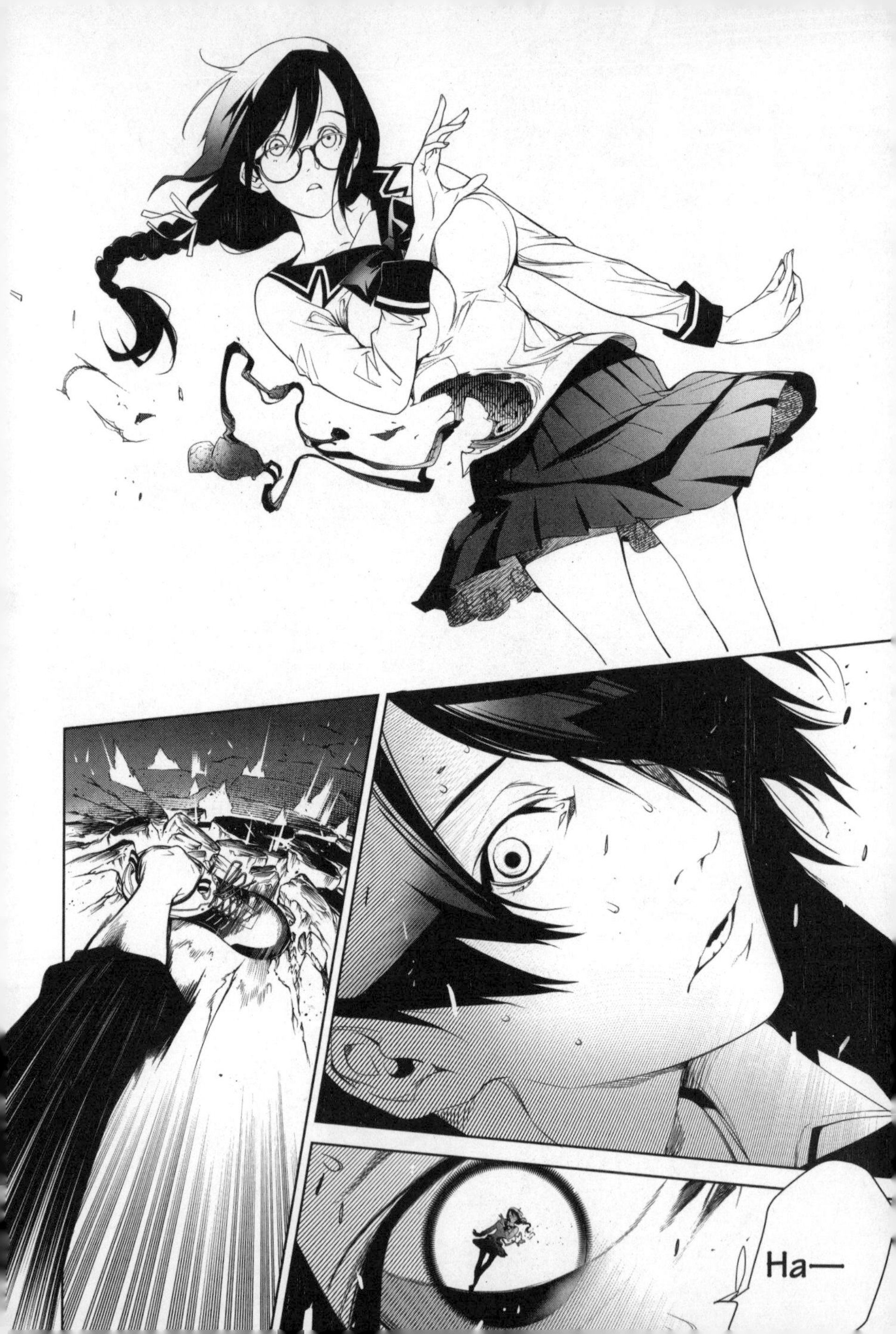
Ha—

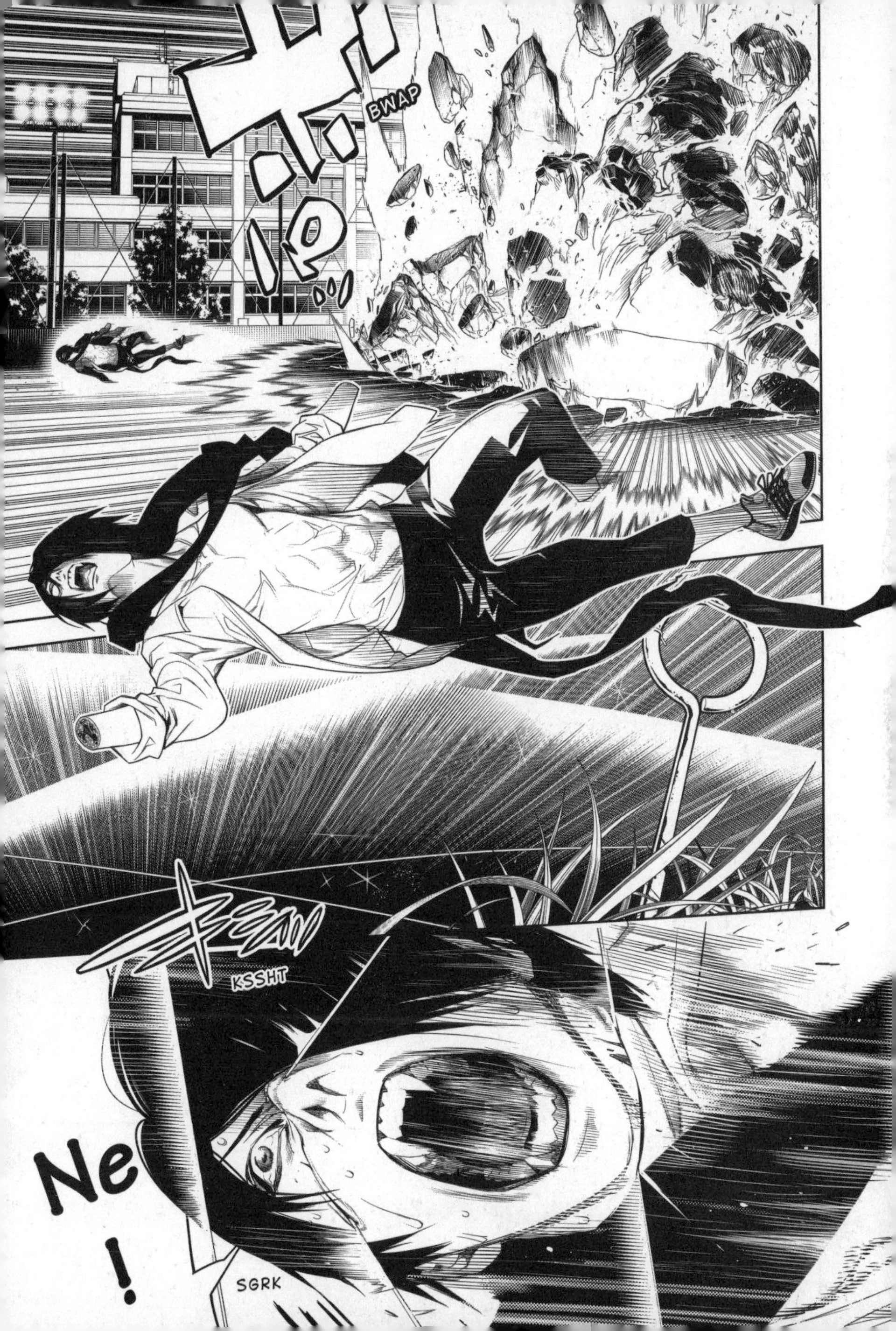
BWAP
KSSHT
Ne!
SGRK

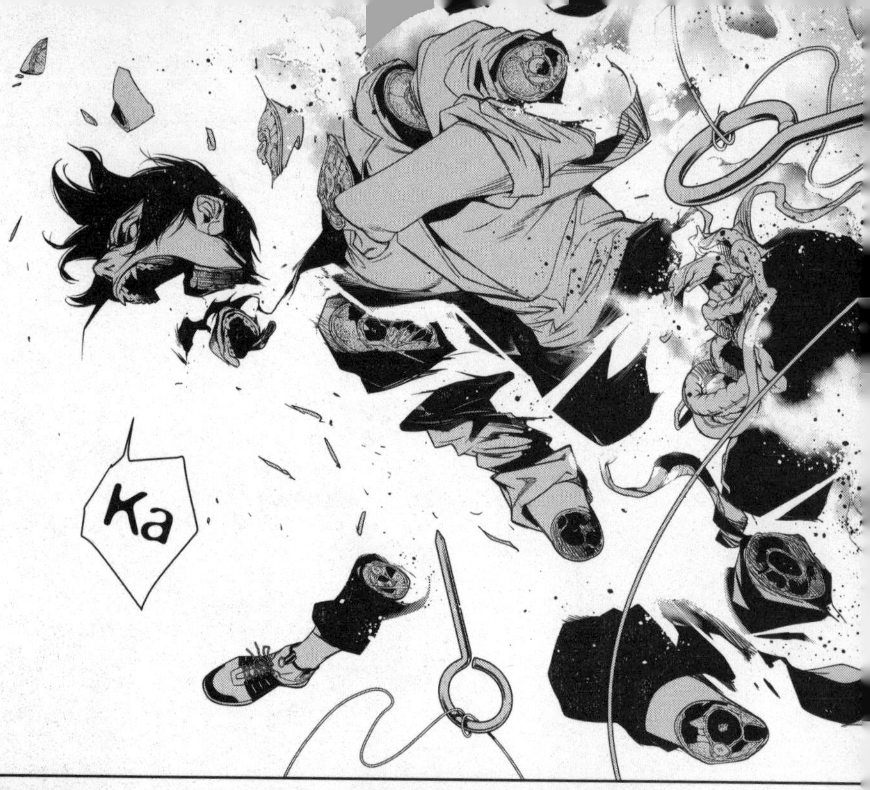
Ka
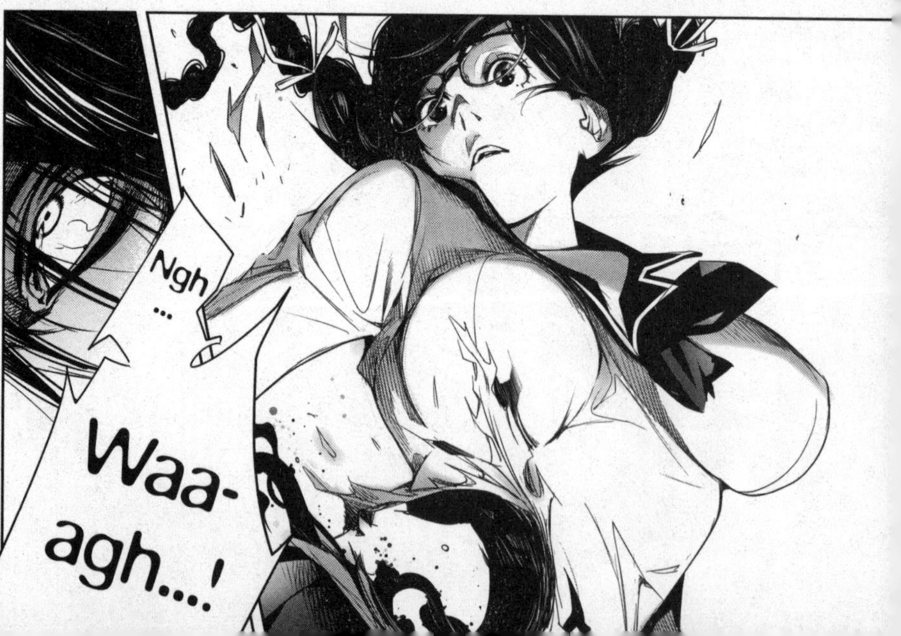
Ngh
...
Waa-
agh...!

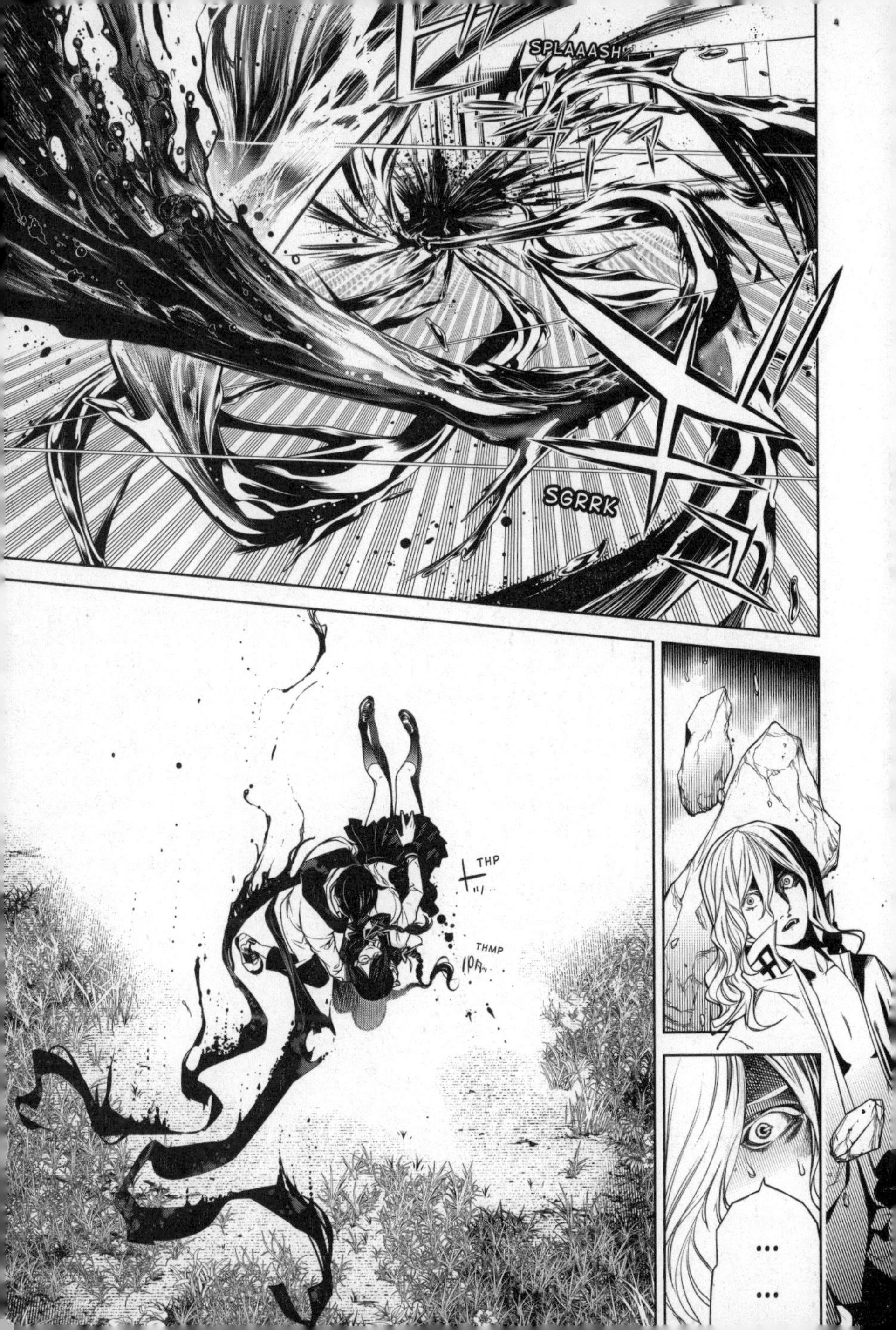
SPLAAASH
SGRRK
...
...
THP
THMP

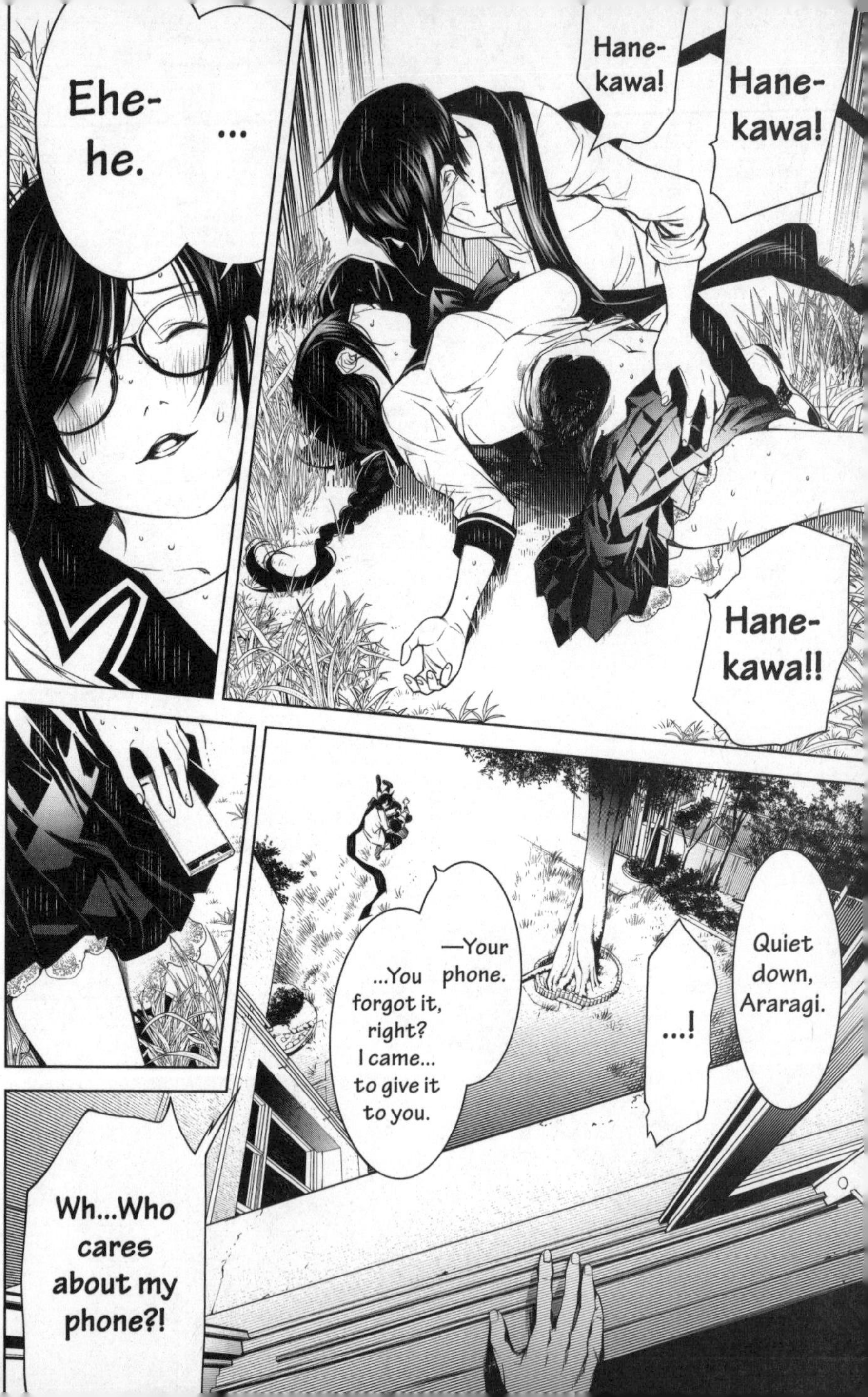
Hane-kawa!
Hane-kawa!
Hane-kawa!!
Ehe- ... he.
Quiet down, Araragi.
...!
—Your phone.
...You forgot it, right? I came... to give it to you.
Wh...Who cares about my phone?!

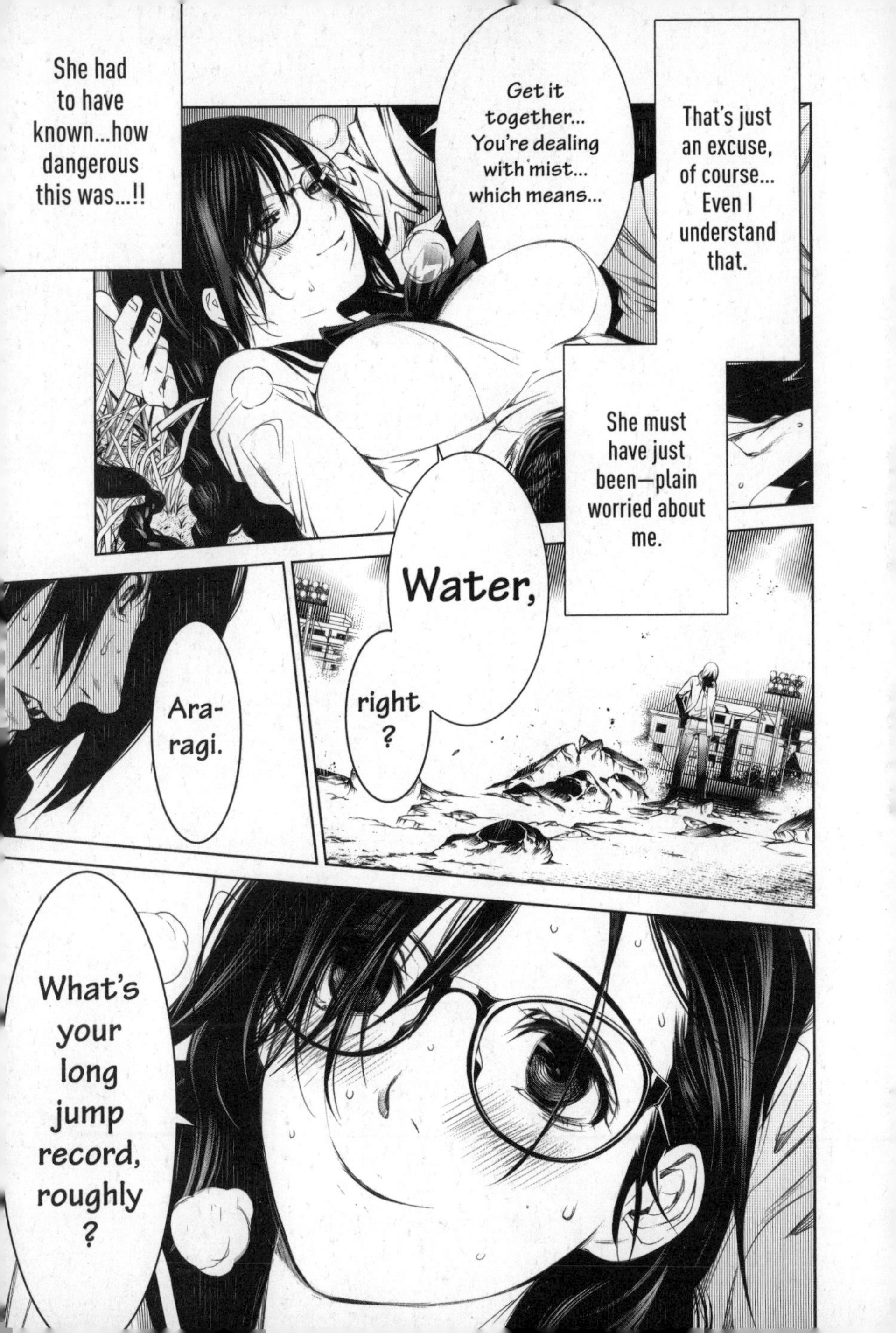
That's just an excuse, of course... Even I understand that.
Get it together... You're dealing with mist... which means...
She had to have known...how dangerous this was...!!
She must have just been—plain worried about me.
Water,
right?
Ara-ragi.
What's your long jump record, roughly?

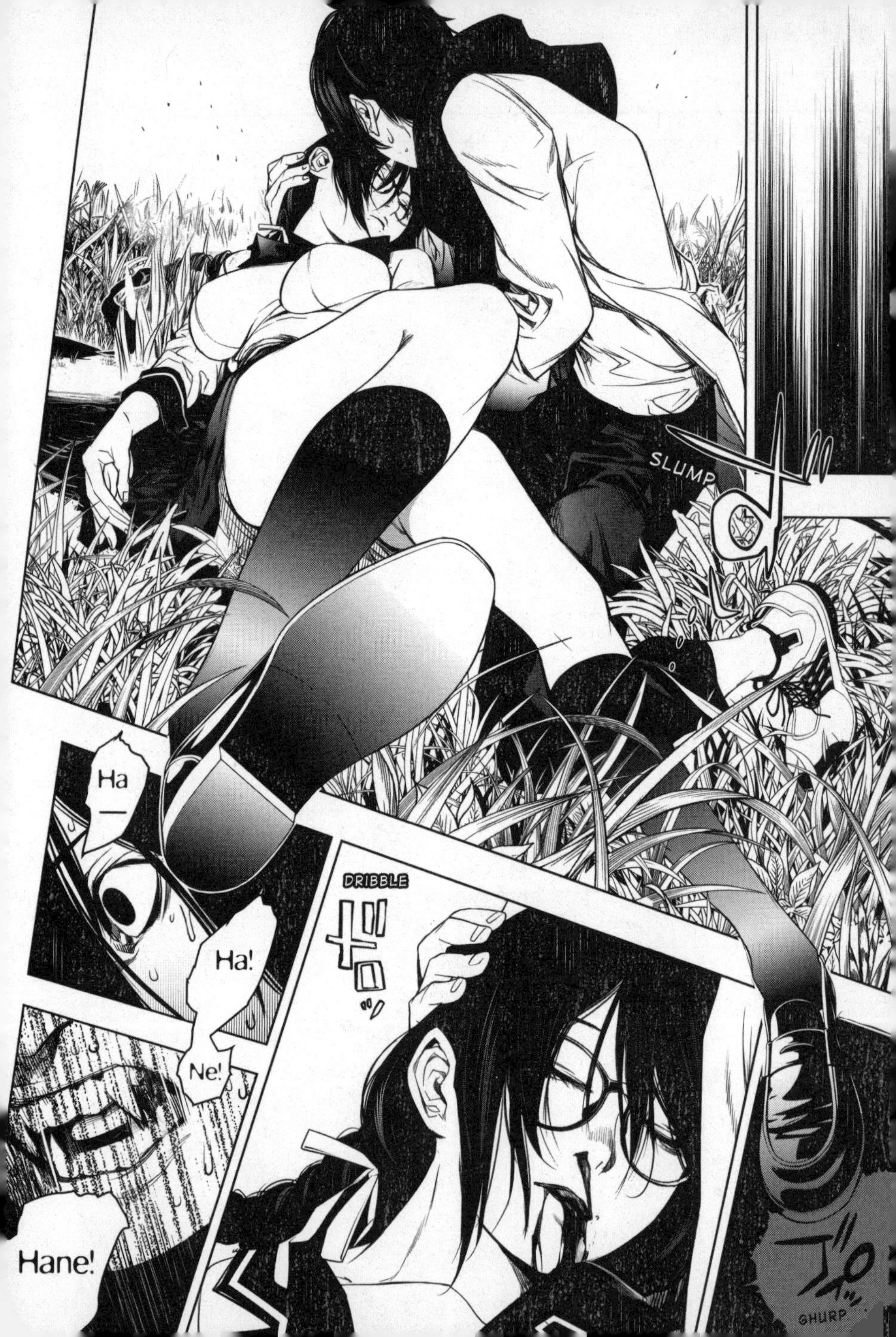
SLUMP
DRIBBLE
GHURP
Ha —
Ha!
Ne!
Hane!

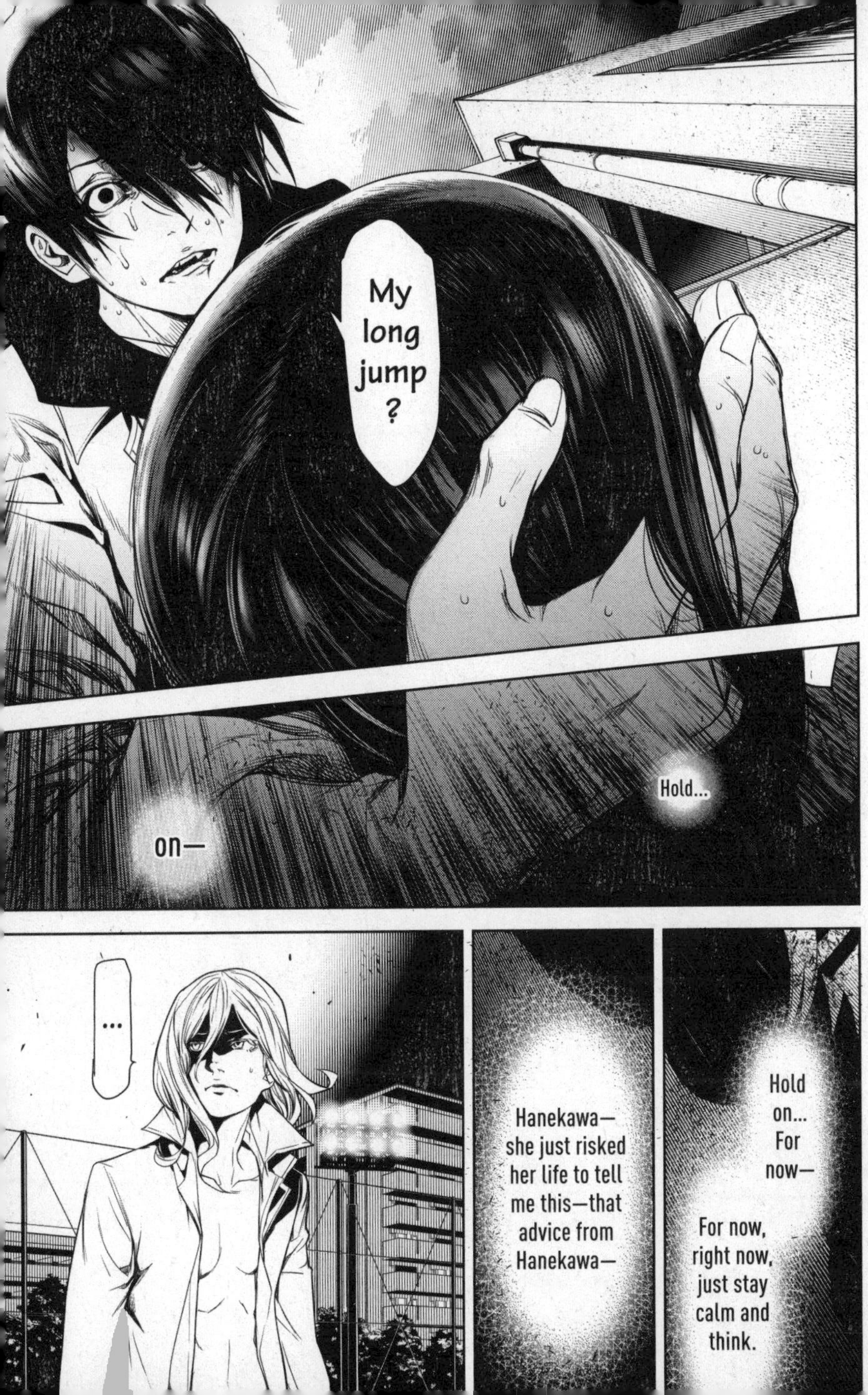
My long jump?
Hold...
on—
Hold on... For now—
For now, right now, just stay calm and think.
Hanekawa—she just risked her life to tell me this—that advice from Hanekawa—
...

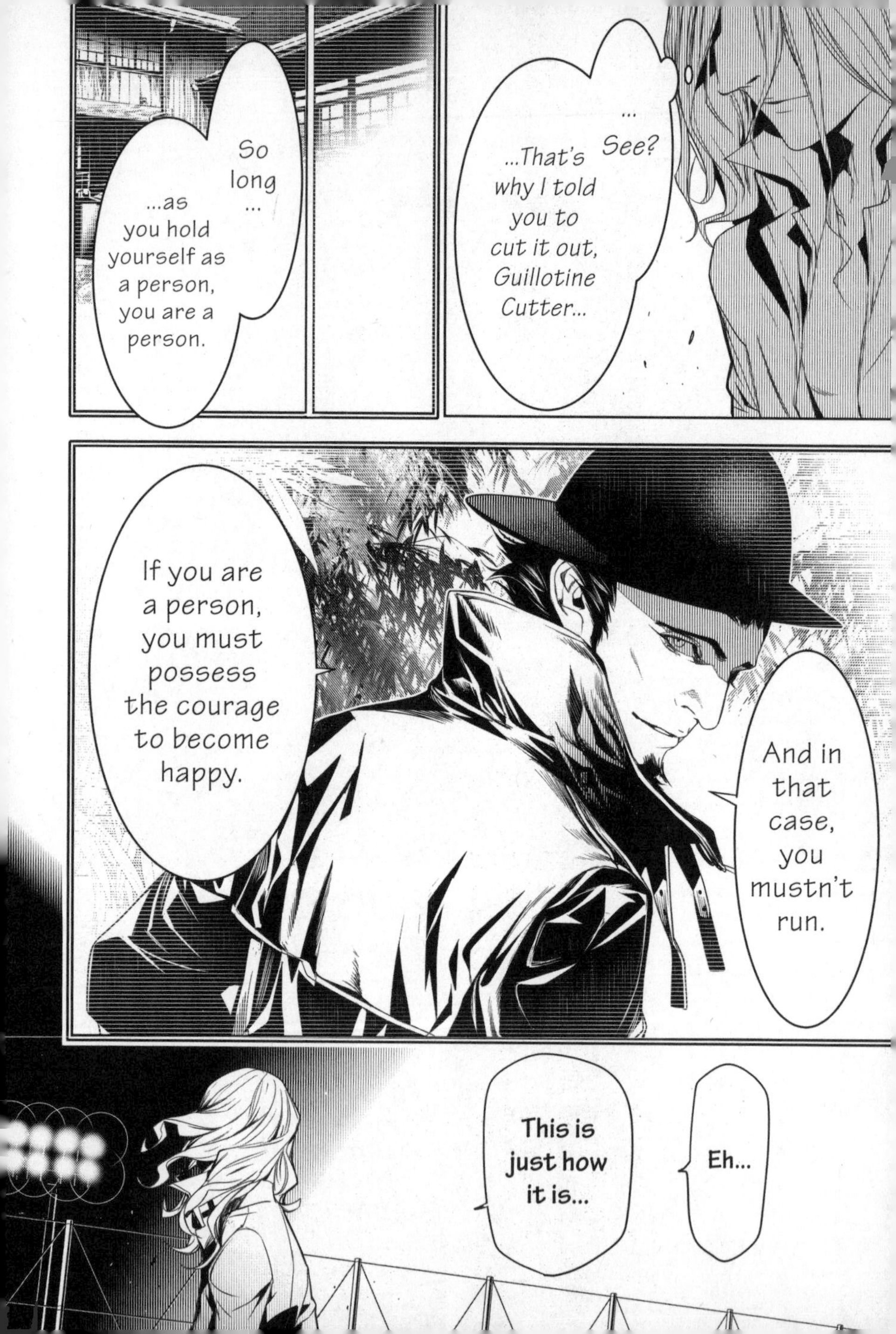
... See?
...That's why I told you to cut it out, Guillotine Cutter...
So long ...
...as you hold yourself as a person, you are a person.
If you are a person, you must possess the courage to become happy.
And in that case, you mustn't run.
Eh...
This is just how it is...

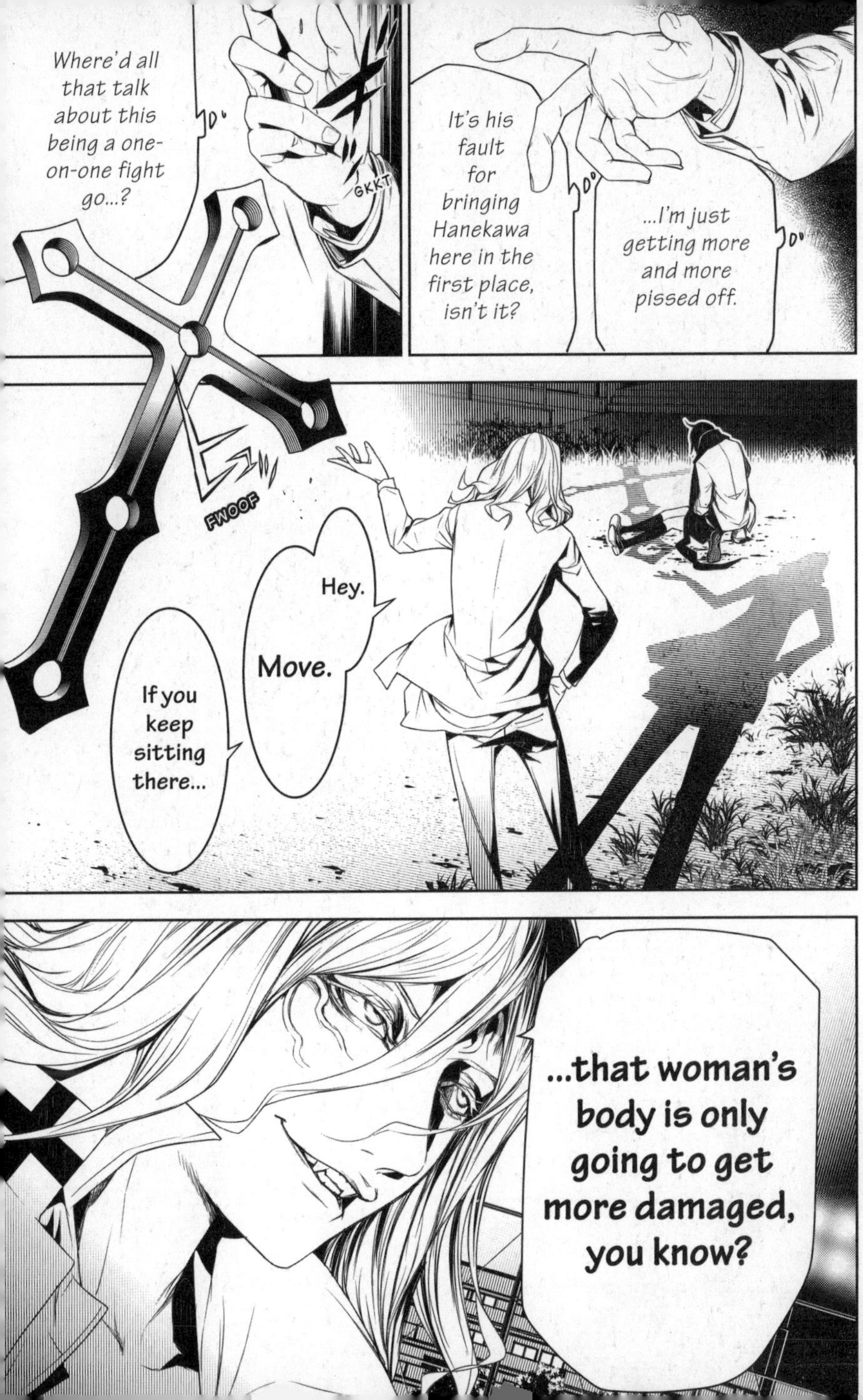
...I'm just getting more and more pissed off.
It's his fault for bringing Hanekawa here in the first place, isn't it?
Where'd all that talk about this being a one-on-one fight go...?
GKKT
FWOOF
Hey.
Move.
If you keep sitting there...
...that woman's body is only going to get more damaged, you know?

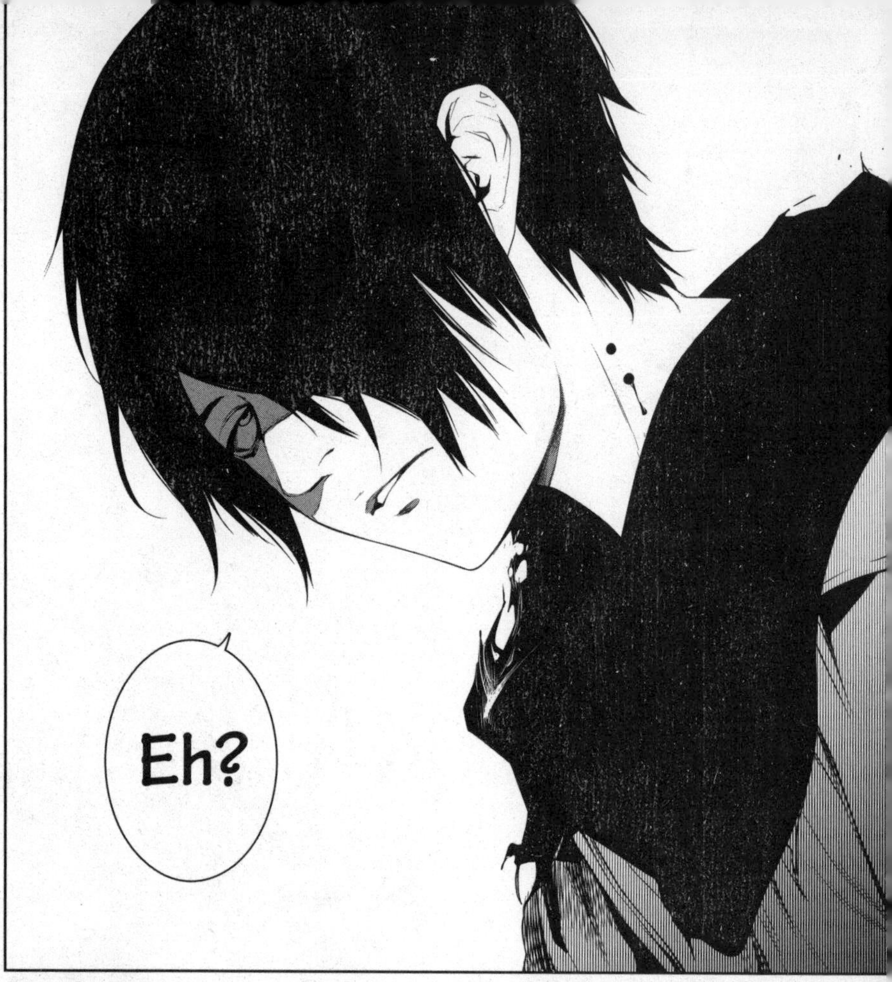
Eh?
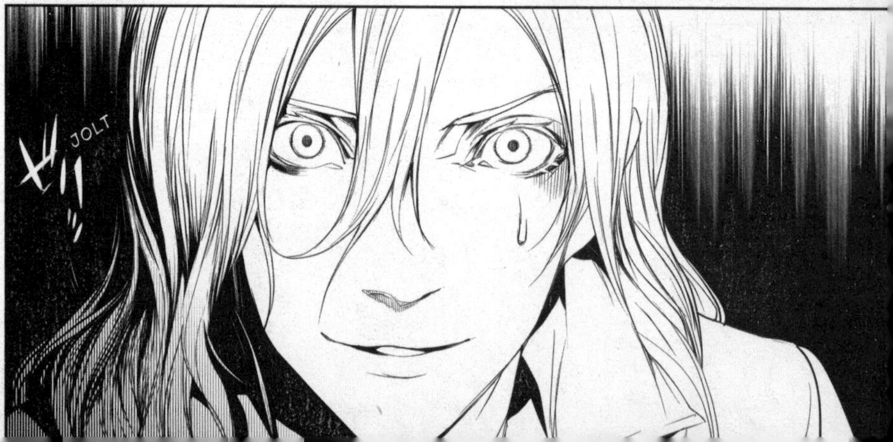
JOLT

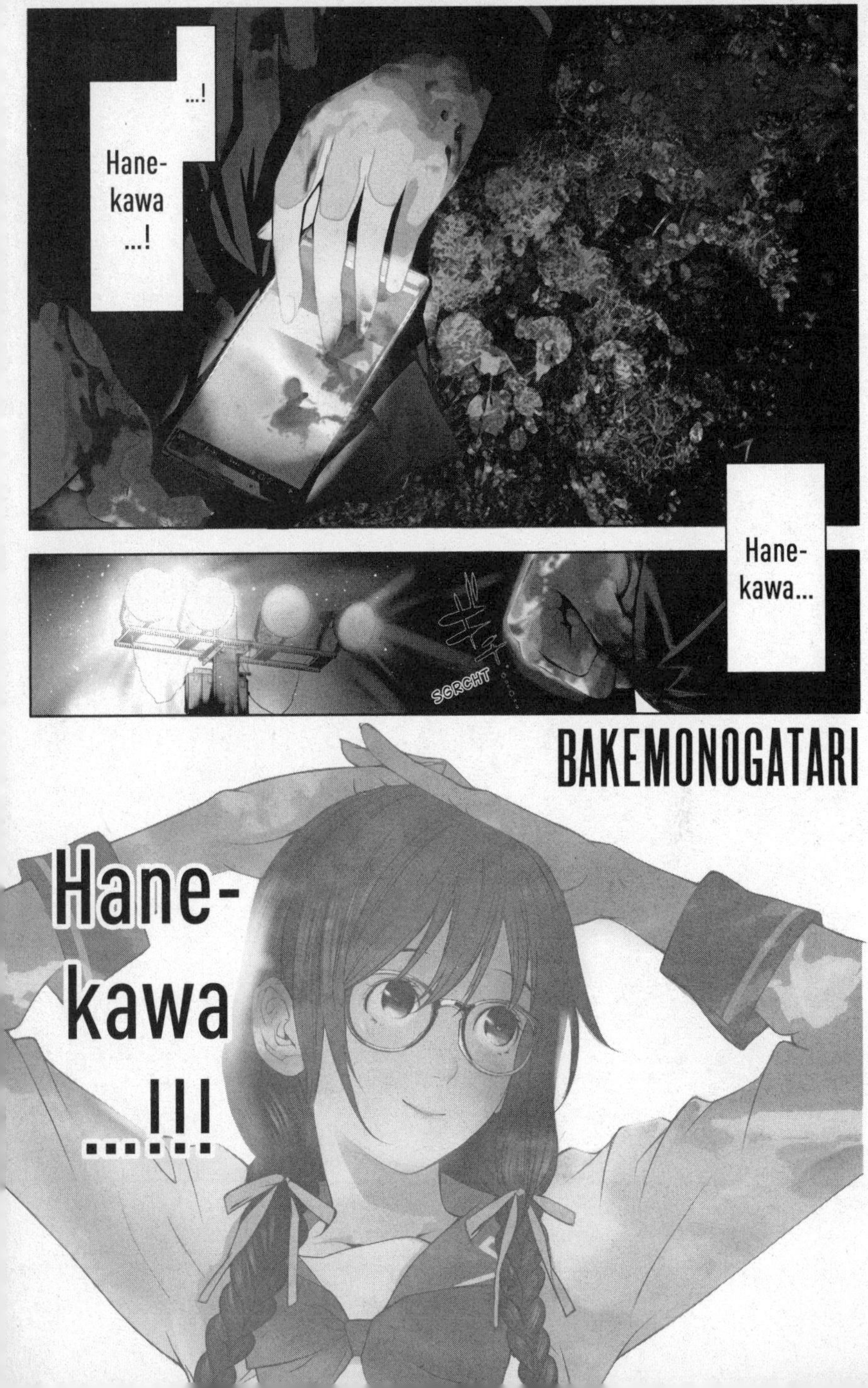
...!
Hane-kawa ...!
Hane-kawa...
SCRCHT
BAKEMONOGATARI
Hane-kawa ...!!!

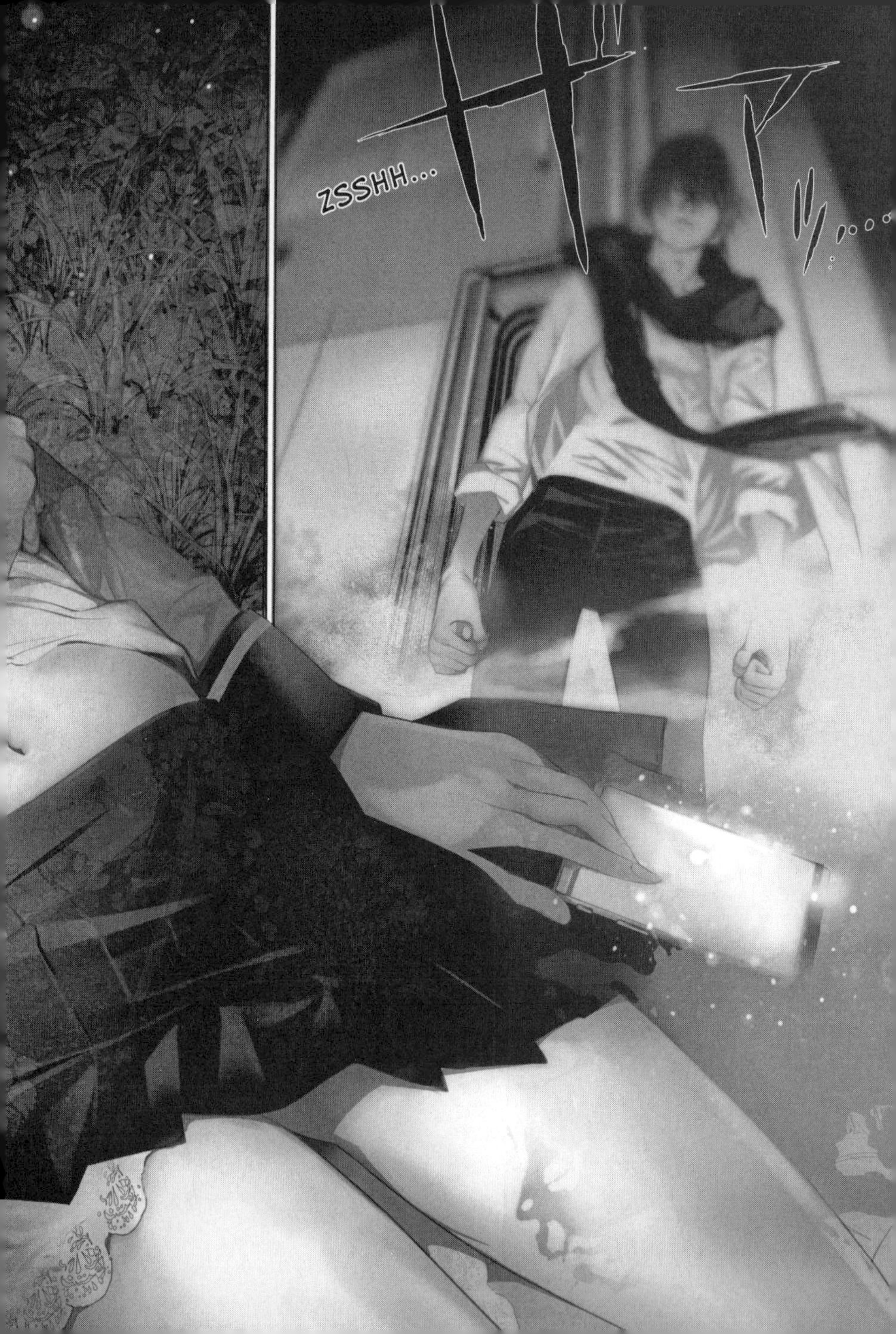
ZSSHH...

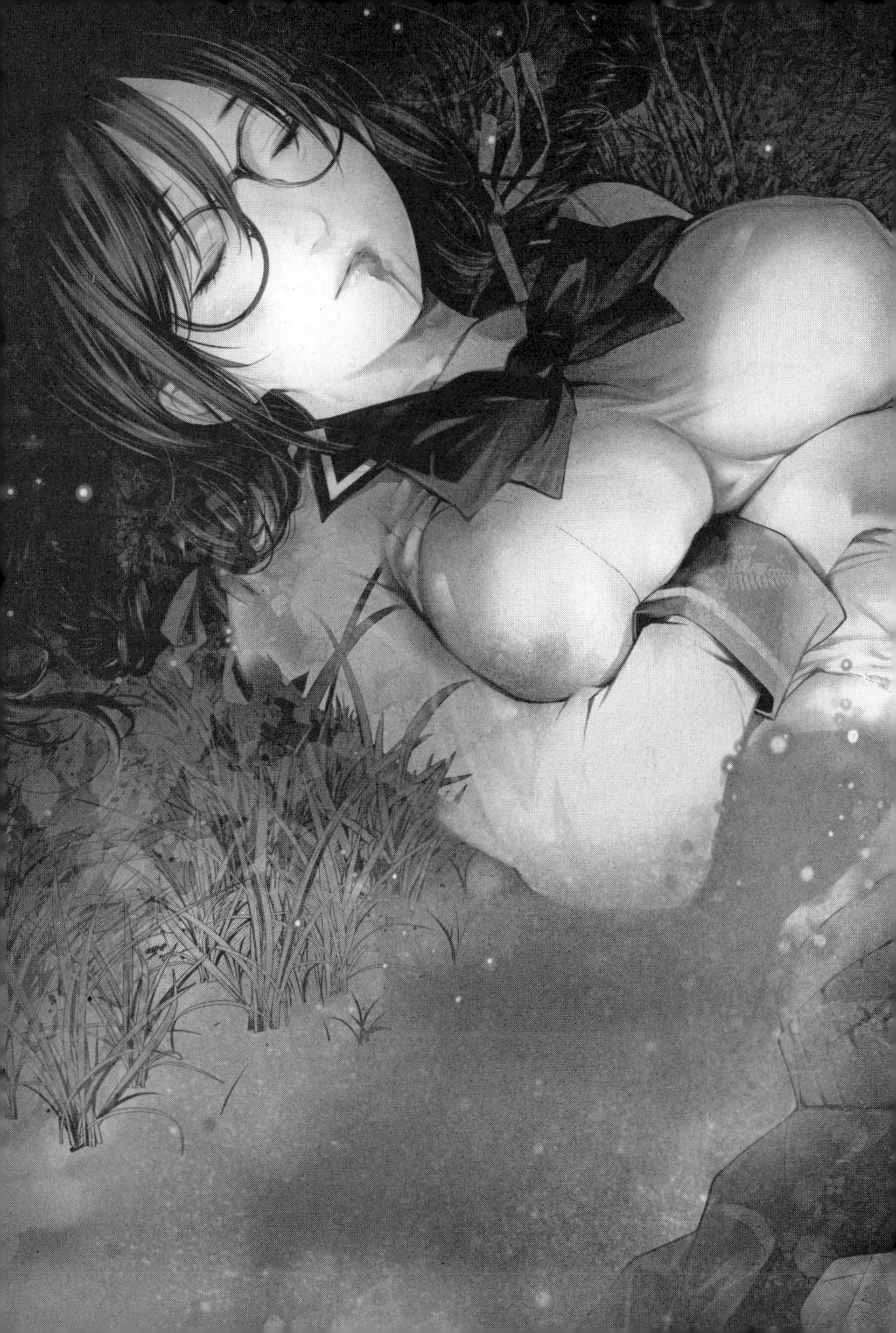

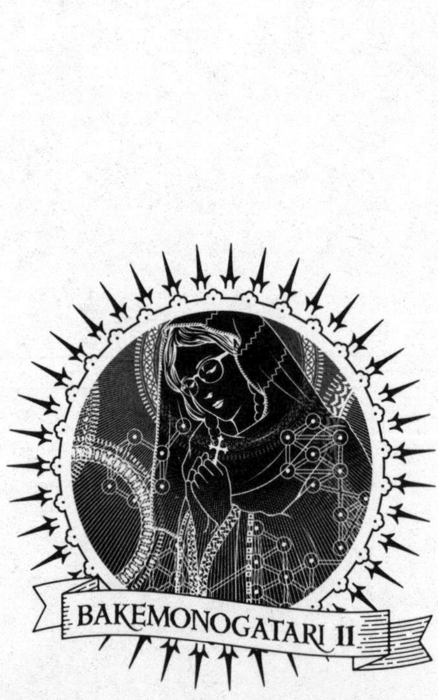
BAKEMONOGATARI II

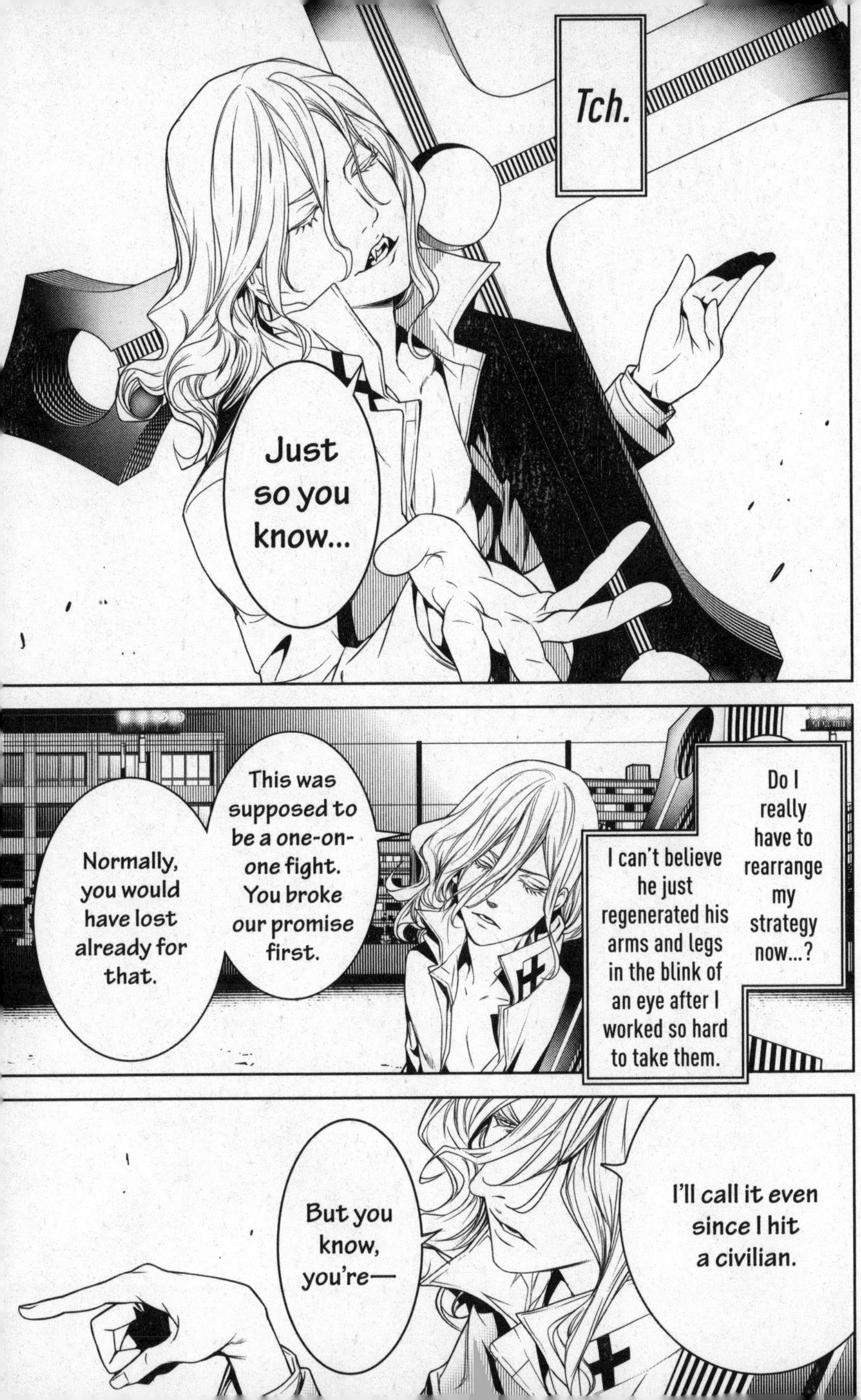
Tch.
Just so you know...
Do I really have to rearrange my strategy now...?
I can't believe he just regenerated his arms and legs in the blink of an eye after I worked so hard to take them.
This was supposed to be a one-on-one fight. You broke our promise first.
Normally, you would have lost already for that.
I'll call it even since I hit a civilian.
But you know, you're—

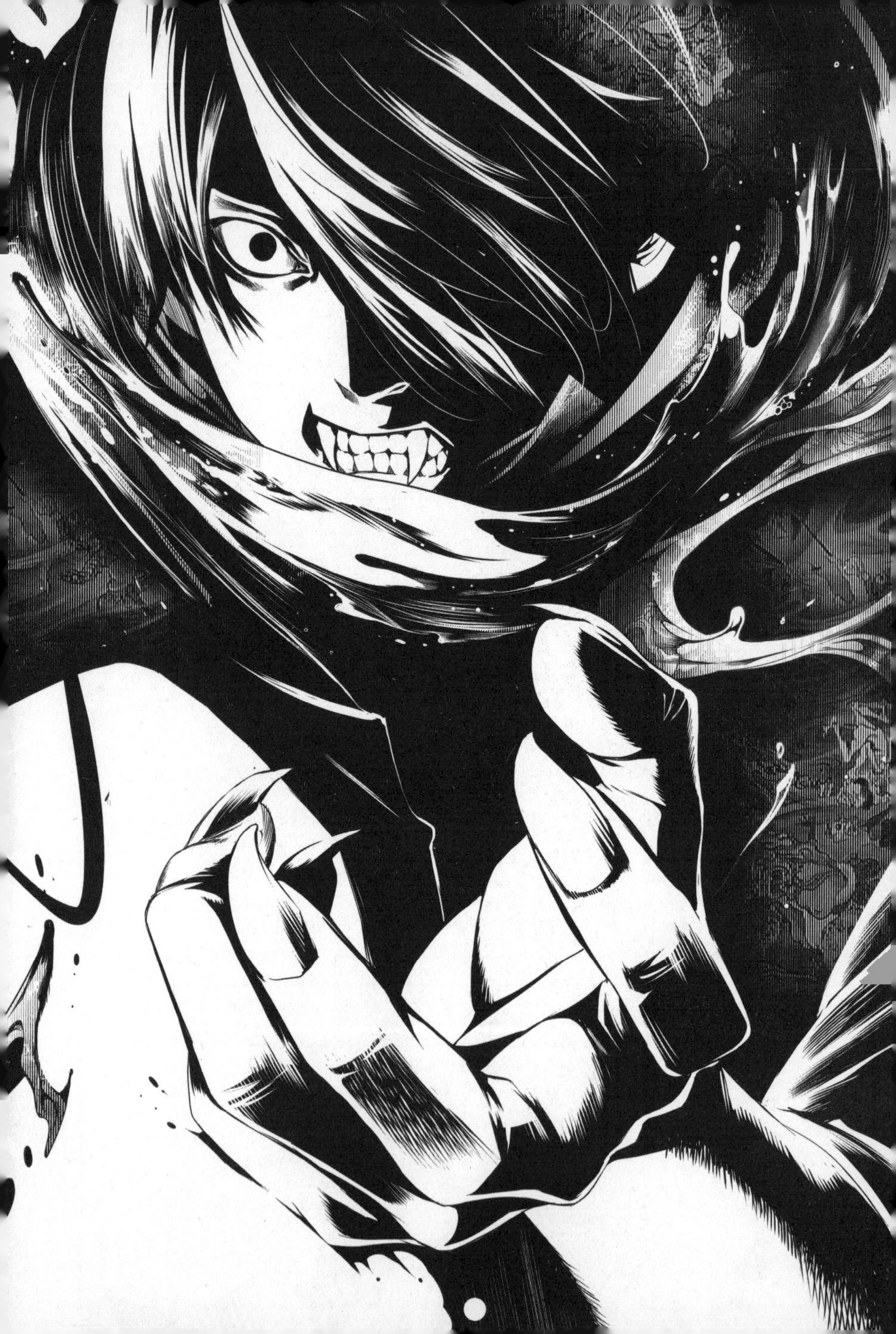

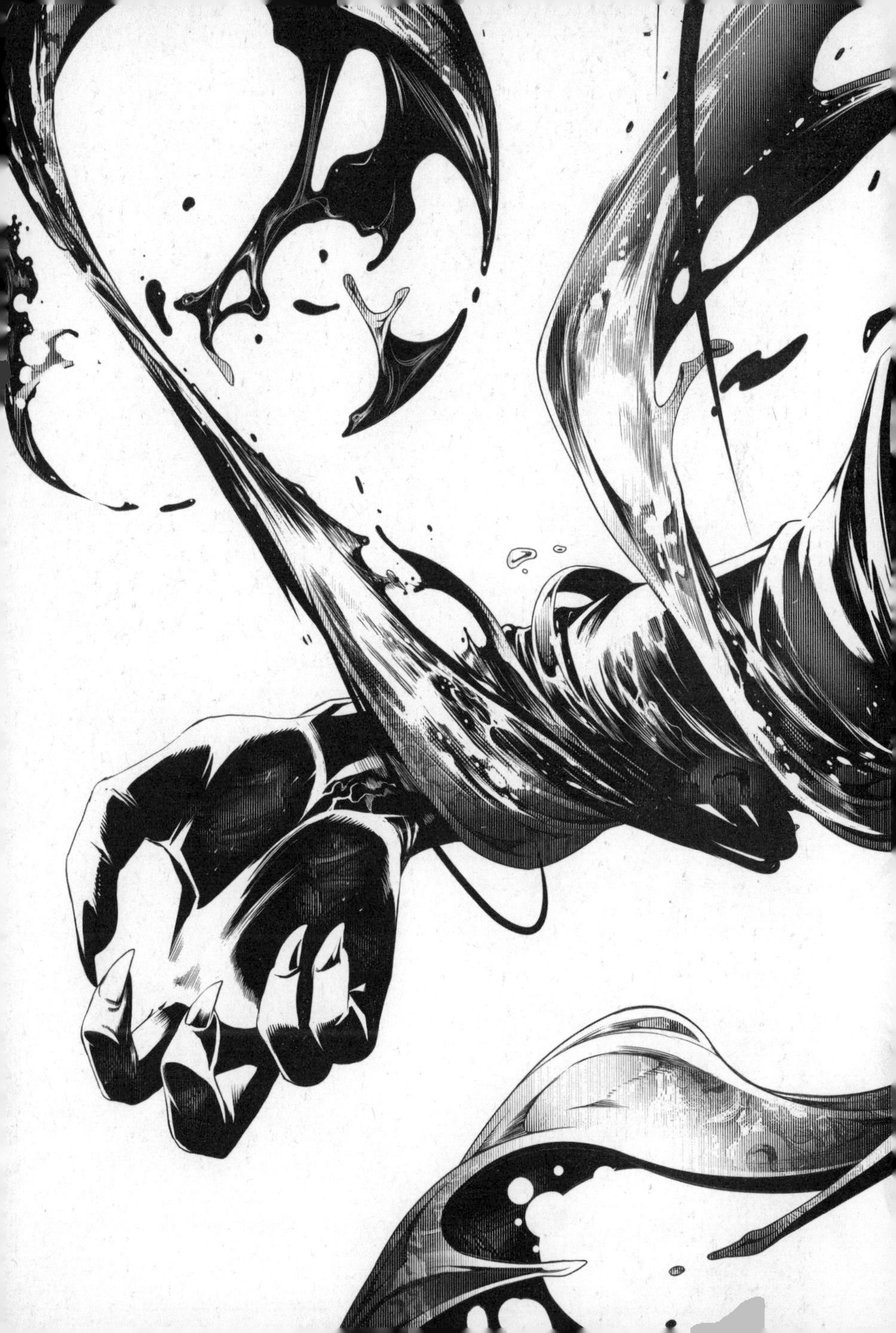

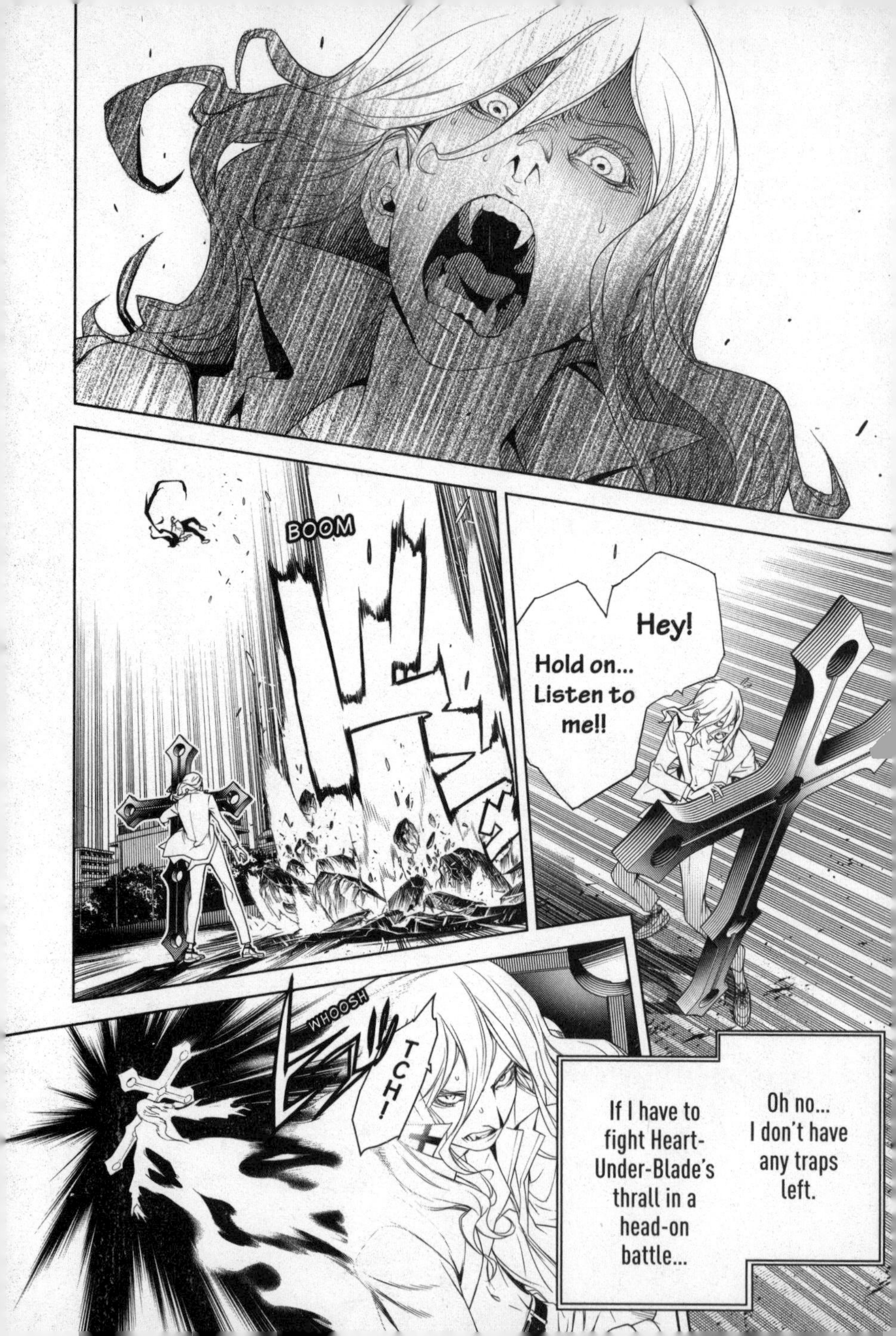
Hey!
Hold on... Listen to me!!
BOOM
Oh no... I don't have any traps left.
If I have to fight Heart-Under-Blade's thrall in a head-on battle...
TCH!
WHOOSH

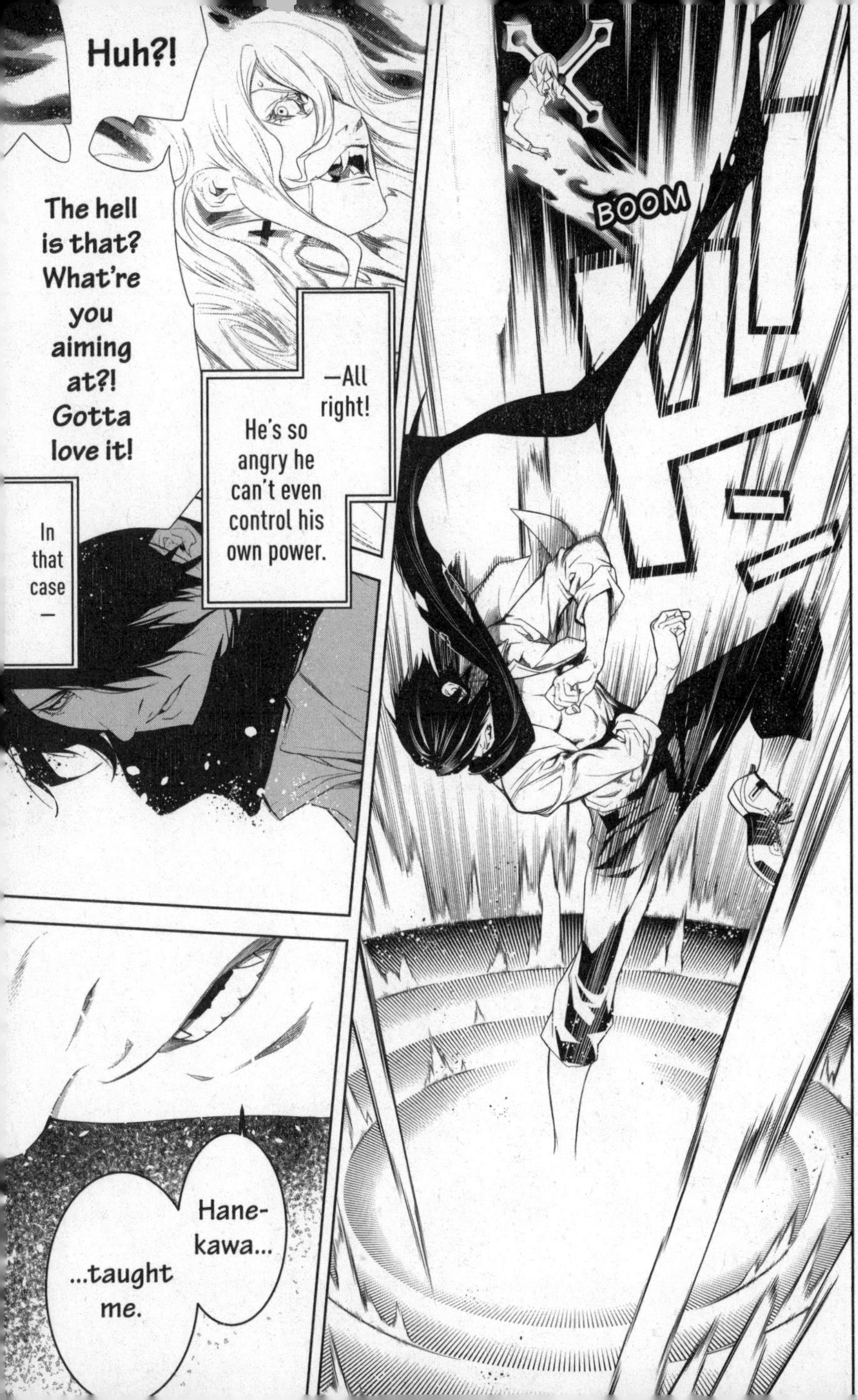
BOOM
Huh?!
The hell is that? What're you aiming at?! Gotta love it!
—All right!
He's so angry he can't even control his own power.
In that case—
Hane-kawa...
...taught me.

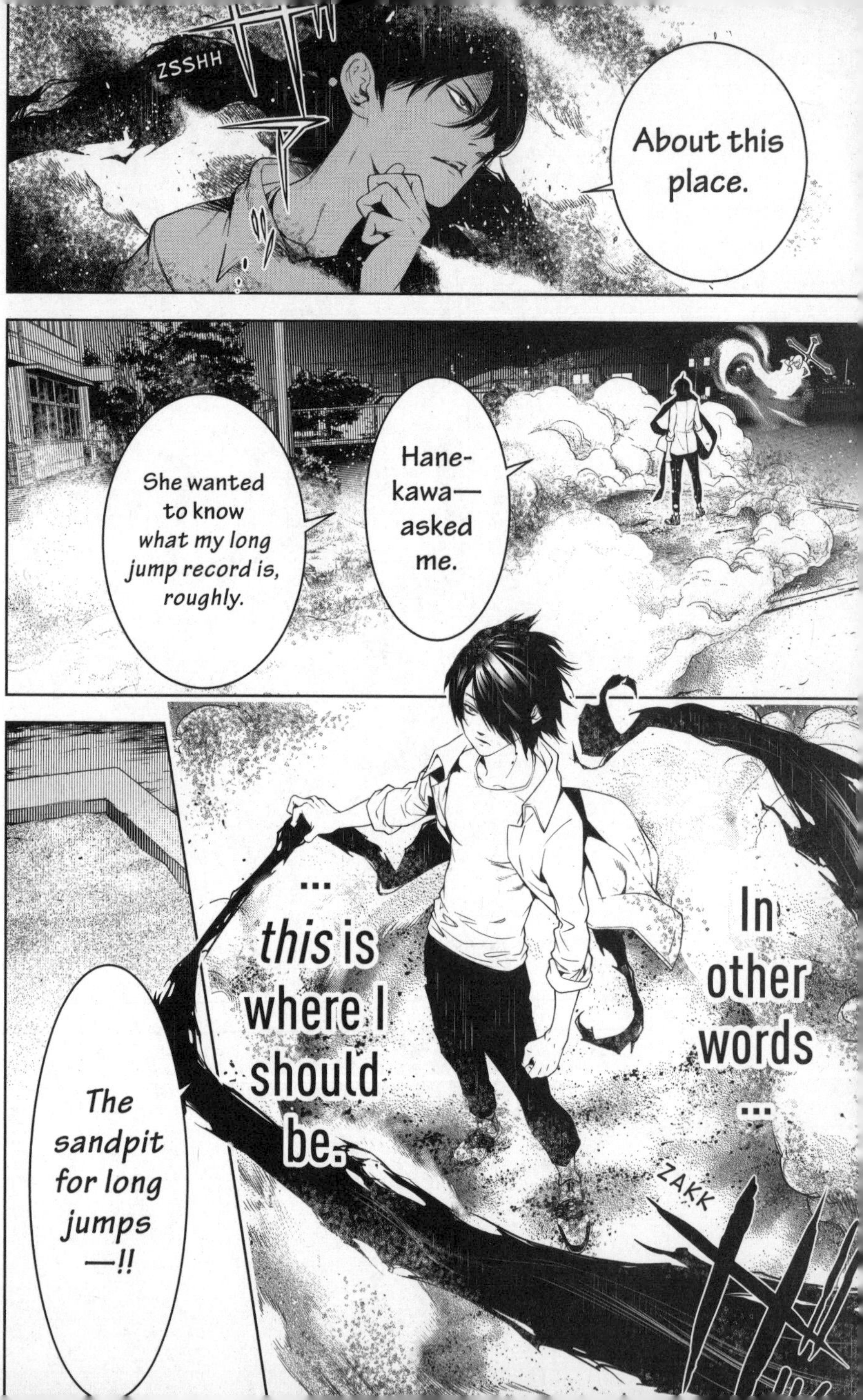
ZSSHH
About this place.
Hane-kawa—asked me.
She wanted to know what my long jump record is, roughly.
In other words ...
ZAKK
... *this* is where I should be.
The sandpit for long jumps—!!

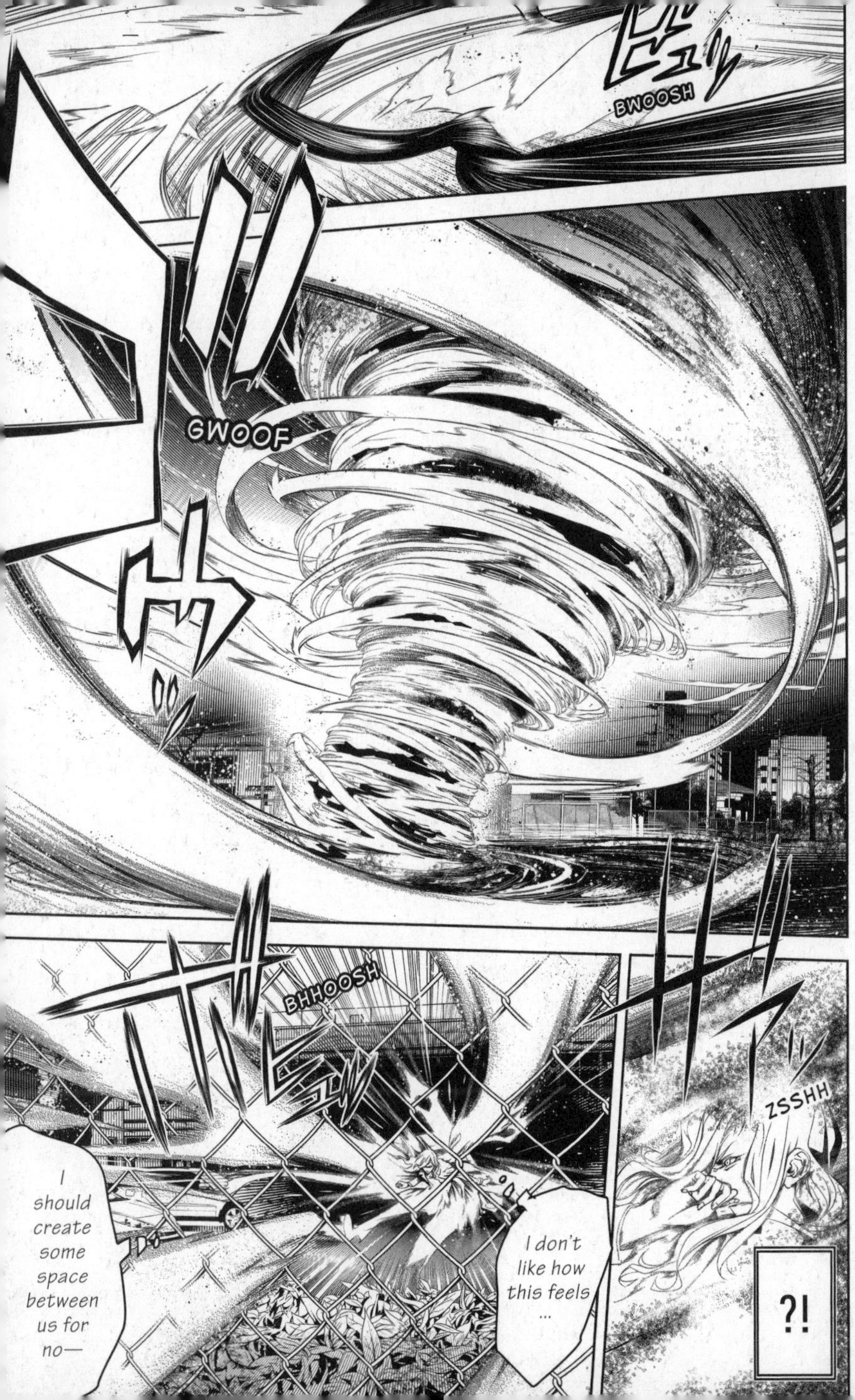
BWOOSH
GWOOF
ZSSHH
BHHOOSH
?!
I don't like how this feels ...
I should create some space between us for no—

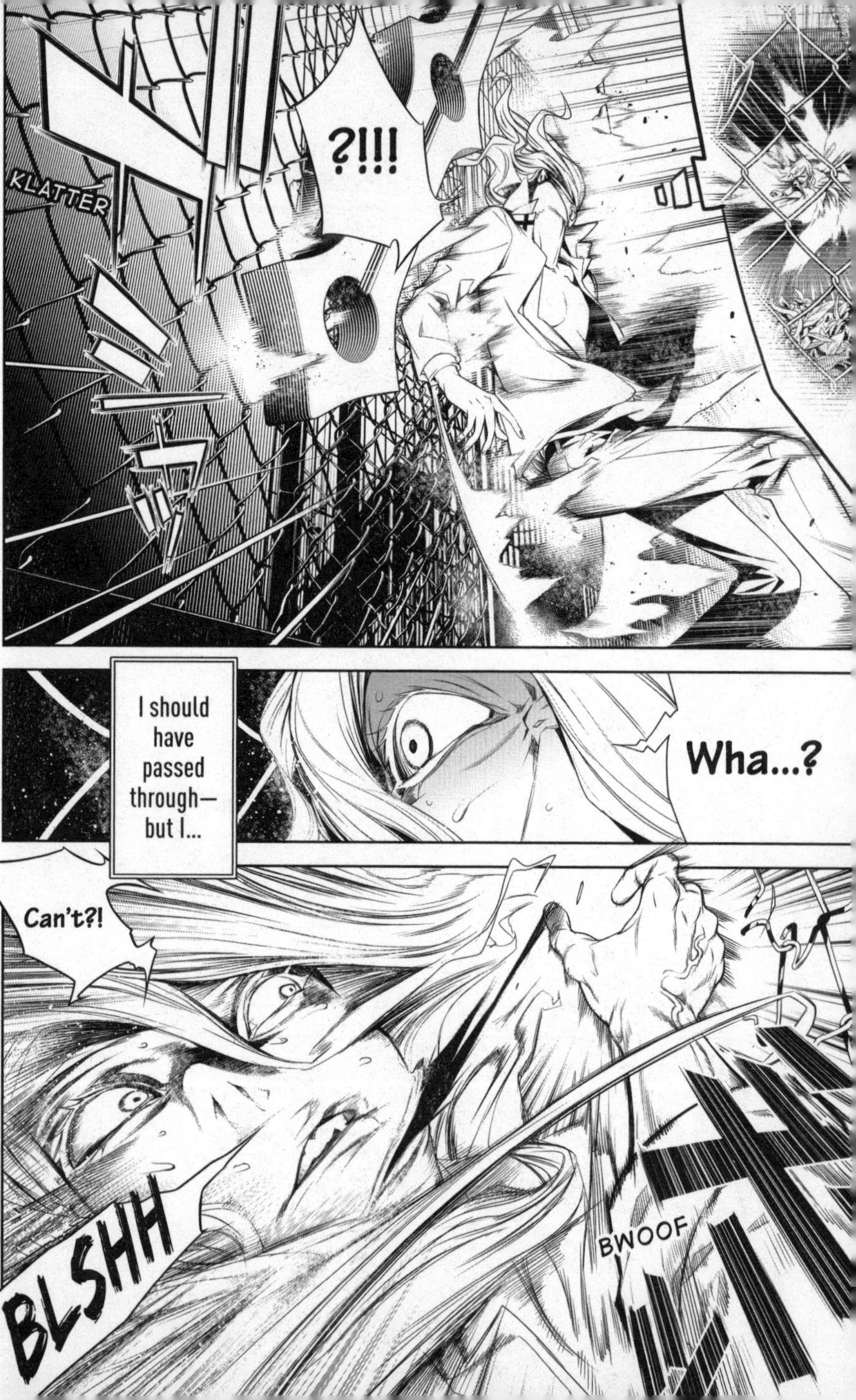
?!!!
KLATTER
Wha...?
I should have passed through—but I...
Can't?!
BWOOF
BLSHH

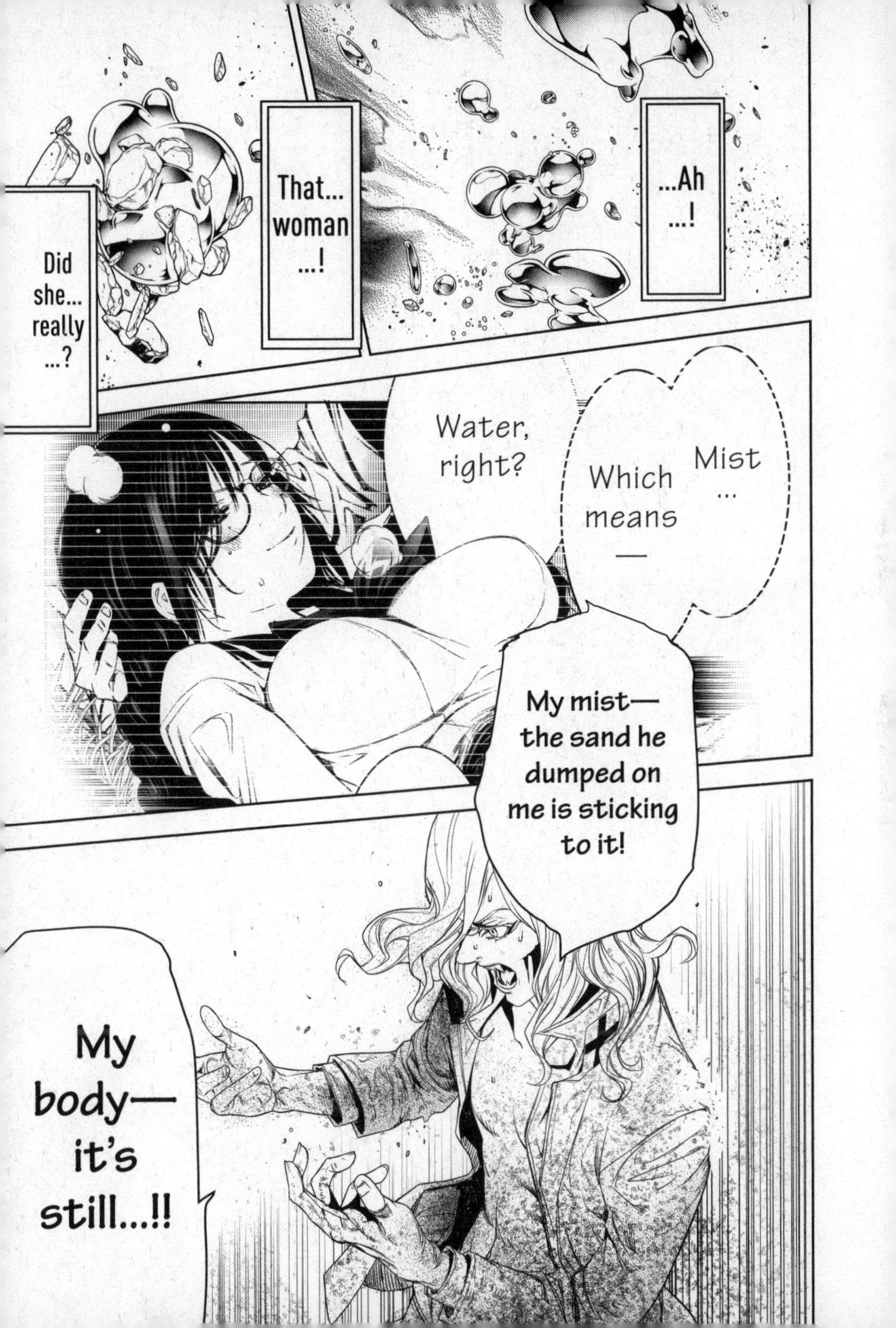
...Ah ...!
That... woman ...!
Did she... really ...?
Mist ...
Which means —
Water, right?
My mist— the sand he dumped on me is sticking to it!
My body— it's still...!!

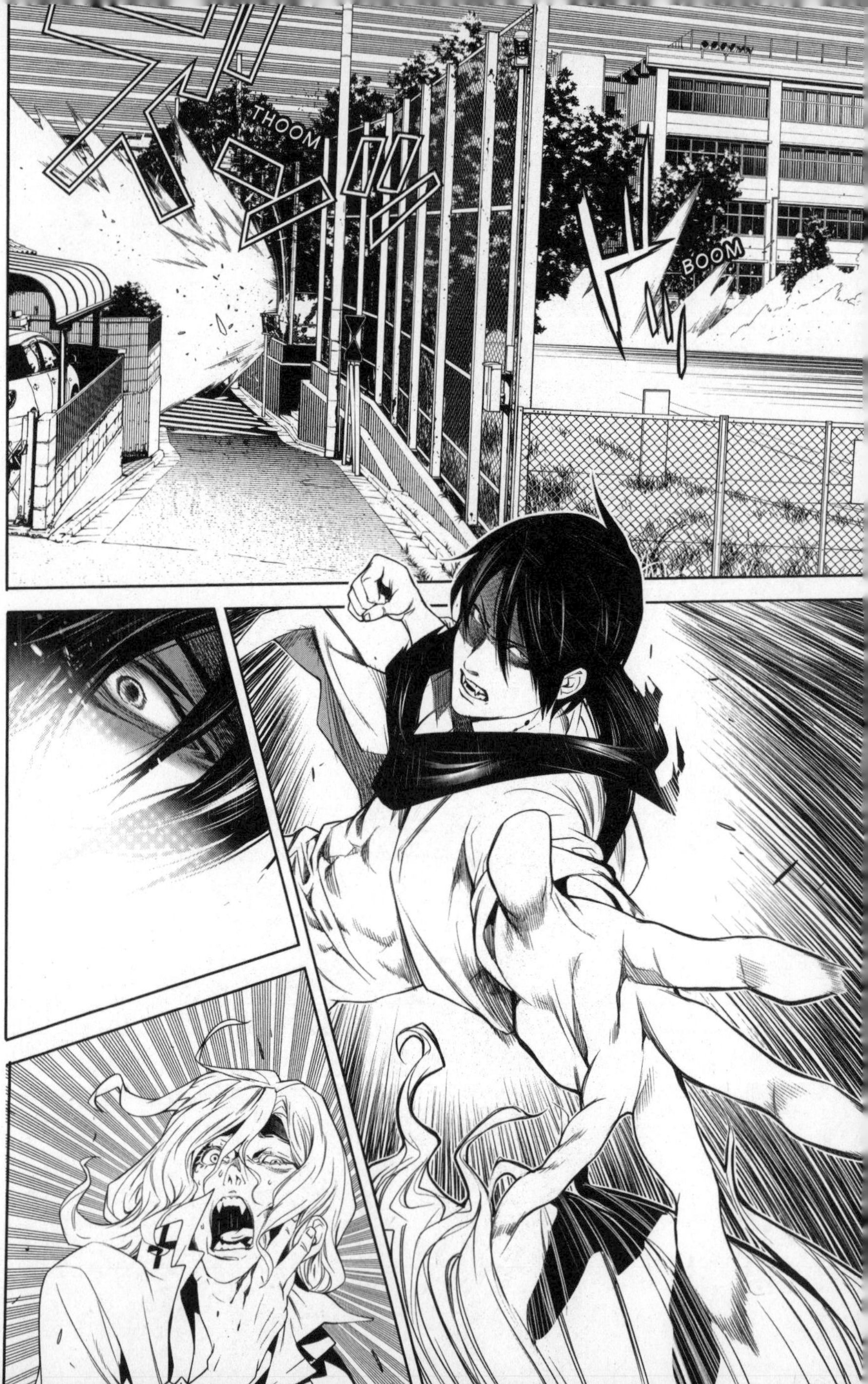
BOOM
THOOM

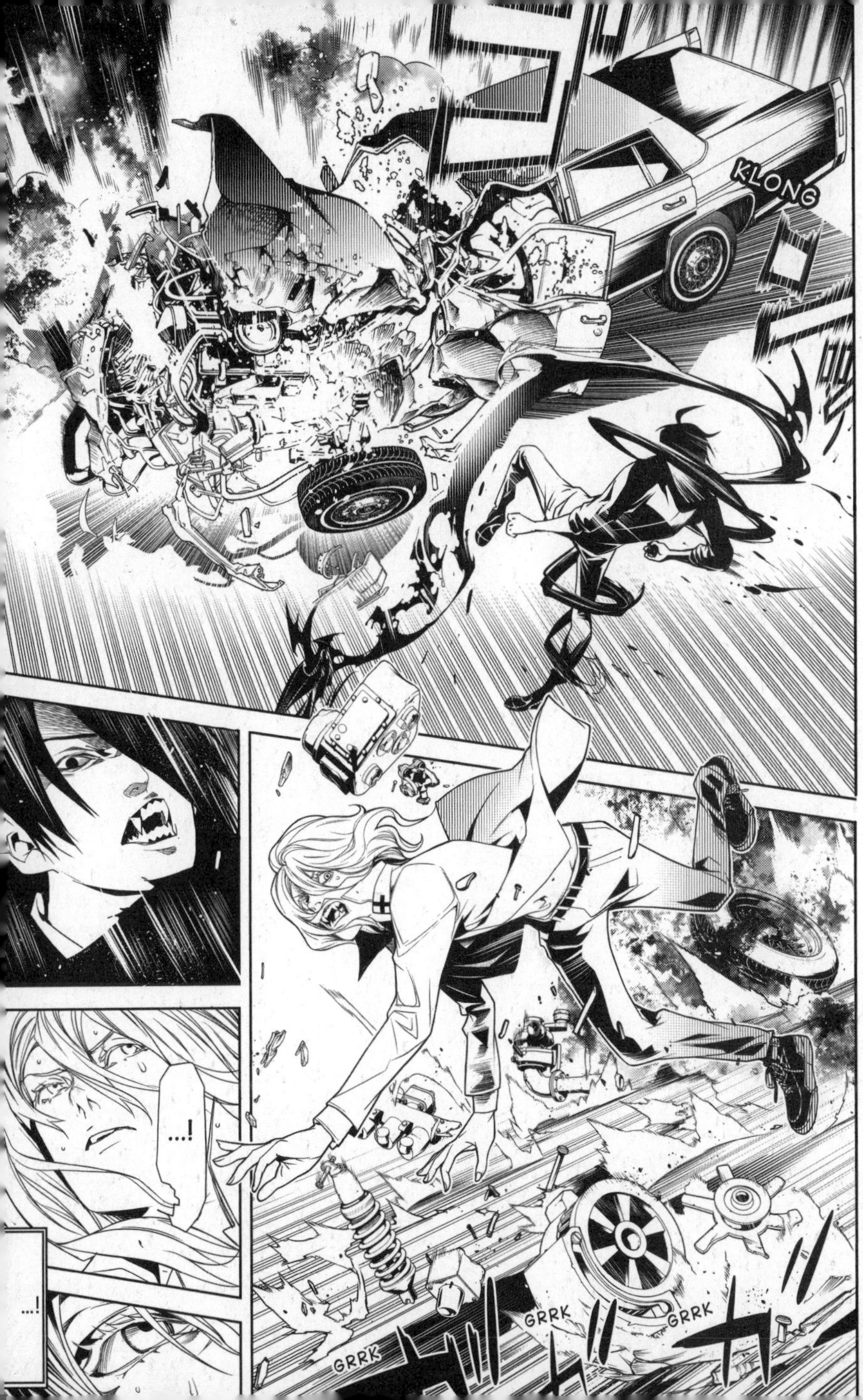
KLONG
GRRK
GRRK
GRRK
...!
...!

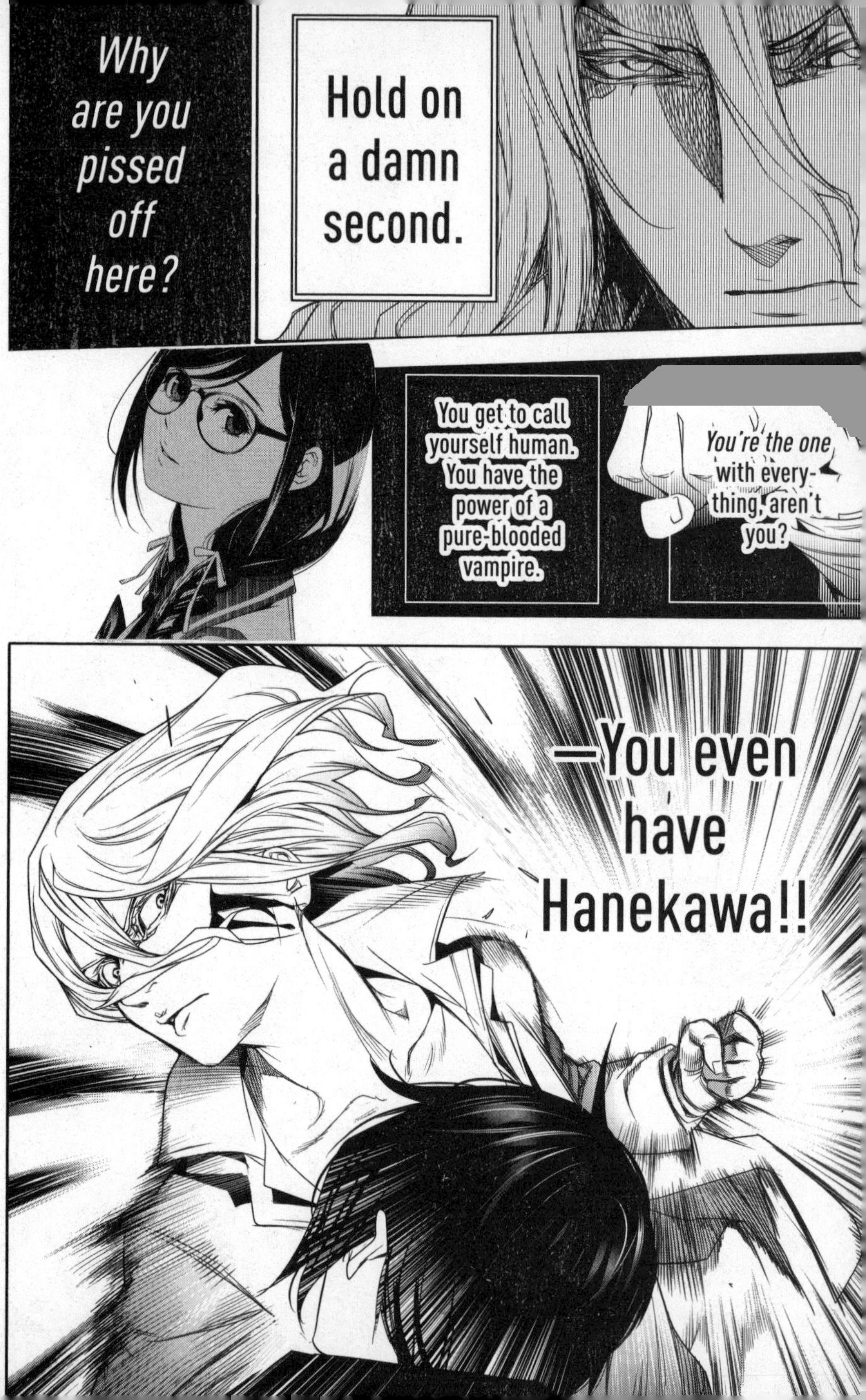
Hold on a damn second.
Why are you pissed off here?
You're the one with every-thing, aren't you?
You get to call yourself human. You have the power of a pure-blooded vampire.
—You even have Hanekawa!!

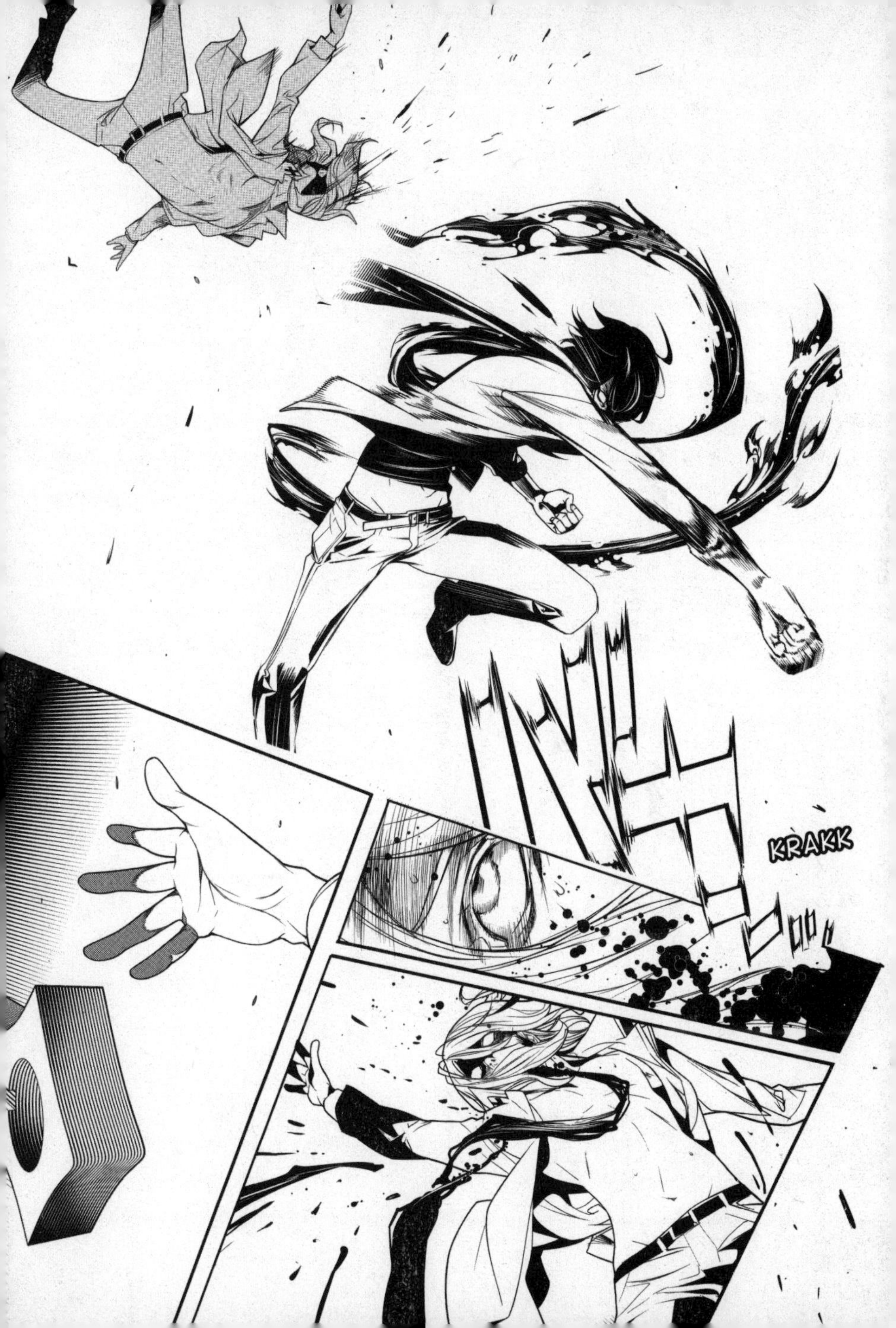
KRAKK

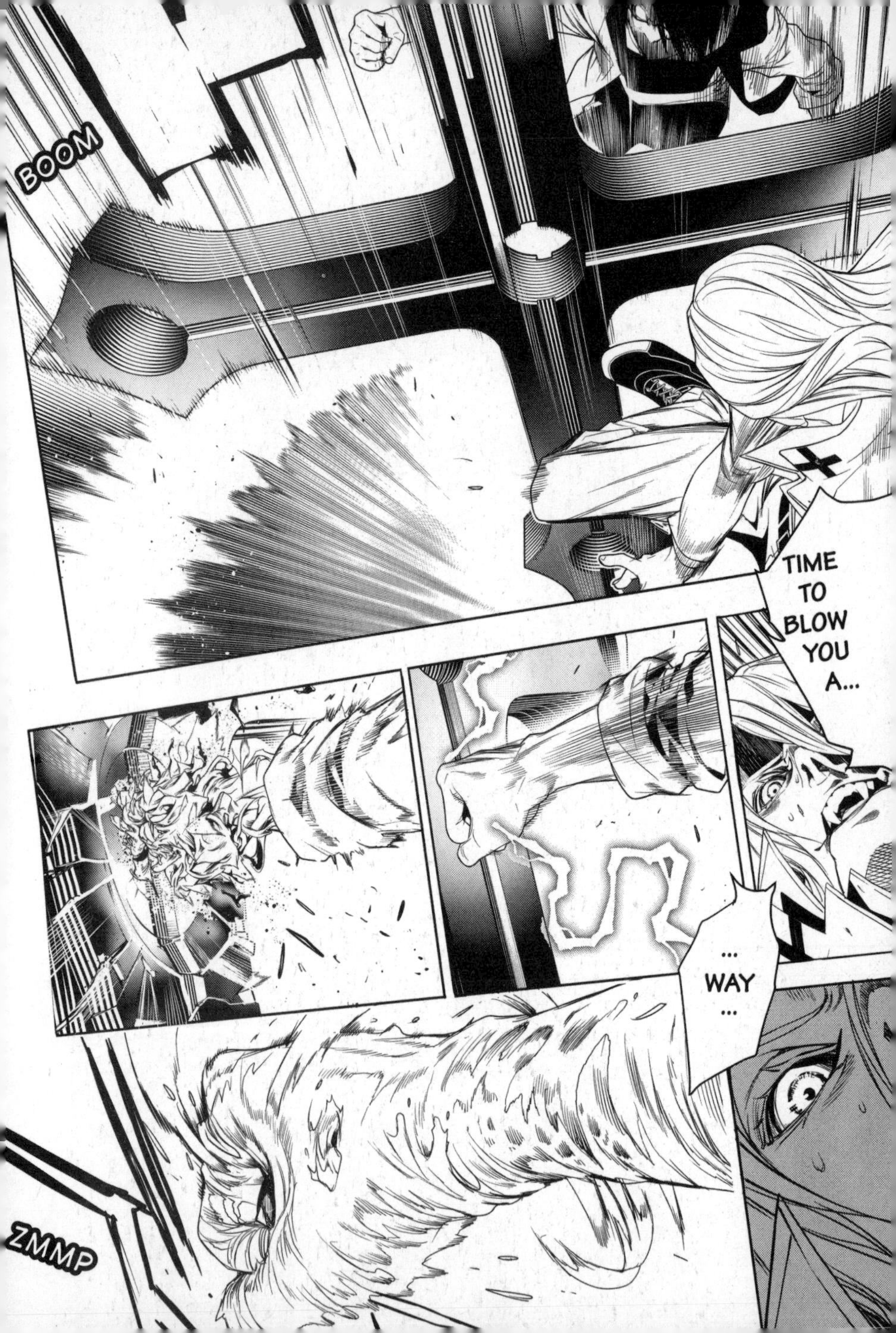
BOOM
TIME TO BLOW YOU A...
... WAY ...
ZMMP

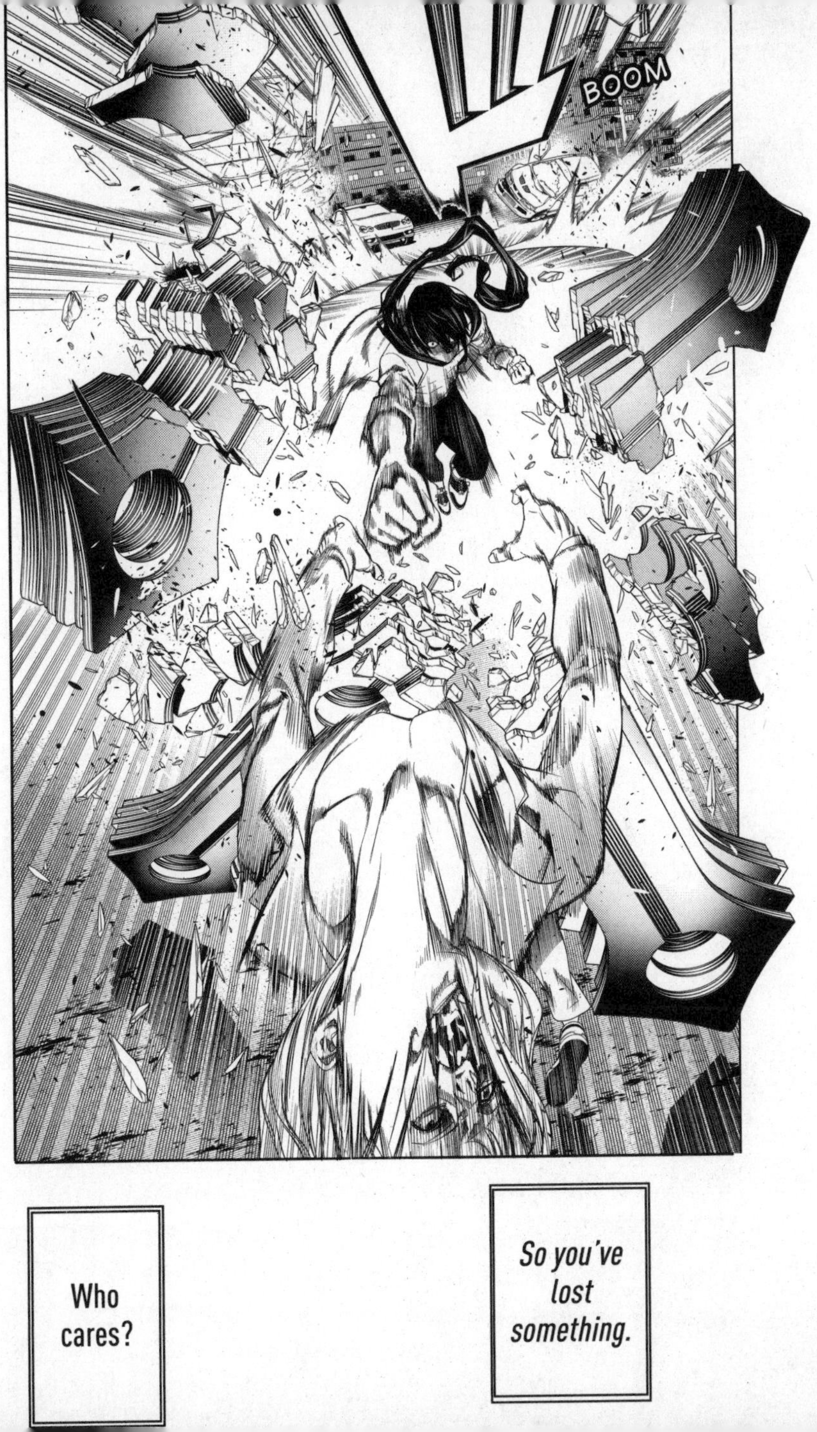
BOOM

So you've lost something.

Who cares?

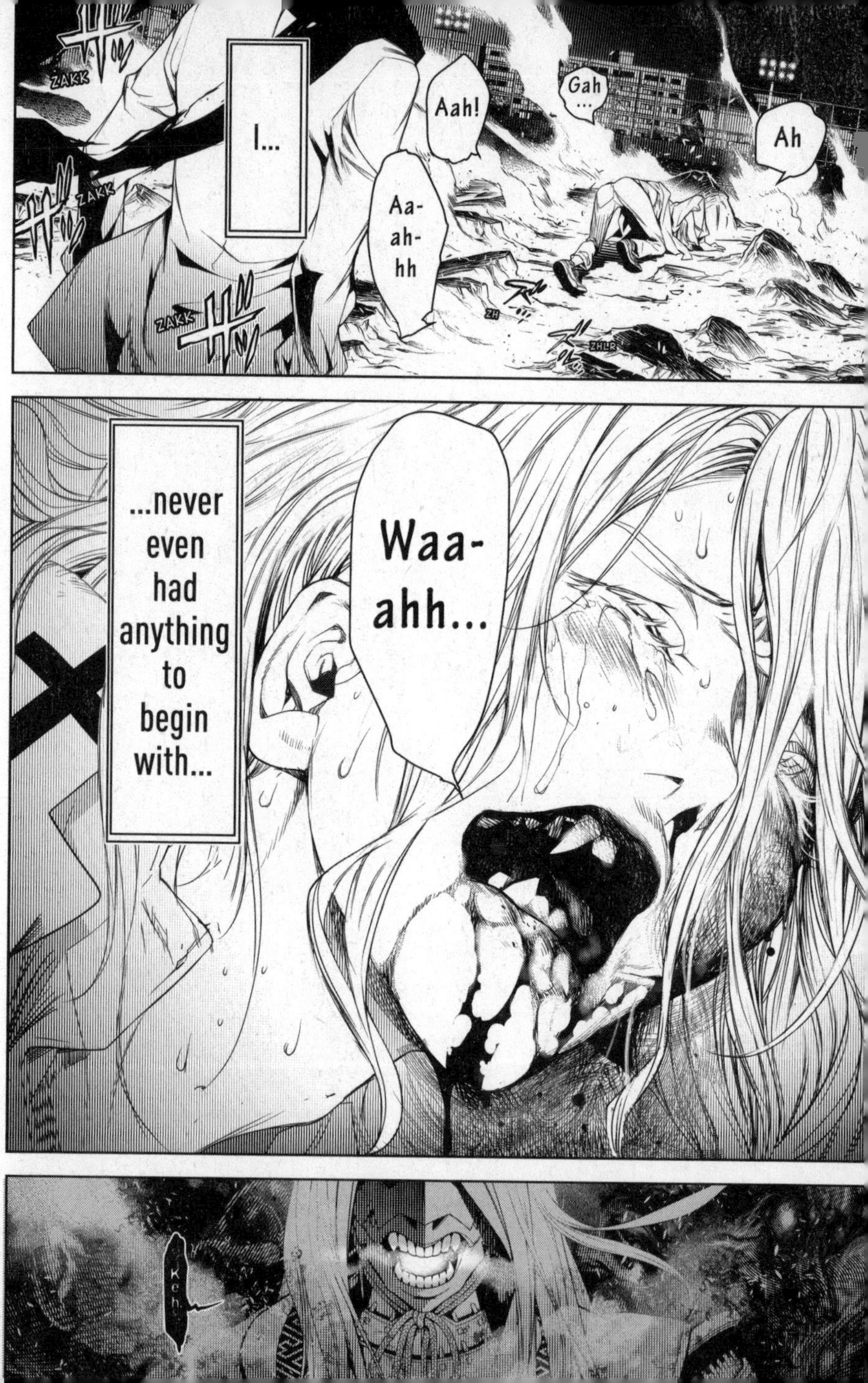

Ah
Gah ...
Aah!
I...
Aa-ah-hh
ZAKK
ZAKK
ZHLR
ZH
ZAKK
Waa-ahh...
...never even had anything to begin with...
Keh

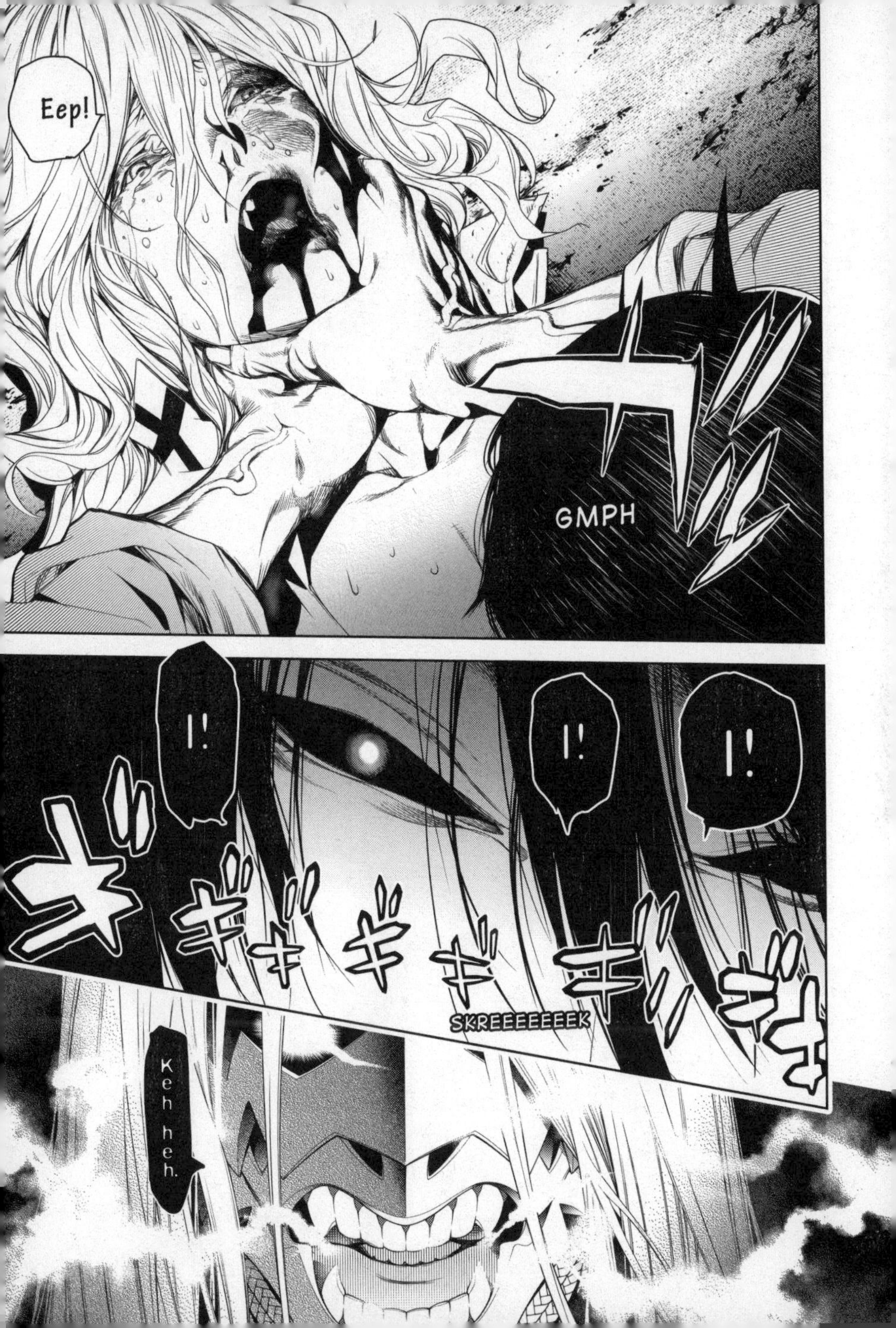
Eep!
GMPH
!!
!!
!!
SKREEEEEEEK
Keh heh.

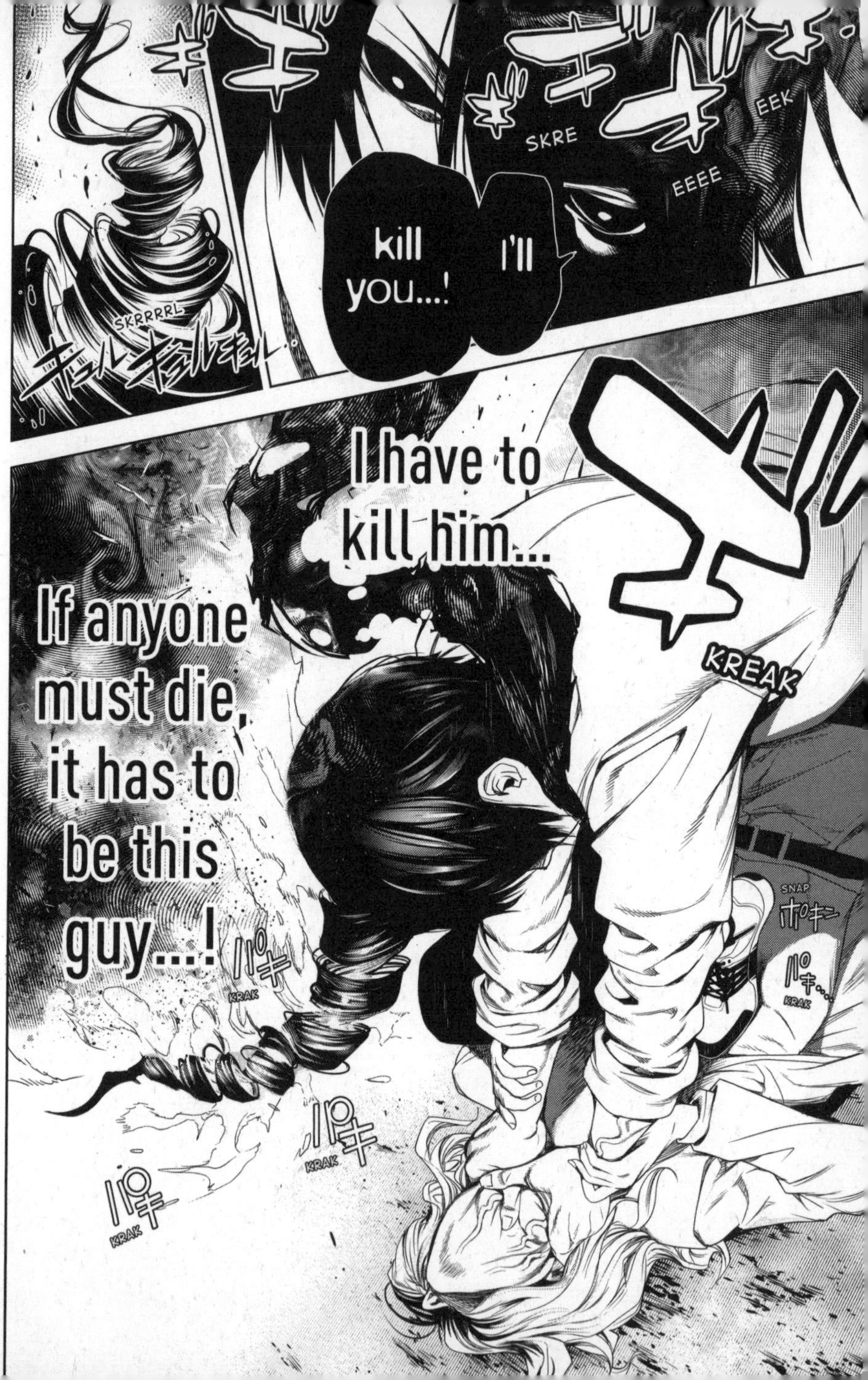

SKRE
EEEE
EEK
I'll
kill you...!
SKRRRRL
I have to kill him...
KREAK
SNAP
ポキン
パキ...
KRAK
If anyone must die, it has to be this guy...!
パキ
KRAK
パキ
KRAK
パキ
KRAK

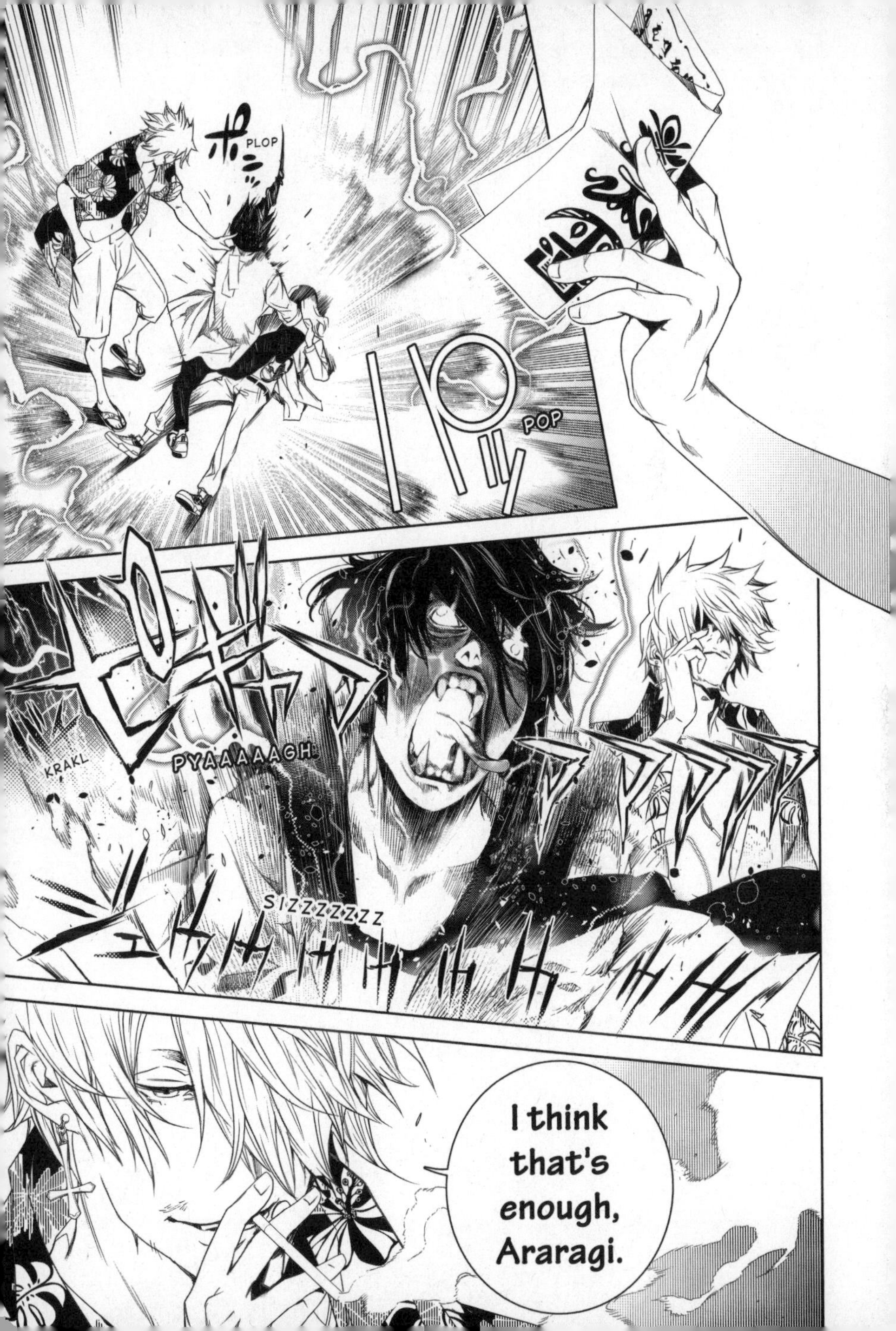
PLOP
POP
PYAAAAAGH
KRAKL
SIZZZZZZZ
I think that's enough, Araragi.

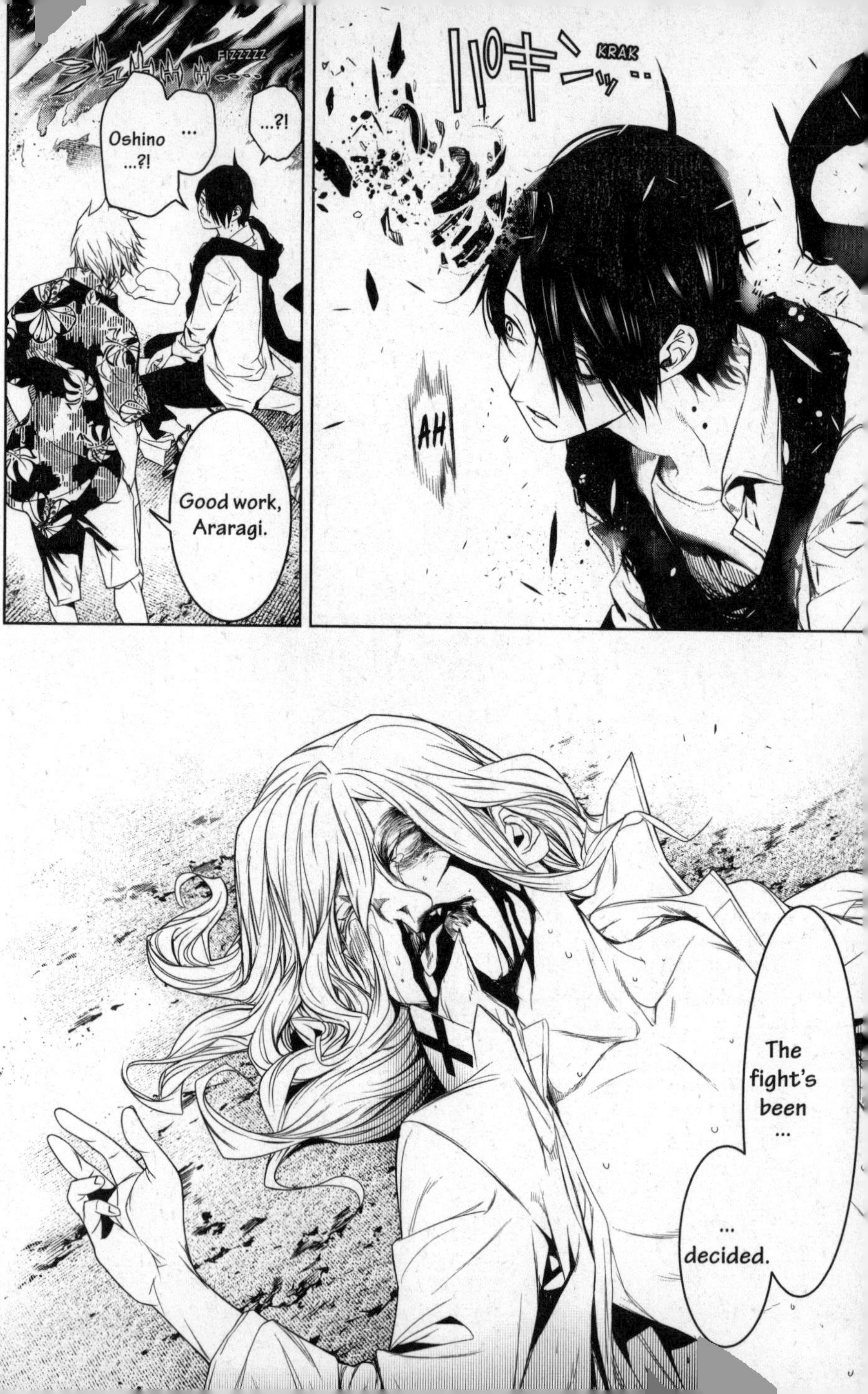
KRAK
AH
FIZZZZZ
...?!
...
Oshino ...?!
Good work, Araragi.
The fight's been ...
... decided.

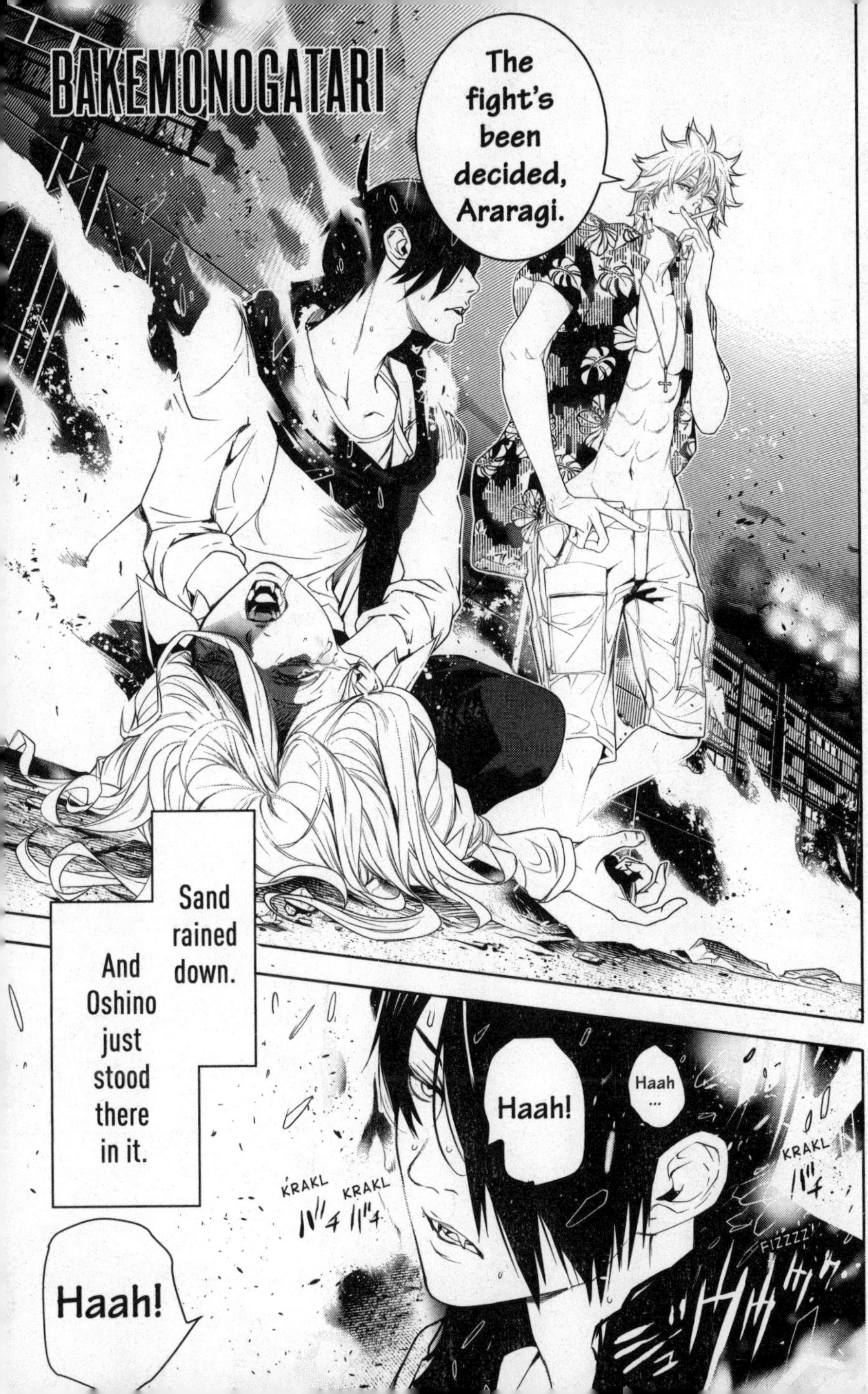
BAKEMONOGATARI
The fight's been decided, Araragi.
Sand rained down.
And Oshino just stood there in it.
KRAKL
Haah ...
Haah!
FIZZZZ
KRAKL
KRAKL
Haah!

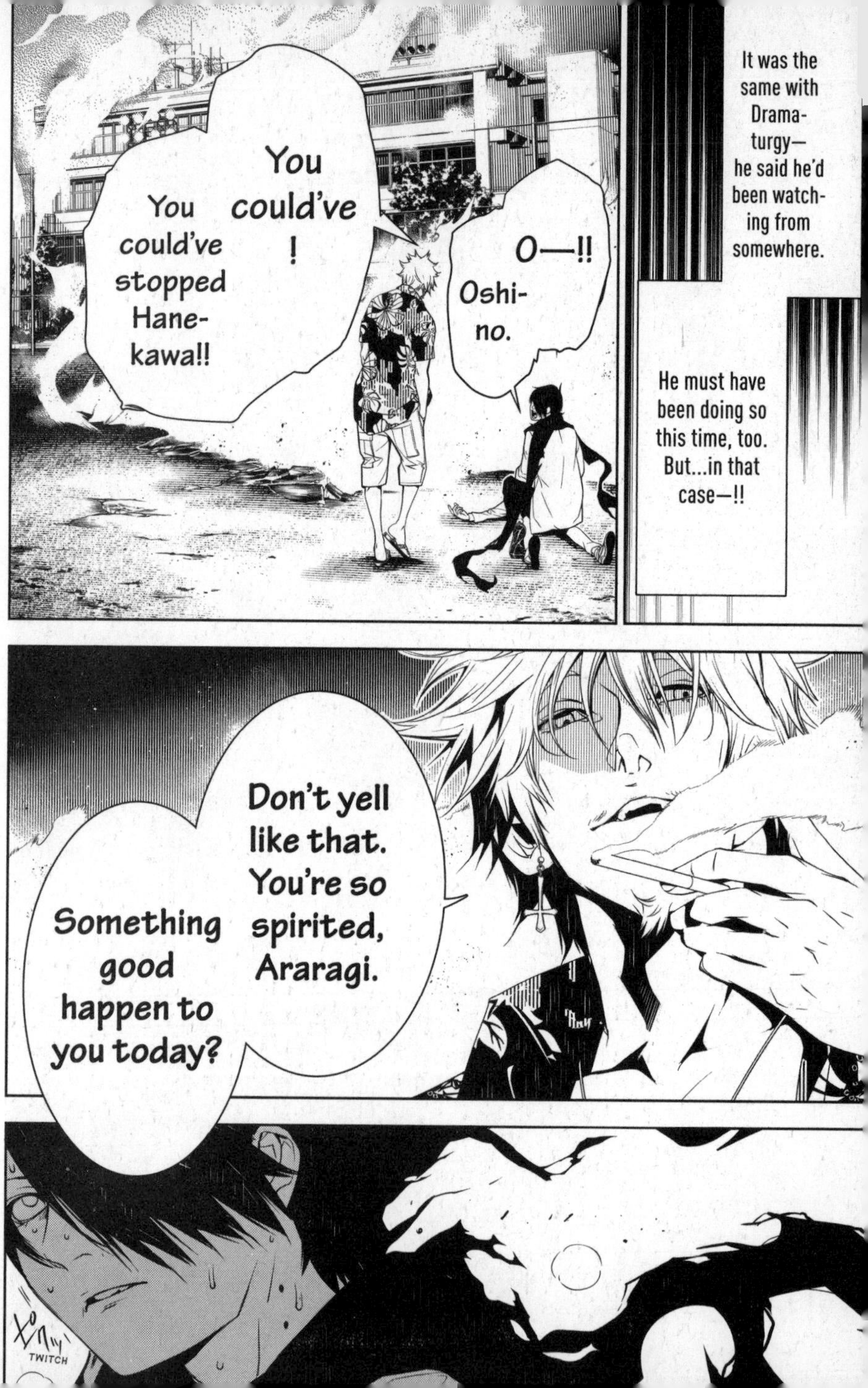
It was the same with Dramaturgy—he said he'd been watching from somewhere.
He must have been doing so this time, too. But...in that case—!!
O—!! Oshino.
You could've!
You could've stopped Hanekawa!!
Don't yell like that. You're so spirited, Araragi.
Something good happen to you today?
TWITCH

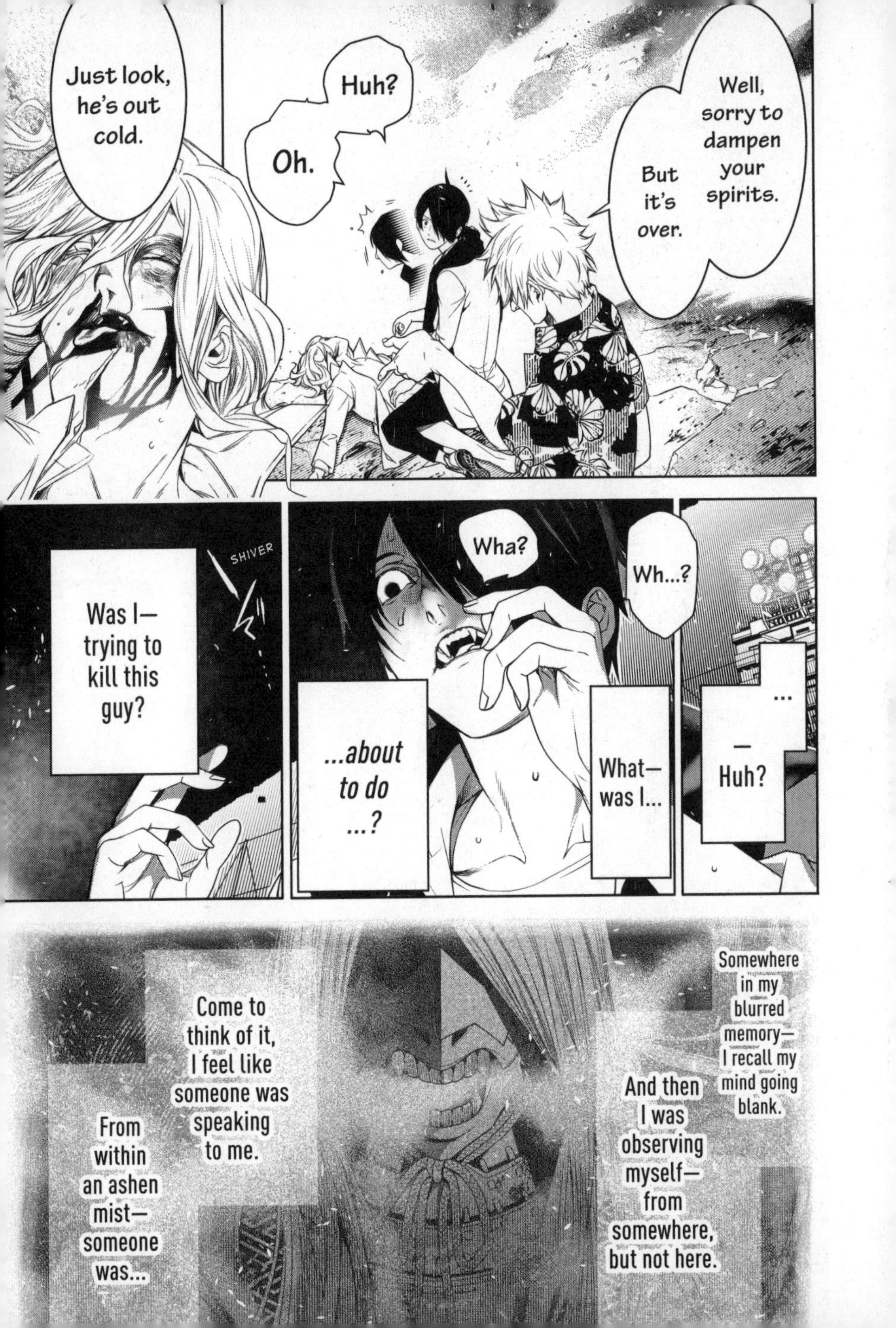
Well, sorry to dampen your spirits.
But it's over.
Huh?
Oh.
Just look, he's out cold.
... — Huh?
Wh...?
Wha?
What— was I...
...about to do ...?
SHIVER
Was I— trying to kill this guy?
Somewhere in my blurred memory— I recall my mind going blank.
And then I was observing myself— from somewhere, but not here.
Come to think of it, I feel like someone was speaking to me.
From within an ashen mist— someone was...

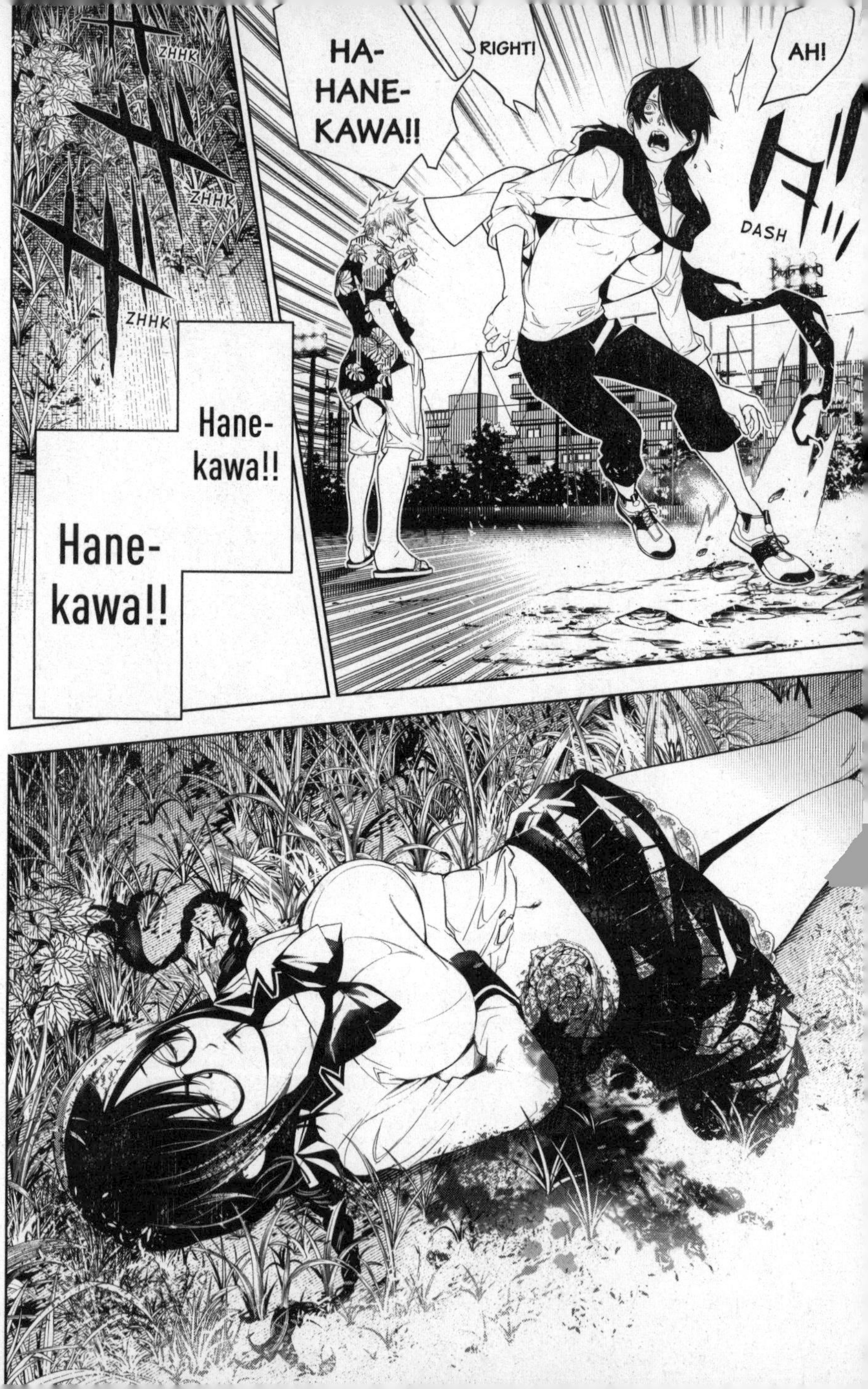
AH!
RIGHT!
HA-HANE-KAWA!!
DASH
ZHHK
ZHHK
ZHHK
Hane-kawa!!
Hane-kawa!!

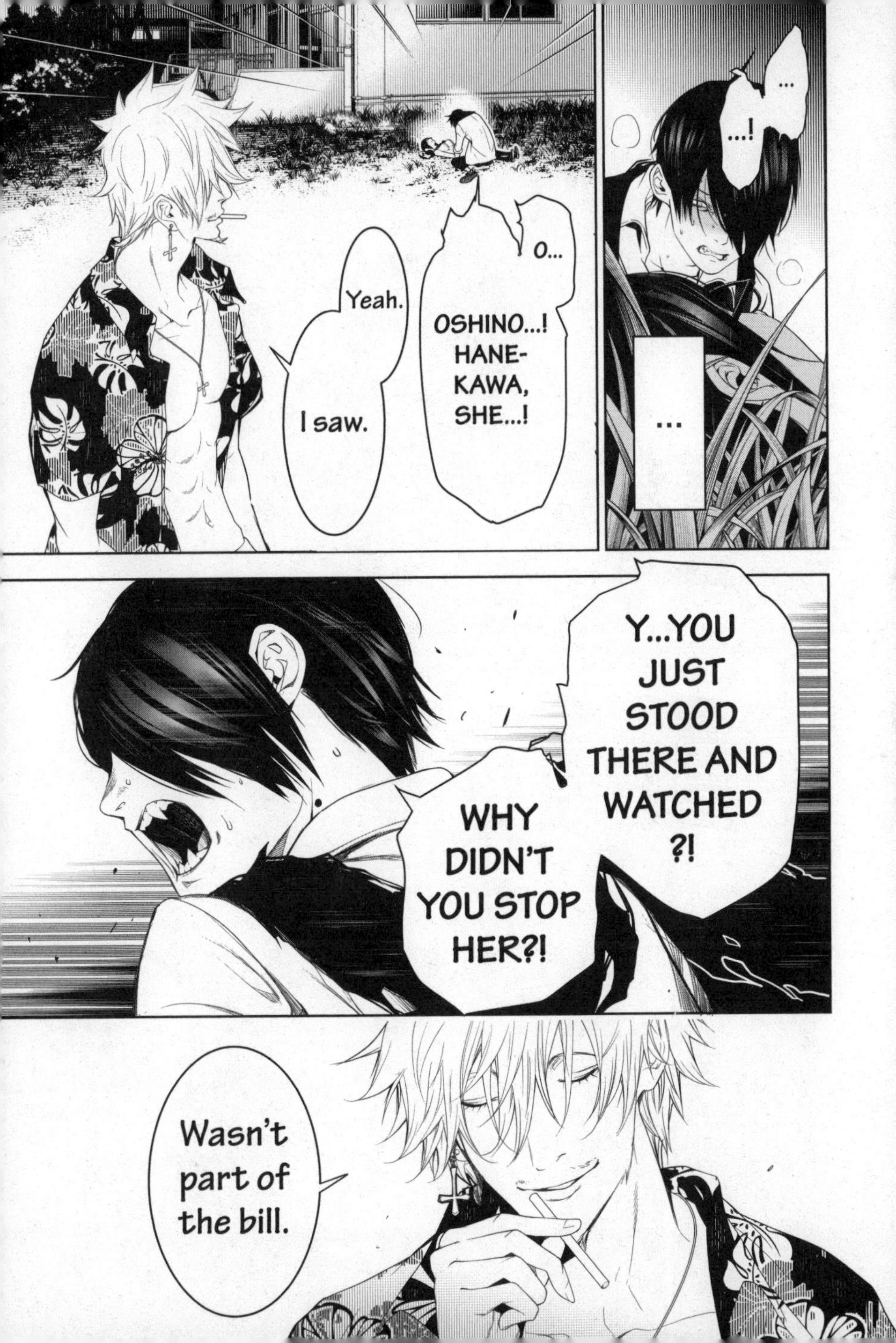
...
...!
...
O... OSHINO...! HANE-KAWA, SHE...!
Yeah. I saw.
Y...YOU JUST STOOD THERE AND WATCHED?!
WHY DIDN'T YOU STOP HER?!
Wasn't part of the bill.

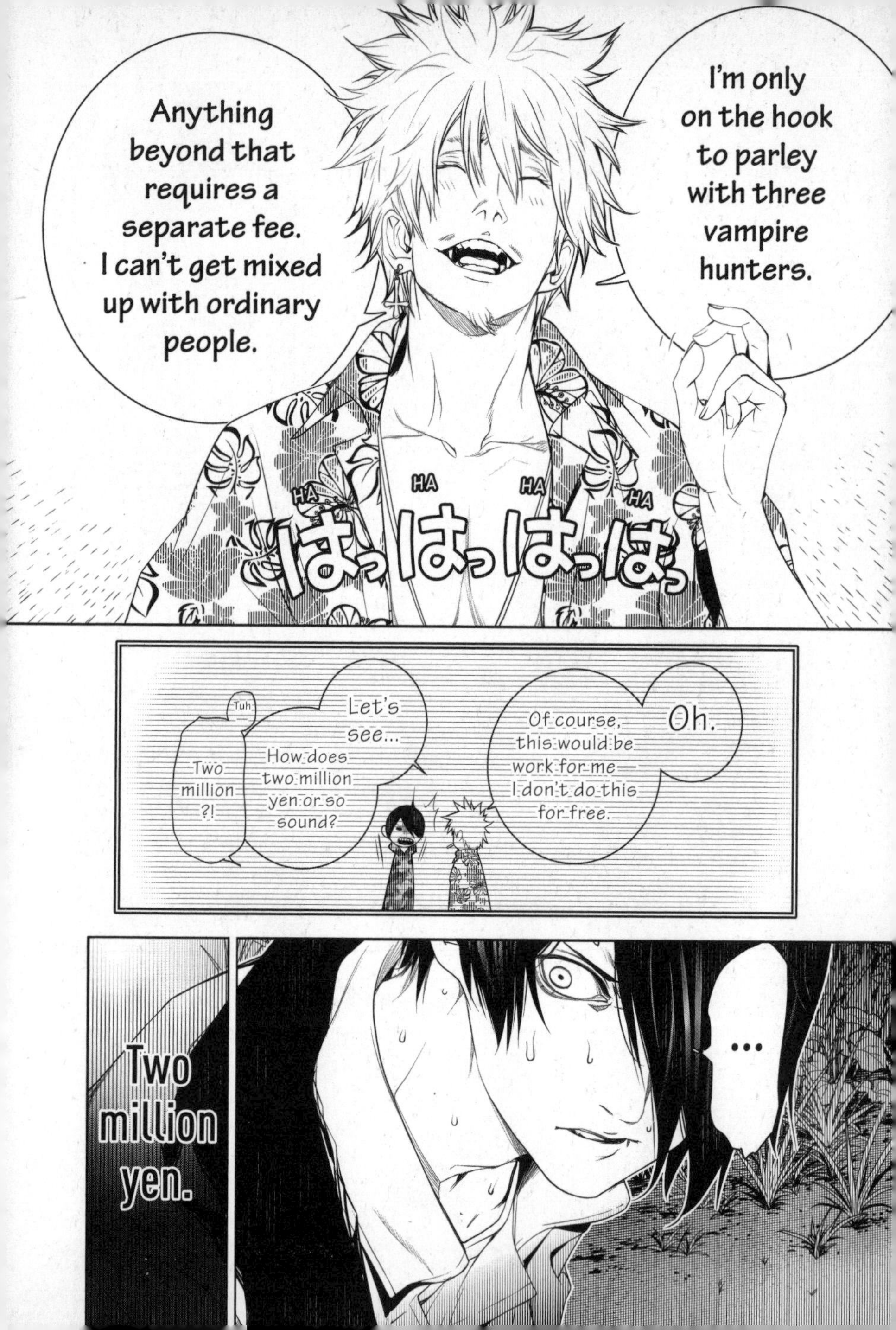
I'm only on the hook to parley with three vampire hunters.
Anything beyond that requires a separate fee. I can't get mixed up with ordinary people.
HA HA HA HA
はっはっはっはっ
Oh.
Of course, this would be work for me—I don't do this for free.
Let's see...
How does two million yen or so sound?
Tuh
Two million ?!
...
Two million yen.

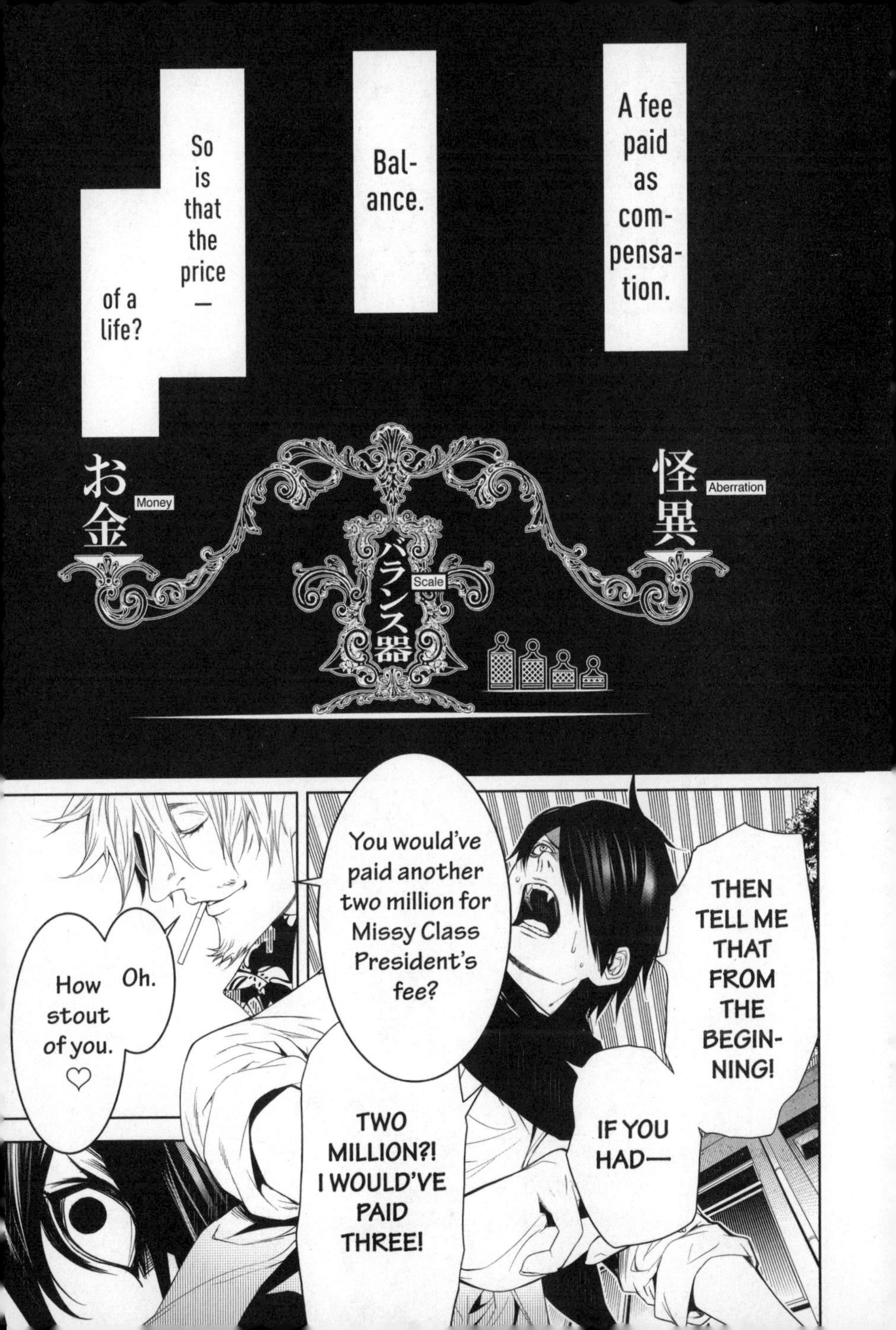
A fee paid as compensation.
Balance.
So is that the price—
of a life?
怪異
Aberration
バランス器
Scale
お金
Money
You would've paid another two million for Missy Class President's fee?
THEN TELL ME THAT FROM THE BEGINNING!
IF YOU HAD—
TWO MILLION?! I WOULD'VE PAID THREE!
Oh.
How stout of you. ♡

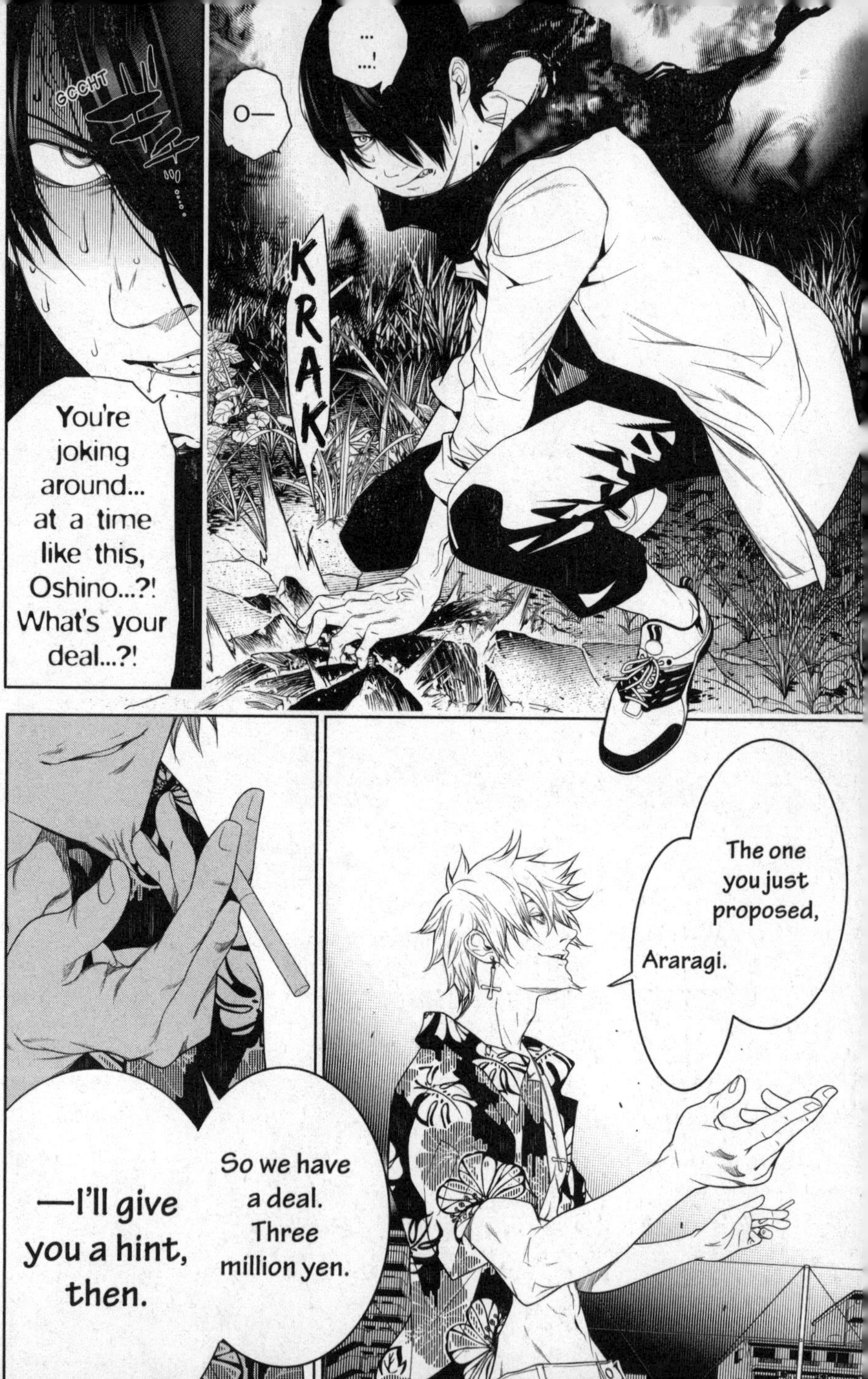
...
!
....
O—
KRAK
GCCHT
You're joking around... at a time like this, Oshino...?! What's your deal...?!
The one you just proposed,
Araragi.
So we have a deal. Three million yen.
—I'll give you a hint, then.

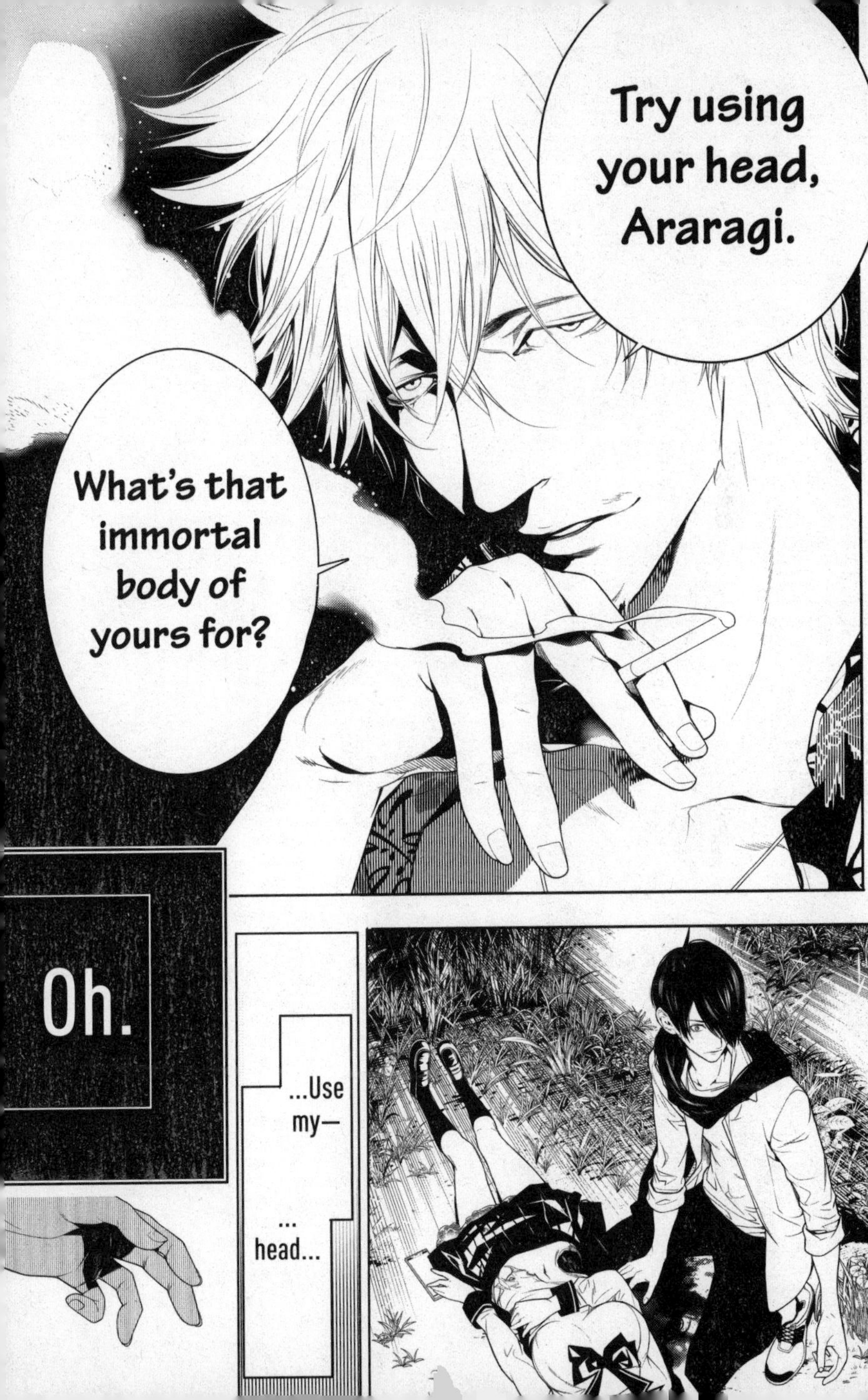
Try using your head, Araragi.
What's that immortal body of yours for?
...Use my—
... head...
Oh.

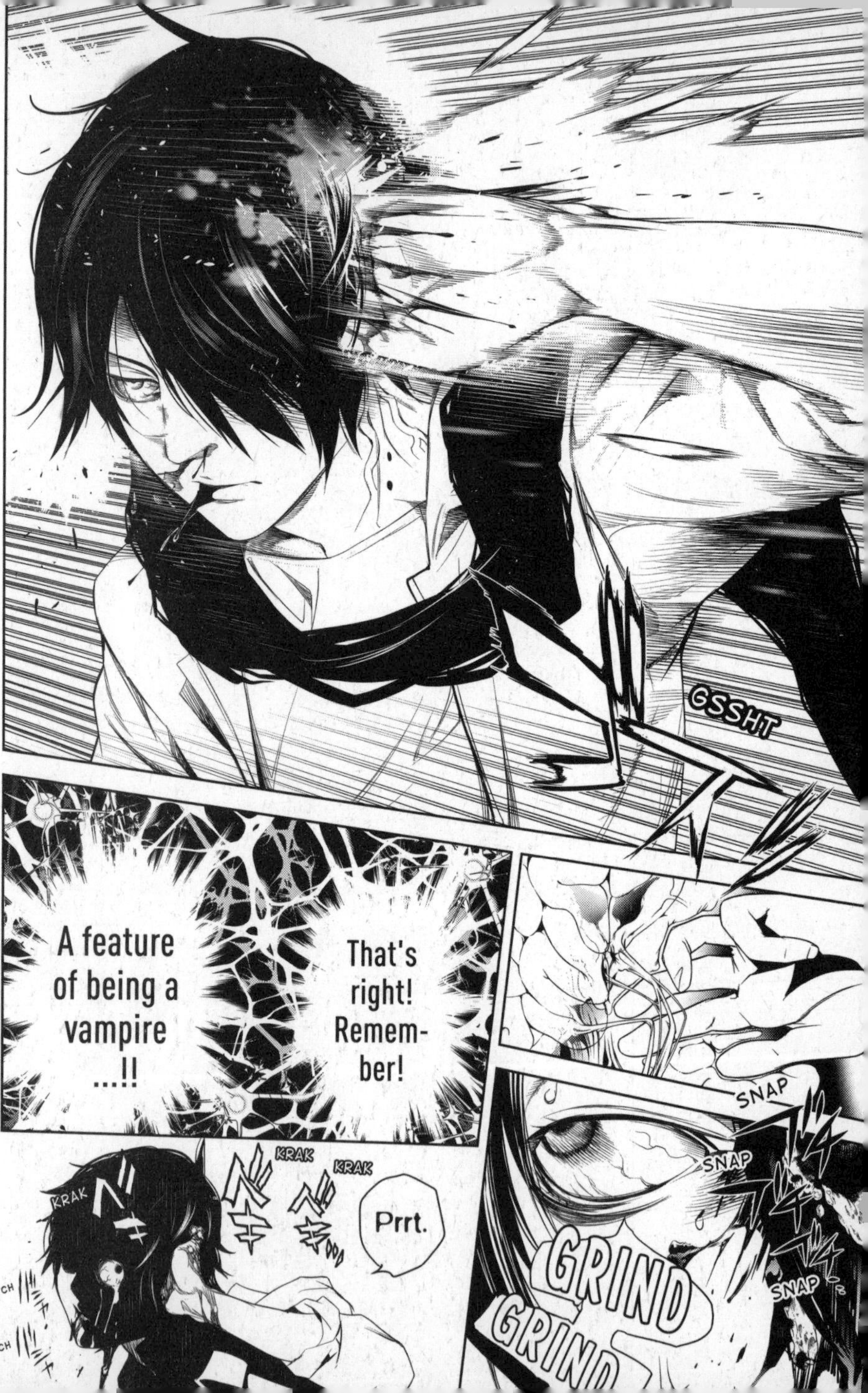

GSSHT
SNAP
SNAP
GRIND
GRIND
SNAP
That's right! Remember!
A feature of being a vampire ...!!
KRAK
KRAK
Prrt.
KRAK
SPLATCH
SPLATCH

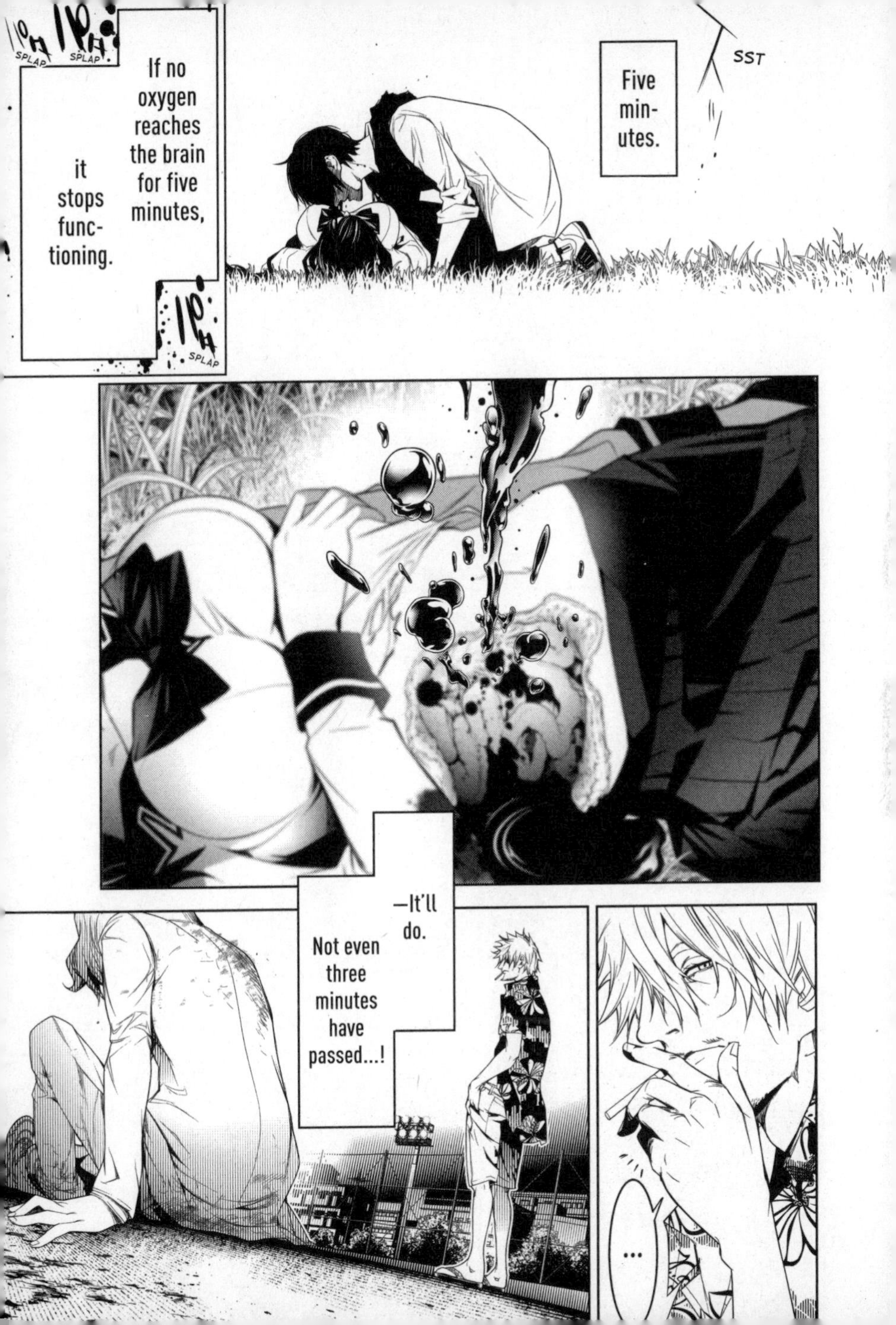
SST
Five minutes.
SPLAP SPLAP
If no oxygen reaches the brain for five minutes,
it stops functioning.
SPLAP
...
—It'll do.
Not even three minutes have passed...!

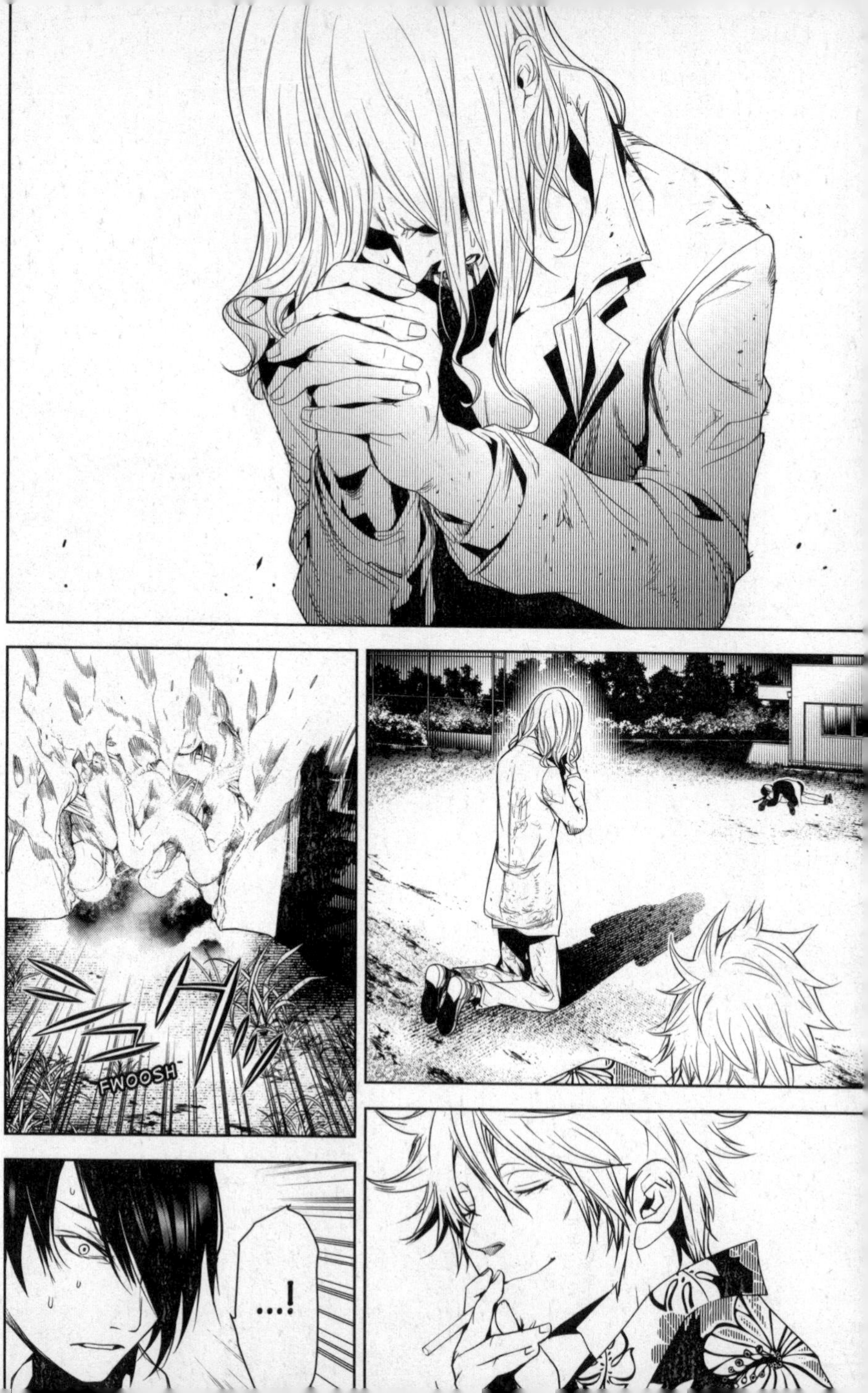
FWOOSH
...!

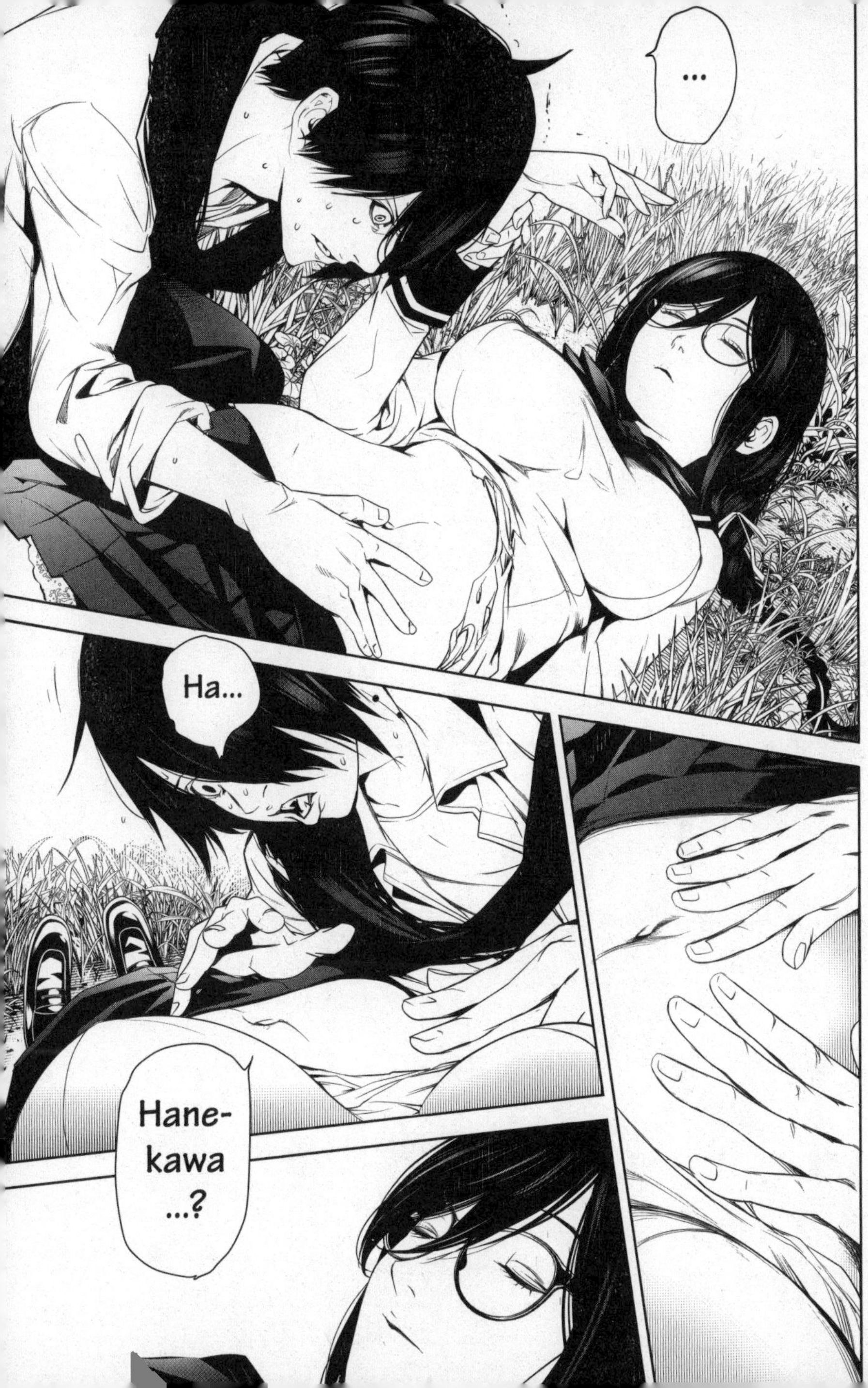
...
Ha...
Hane-kawa...?

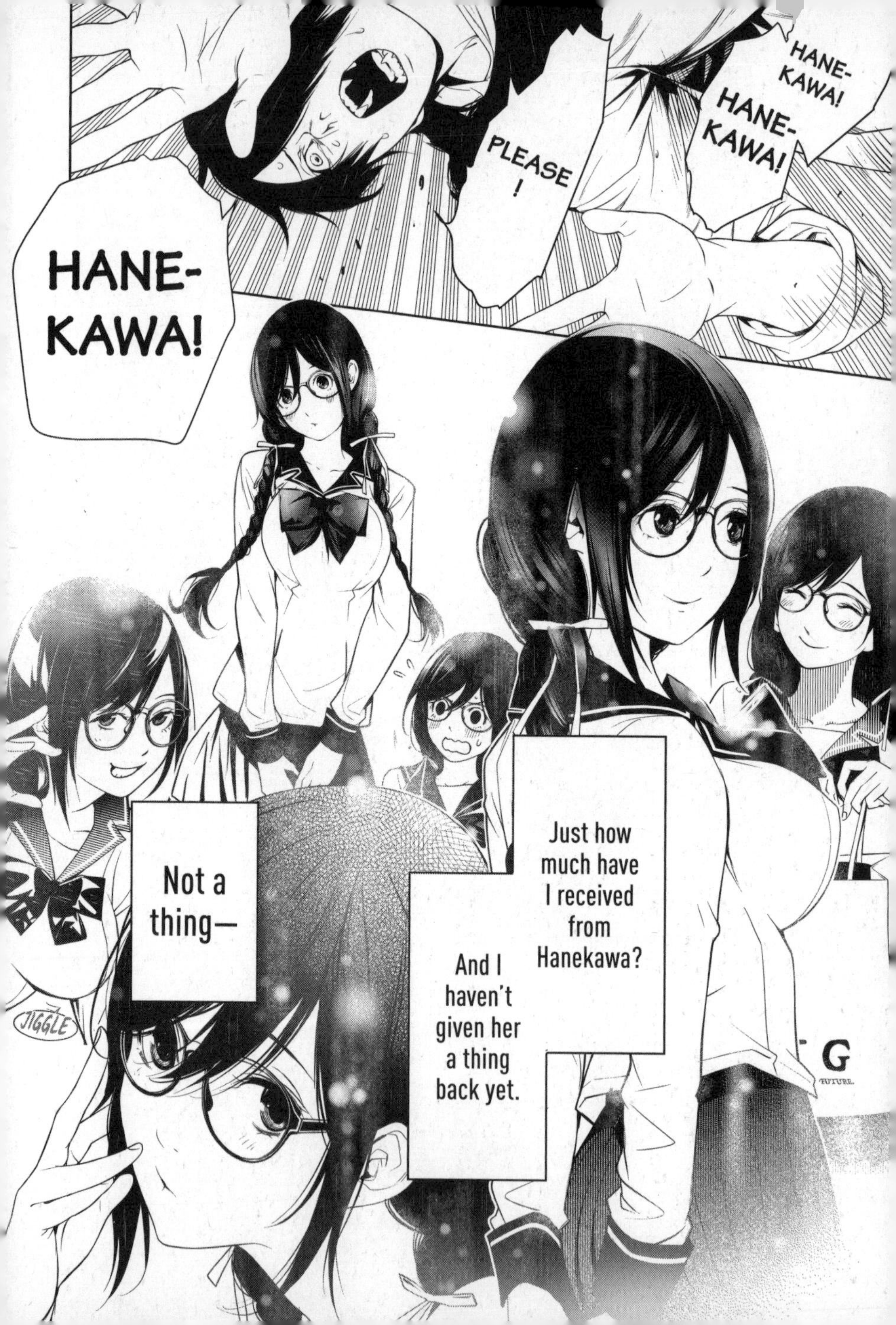
HANE-KAWA!
HANE-KAWA!
PLEASE!
HANE-KAWA!
Just how much have I received from Hanekawa?
And I haven't given her a thing back yet.
Not a thing—
JIGGLE

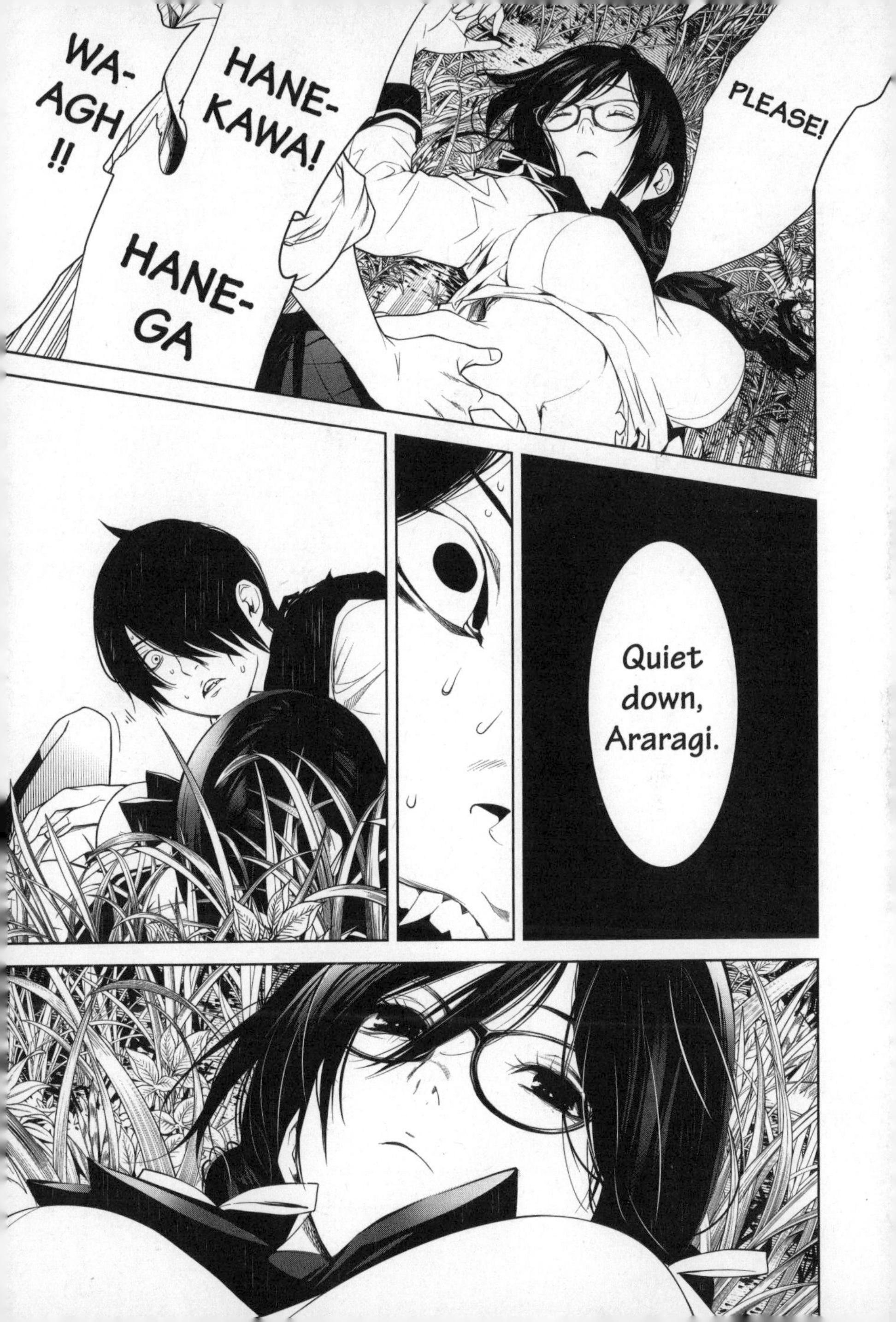
PLEASE!
HANE-KAWA!
WA-AGH!!
HANE-GA
Quiet down, Araragi.

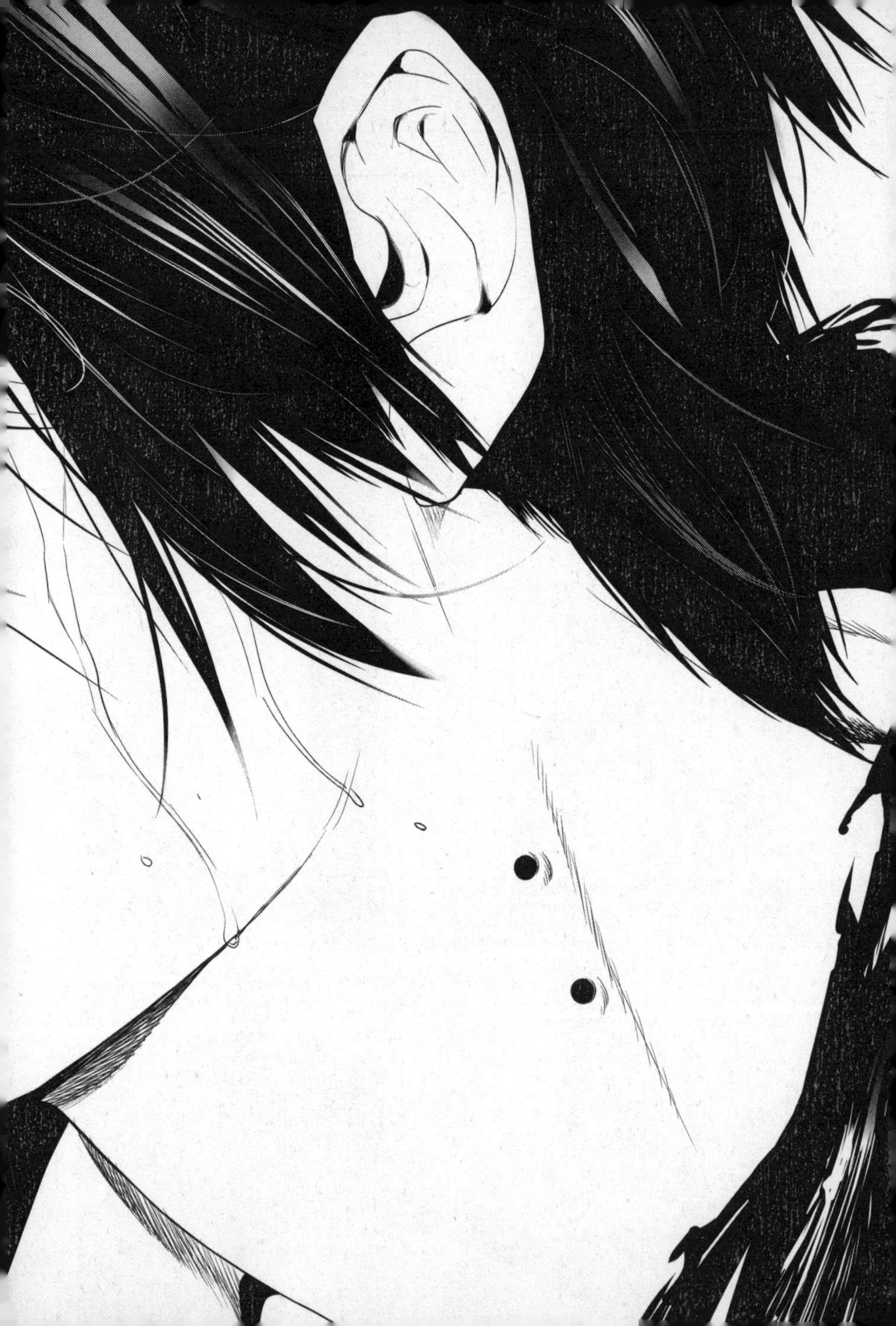

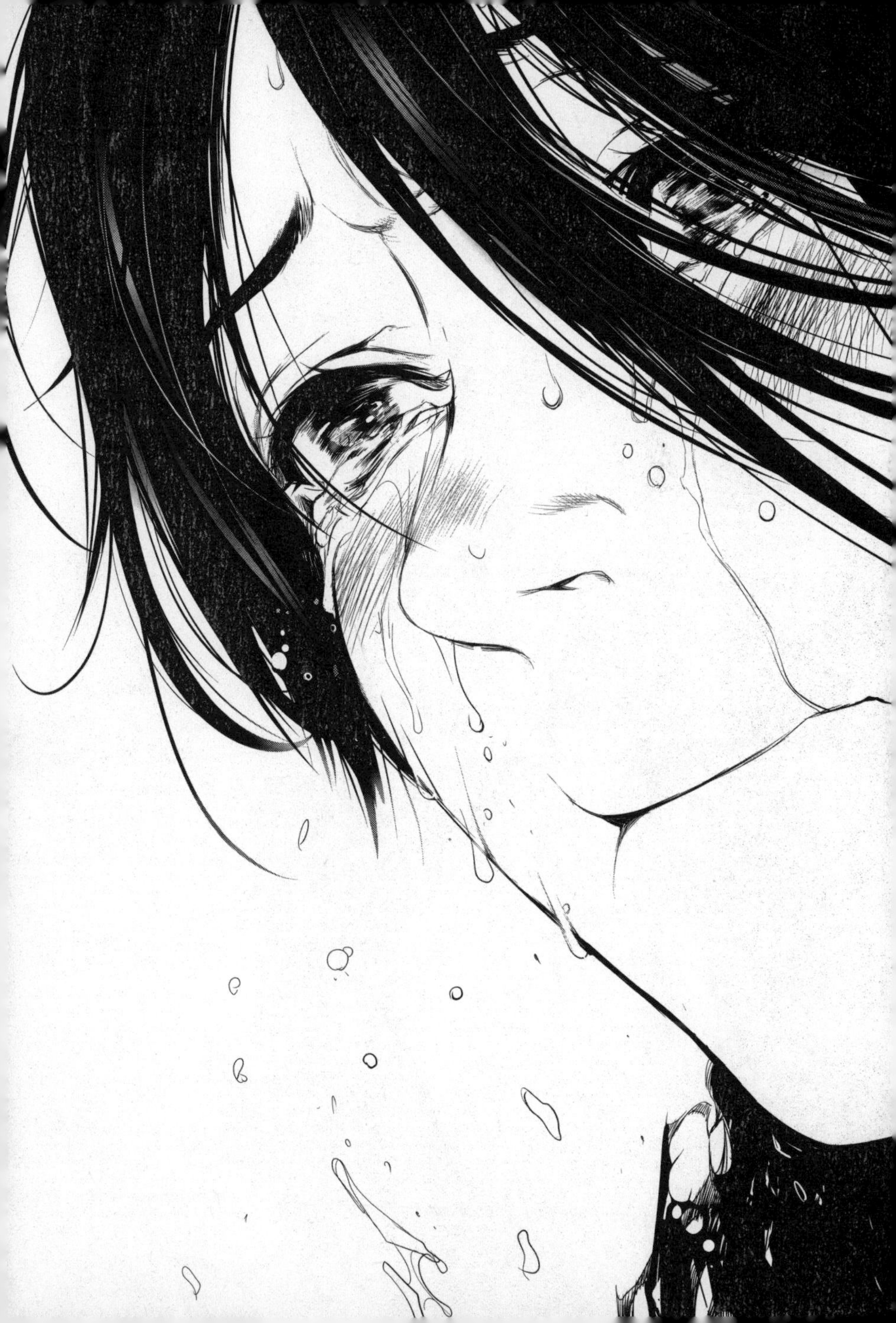

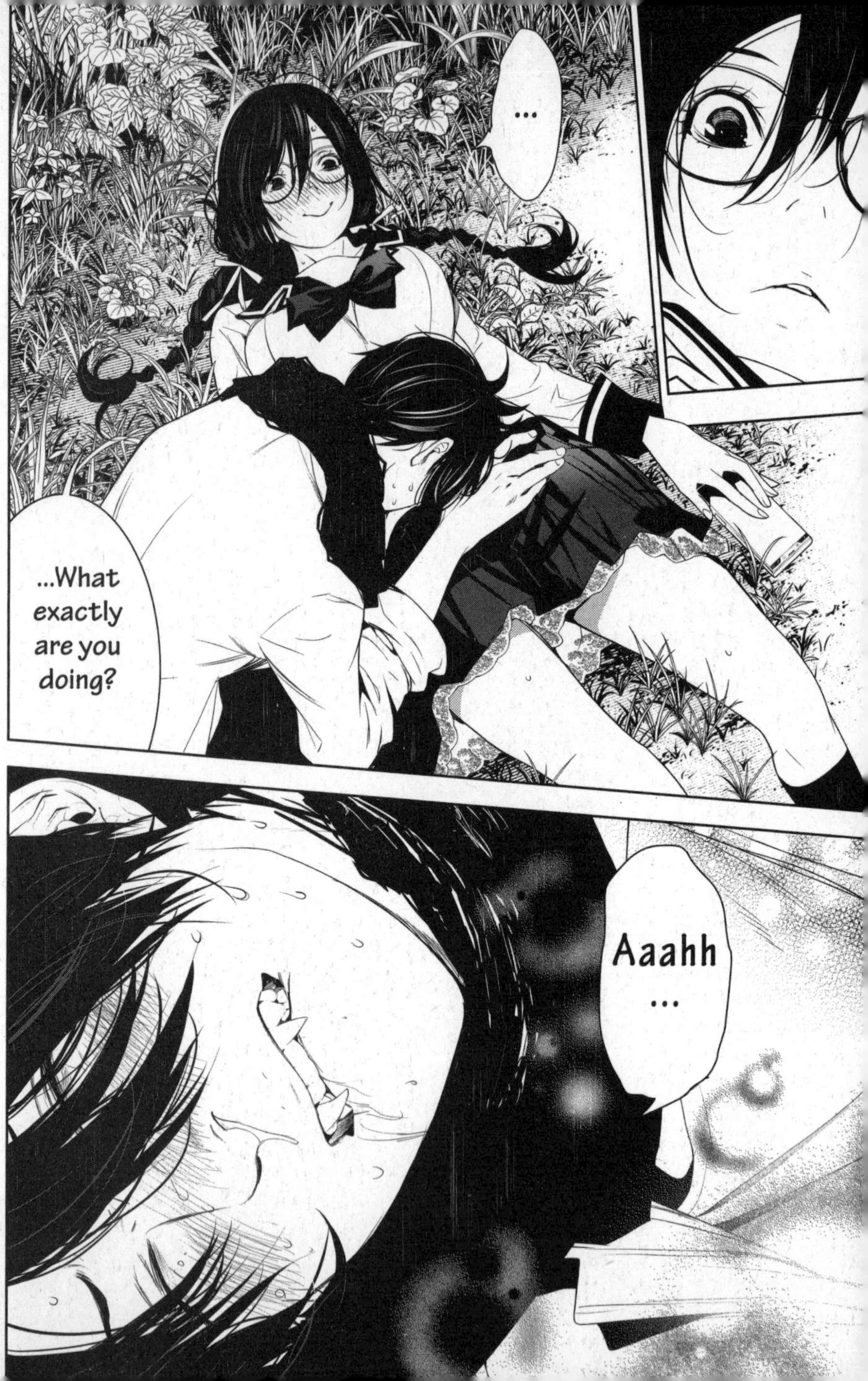
...
...What exactly are you doing?
Aaahh ...

BAM

?!

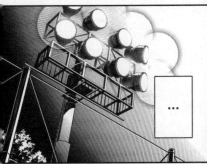

...

My...uniform appears to be torn. Should I chalk this up to you, too?

They say people don't always remember the moments before they lose consciousness.

My bad... Hane-kawa.

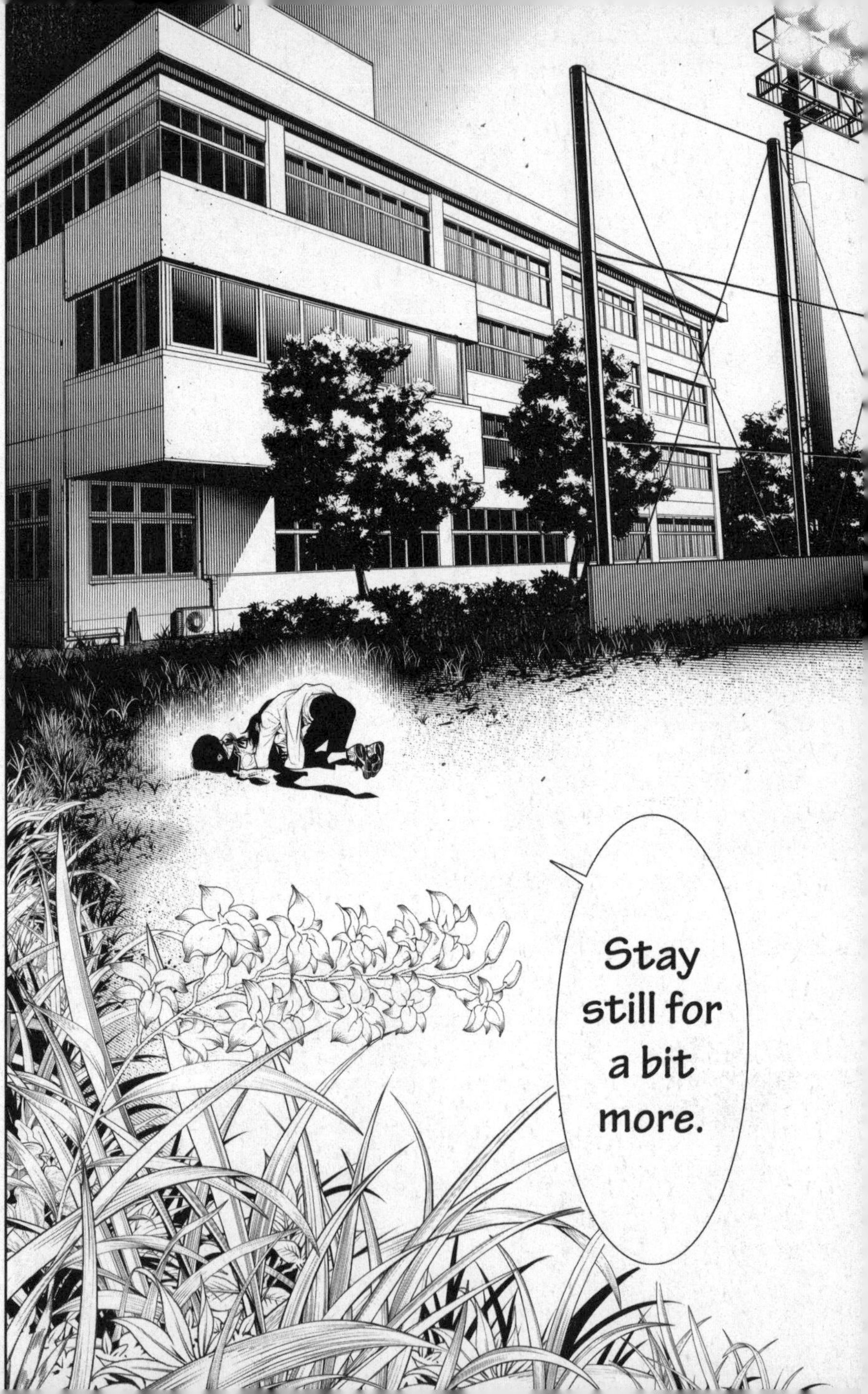
Stay still for a bit more.

Continued in Volume 12

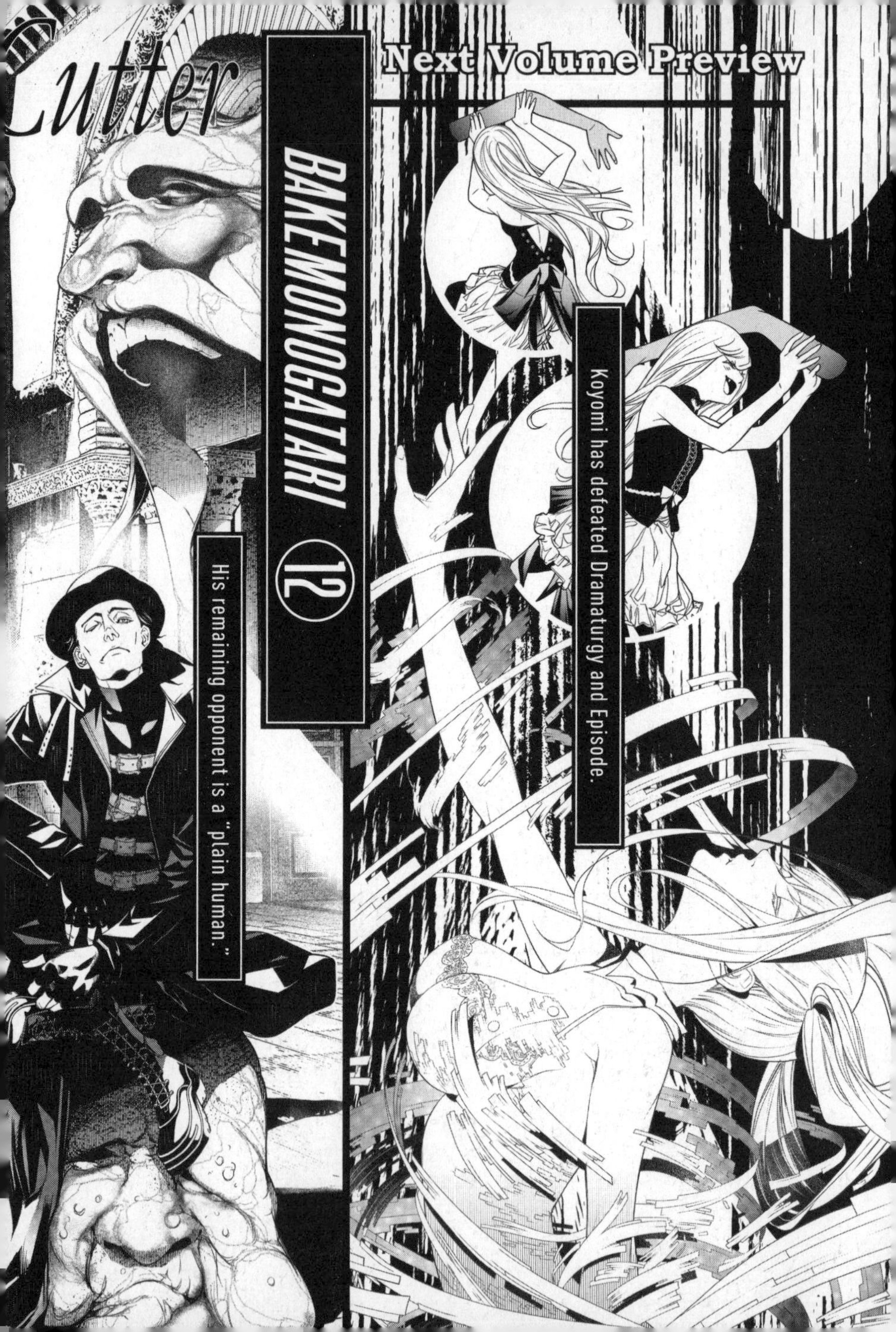
Next Volume Preview
Koyomi has defeated Dramaturgy and Episode.
BAKEMONOGATARI 12
His remaining opponent is a "plain human."
Cutter

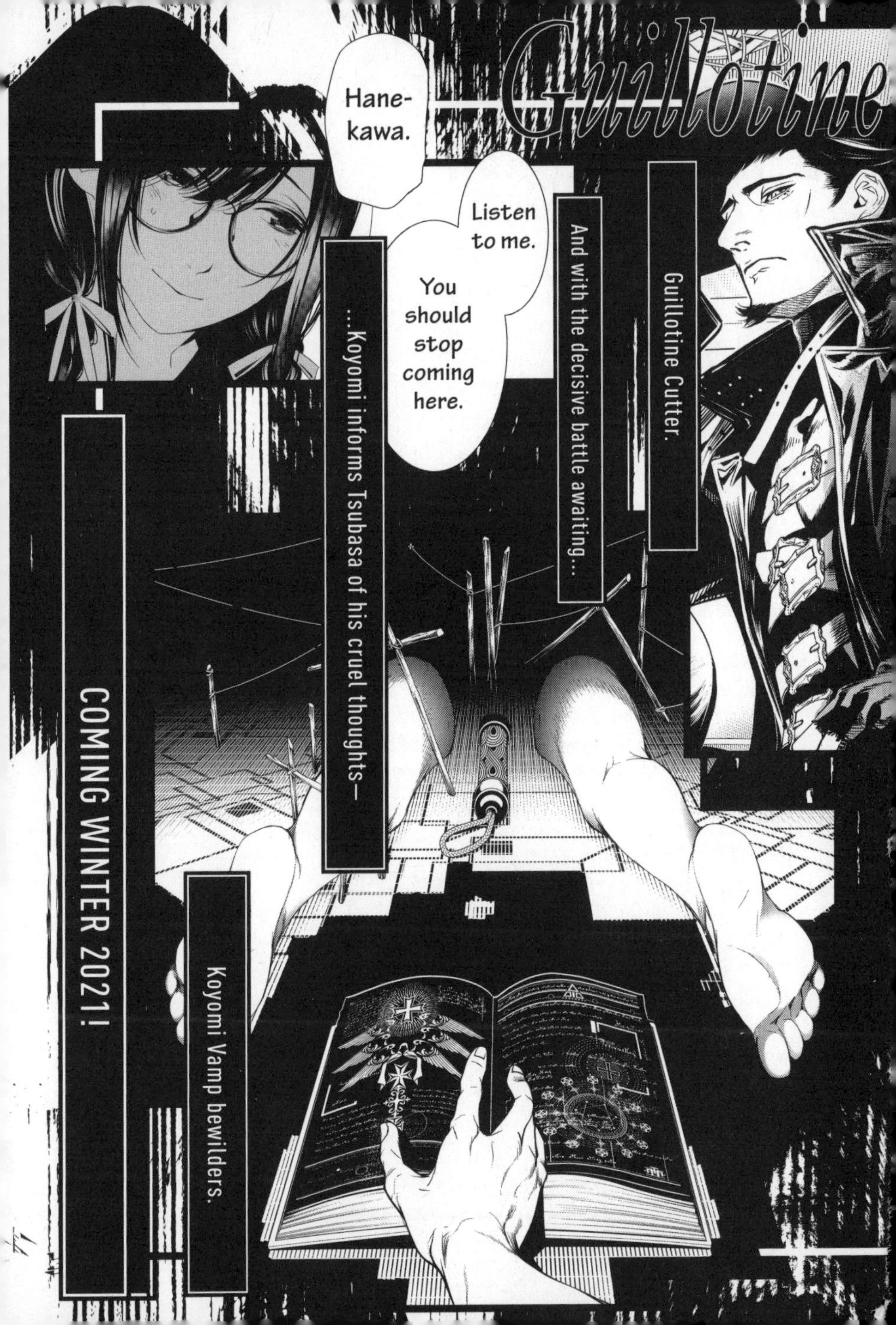
Guillotine
Guillotine Cutter.
Hane-kawa.
Listen to me.
You should stop coming here.
And with the decisive battle awaiting...
...Koyomi informs Tsubasa of his cruel thoughts—
Koyomi Vamp bewilders.
COMING WINTER 2021!

BAKEMONOGATARI
volume 11

A Vertical Comics Edition

Editing: Ajani Oloye
Translation: Ko Ransom
Production: Grace Lu
 Hiroko Mizuno
 Anthony Quintessenza

First published in Japan in 2020 by Kodansha, Ltd., Tokyo
Publication for this English edition arranged through Kodansha, Ltd., Tokyo
English language version produced by Vertical Comics,
an imprint of Kodansha USA Publishing, LLC

Translation provided by Vertical Comics, 2021
Published by Kodansha USA Publishing, LLC, New York

Originally published in Japanese as *BAKEMONOGATARI 11* by Kodansha, Ltd.
BAKEMONOGATARI first serialized in *Weekly Shonen Magazine*,
Kodansha, Ltd., 2017-

This is a work of fiction.

ISBN: 978-1-64729-064-1

Manufactured in the United States of America

First Edition

Kodansha USA Publishing, LLC
451 Park Avenue South
7th Floor
New York, NY 10016
www.kodansha.us

Vertical books are distributed through Penguin-Random House Publisher Services.